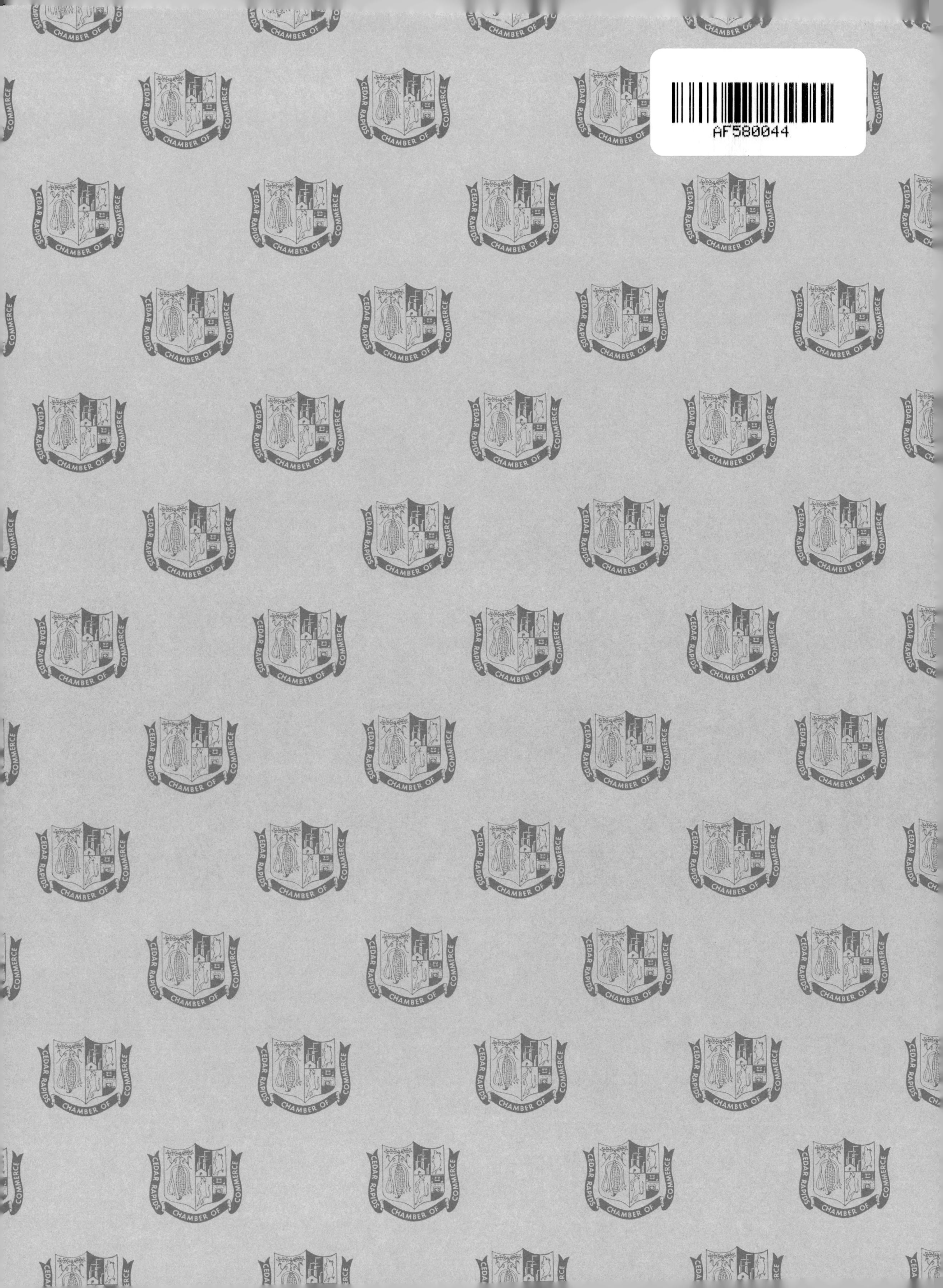
AF580044
CEDAR RAPIDS
CHAMBER OF COMMERCE

Cedar Rapids

150

Prologue & Promise

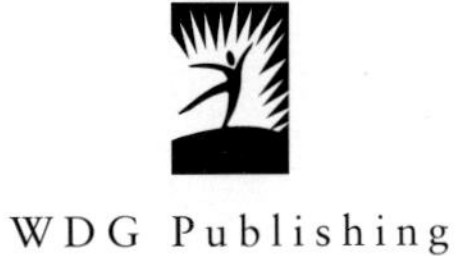

WDG Publishing

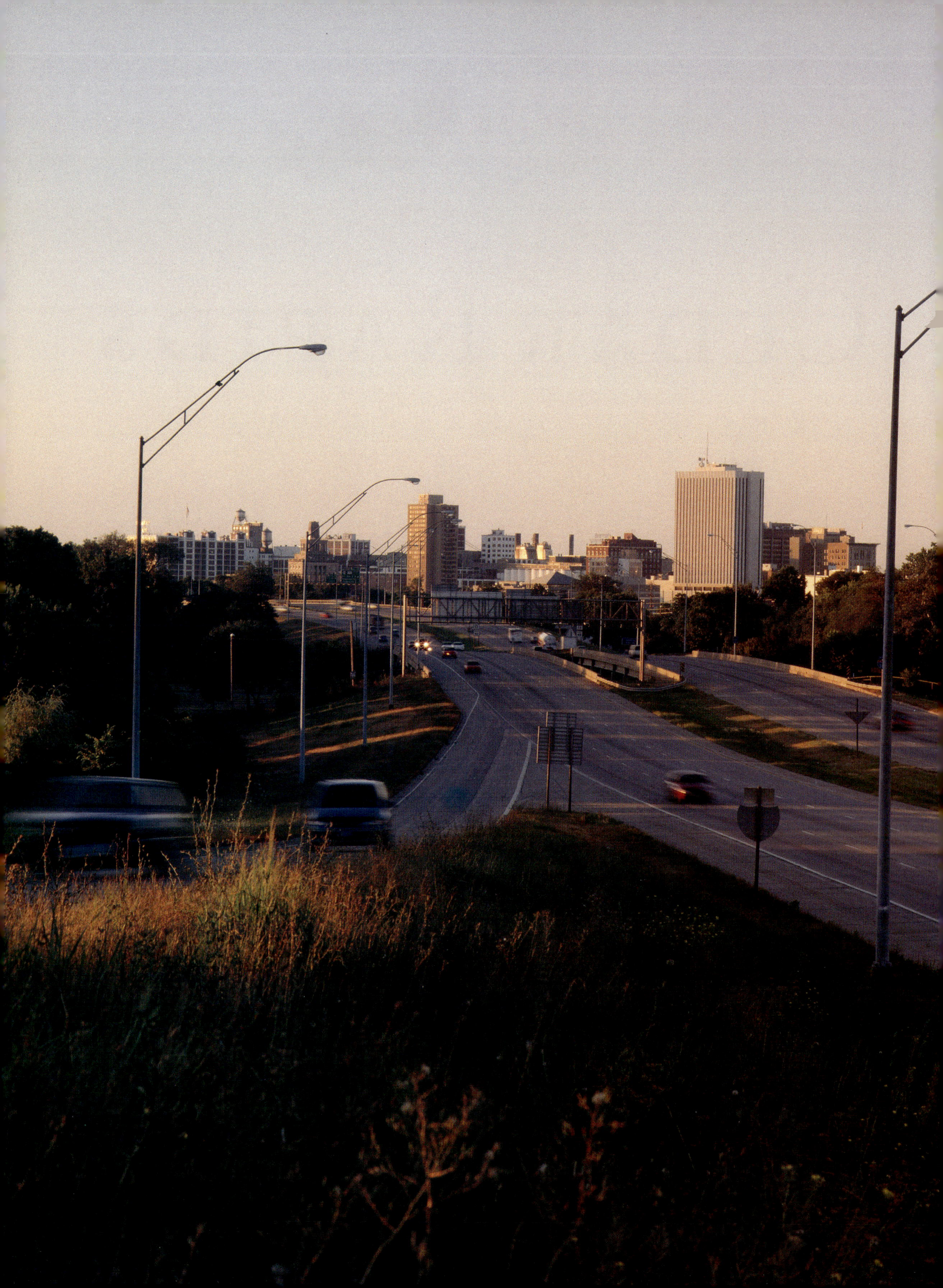

Cedar Rapids 150

Prologue & Promise

One Hundred & Fifty Years of Cedar Rapids Progress

Bernard Smith ■ Susan Davis Smith

Neil R. Baumhover

Frontispiece: Interstate 380 at dusk by Ron Dreasher

Published by WDG Publishing

Acknowledgements

Special thanks to Linda Langston, executive director of the History Center, for the generous amount of time and effort she gave in helping with this book. Her advice was invaluable and her guidance greatly appreciated.

Prologue & Promise
150 Years of Cedar Rapids Progress

Published in partnership with
The Cedar Rapids Area Chamber of Commerce

Editorial Director: Elinor Day
Art Director: Duane Wood
Design: Michael Bentley
Duane Wood

First published in the United States of America by:

WDG Communications
3500 F Avenue NW
Post Office Box 9573
Cedar Rapids, Iowa 52409-9573
Telephone (319) 396-1401
Facsimile (319) 396-1647

ISBN 0-9651620-1-X

10 9 8 7 6 5 4 3 2 1

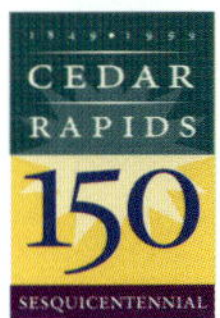

Partners in Progress

These Cedar Rapids area businesses showed their community support with their commitment to this sesquicentennial commemorative volume.

ADM Corn Processing

APAC Teleservices

Alliant Utilities

Al Wells Homes, Inc.

Apache Hose & Belting Co., Inc.

CRST International, Inc.

Cargill

Cedarapids, Inc.

Cedar River Paper Company

Climate Engineers, Inc.

Czech Cottage

Diamond V Mills, Inc.

Evergreen Packaging Equipment

Farmers State Bank

First National Bank

The Gazette Family of Companies

Goss Graphic Systems, Inc.

Guaranty Bank & Trust

Intermec/Norand Mobile Systems Division

In Tolerance

Iowa Midland Supply, Inc.

King's Material, Inc.

MCI WorldCom

McLeodUSA Incorporated

Mercy Medical Center

Network Data Processing

OB-GYN Associates, P.C.

Pineview Properties

Pioneer Office Products

Point Builders, Inc.

The Quaker Oats Company

Rinderknecht Associates, Inc.

Rockwell Collins

SCI Financial Group, Inc.

St. Luke's Hospital

Shive Hattery, Inc.

Souvenir Group

Square D Company

Teahen Funeral Home, Inc.

United Way of East Central Iowa

West Side Sewing

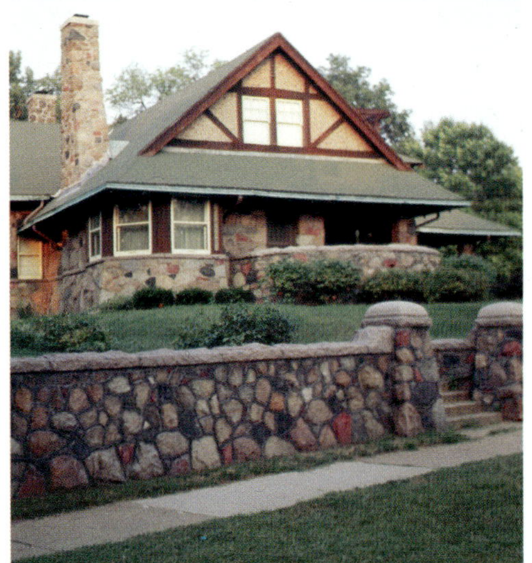

Neighborhoods

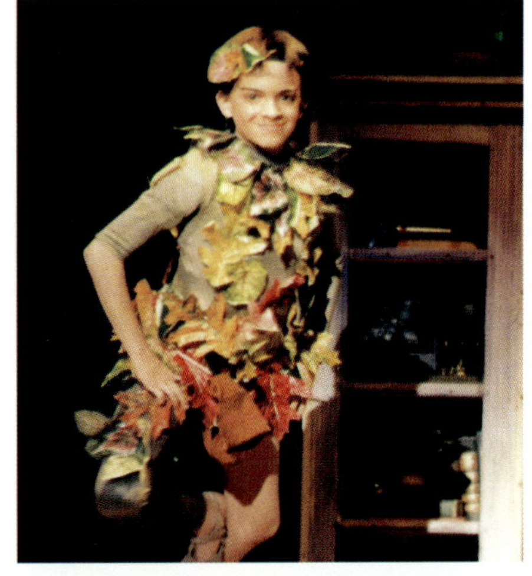

The Arts

Festivals

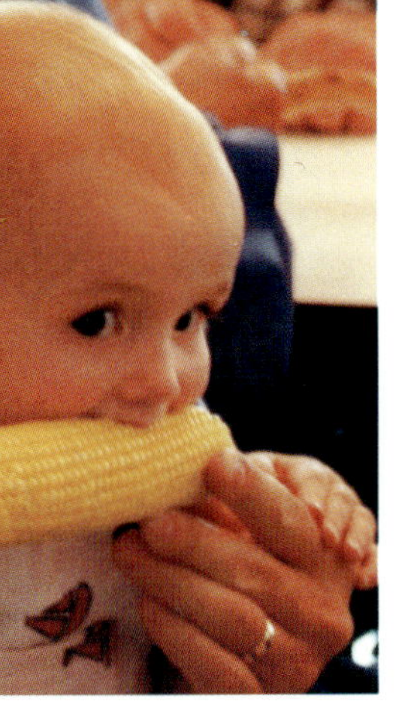

Government

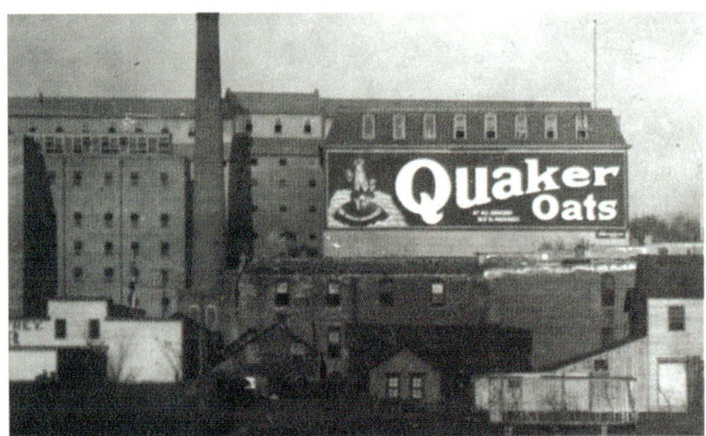

Heritage

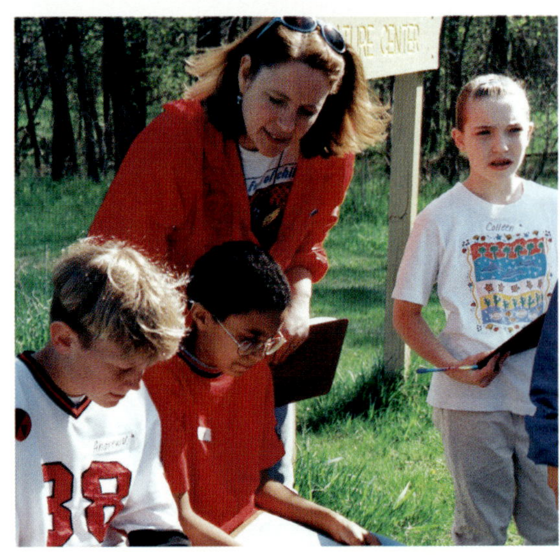

Education

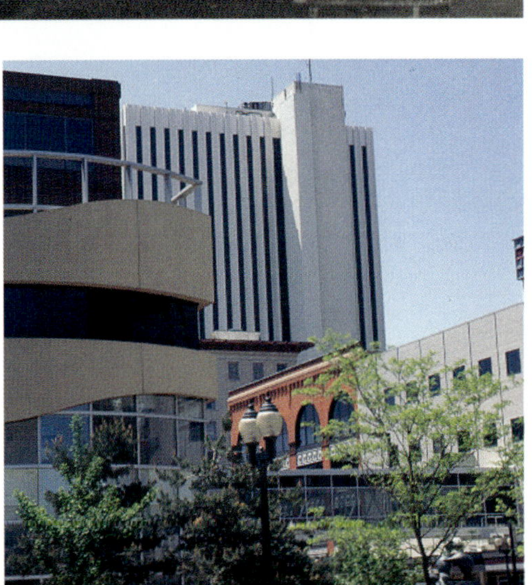

Commerce

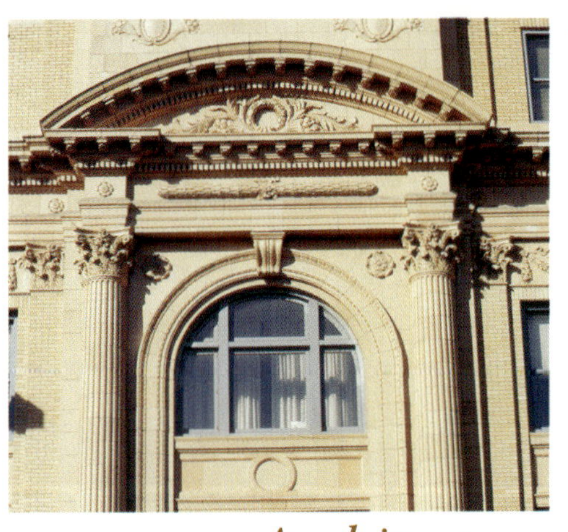

Architecture

Cedar Rapids
Prologue & Promise

1. Partners In Prologue and Promise
Support from the business community.

3. Contents

4. The Rock and High Water
An introduction.

6. Who Are We, Anyway?
A city with its own personality, history and legends.

24. The Quality of Our Lives
What makes this a good place to live?

62. Rome on the Prairie
Art, theater, music and more.

78. Acts of God and Government
Roots and deeds of the commission form.

90. Ginseng and Gall Bladder
Cedar Rapids goes a'courting.

107. Business Profiles

167. Photographers

168. Index

171. Bibliography

Endpaper artwork is a logo for the Cedar Rapids Chamber of Commerce from the 1930s by Grant Wood.

The rock and high water

Just off the eastern bank of the Cedar River, a few yards from the Five-in-One Dam and the Tree of Five Seasons, sits a boulder that used to mean something around here. The sight of the "high water rock" told early settlers that the river was low enough to allow them to cross safely. When the rock was submerged, it was best to stay put.

My, how things have changed.

Now, we rarely give the rock a second glance or second thought, if we've noticed it at all, as we fly across the river on a nearby bridge in our cars and trucks, our vans and SUVs. In our busy lives, we don't often give much thought to our community's past, either. We need to handle a thousand details a day, and we need to look ahead to make family plans, business plans, retirement plans.

Still, there are times when looking back is especially appropriate. Times like the present, as we celebrate our sesquicentennial year—our 150th anniversary. We can learn from our past and take pride in our past. Understanding where we've been and how we came to be what we are today can make it easier to understand where we're going.

In the introduction to their 1911 "History of Linn County, Iowa," writers Luther A. Brewer and Barthinius L. Wick described their meticulous documentation of the county's early history by noting, "We have done some things which need not be done again by any one who follows us."

Most would agree that their history of the earliest days need not be done again, so the sesquicentennial writings you'll find in this new volume focus on more recent noteworthy events and the people and causes behind them.

They deal with a different kind of high water mark than that represented by the rock in the river. They are about turning points, about passages in the life of our community.

Brewer and Wick considered themselves highly fortunate to live when they did, especially when they compared their times with those of Iowa's pioneers of the 19th Century. They wrote of "living in a day crowded with all the conveniences of the 20th Century."

My, how things have changed at the other end of that century.

Fur trapping, agriculture, milling and related basic industries consumed the lives of our earliest citizens, and many of those same activities continue to underpin our economy today. The river was first an obstacle, then a source of transportation, which gave way to the railroads, which gave way to highways and electronic commerce. We've grown up.

Even our language has changed as we evolved, to reflect technology in many cases and to reflect new ways of thinking in others.

CRST International, for example, was once a trucking company. Now it markets its services as a logistics company, a transportation solutions company. Not so long ago, the newspaper used hot metal type to publish the news. Now we can get news through the Internet from the newspaper itself, as well as from radio and television stations.

We are online through our library. We're connected. We're a digital community with our roots still in the fertile Iowa soil.

We've grown, and we're still growing. New development takes us farther and farther out from the city's downtown heart but we come back downtown to congregate on special occasions. We like to get together, for fireworks, for music, for parades, for celebrations.

Some things haven't changed. It's time for a celebration.

Who are we, anyway?

The city of Cedar Rapids is the product of 150 years of life. It has its own personality, its history, its legends. At one time it was the front door of the frontier. People came from the East looking for land. Others were hunters and trappers. Legend tells us Osgood Shepherd was one of those trappers, possibly also a horse thief and the city's first settler. If he was the first, he wasn't alone for long.

We are a community built on the efforts of people like Alexander and John Ely, Sampson Bever, Judge George Greene, Frank Carpenter, A.M. Smulekoff, Oscar Solomon, Abraham Becker, Sutherland Dows and later the Douglases, Sinclairs and Halls. Descendants of many of our early families continue to provide leadership in the community today.

These founding families had an image of Cedar Rapids. It was to be an upright, clean, well-kept community. A parlor city. They pictured people getting off the train in Cedar Rapids, and they wanted a park to be the first thing those people would see. Today, we know that park as Greene Square Park.

Their vision also included the city's architecture. Some of the city's buildings tell those stories. City Hall, with its island location and Grant Wood's stained glass window, is a symbol of solidity and individuality. Today, the renovated Paramount Theatre—once a movie theater—attests to the city's commitment to the arts.

The Guaranty Bank building took the downtown community into the 20th century. Built in 1895, it was the city's first skyscraper, and its six

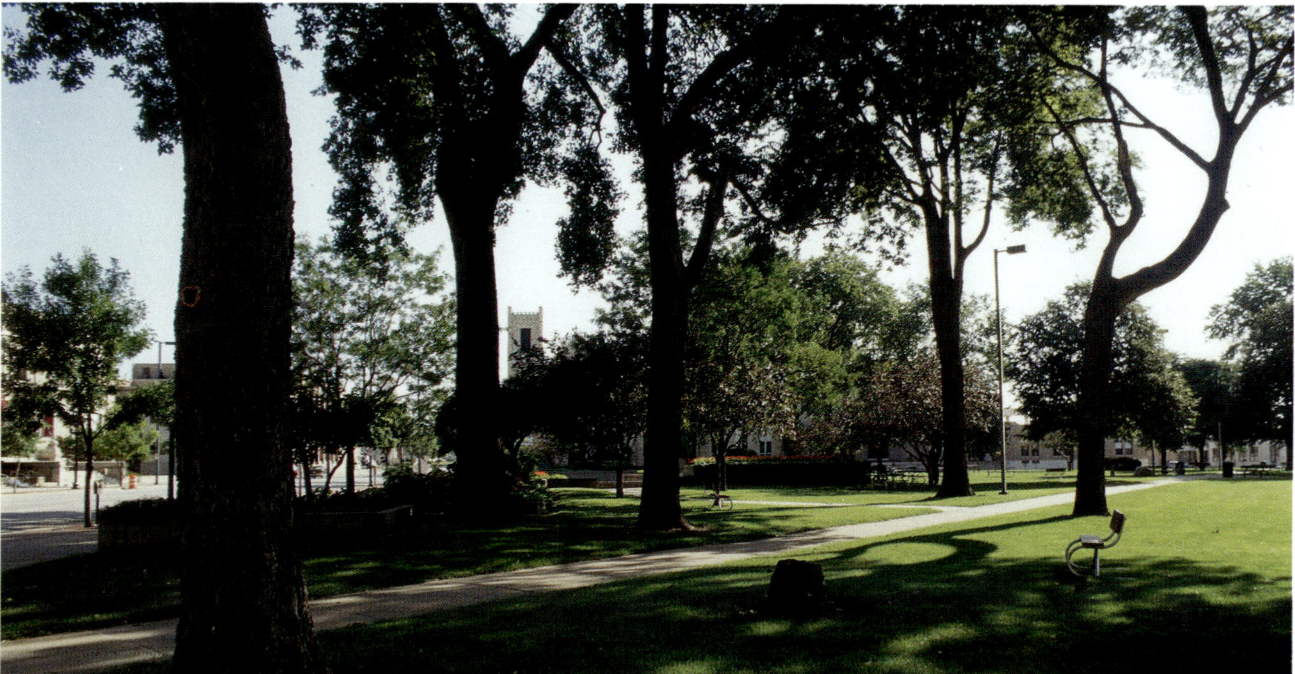
David Van Allen

Greene Square Park

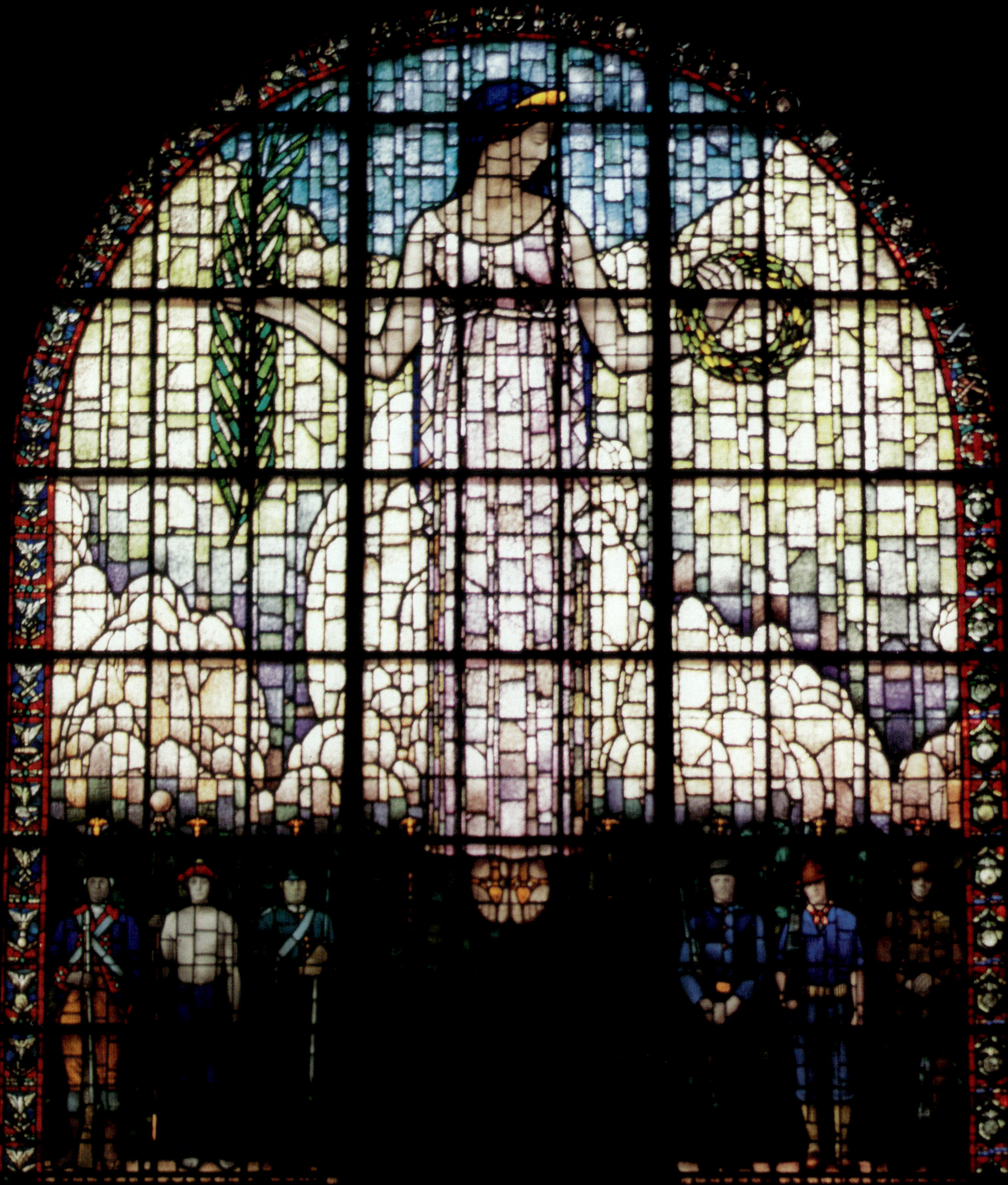

floors and elevators—another first—set a standard of business that had not been seen before. Likewise, what was then the IE Tower set the standards of a new era when it was built in 1972—standards that said Cedar Rapids was a leader in business.

Reminders of who came before us can be seen on many buildings today: Higley, Grandby, Armstrong, Kubias and Turner. CSPS Hall reminds us of the Czech immigrants who settled in the city's southwest neighborhoods. It was where hard-working people came to meet and socialize. It was also a fraternal organization that offered benefits to Czech workers, which would eventually become the insurance company that exists today, Western Fraternal Life Insurance. Other buildings share recognition with who built them. The former Peoples Savings Bank was designed by nationally renowned architect Louis Sullivan.

As the city grew more industrial, neighborhoods grew away from downtown. People settled south, west and east. Today's neighborhoods of Mound View, Wellington Heights, Kingston, Vernon Heights, Czech Village and Kenwood remind us of families who sought refuge from the city's sounds and smells. Today's families move to be near work, school, shopping and transportation. Entire neighborhoods grew around the ever-expanding company built by Arthur Collins. Homes now line both sides of Interstate 380.

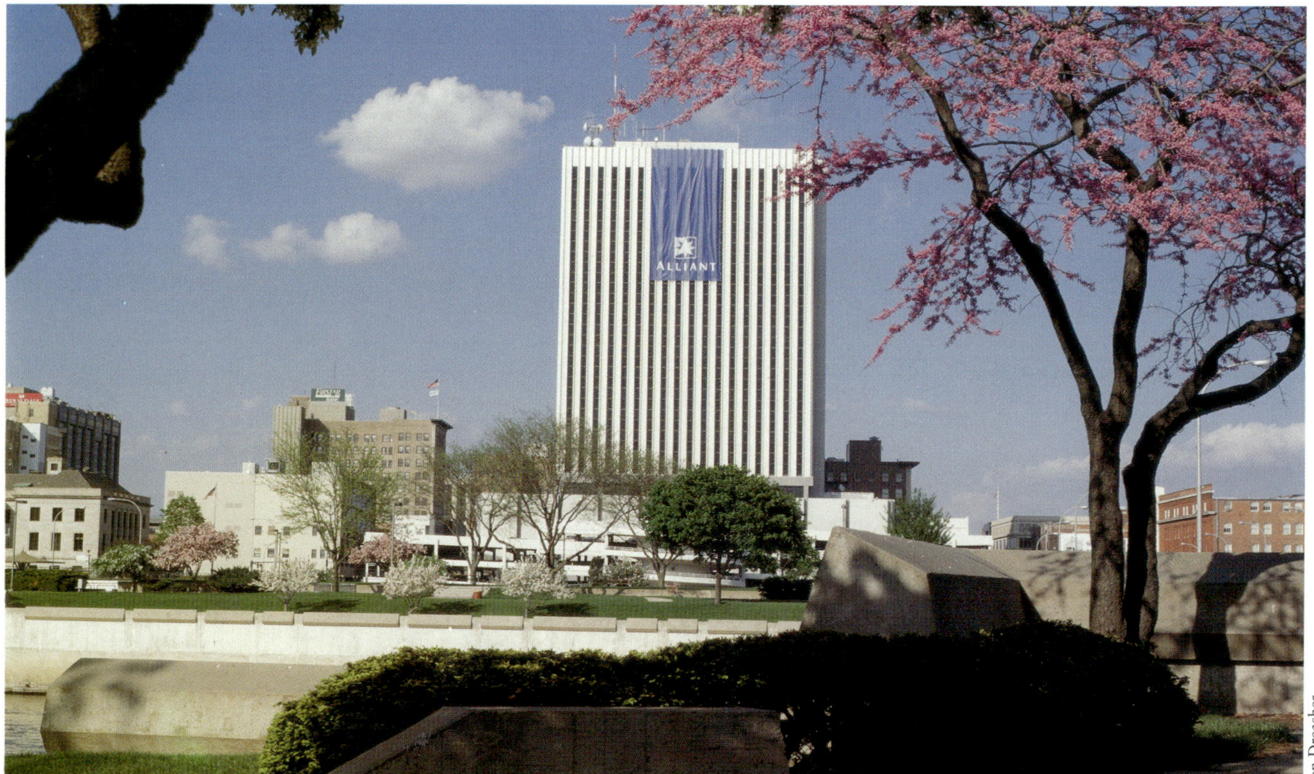

Ron Dreasher

Cedar Rapids' first real skyscraper—built in 1972—forever changed the city's skyline.

An industrious people

Both the nature of our work and where we work also changed to a great extent as the city's economy evolved. A once heavily agricultural and manufacturing-oriented economy became a much more service-oriented economy.

Downtown Cedar Rapids, for example, was once a thriving retail center. While it is once again a thriving area, it has become more of what Jon Dusek, president of Armstrong-Race Realty, describes as "an urban office park." The area was once home to local retail mainstays such as Killian's and Armstrong's, which lasted for 100 years before succumbing finally in the '80s.

While Smulekoff's and a few others maintain a retail presence in downtown Cedar Rapids, many other retailers closed or migrated to Lindale Mall, Westdale Mall and other shopping centers closer to new residential developments. As urban renewal efforts and private investment subsequently rebuilt, rejuvenated and beautified the downtown area, a new type of business clientele moved in.

"In the old days we had more individual entrepreneurs, and now we've evolved into a more corporate mentality," Dusek said. Individual wealthy investors are less likely to own downtown property now than are corporate investors, and the buildings are largely office buildings rather than retail shops. At the same time, Dusek said, the 14,000-some people who now work downtown are

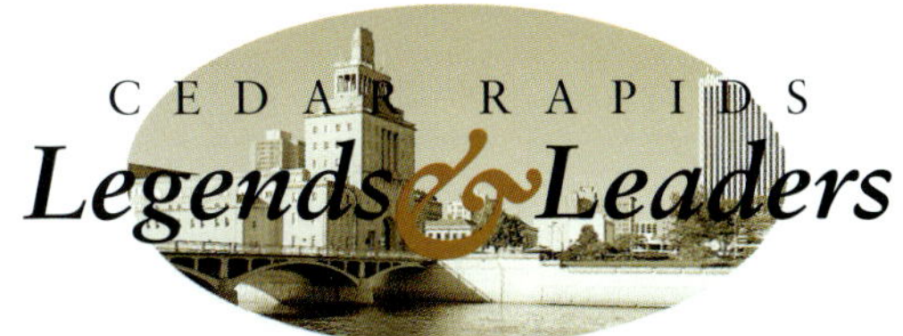

Judge George Greene
1817-1880

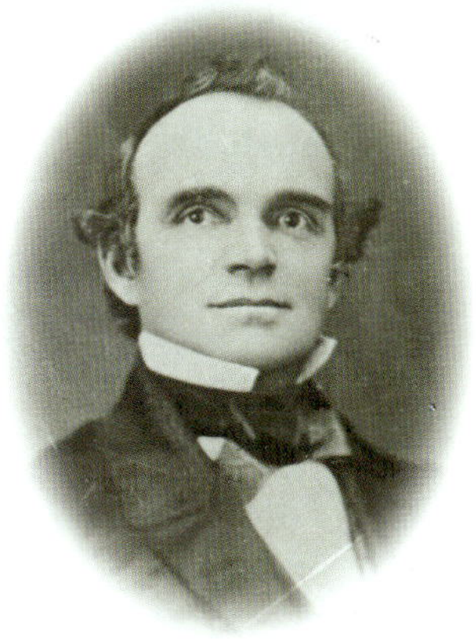

One of the founders of Cedar Rapids, Judge George Greene was also one of the most influential people in the city's growth. Greene came to Iowa in 1838 as a land surveyor. By 1849 he had become an attorney, worked on a newspaper and was an early member of the territorial legislature.

Greene became one of the founders of Cedar Rapids by helping to survey and lay out the original town. He was also active in bringing the railroad to Cedar Rapids and in his financial support of building projects within the city, including the city's first hospital.

Greene served one year as the mayor of Cedar Rapids in 1855. He lived in Cedar Rapids until his death. Greene Square Park was named for this founding father.

Photo: Iowa State Historical Society

Neighborhoods

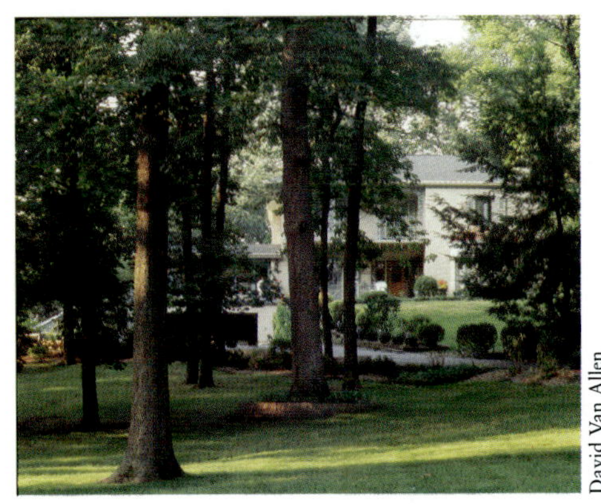
David Van Allen

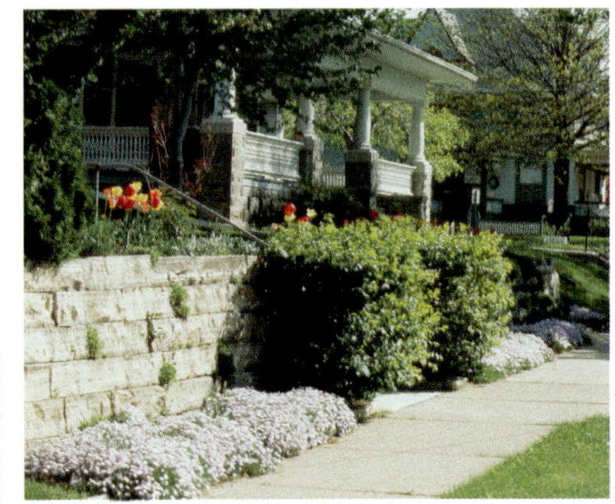
French Studios

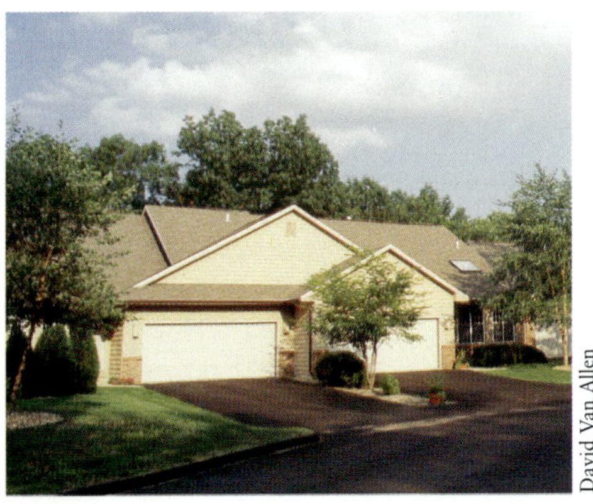
David Van Allen

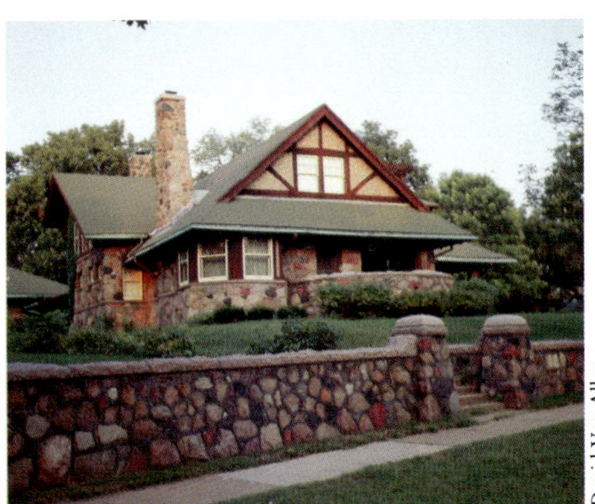
David Van Allen

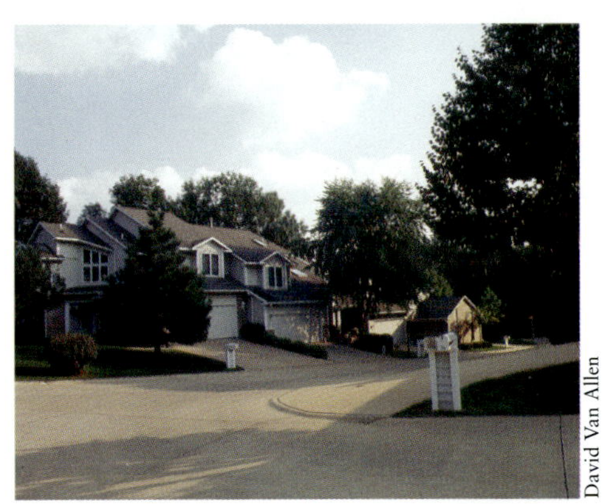
David Van Allen

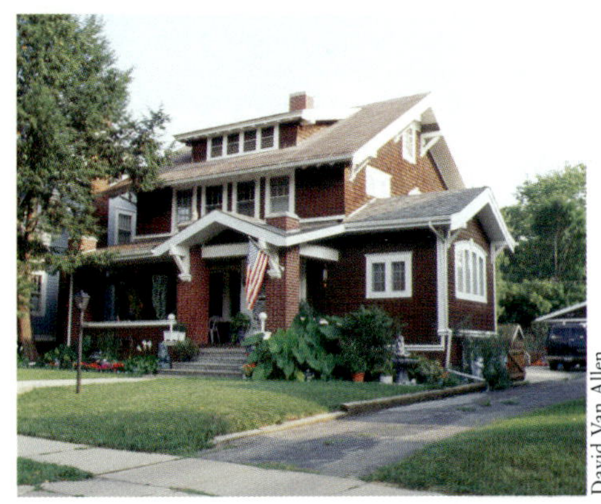
David Van Allen

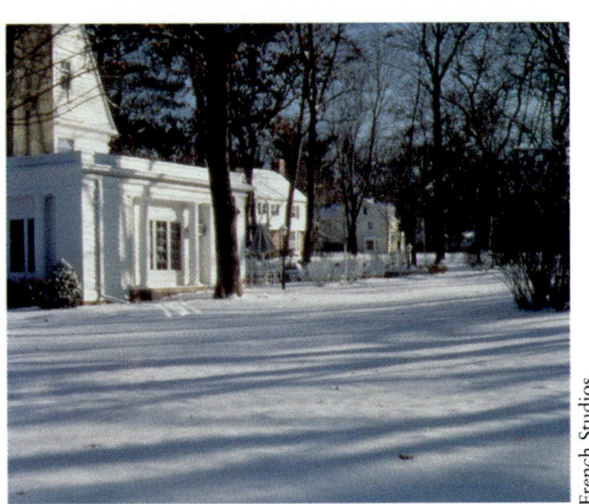
French Studios

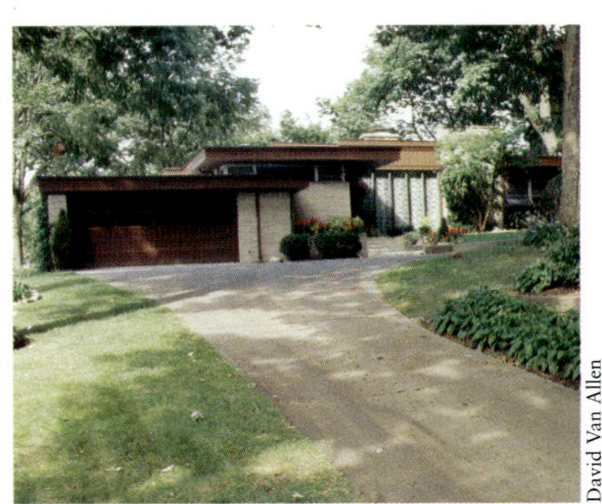
David Van Allen

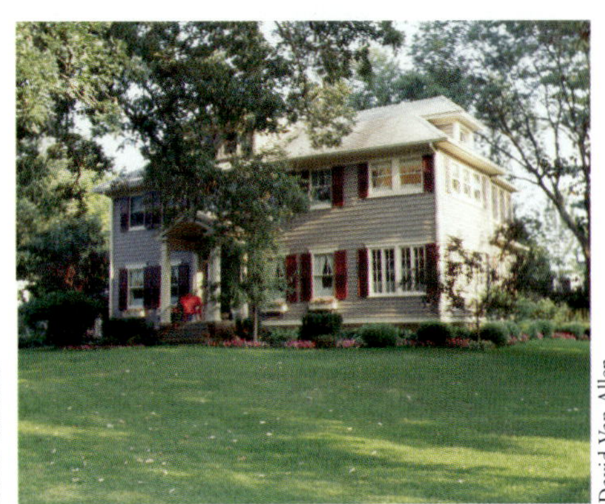
David Van Allen

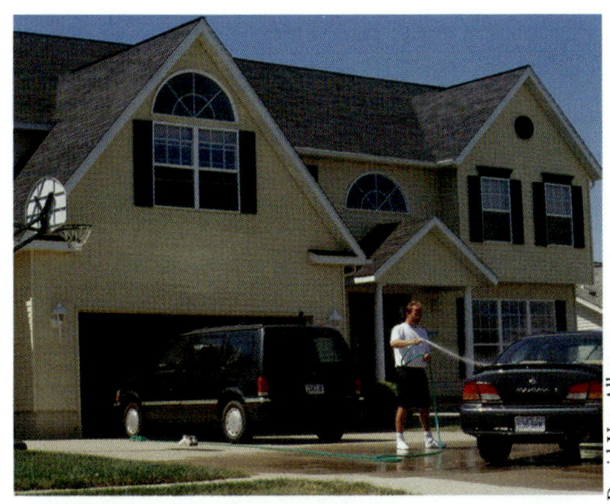
David Van Allen

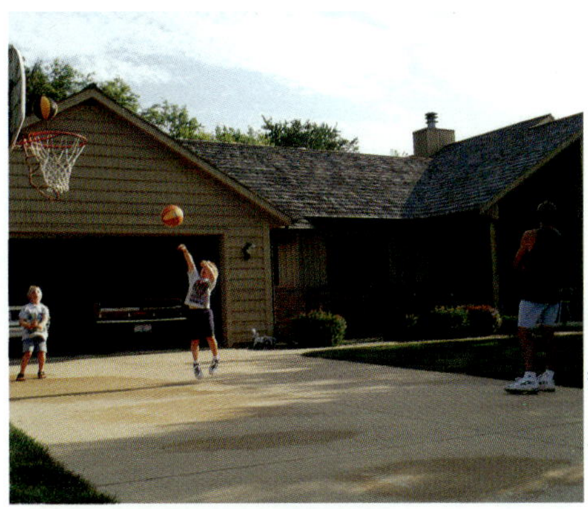
David Van Allen

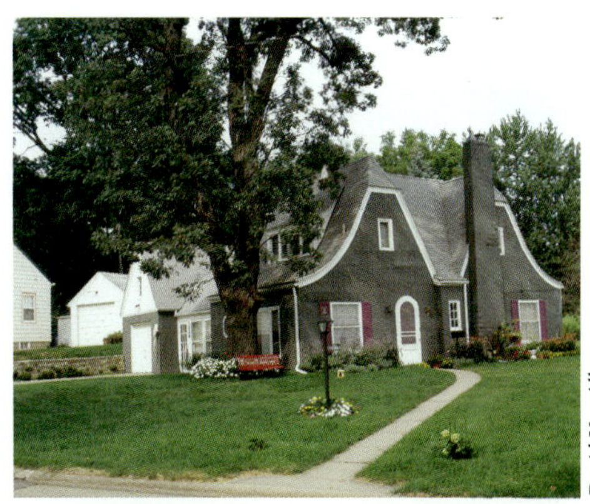
David Van Allen

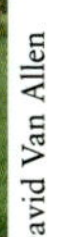

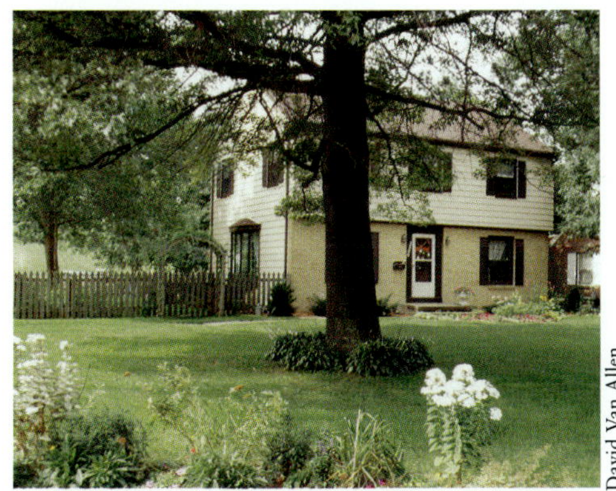
David Van Allen

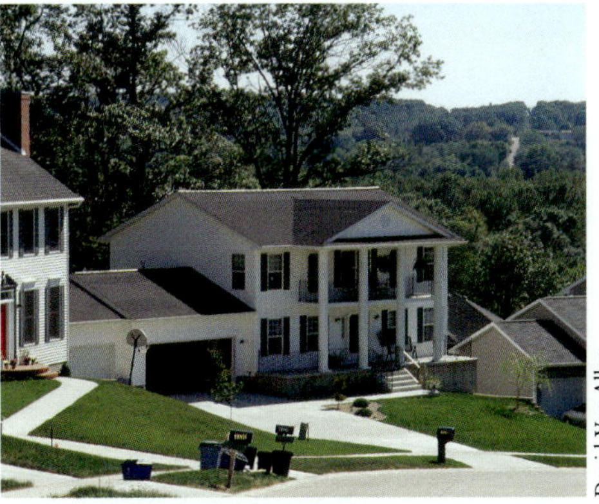
David Van Allen

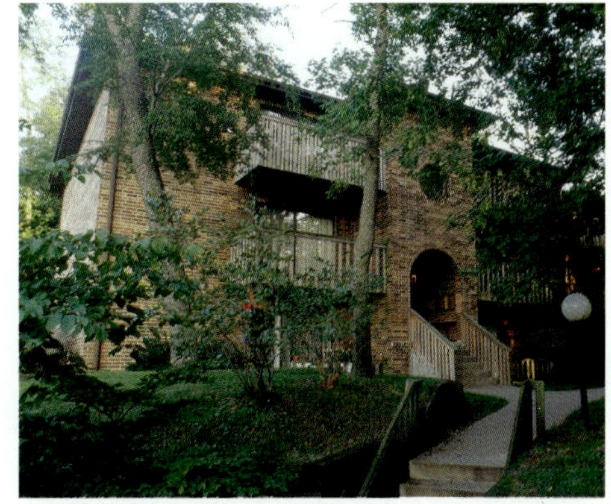
David Van Allen

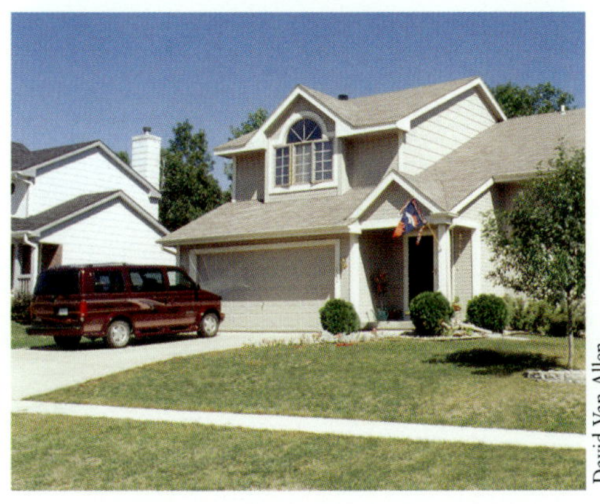
David Van Allen

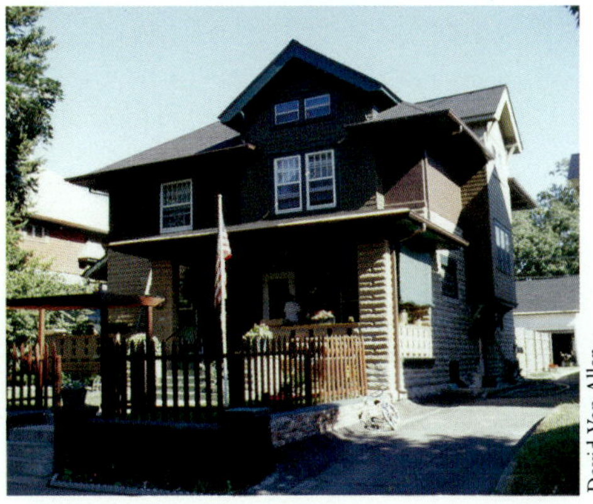
David Van Allen

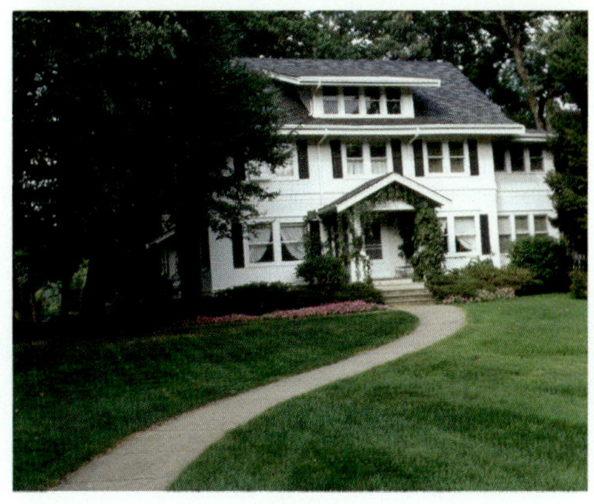
David Van Allen

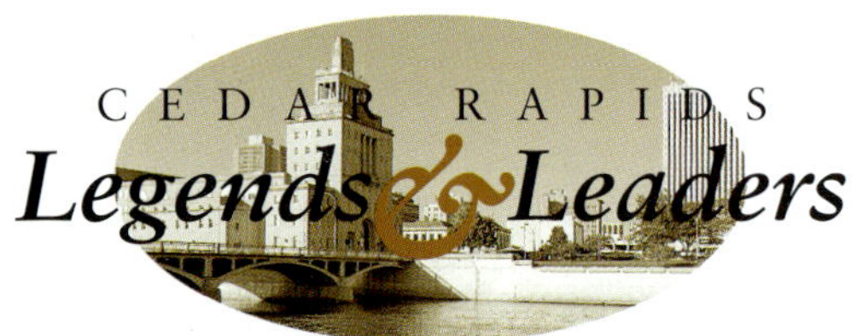

Edward Rudolf Kuba
_1911-1998_

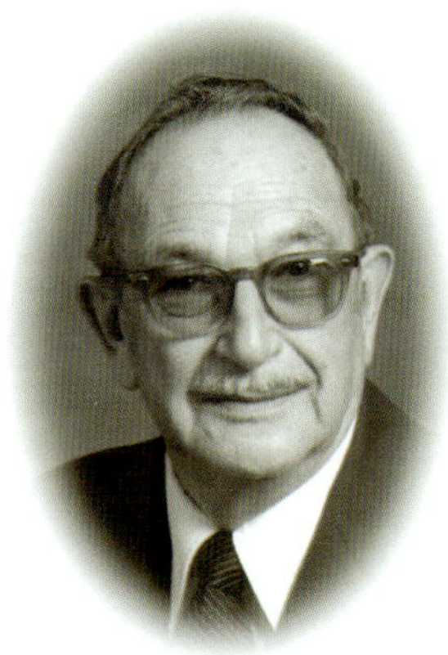

Pride in his Czech heritage was a hallmark of Ed Kuba's life. Born in Cedar Rapids, he ran a successful business and kept Czech culture alive in Cedar Rapids. He spoke Czech, knew its history, and among the Czech community is credited with the survival of the Czech school where youngsters learn to read and write in Czech and study its history.

Kuba was also influential with two projects that were completed in the years just before his death. He was instrumental in renovating the 16th Avenue Bridge, an artery that runs through Czech Village. Even as construction was to begin, Kuba insisted on carrying out the old Bohemian tradition of mixing eggs with the concrete that went into the bridge.

He also played a role in the development of the National Czech and Slovak Museum and Library, a national institution that promotes Czech history to all.

Photo: Papich Kuba Funeral Home

largely employed in higher-paying jobs than the older retail downtown ever supported. Financial services companies and communications companies and other service businesses replaced department and specialty stores.

The new vision of the downtown area includes a hope for more recreational opportunities, day care facilities and other amenities that might aid in recruiting new workers.

Many business leaders say they expect Cedar Rapids' evolution toward a more service-oriented, high-tech community to continue even while we maintain our deep roots in agriculture and continue to grow in manufacturing strength. Longtime anchors such as Quaker Oats, Rockwell Collins and Penford Products (Penick & Ford) still are large presences near the city center, while others have located in outlying industrial areas.

Proud of our heritage

Cedar Rapids is home to many cultures. This is a community where Russian peddlers became professional businessmen. Where Somalian and Vietnamese refugees have found a new home.

Between 1859 and 1870 Cedar Rapids grew from 12,000 people to a population twice that. This was due in large part to immigrants who sought jobs and land—two things that were readily available in Cedar Rapids.

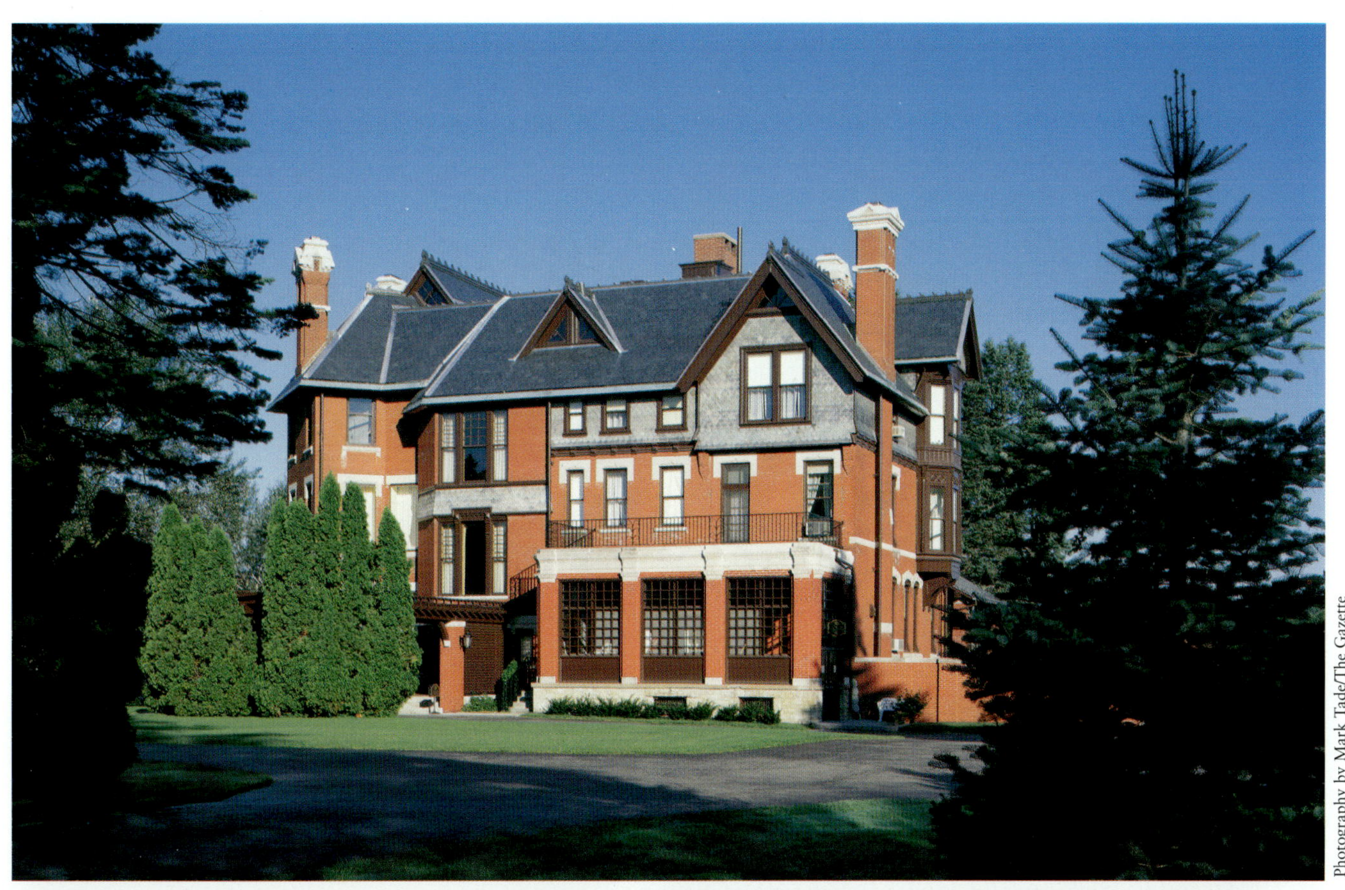

Photography by Mark Tade/The Gazette

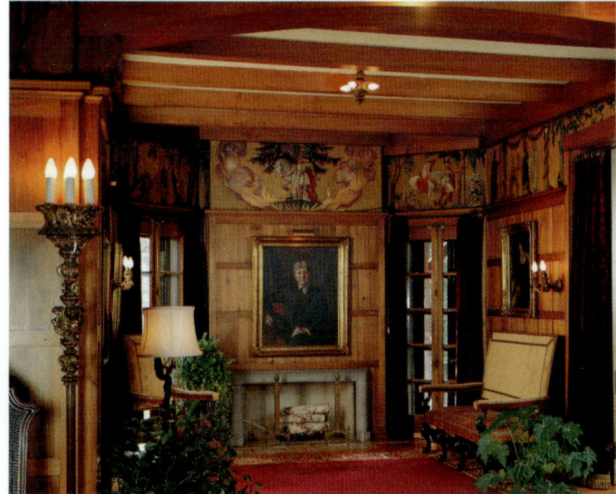

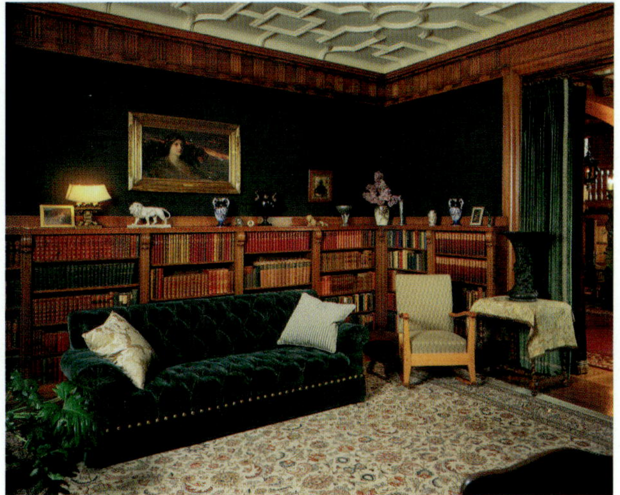

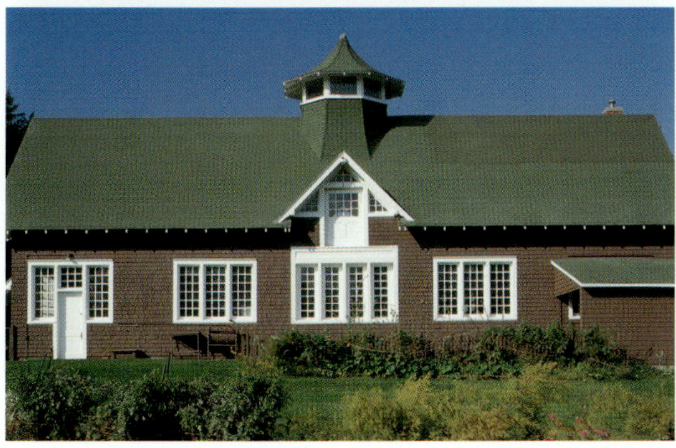

Brucemore has been a Cedar Rapids landmark since 1886 when Caroline Sinclair, the widow of businessman T.M. Sinclair, built the Queen Anne-style mansion. Later, Sinclair traded the park-like estate with the George Douglas family, who owned the home until Margaret Douglas Hall's death in 1981. The estate, the site of many special events throughout the year, is now a property of the National Trust for Historic Preservation.

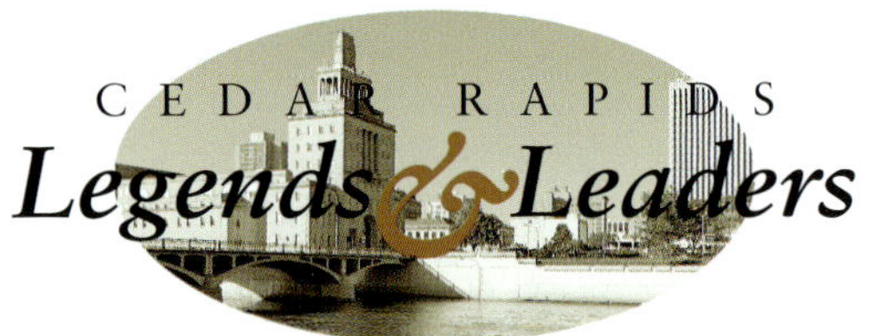

Viola Gibson
1905-1989

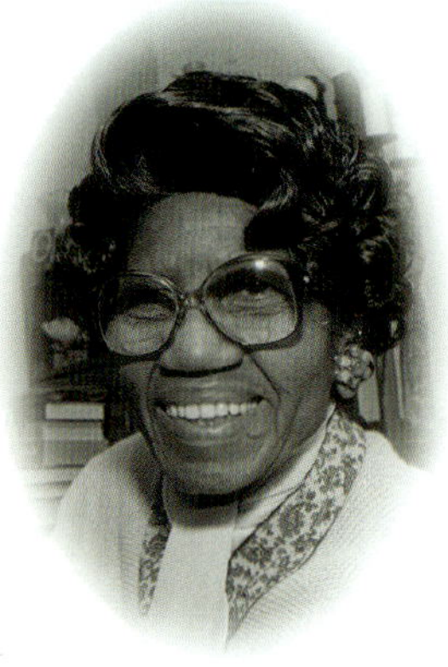

The children who attend Linn County Day Care Center or learn how to swim at Bender Pool benefit from the works of Viola Gibson.

Gibson, who was trained as a nurse and at the age of 49 was ordained a minister, gave more than 40 years of service to Cedar Rapids' civic and religious organizations. Because African-Americans were denied the right to use Ellis Park Pool, in 1942 Gibson rallied support to start the Cedar Rapids branch of the National Association for the Advancement of Colored People (NAACP). She served as president and secretary and remained an active member until her death.

Her interests in religious and community organizations benefited the Oak Hill neighborhood. As a member of the Mayor's Committee for Oak Hill Citizens, she was involved in the building of senior and low-income housing, the Jane Boyd Community House and Bender Pool.

Photo: The Gazette

By far the largest concentration of newcomers were the Czechs. They emigrated in large numbers, brothers and sisters, entire families. Settled, they created a distinct enclave like no others in Cedar Rapids. They lived in certain neighborhoods. They established their own retail shops, they attended their own churches.

"There is a Czech *community* here in Cedar Rapids. That's an important distinction. It helps define why there are so many Czech organizations here and why we maintain its heritage," explained Dan Baldwin, executive director of the National Czech and Slovak Museum and Library, which opened in 1995.

Twenty-five percent of Cedar Rapids' population today claims Czech heritage, a sizable concentration in one city. Their imprint on the community is just as sizable. They built St. Wenceslaus and later St. Ludmila Catholic churches. They were a large percentage of the manpower at companies like T.M. Sinclair Meatpacking, Penick & Ford, Wilson Foods and Iowa Steel and Iron. The importance of family can be seen in their homes. First a smaller home was built. Then, as the family became more prosperous, a larger home was built on the same lot and other family members moved back to the smaller, first house. When they died, they were buried in the Czech National Cemetery.

Being proud of their heritage hasn't always been easy. Baldwin says their history in Cedar Rapids included being the butt of jokes or of being misunderstood. Some Czechs denied their ancestry.

The development of the National Czech and Slovak Museum and Library changed some of that, Baldwin said. The institution, which has a high profile nationally and internationally, has restored a sense of pride in this Czech community. This resiliency—a heritage of survival—is also a part of their history, Baldwin said.

"What makes the Czech story so compelling today is that starting in 1620 the Czechs lost their self-rule. They didn't have a national identity until 1918. They were under the rule of another country. If you could imagine the Portuguese taking over our country for 300 years, do you think American culture could survive during that time? And yet the Czech culture survived," he said.

Two things have given this museum and Cedar Rapids national recognition: The appearance of three presidents—President Bill Clinton, Czech President Vaclav Havel and Slovak President Michal Kovac—during the building's dedication ceremony; and the international exhibit, "A Thousand Years of Czech Culture," which drew thousands to Cedar Rapids.

"Awareness of this facility goes way beyond Cedar Rapids, Iowa," Baldwin said. "It has national

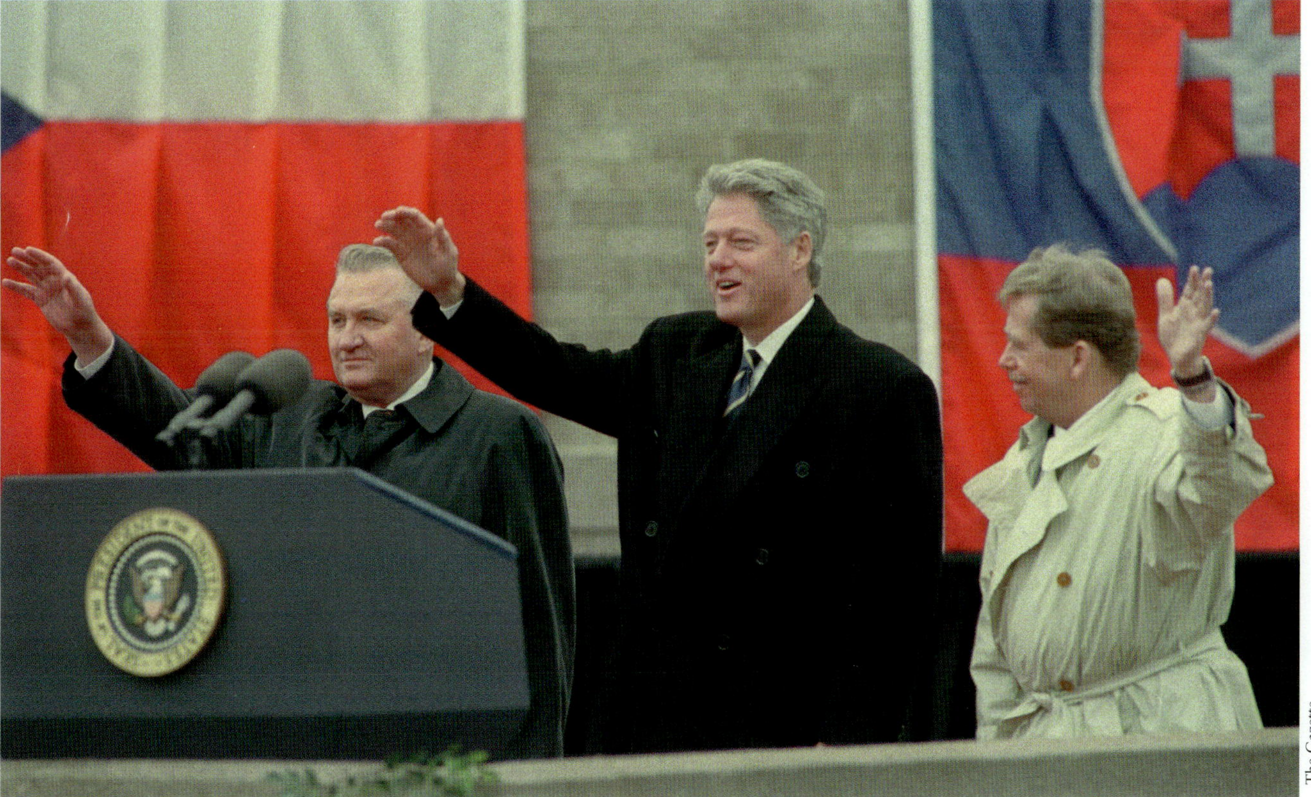

The Gazette

Slovak President Michal Kovac, President Bill Clinton and Czech President Vaclav Havel dedicated the National Czech and Slovak Museum and Library in 1995.

Proud Diversity

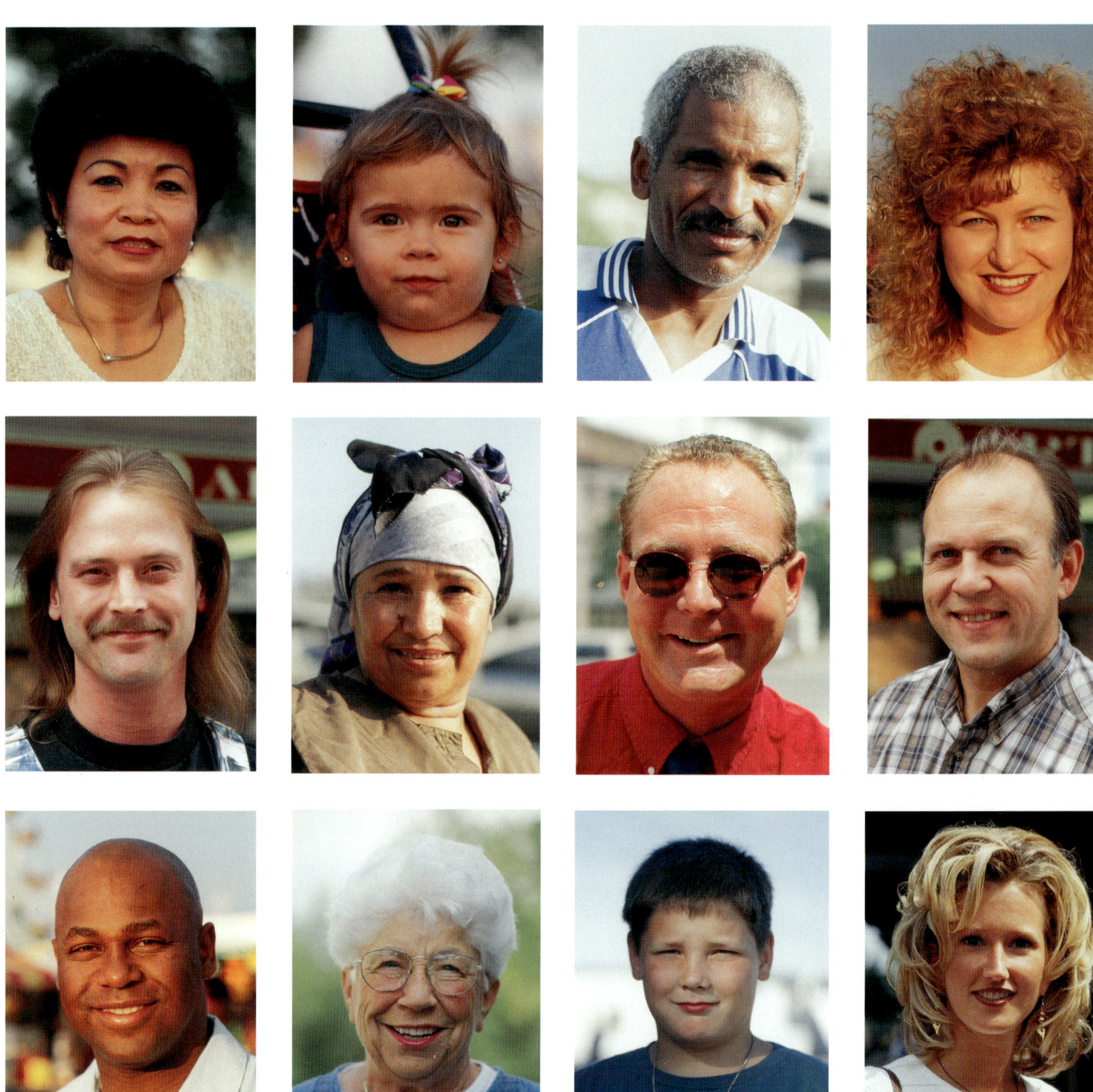

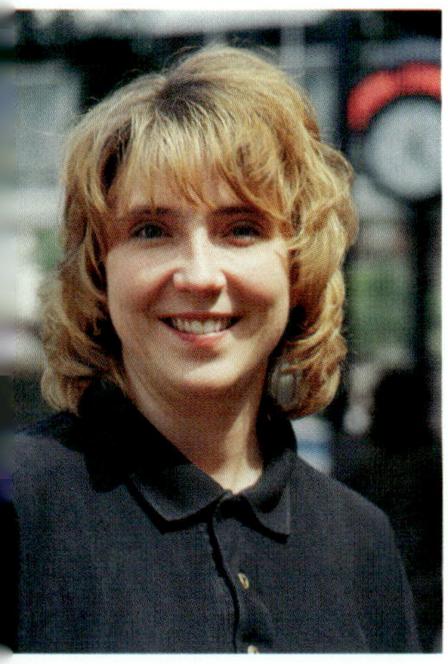

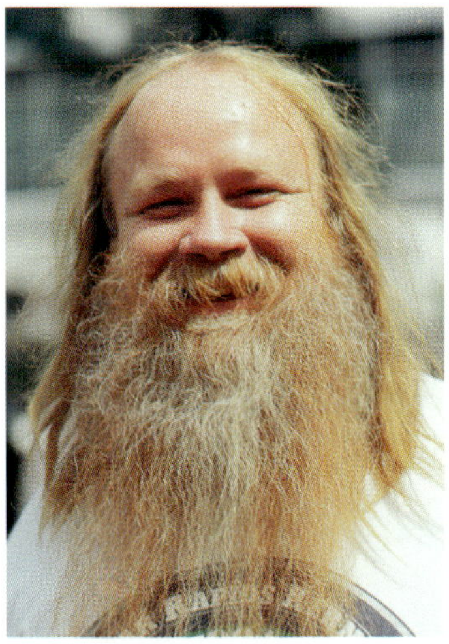

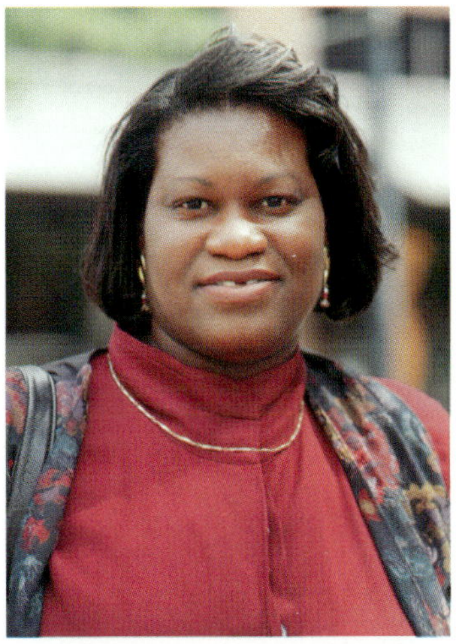

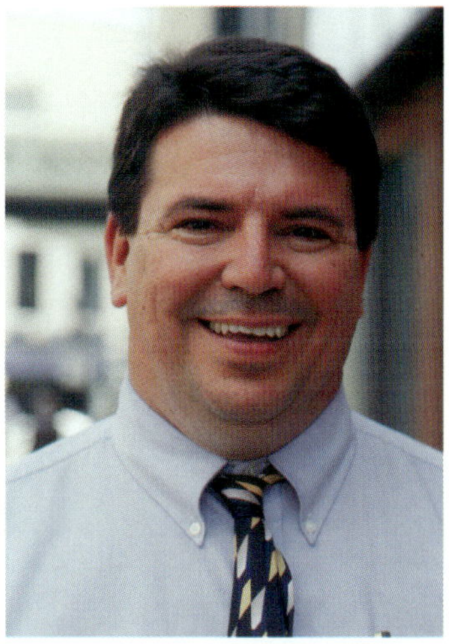

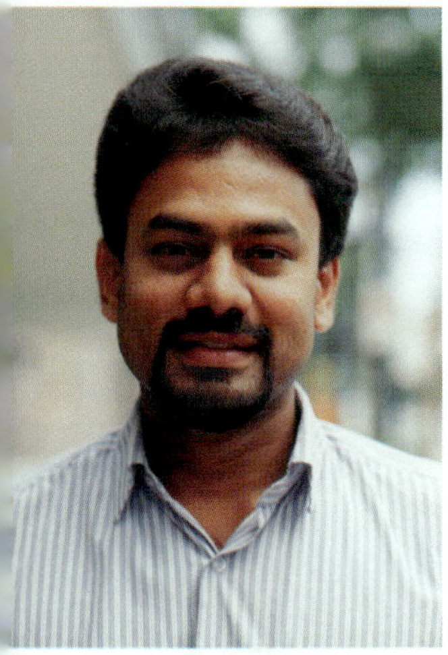

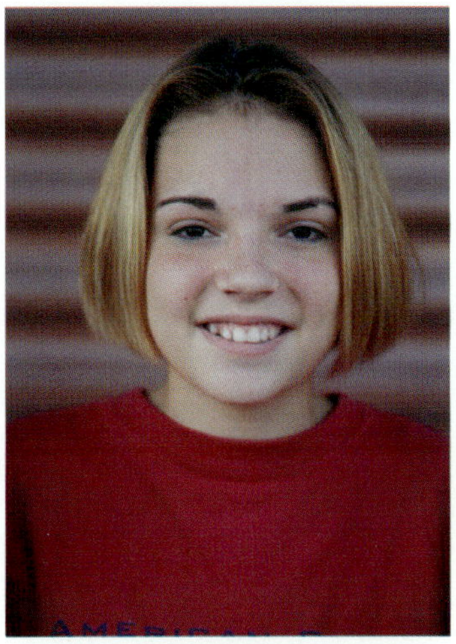

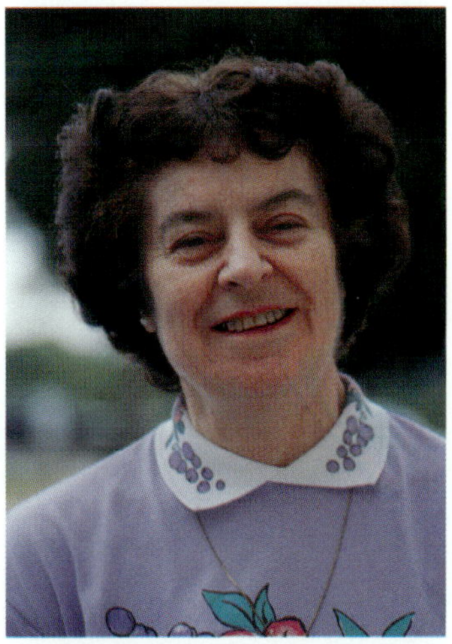

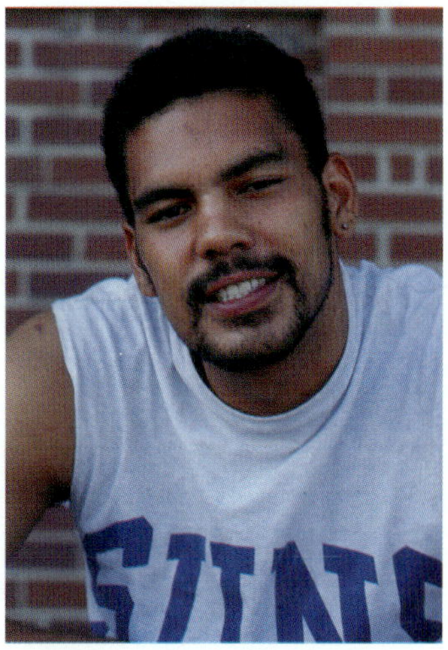

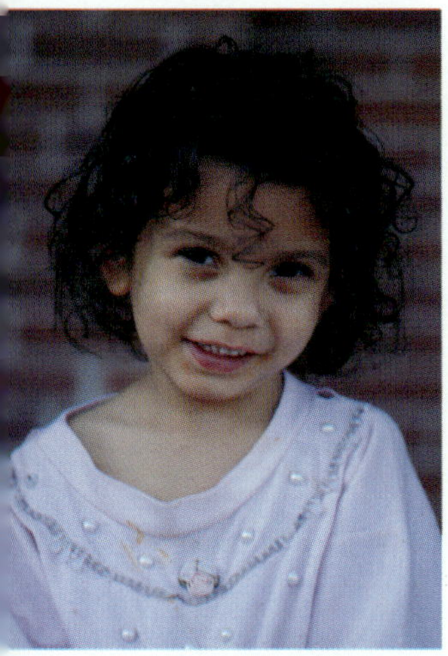

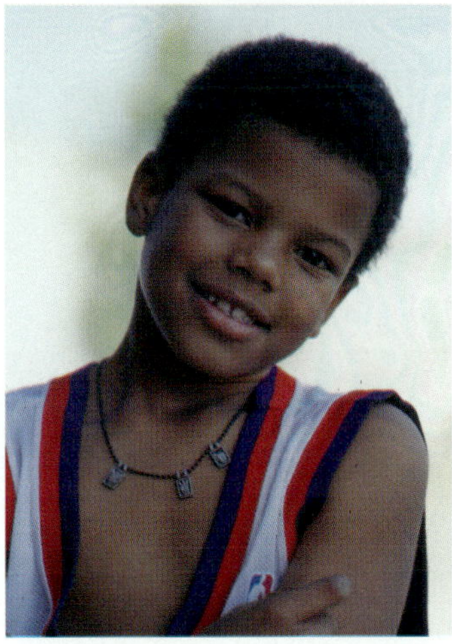

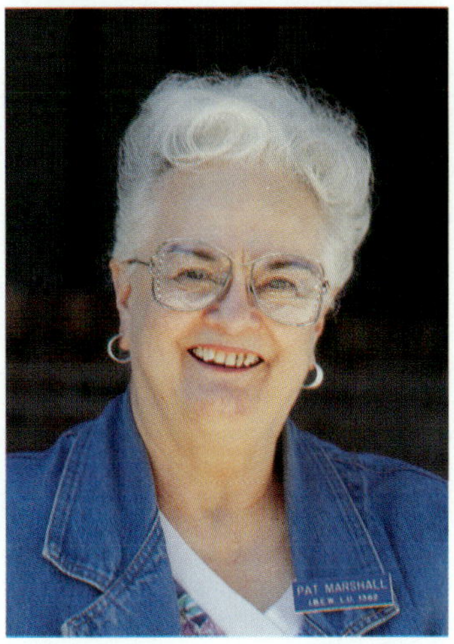

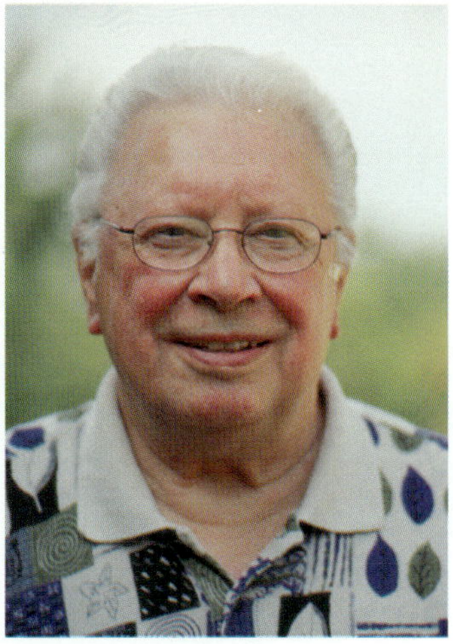

Photography by David Van Allen

appeal where people of Czech heritage travel from all over to come here. It's become the national museum for the Czech community."

A generous people

Philanthropy opens its arms to serve all areas of Cedar Rapids. Judge George Greene set the stage in 1878 when he donated land for the city's first hospital. Today philanthropy's mark is felt in all areas of life in Cedar Rapids. The generosity of the community supports arts and culture, historic preservation, education, human services, health, environment and community affairs.

"We are a generous people," said David Roosevelt, executive director and CEO of the Greater Cedar Rapids Foundation. "I don't know if it's a Midwest mentality, but this kind of generosity is something I've rarely seen before."

The Greater Cedar Rapids Foundation and the Hall-Perrine Foundation were founded in the late '40s and early '50s. The Greater Cedar Rapids Foundation represents gifts from many, many businesses and individuals in the community. The Hall-Perrine Foundation exists because of the generosity of two families, explains Bill Whipple, who has been involved in the Hall-Perrine Foundation for 23 years. Over the

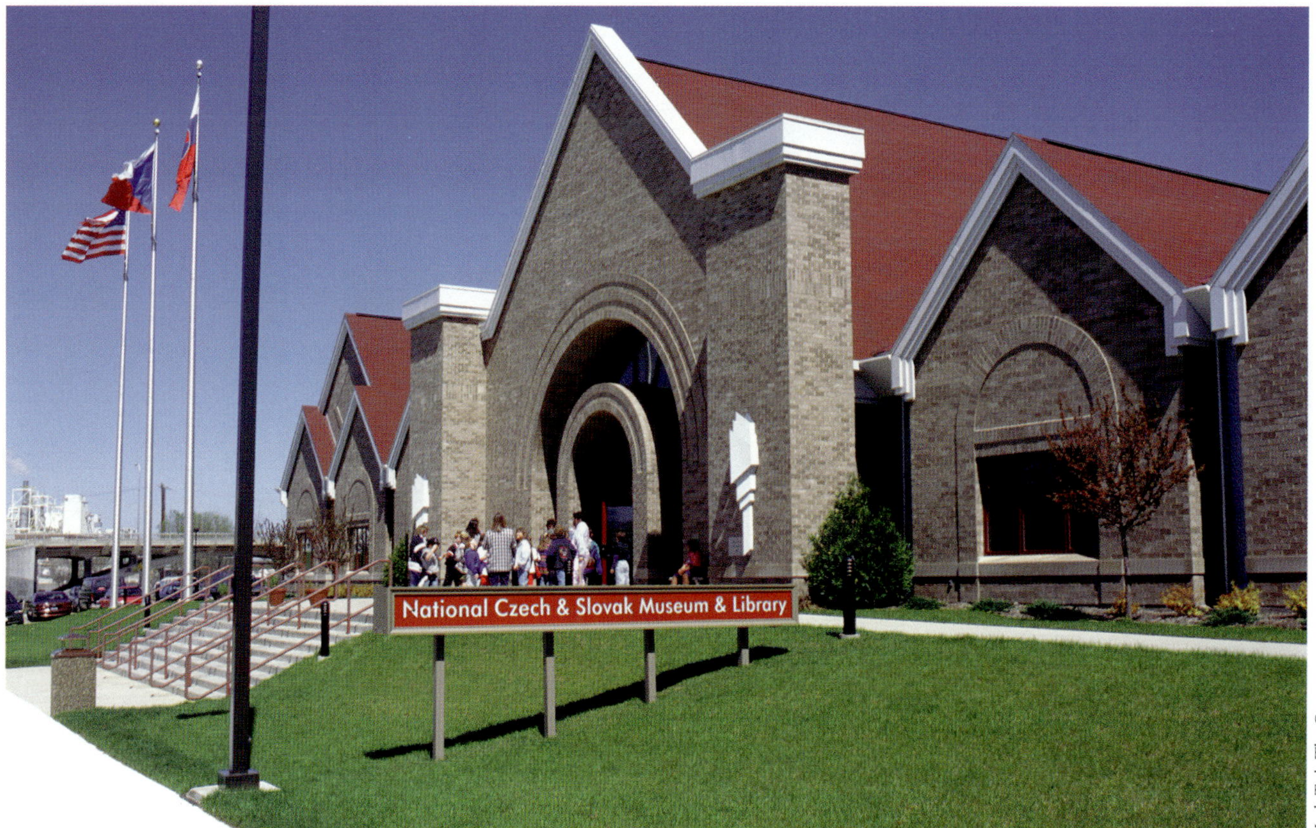

Mark Tade/The Gazette

Exhibits such as "A Thousand Years of Czech Culture" draw thousands of visitors to Cedar Rapids.

years, these two foundations have grown and as their resources expanded, so has the need.

"The non-profit community serves a purpose for needs that cannot be met by business alone or by the government," Roosevelt said. "In this day and age when we are seeing cutbacks in state and local areas for support of quality of life services, the non-profit community, particularly the philanthropy sector, must step forward and help fill the void."

It was philanthropy that built the Cedar Rapids Public Library. When several bond referendums failed, the Hall-Perrine Foundation gave a $6 million gift to the community. "We also required the community to raise $1 million in a relatively short period of time," Whipple says. "Hundreds of people in Cedar Rapids went out and raised that million in short order, which I think is a good demonstration of the concern and compassion of the community."

People in Cedar Rapids also reach out and offer their help in other ways. Thousands support local United Way organizations and campaigns. Junior League members focused their volunteer efforts into building the Madge Phillips Center, a shelter for homeless women and children. Still other individuals give time and money to area youth, churches and service organizations. When push comes to shove, Roosevelt says, Cedar Rapids comes together.

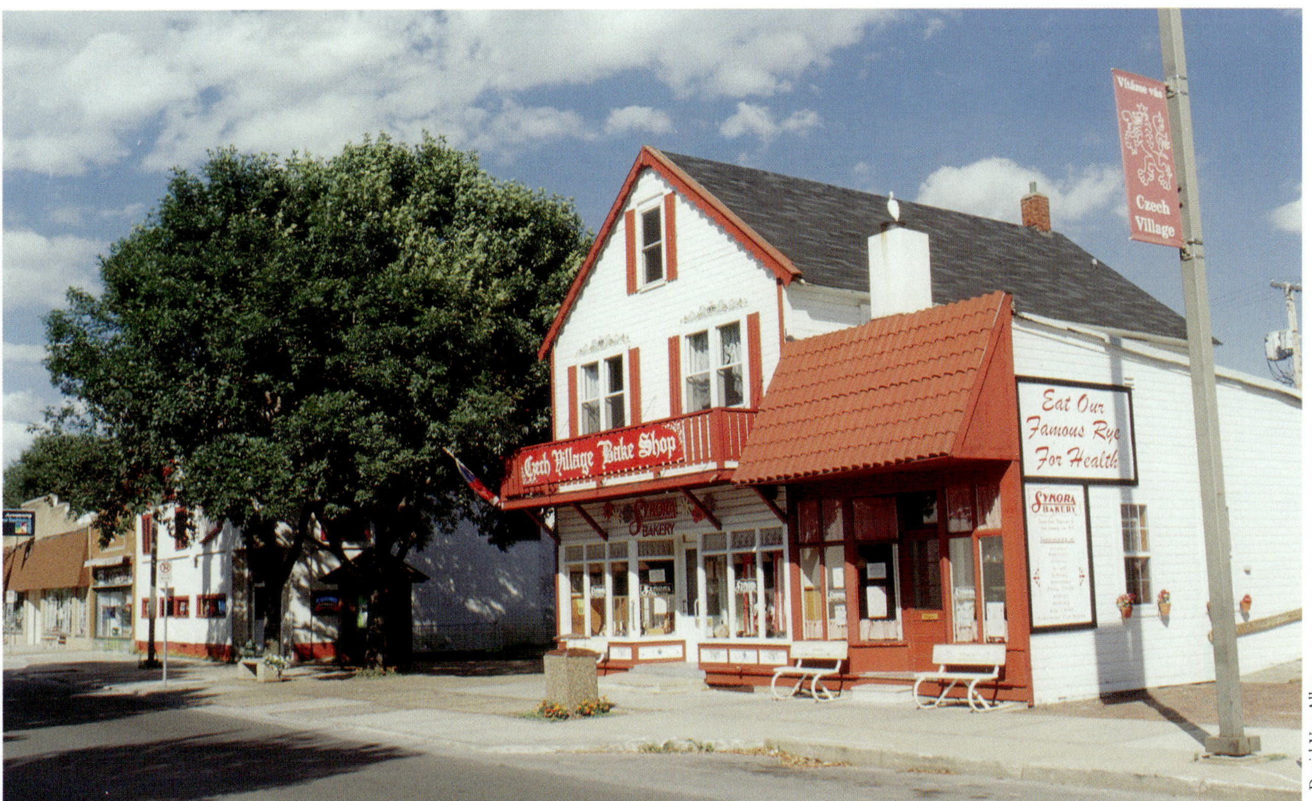

David Van Allen

Sykora's Bakery, a local Czech landmark.

We look back, but we also look forward

When high unemployment dealt Cedar Rapids a serious blow in the 1980s as many large, long-time employers were lost, the city and business communities made a commitment to restoring our economic health. Mike Blouin, Chamber of Commerce president, said it began to become obvious in the '90s that the economic development battle finally was being won, that "the glass was getting full."

"We started out 15 years ago to fill the glass up, to get the economy back up to full employment, and the glass was getting pretty close to the top," Blouin said. "As a community, it was time to look forward, to look out a number of years, and figure out what we wanted to be when we grew up."

The community's way of looking forward became the project known as Foresight 2020, which was formed to develop a vision of the future for all of Linn County. Much of that vision, articulated by a group of more than 80 citizens from all walks of life, revolves around maintaining and enhancing our quality of life and the physical and social amenities that contribute to it. It's about finding a balance between the needs of individuals, the needs of families and the needs of business, and recognizing the limits and fragility of our environment.

"We know that a lot of companies need entry-level workers, and a lot of people need entry-level jobs, to start their careers somewhere. We need to find a way to make the community more affordable for those folks," said Blouin. "At the same time, we need to make sure that the quality of life we have here not only continues but is actually enhanced—enhanced for people regardless of economic levels."

Quality of life probably means something different to each of us. For some, it is an opportunity for a good education. For most of us, it includes feeling safe in our homes and elsewhere in our city. We want a clean, healthy environment for our children. We want to work at good jobs, and we want to be able to enjoy our culture and our spare time in many different ways.

If our history is any indication, we will probably continue to get what we want.

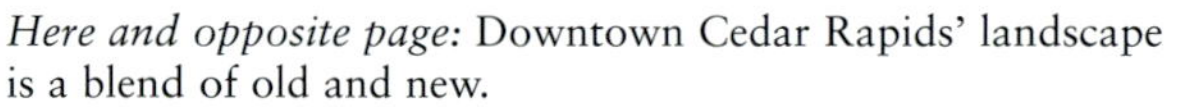

Here and opposite page: Downtown Cedar Rapids' landscape is a blend of old and new.

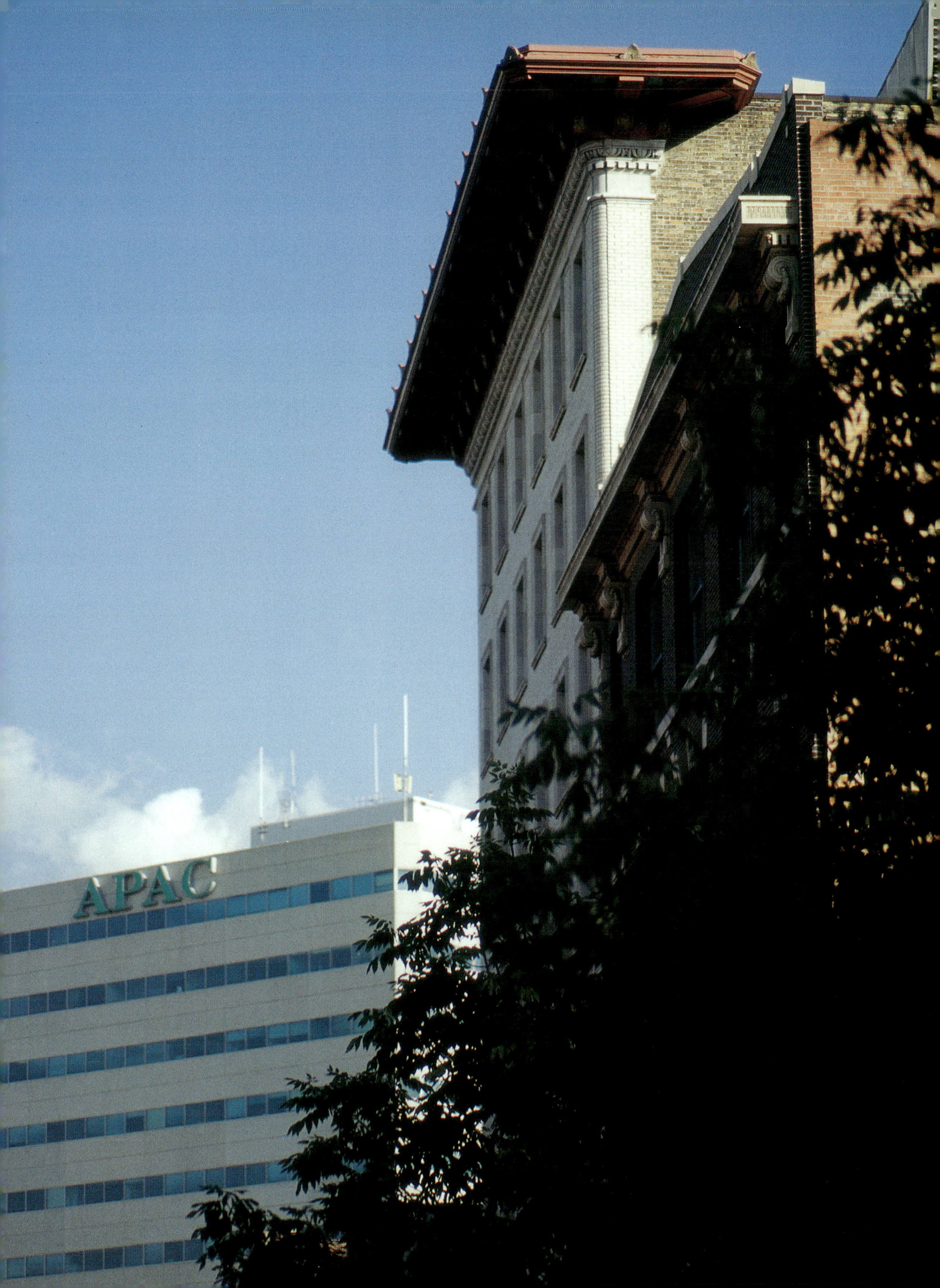
APAC

Tragedies and Natural Disasters

Tragedies and natural disasters have shaped our landscape and strengthened our resolve.

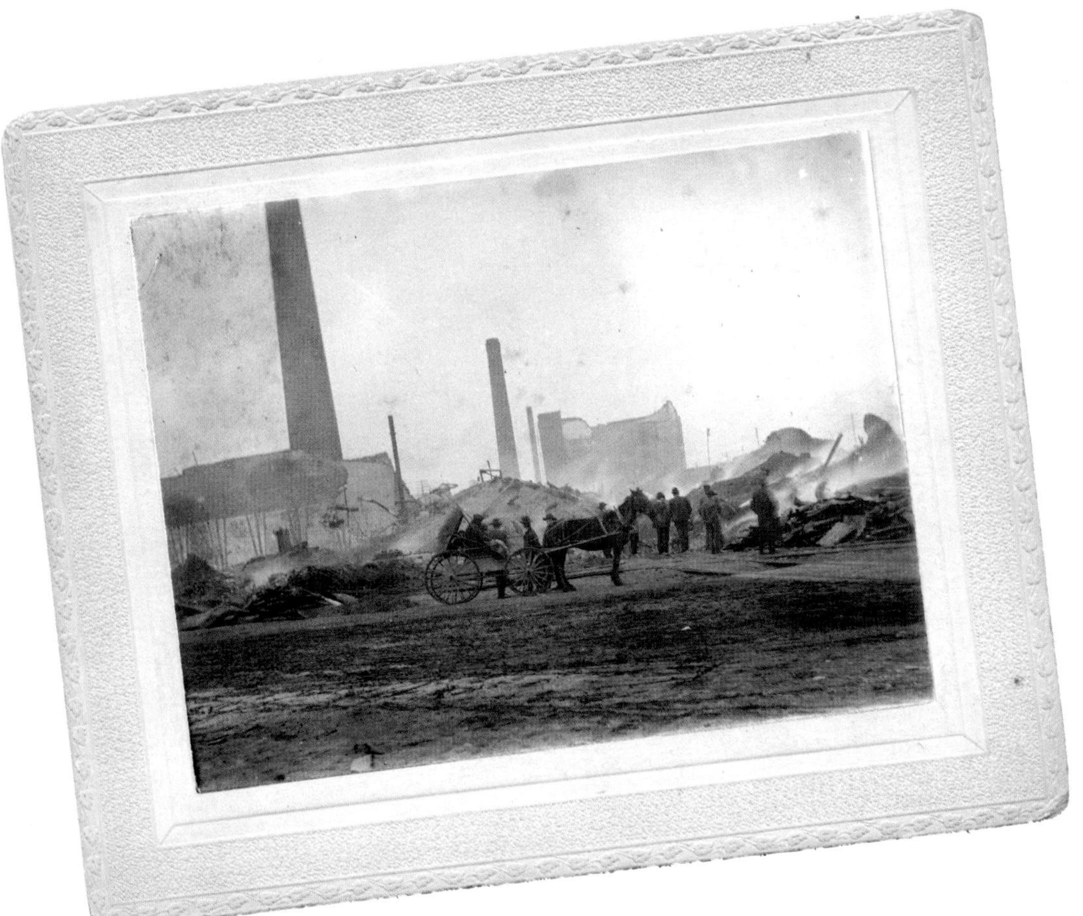

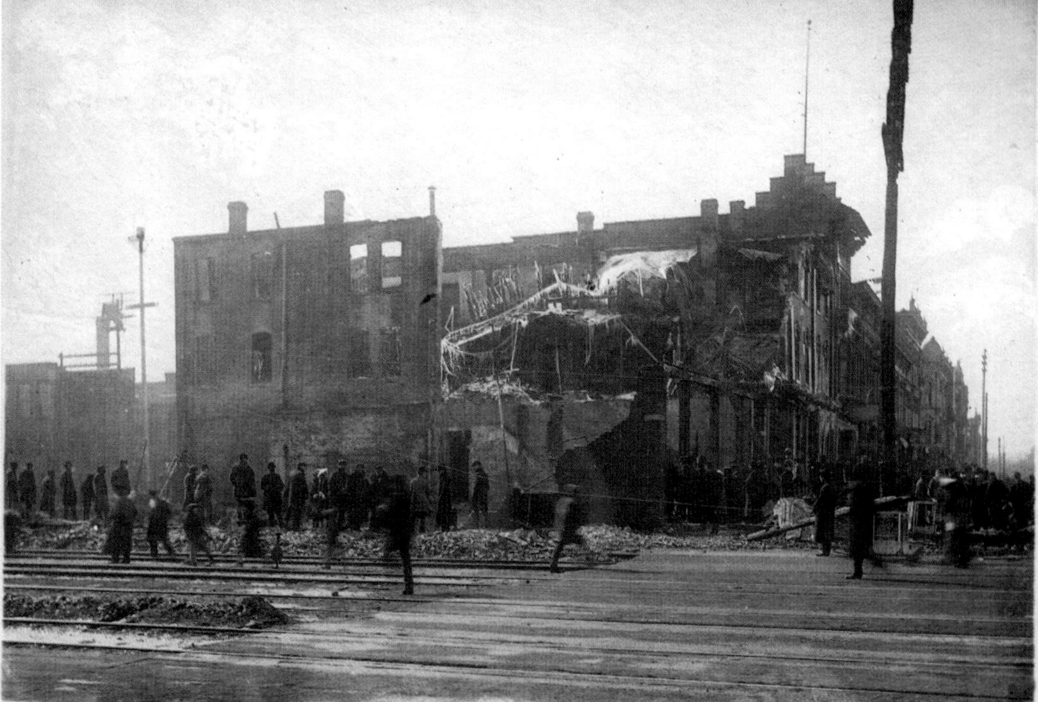

Grain dust sparked an explosion at Quaker Oats in 1905 *(top)*. A fire destroyed the Clifton Hotel *(bottom)* in 1903. A massive explosion in 1919 at Douglas Starch Works *(top, page 23)* broke every window in the downtown area. Forty-eight people were killed. In 1929, spring floods soaked downtown Cedar Rapids.

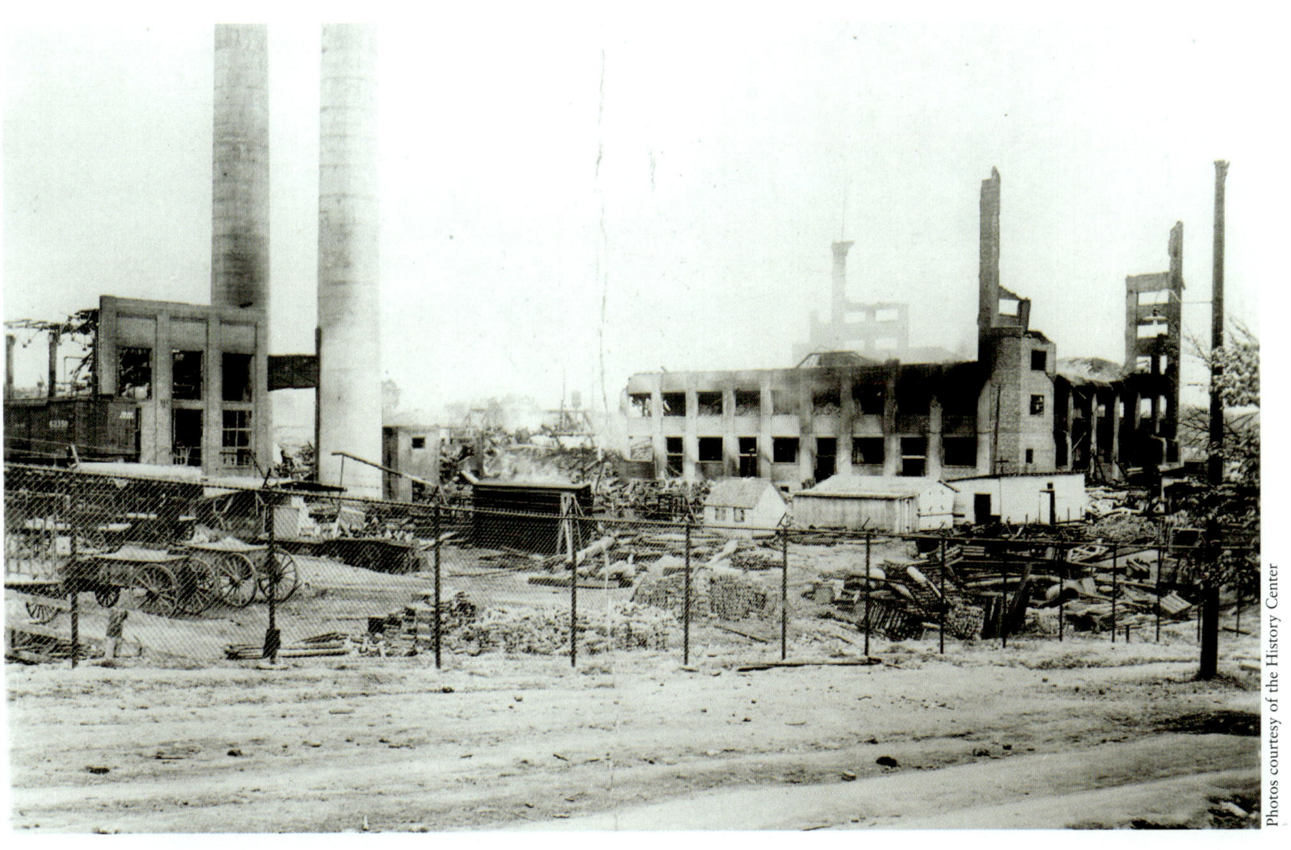

Photos courtesy of the History Center

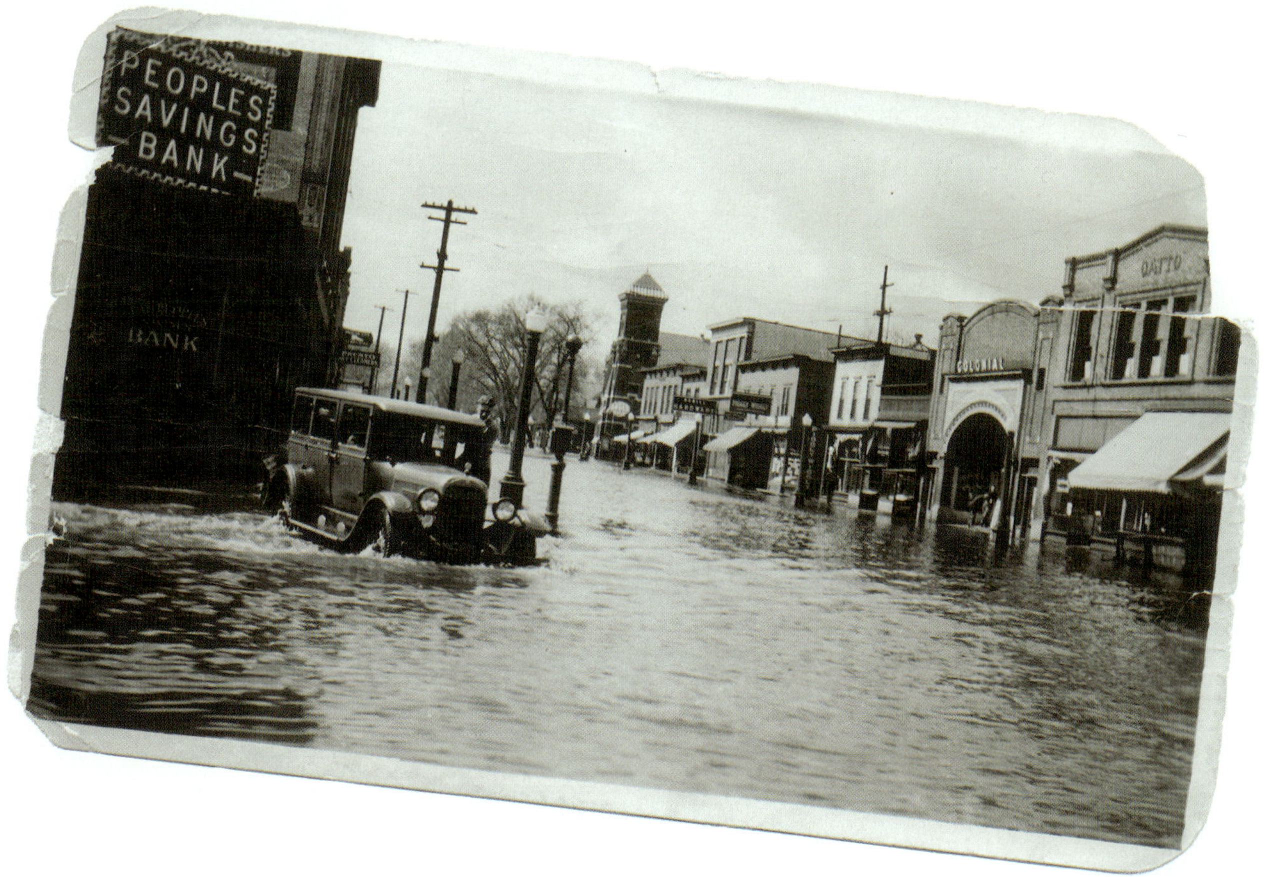

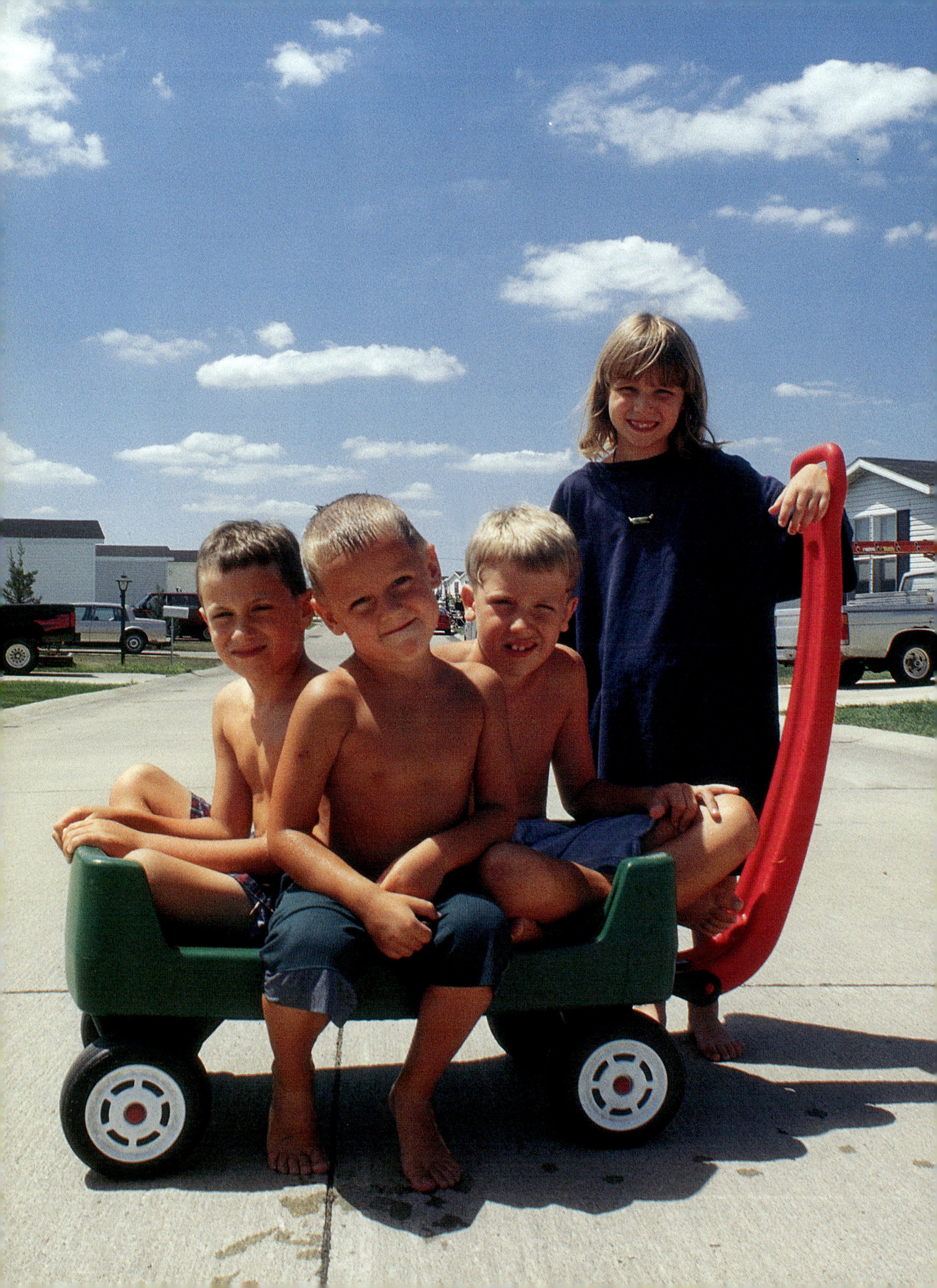

The quality of our lives

To the thousands who read, research and enjoy the search for knowledge, quality of life means a strong public library. To the people who regularly need health care, quality of life is a community with hospitals and an interest in maintaining good health. To families, young adults and people interested in new careers, educational opportunities improve the quality of life.

Just as Cedar Rapids has about 114,000 people, it also has 114,000 definitions of quality of life. Some you will hear mentioned over and over again: good jobs, safe neighborhoods, availability of the arts, a strong workforce. What most would agree on is that all of these things make Cedar Rapids a place where we want to be.

The quality of life is as important today as it was when Cedar Rapids was incorporated in 1849. The early settlers knew that the basic infrastructure of the city was important, but it wasn't enough. Neighborhoods needed parks, children had to be educated and the spiritual life needed tending as much as the physical life. These needs haven't changed in 150 years, but how they are met has changed. The city still has its parks, but it has added walking trails and swimming pools. The public library lends thousands of books but also provides

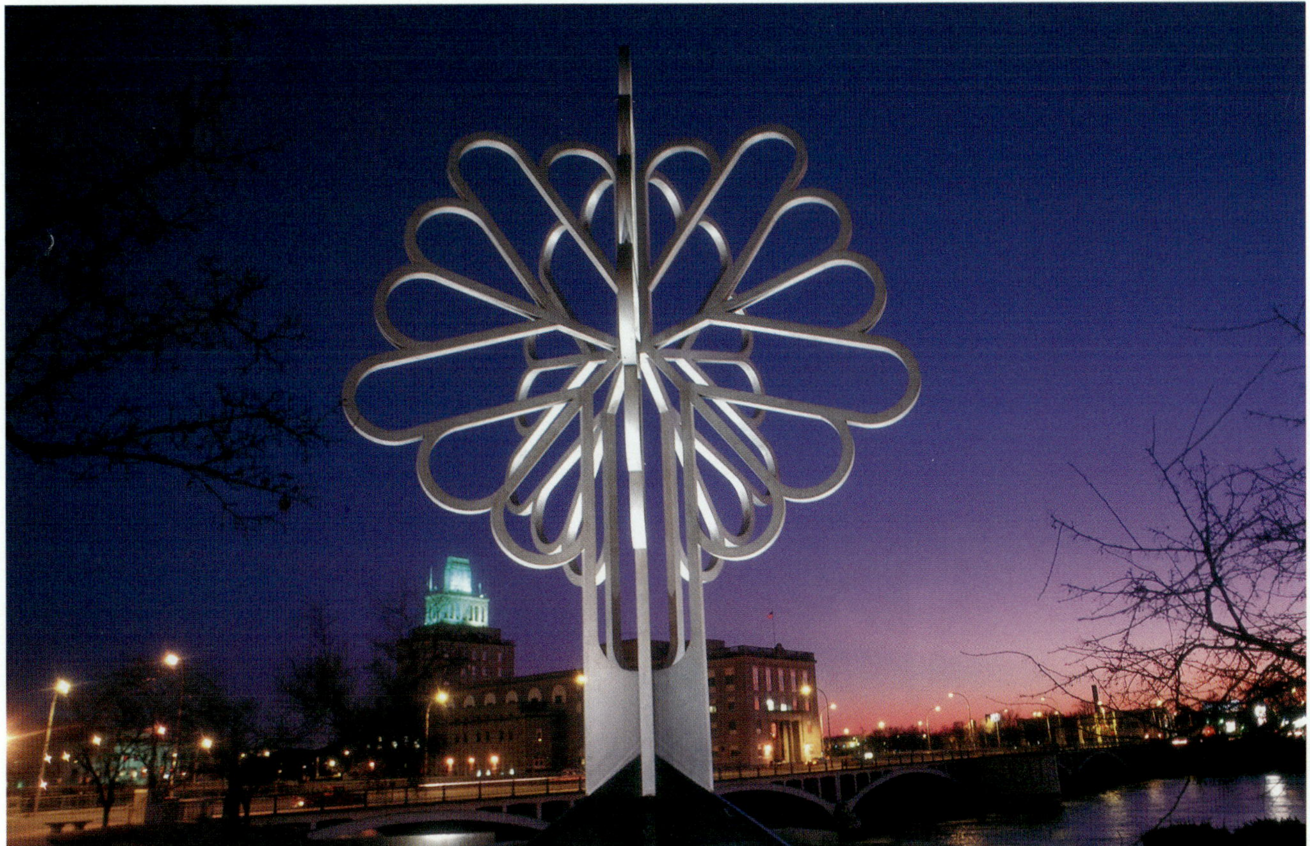

Mark Tade /The Gazette

The Tree of Five Seasons commemorates the city's Fifth Season—time to enjoy the other four.

access to collections all over the world through the Internet.

Just as individuals prepare and grow for the future, so do cities and the structures that add to the quality of our life: religion, health, recreation, library, education.

Religion

Close to the end of the 20th Century a strong ecumenical spirit thrives in Cedar Rapids. Nearly half of Cedar Rapids residents describe themselves as adhering to Christian beliefs. The other half belong to a diverse number of faith groups: Jewish, Islamic, Baha'i, Mormon, Unitarian-Universalist, Taoism and Hindu among them.

"Cooperation between the area's faith groups is one of the biggest changes I've seen in my 32 years in this community," says the Rev. Cedric Lofdahl, pastor of Holy Redeemer Lutheran Church and a co-founder of the Cedar Rapids Inter-Religious Council.

"There is a sense today that we have many things in common while respecting our differences," Lofdahl says, attributing that change to the formation of the Inter-Religious Council in 1993. Generations ago you might not have found that cooperation. But an incident in Cedar Rapids' history foreshadows the

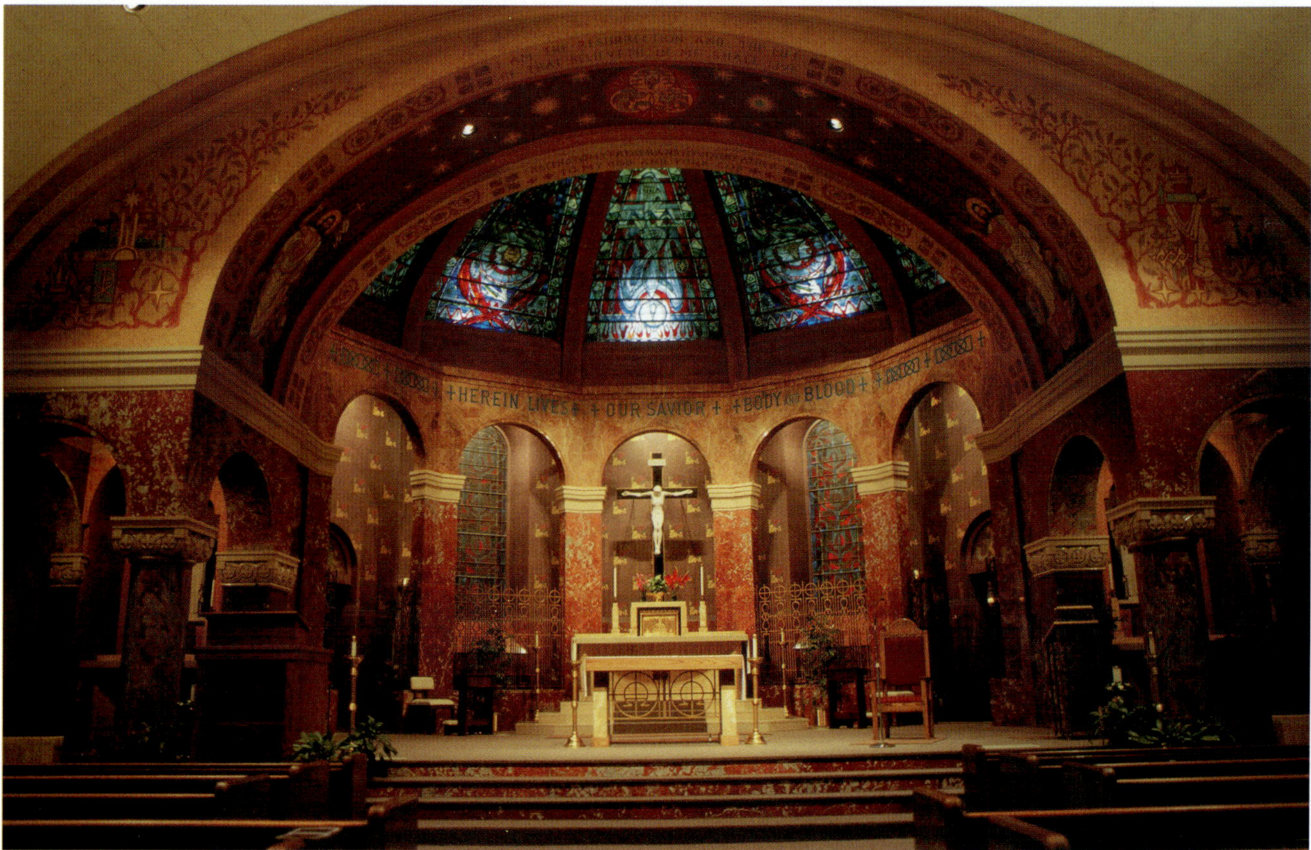

David Van Allen

Clockwise from upper left: First Lutheran Church; minaret of the Islamic Center of Cedar Rapids; St. George's Greek Orthodox Church. *Opposite:* The interior of St. Patrick Catholic Church.

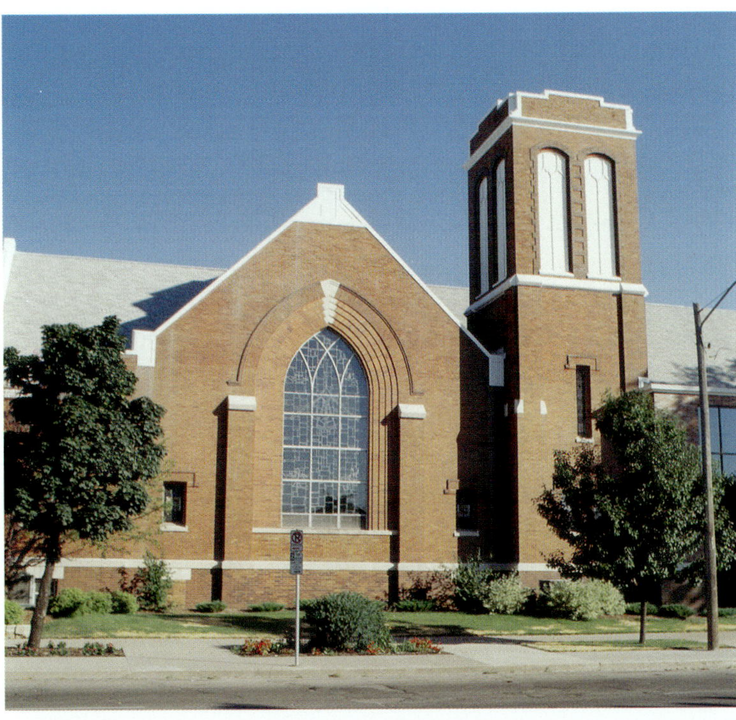

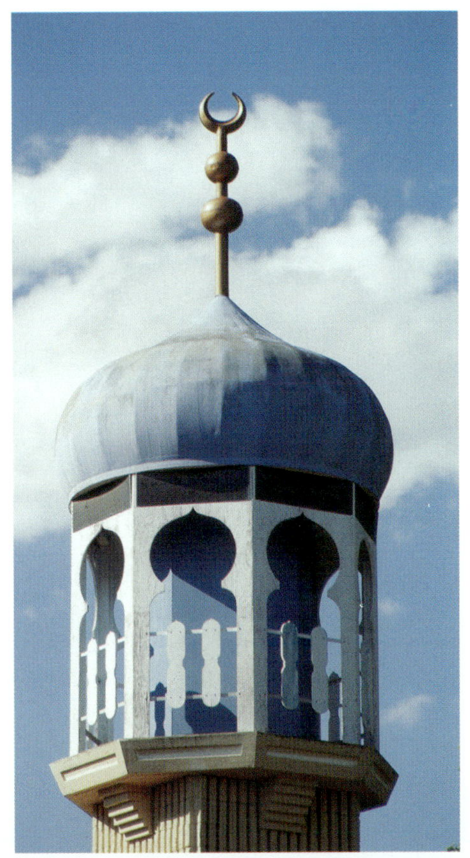

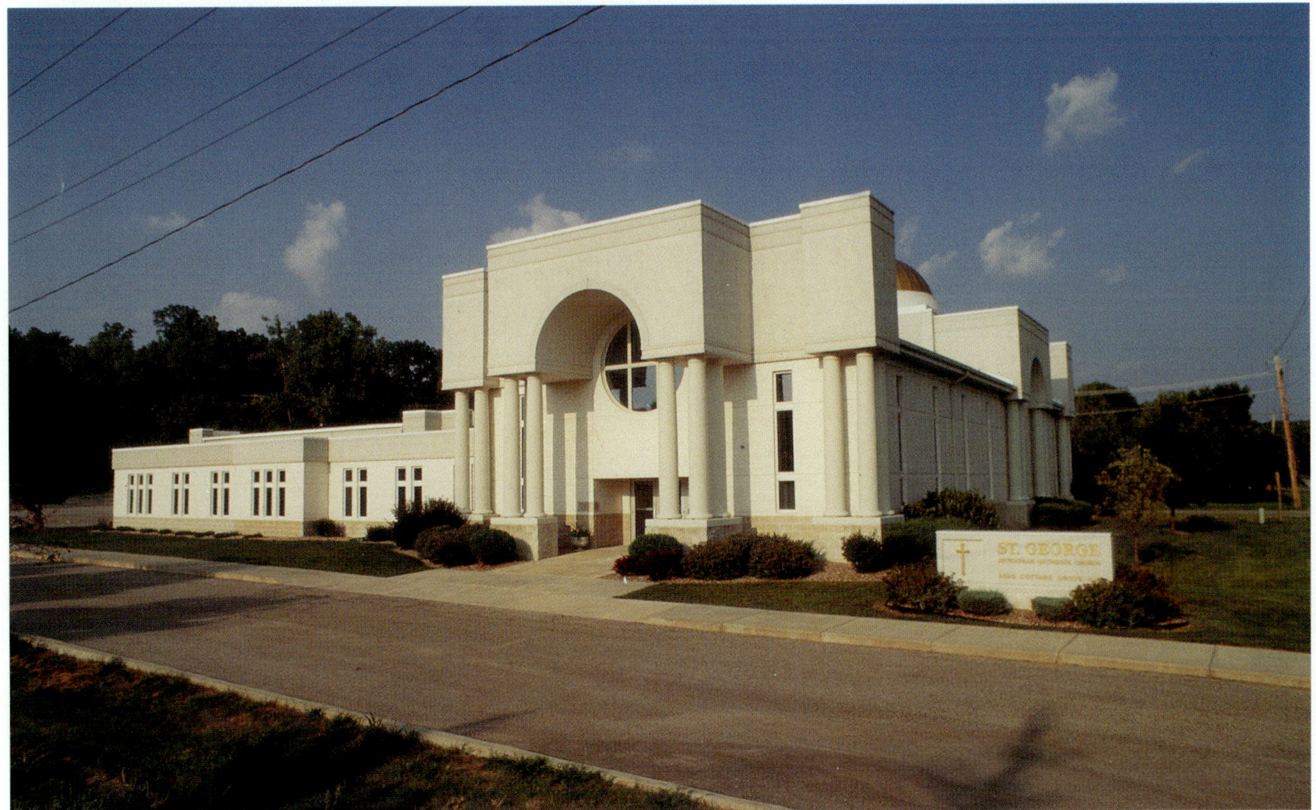

Photography by David Van Allen

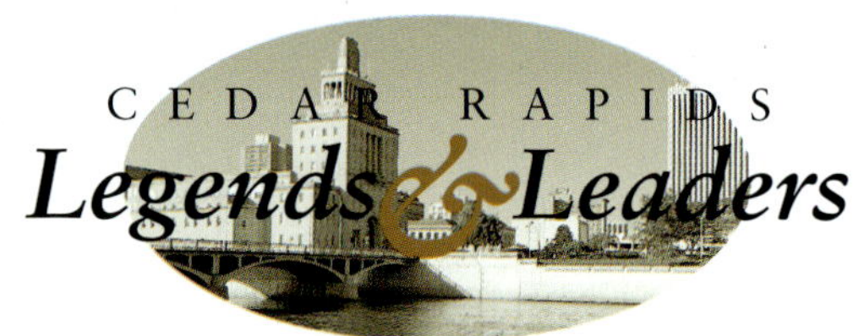

Lydia Jane Boyd
1869-1932

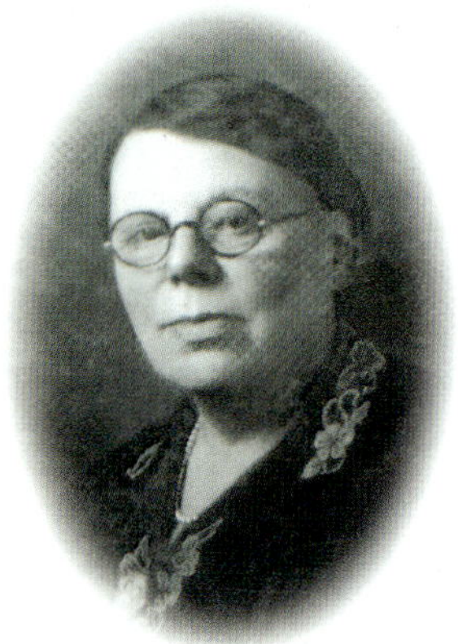

Social work pioneer Lydia Jane Boyd, who was rarely called by her first name, was born in Tipton on November 2, 1869. She became a teacher at Tyler School in 1894 and served there as a social worker from 1918 to 1929.

The Community House that was later named for her was founded in 1921. Boyd persuaded a civic group to fund a milk program for kindergartners, helped disabled children get medical help through the University of Iowa Hospitals, and established Camp Conservation for needy children in 1930. She also started a sewing project to provide clothing for the poor.

Her community service ultimately led to her death in 1932, when she contracted blood poisoning from a rusty pin while washing some used clothes to be given to the poor. She was eulogized by Dr. Harry Morehouse Gage as "a modern saint."

Photo: Jane Boyd Community House

ecumenical spirit that lives today.

The first Jewish congregation in Cedar Rapids formed in 1896. Members met in rented halls to celebrate their religious holidays until a building could be built in 1906. Later, members split into two groups —the Reform and the Orthodox—and the Reform congregation was without a place of worship.

They proceeded with developing a religious school without a building. And in November 1924, the school began meeting every Saturday morning at People's Unitarian Church. People's generosity toward the Jewish community led to close ties for many years between the two denominations.

"I call it forward thinking," says Linda Langston, executive director of the History Center, as she tells the story nearly 75 years later. And the Rev. Lofdahl agrees.

The Inter-Religious Council was also a long time in coming, he says: "Prior to 1993 we had Churches United, a group of Christian churches. Representatives from the Islamic community sat in on our board meetings, but without a vote."

There was an interest, though, between all faith groups to form a council that could explore what they had in common. In seeking a common ground, they met at the Mother Mosque in Cedar Rapids to learn more about the Islamic community. Jewish-Christian dialogues were held at the Temple. Out of these first meetings came a project that Lofdahl describes as unifying.

"We all appreciated that we were all working together to meet human needs. And there was the concern of how we could better instill values in a society that seems to be more violent," he said.

The council put together a project, the Community Character Initiative, to find out the values each religious group in Cedar Rapids shared in common.

"Like cream coming to the top of the milk," Lofdahl says, four values emerged that all shared in common. "We identified caring, honesty, respect and responsibility as the values most prized by Cedar Rapids residents," he said.

The task the council faces at the end of the 20th Century is to unite the community—schools, businesses and other organizations—in encouraging and teaching the values.

"We are already a particularly caring community and you see that in the success of our food banks and in our success in resettling refugees in our community," Lofdahl said.

In some ways, this kind of project is not unlike the work churches used to undertake years ago. Churches have always tried to reinforce the values of a community, Lofdahl said. What's unique about this project is that we are doing it together.

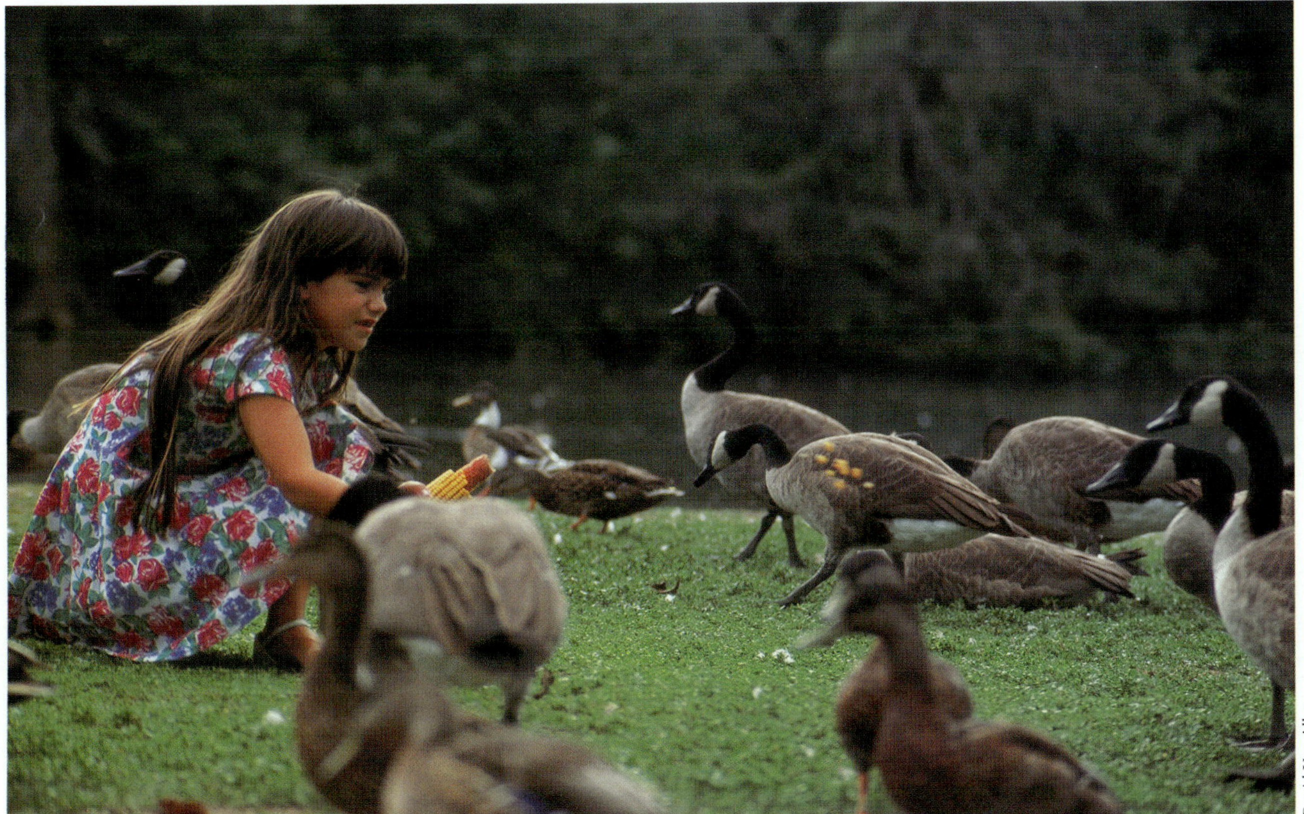

David Van Allen

Feeding the geese at Ellis Park is a popular pastime.

Health

The need for a healthy community is no different in the late 1990s from what it was when a minister posed the challenge to build a hospital in a very young Cedar Rapids.

What more and more cities—and Cedar Rapids is one of them—now focus on when they look at health care is taking the focus off the hospitals and placing it on community health improvement. "This is the glimpse of the future when it comes to health care," said Liz Selk, the director of Healthy Linn Care Network, a partnership of organizations that work to improve the health status of people in Linn County.

What makes up a healthy community extends beyond a person's physical being, Selk explains. "We realize now that to have a healthy community you have to have a healthy environment, make good lifestyle choices, have safe streets in your neighborhood, green areas for play and good stress management skills. Plus an acute care hospital," she added. "There's never a choice between the two, but a partnership."

Both St. Luke's Hospital and Mercy Medical Center play an active role in Healthy Linn Care Network, as do more than 100 other agencies in Linn County. Started in 1990 (as Healthy Linn 2000), this health care network focused its first efforts on prevention.

As baby boomers age and drive the health-care market even more, Selk said, it will make sense for the network to look at factors that influence aging. "We don't want aging like our parents," she said. "We want to be healthy elders. And we've been told for years that to be healthy in old age we have to take care of ourselves now."

Prevention efforts include offering screenings for diabetes, smoking cessation classes, educational programs and school-based health services that emphasize the need for healthy living. Programs in schools, such as one being planned for Franklin Middle School, will combine information on nutrition, increasing activity, avoiding tobacco and learning stress management. It will be available not only to students, but parents and staff.

"We'll also do baseline testing and help people set individual goals to be a healthy person or family," Selk said. "We'll build incentives. These are the kinds of projects that we will see more of in community health care. People won't have to go to the hospital to get this information. It will be offered at the community level—in schools and churches."

Also driving health care changes have been financial realities. Caring for everybody in a hospital setting has been an expensive way of doing business.

"It's hard to predict the future of health care because of the technological changes, but I think we will continue to see a blend of high tech and low tech," Selk said. "If I have high blood pressure, yes, I may need medications, but you can also look into

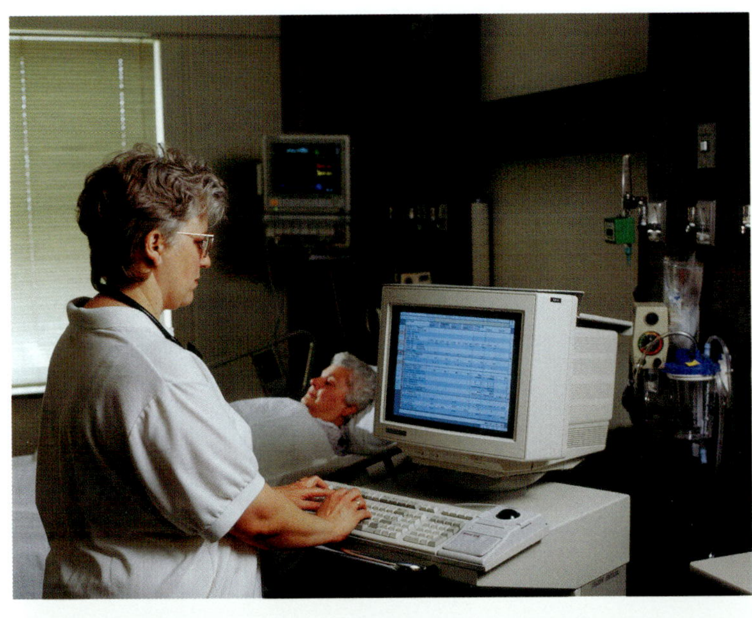

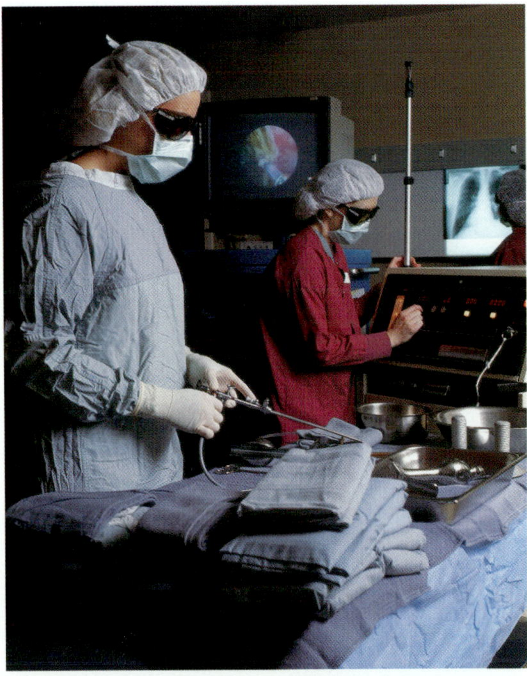

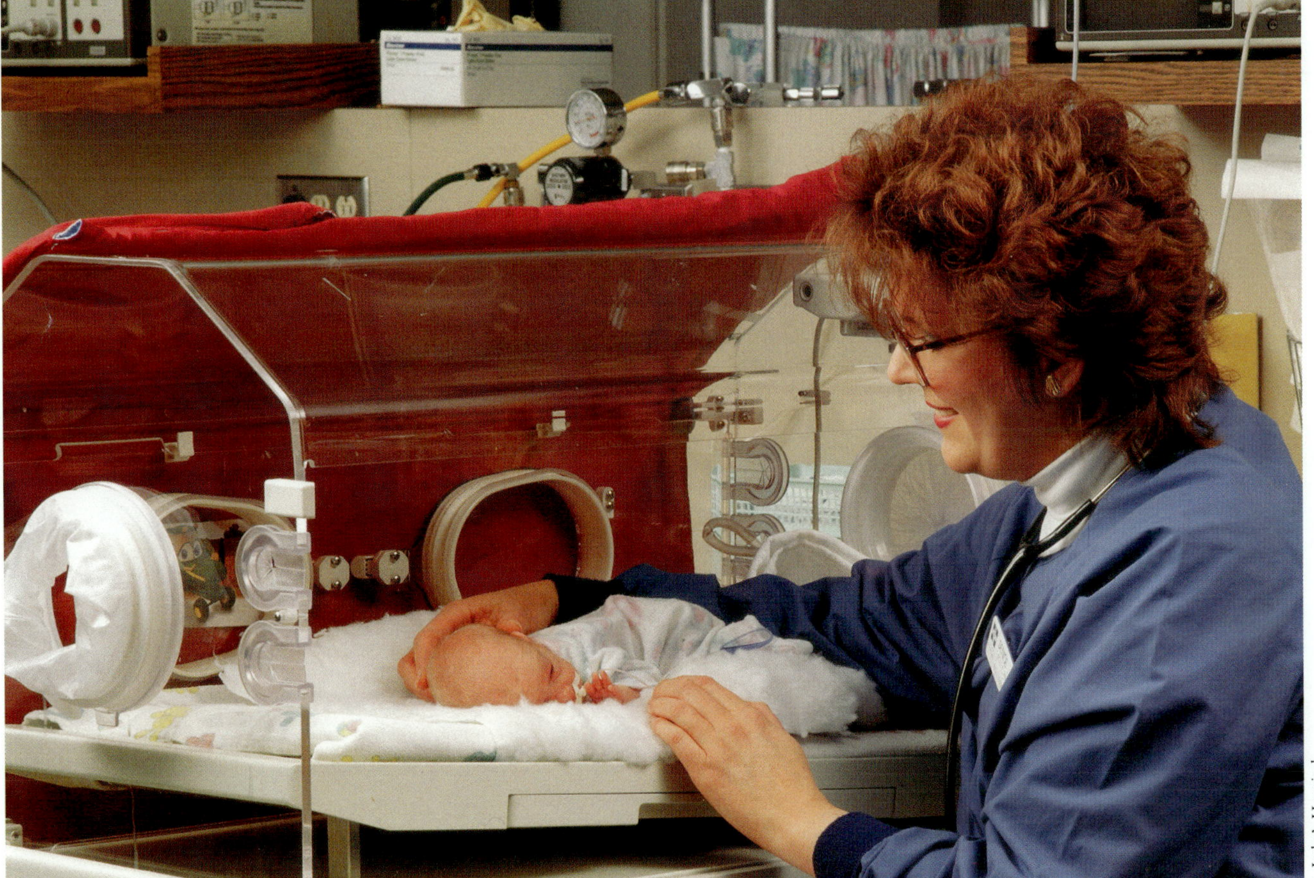

St. Luke's Hospital

Computer technology in Eastern Iowa helps improve patient diagnosis and treatment and reduce hospital stays. Community partnerships have supported advanced cardiac care and a neonatal intensive care unit at St. Luke's Hospital to improve the health of people throughout Eastern Iowa.

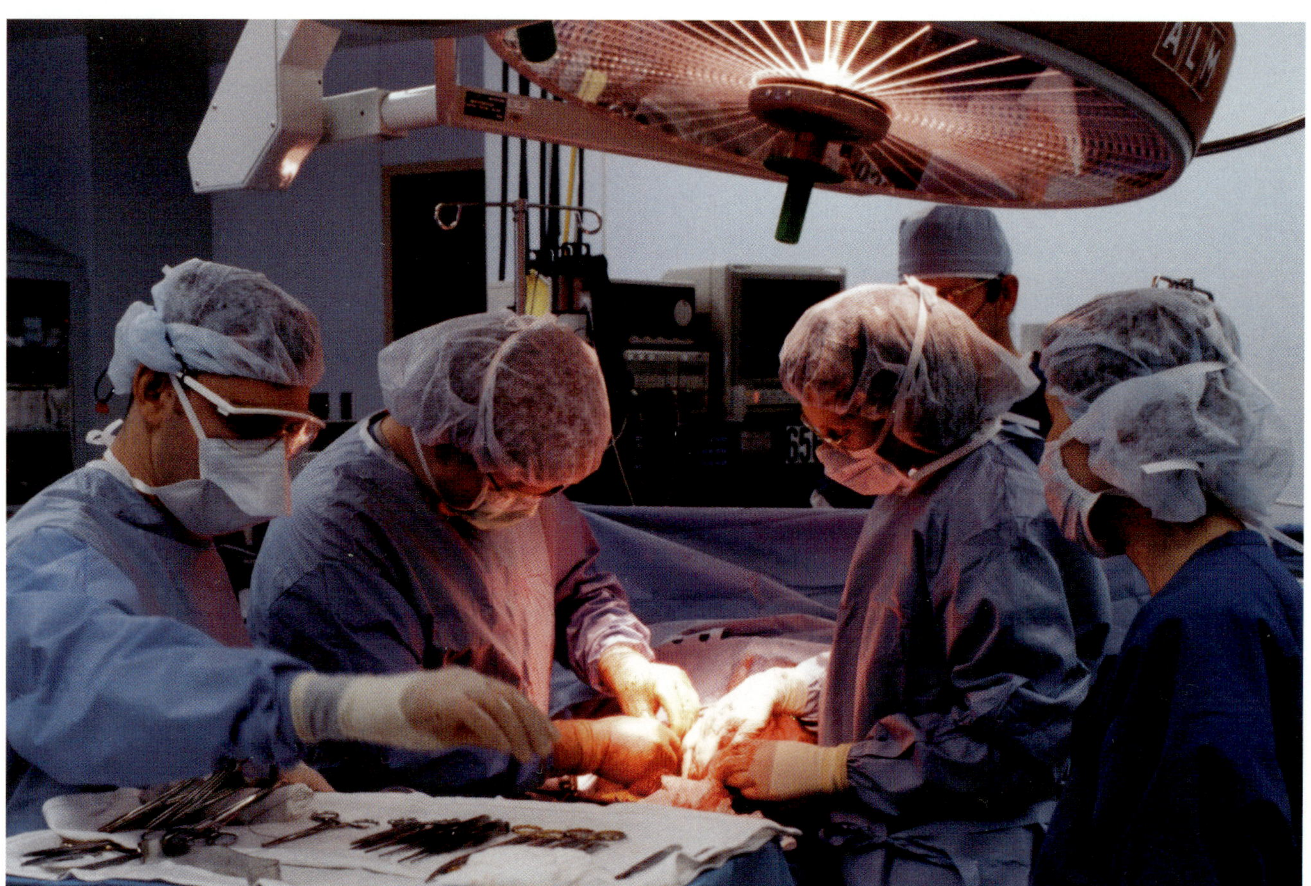

Mercy Medical Center

Mercy Medical Center

Above: State-of-the-art surgical suites and highly skilled surgical teams at Mercy Medical Center are in constant readiness for inpatient, outpatient, and emergency surgeries.
Right: The annual "Especially For You" Women's Race Against Breast Cancer, sponsored by Mercy Medical Center and General Mills, draws women from across the state and country. This October event raises money to provide mammography services for women in need.

other therapies. If I have cancer give me chemotherapy, but I may also need meditation and massage. It's never about either/or anymore."

Recreation

When Nancy Wendler was growing up in Cedar Rapids, her family celebrated the Fourth of July as many did—with parades, picnics and fireworks.

Wendler, now the executive director of the Freedom Festival, the city's annual Fourth of July celebration, falls back on those memories in planning the festival. "We're building on a formula that works with the values that represent what this community is about. Affordability, accessibility and patriotism," she said from her office in downtown Cedar Rapids.

The annual festival is one among many of the recreational opportunities in Cedar Rapids. Leisure time activities may include an evening at the symphony as well as a night at the ballpark watching the city's minor league baseball team. Art museums, night life, and boating on the Cedar River or nearby Coralville Lake attract the people who live in the community as well as surrounding towns.

Our ideas of recreation and leisure change from generation to generation, and the city bears witness

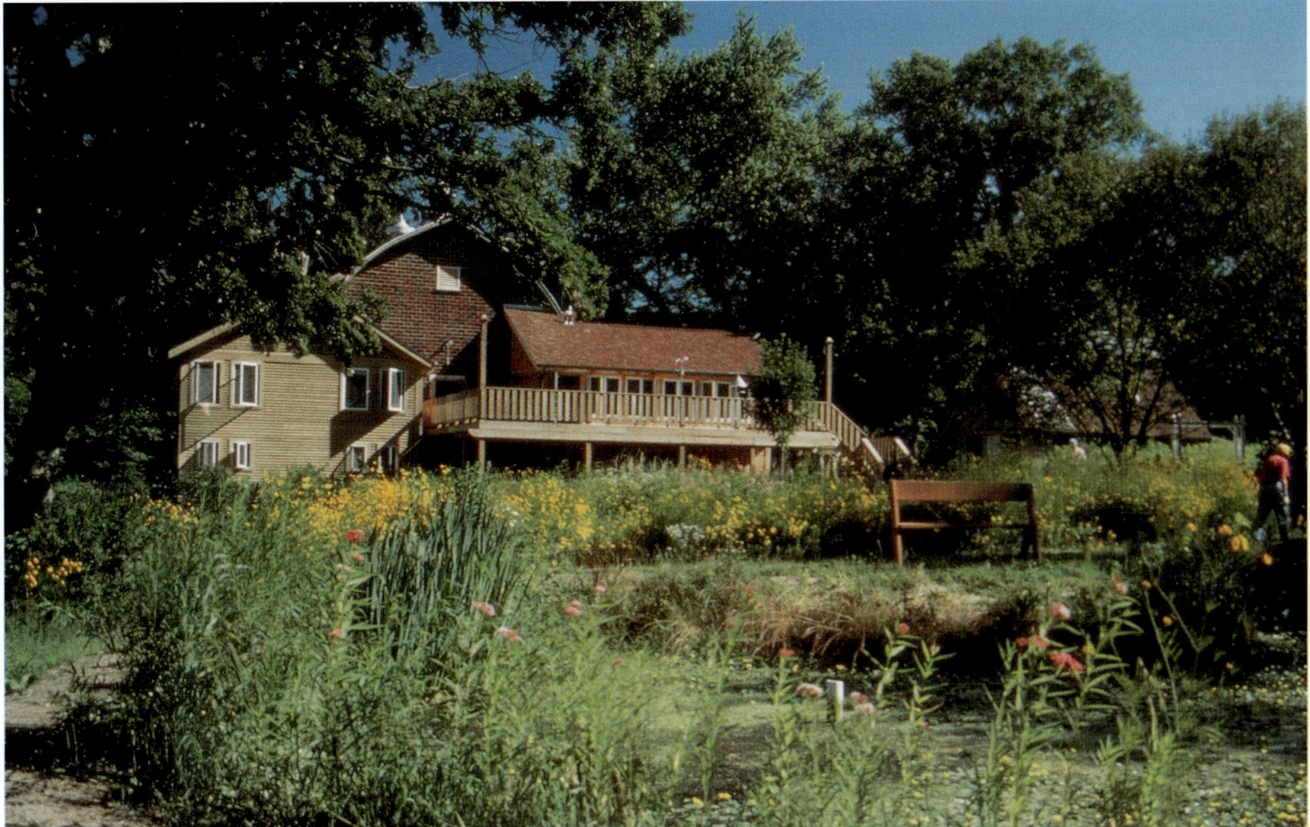

Rich Patterson

Indian Creek Nature Center offers recreational and educational opportunities, and quiet walks in the woods.

to the trends. Twenty years ago you couldn't build enough tennis courts, explained Dave Smith, the Cedar Rapids parks superintendent. "Thirty and 40 years ago, you couldn't do enough for playgrounds, swimming pools and park pavilions."

Some activities attract people year in and year out. Golf is always popular. The city's 4,000 acres of parks offer a refuge of greenery and recreation with their pools and walking trails. On the horizon, though, is change. There is more interest in walking and jogging paths. Requests are up for park space to play rugby and cricket, to rollerblade and skate-board.

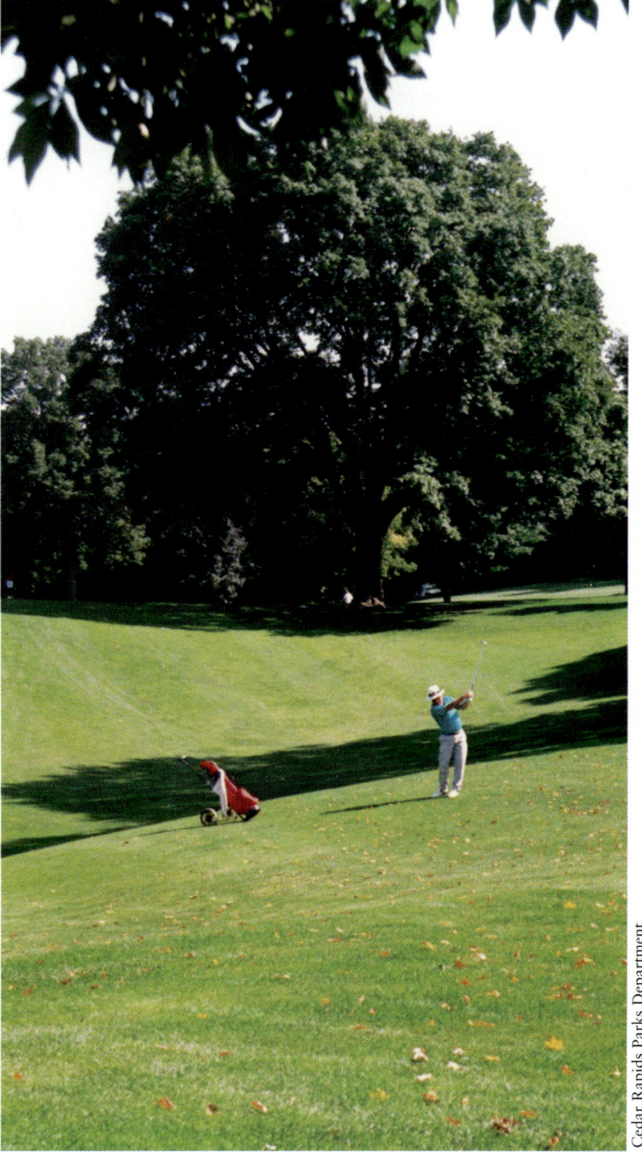

Cedar Rapids Parks Department

People today also need solitude away from the city's hustle and bustle, and the community was ahead of others when it developed the Indian Creek Nature Center. South of the city, the 1,000 acres of land provide the opportunity to walk, bicycle and cross-country ski on a network of trails. In 1975, the Sac and Fox Trail became the first National Recreational Trail in Iowa.

The center was founded by two area women, B.B. Stamats and Jean O'Donnell, said Rich Patterson, who has been the Nature Center's director since 1978. "The women had seen places like this in other cities and thought the idea could work in Cedar Rapids," Patterson said. A fund-raising campaign generated money to start the center. The city leased the land and buildings to the center for $1 a year. Twenty-five years after its opening, this arrangement continues.

Cedar Rapids is home to several public and private golf courses, and many others are within easy driving distance of the city. *Facing page:* From May through October, vendors sell fresh homegrown fruits, vegetables, flowers, baked goods and crafts at the city's Farmers Market in Czech Village.

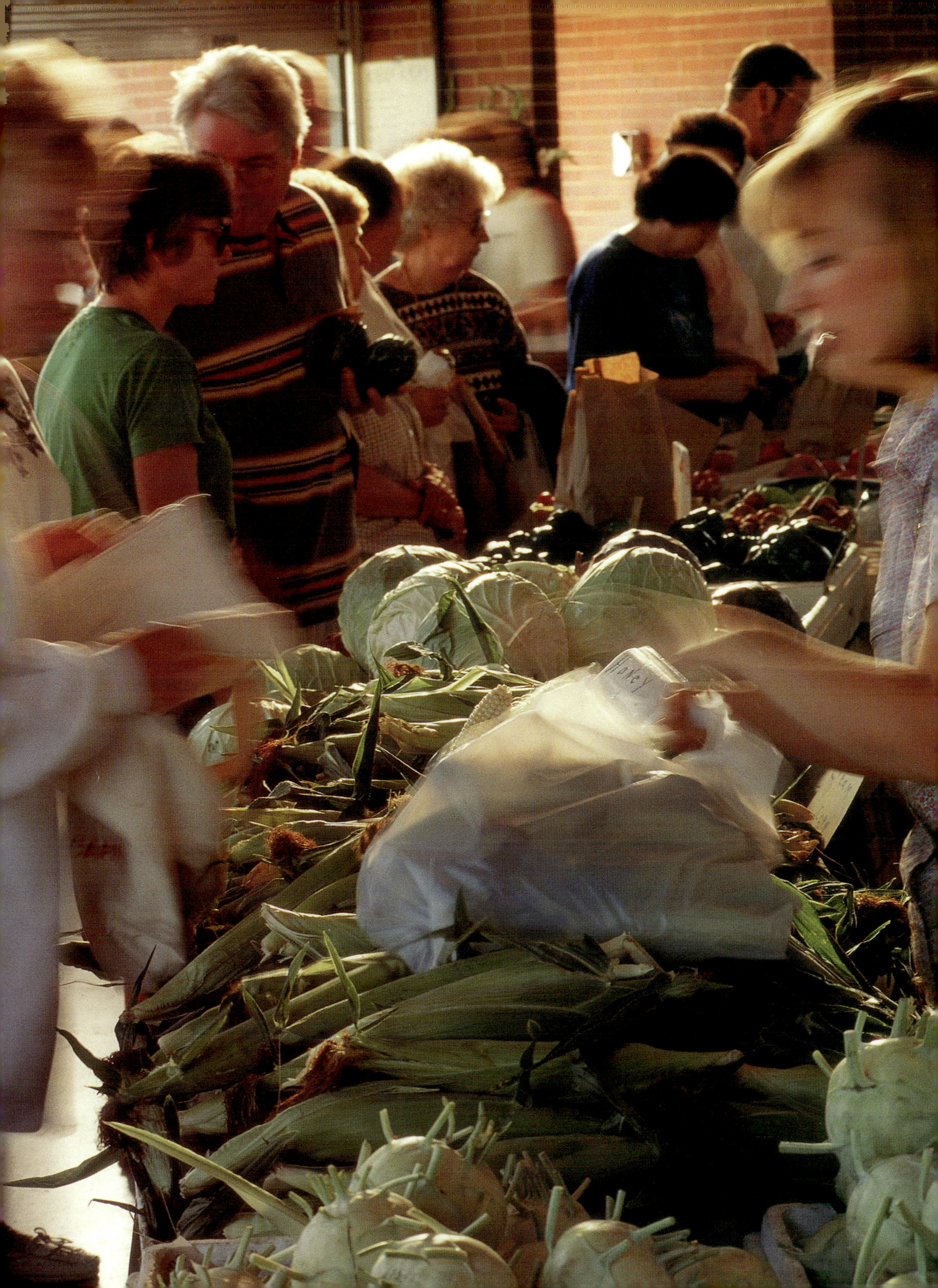
Honey

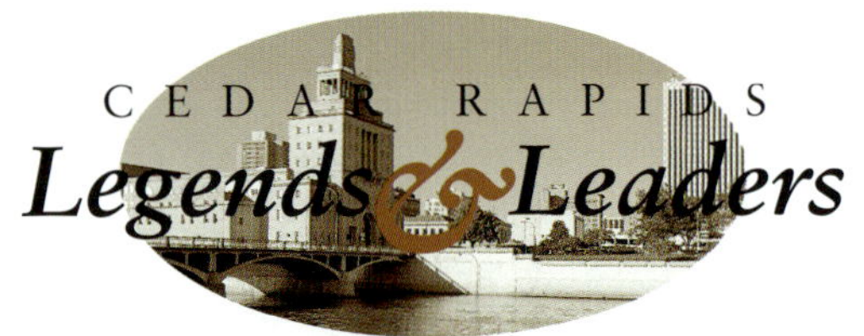

Elizabeth Bender
1903-1992

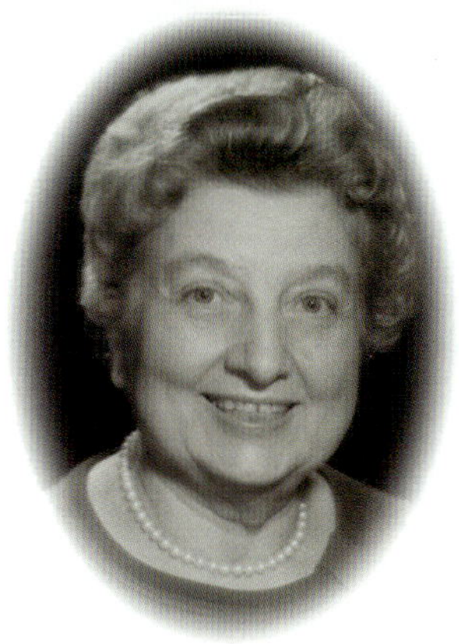

36 *A physician's daughter and Coe College graduate who became known as a member of the "Old Guard" of social reformers, social worker Elizabeth Bender operated a soup kitchen during the Great Depression and served for more than 40 years—from 1927 to 1968—as director of the Jane Boyd Community House.*

Bender's dedication to helping low-income families and promoting harmony among people of all ages and races left a lasting mark on the community. A fund drive spearheaded by the Jane Boyd Community House board of directors toward the end of her tenure as director resulted in the construction of Bender Pool and fulfilled her longtime dream of providing more recreational opportunities for youngsters in the Oak Hill Neighborhood. She is buried in Oak Hill Cemetery, not far from the pool that bears her name.

Photo: History Center

As the city grows around this haven of nature, Patterson expects our need for places like the Nature Center to grow. "People have a desire for nature and for solitude. I think they want time with family and friends, without the distractions."

Library

Lovers of books never take a public library for granted. It is the one place in a community where the door opens and the world is within your grasp—at no cost. Ada Van Vechten knew that. So does Nancy McHugh. Both women had a lasting effect on the Cedar Rapids Public Library.

Ada Van Vechten was the force behind establishing the first public library in Cedar Rapids. In 1896 women could vote only for city improvement referendums. And while many of the male leadership didn't see value in a public library, Van Vechten did. She garnered support among her female friends and it was their votes that assured the city of a public library. Nearly a century later, Nancy McHugh led another crusade. She propelled a building campaign that culminated in a new $9 million library.

In 1985 the Cedar Rapids Public Library left the stately, traditional Carnegie era for the high-tech modern era.

The library also left behind the concept that the only way to use the library was to walk through its doors. Technology allows patrons to access the library through fax machine, telephone and computer.

"It's not just the information in the community library you can access, but you can go anywhere in the world and that is really quite amazing," said library director Tom Armitage.

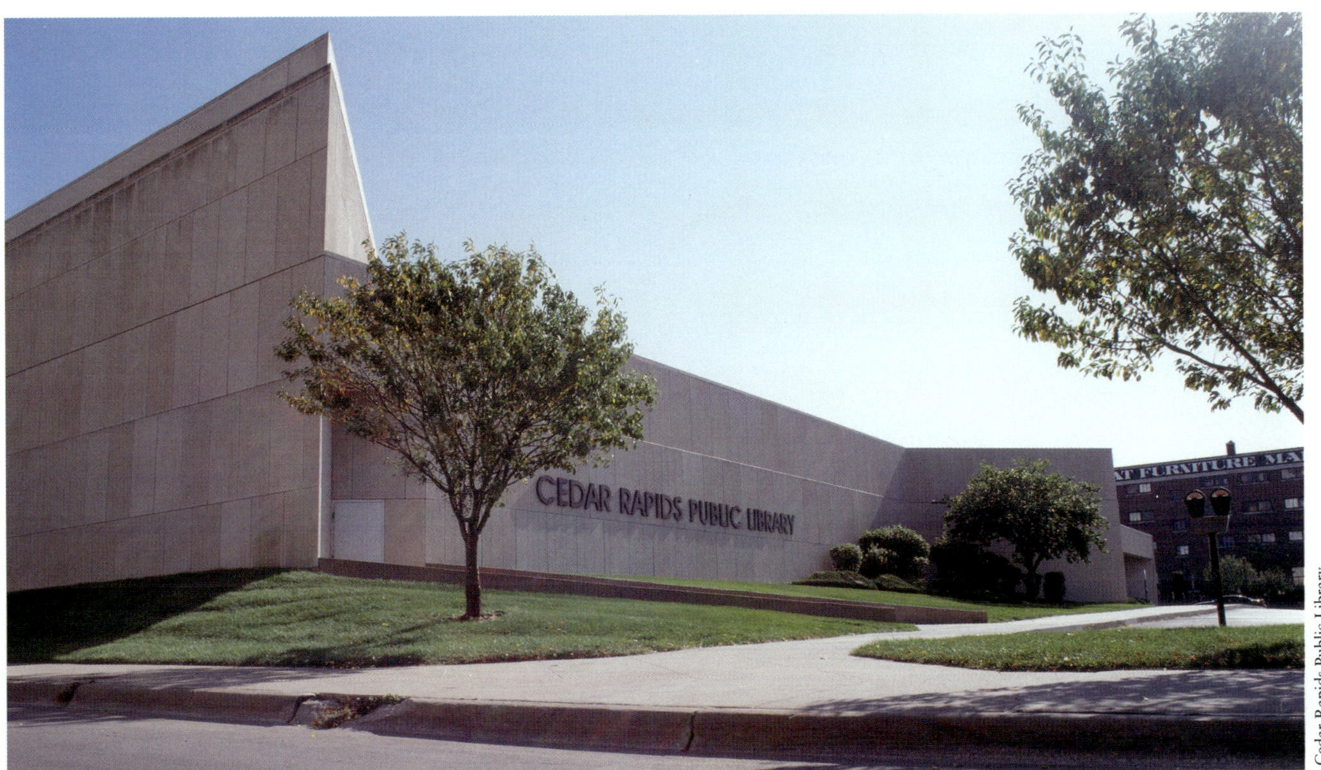

Cedar Rapids Public Library

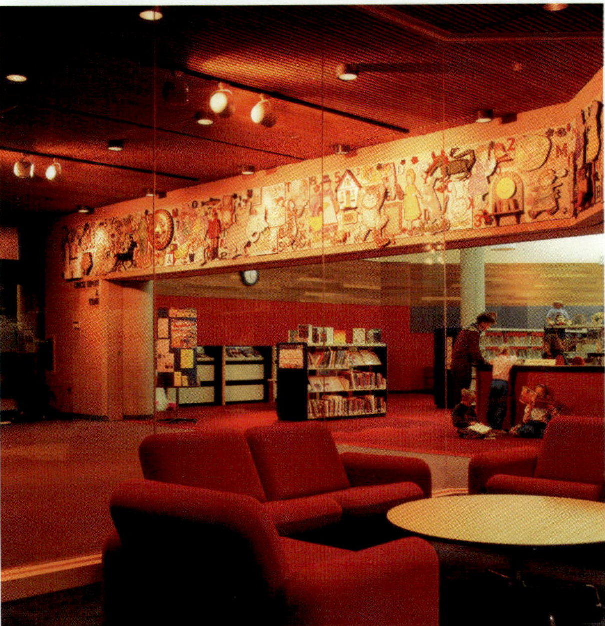

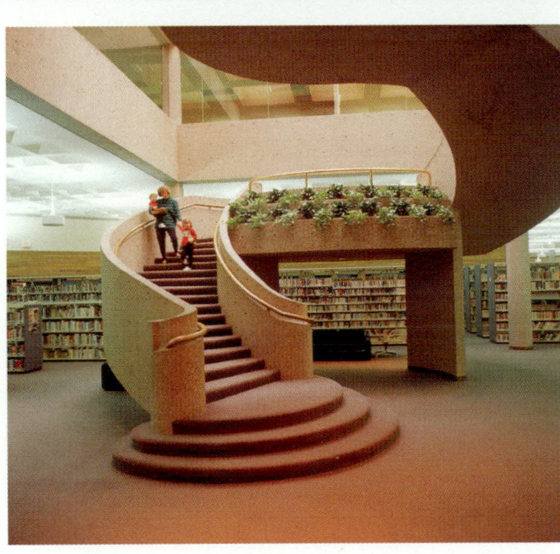

A building campaign culminated in a new $9 million library in 1985. A wood sculpture by the late Richard Pinney greets visitors to the children's area *(lower left)*. The library incorporates the latest technology, allowing patrons access through fax, phone and computer.

The greatest challenge facing the library today, he said, is how to bring the 75,000 borrowers—35,000 of whom are regulars—with you when the technology changes so rapidly.

"You hold classes. You have a rover who's on duty and taps people on the shoulder to offer help. You create a culture here of openness and service," he said.

The goal in replacing card catalogs with computers is for people to use the computers as effectively as they once did the catalogs. A library, after all, is the one place in a community where any question you might have can be answered, said Mary Russell Curran, the current president of the library board of directors. "The library has that practical role. It is the only place in the community, outside of secondary education, where you can come free of charge and learn," she said.

"The range of services we offer, from access to materials, to education, I don't think anyone else can compete with us," added Armitage. "We serve a professional, recreational and educational role. It's the greatest possible reach and that's quality of life right there."

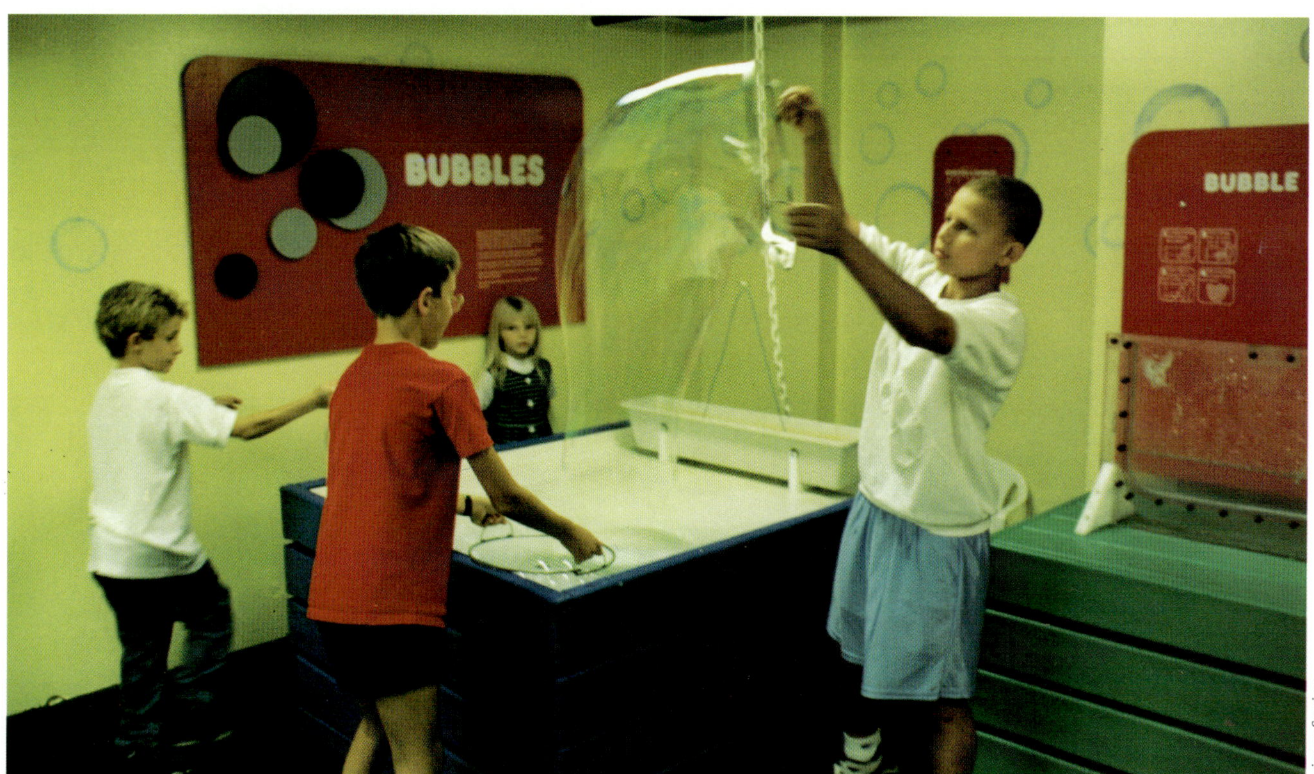

Science Station

Area youths explore scientific theories at the Science Station.

Education

It was a sense of community that attracted Lew Finch to the Cedar Rapids Community School District. It has been community support for its schools that has kept him here.

By most standards, Finch said, Cedar Rapids schools are good. The evidence of that can be seen in the students' performances on standardized tests, school attendance, good parental involvement and solid progress of integrating technology into the schools.

"The biggest challenge we're faced with is a sense of complacency that comes along when you think you're good," he said.

Complacency, he hopes, will not become a part of Cedar Rapids school curriculum. Learning in the 21st century will require change, he insists. It will be more authentic-based and focused on real-life projects. In a sense, learning will become a partnership between schools and the outside world.

"I think schools will have to take on a different role from the one we've had as the only dispenser of knowledge to children," Finch predicts. "With computers offering information they can get at home, I see our role changing to more of a function of guiding and leading students through that huge amount of information."

In some ways, the idea of real-life learning is not unlike that already found in Cedar Rapids colleges. Partnerships involving on-site training or internships

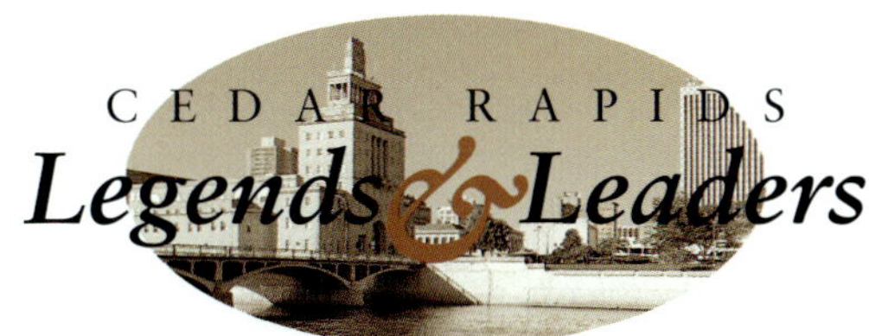

Sutherland C. Dows
1891-1969

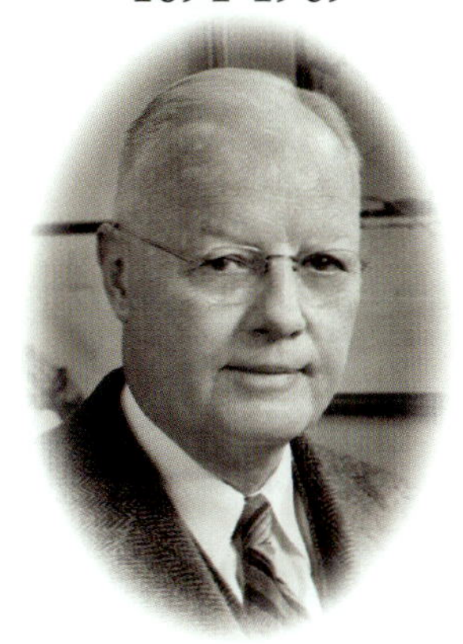

The first Iowa Electric Light & Power Co. employee to receive a 50-year pin, Sutherland Dows was the grandson of railroad builder and philanthropist Captain Stephen L. Dows and the son of railroad man, soldier and power company president William G. Dows.

He joined the company in 1913, and served as president from 1941 to 1961. He was chairman of the board from 1961 until his death.

Dows led the company through the challenges of a wartime economy. In 1955, he was named by the U.S. Congress to a civilian panel, formed "to study the impact of the peaceful uses of atomic energy on the American economy."

Dows served on the Coe College Board of Trustees for 49 years, and also was a member of the board of several other colleges and financial institutions. He and his family gave many gifts to the Cedar Rapids and Eastern Iowa educational and cultural communities.

Photo: Dows Family

are an important part of the learning process for students at Coe and Mount Mercy Colleges and Kirkwood Community College.

"No one can do the job alone in educating people today," said Norm Nielsen, president of Kirkwood Community College. "What we found the employer wants and has asked for are the skills that come in arts and science programs, but also in technical training."

Kirkwood, which serves 11,000 students, has been involved in more than 60 partnerships with area businesses, providing workforce development, continuing education and job training.

An example of Kirkwood's influence in Cedar Rapids' industrial community is Cedar River Paper Company. As the new company made plans to build a plant in the city, Kirkwood became involved in the training for 160 jobs. It has done the same at McLeodUSA and Diamond V Mills in recent years.

Coe College and Mount Mercy College also have a good town-and-gown relationship with Cedar Rapids. Both colleges rely on area hospitals and schools for cooperative learning experiences. The business community also supports internship opportunities.

Recently Mount Mercy, a small Catholic college, teamed up with Kirkwood Community College in a partnership geared to educating the working adult.

In the Advance Program, students take accelerated courses—five weeks instead of the traditional 10 or 13—as they work toward a bachelor's degree in applied business. The impetus to doing this, said its dean, Dr. David Hennessy of Mount Mercy College, "is to improve our responsiveness to the business community's needs."

"For the student, the Advance Program is a blend of theory and practice," he said.

Likewise, Coe College alumni have found that a blend of theory and practice prepares them for the realities of life. Since 1979, Coe students have performed nearly 500 full-time internships in Cedar Rapids and Marion businesses. So important are internships that, beginning in 1998, all Coe students are required to complete a practicum experience.

Small schools like Coe also provide opportunities not found in larger institutions, says William Whipple, a 1935 Coe graduate who is now a life trustee of the school.

"I was in athletics but I was no superstar," Whipple said. "I wasn't a great speaker, but I participated in many debates, and I certainly wasn't an actor, but I participated in four or five plays. I also wrote for the newspaper. The point is, in a larger institution I might have been able to be in one of those, but not all. And drawing on those experiences helped me throughout my career."

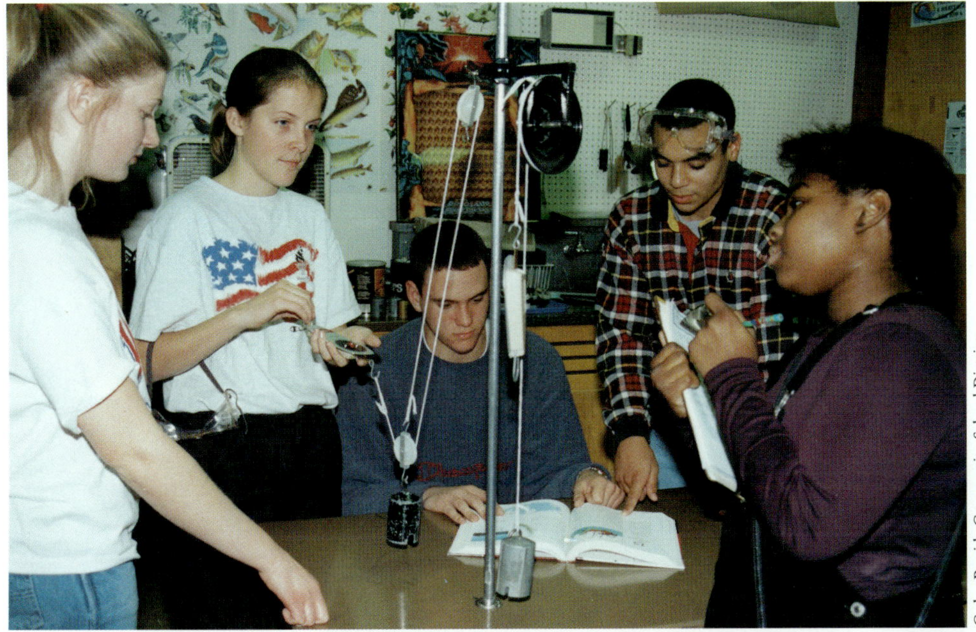

Cedar Rapids Community School District

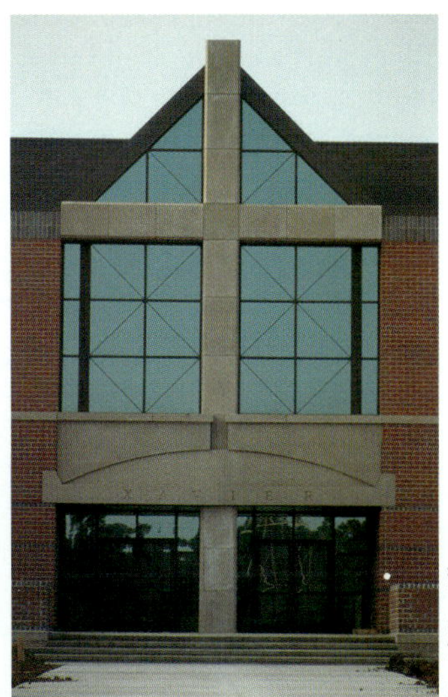

David Van Allen

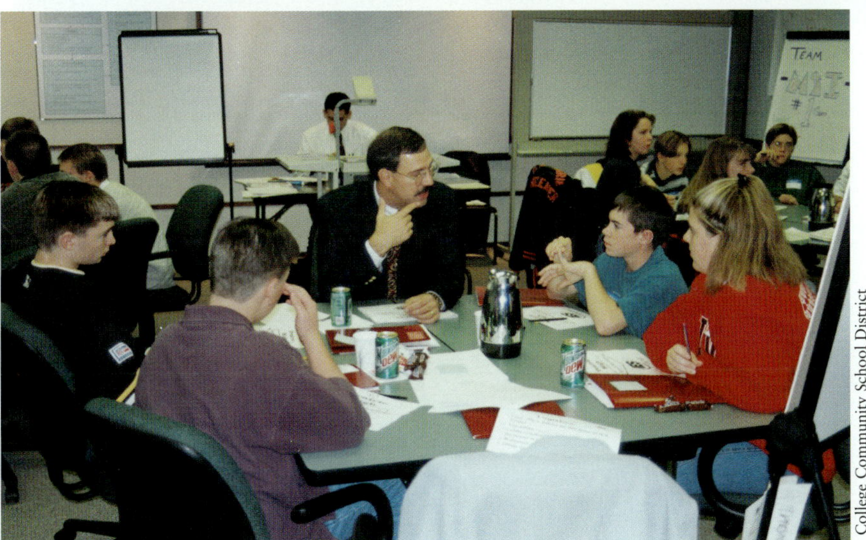

College Community School District

Cedar Rapids Community School District

Clockwise from upper left: Washington High School science students learn through hands-on activity; the main entrance to Xavier High School, which opened in September 1998 with approximately 700 students, following the merger of Regis and LaSalle Catholic high schools; elementary students learn about the environment at Indian Creek Nature Center; Prairie High School students meet with local executives in a program pairing business people with College Community School District students to give the youngsters practice solving business problems.

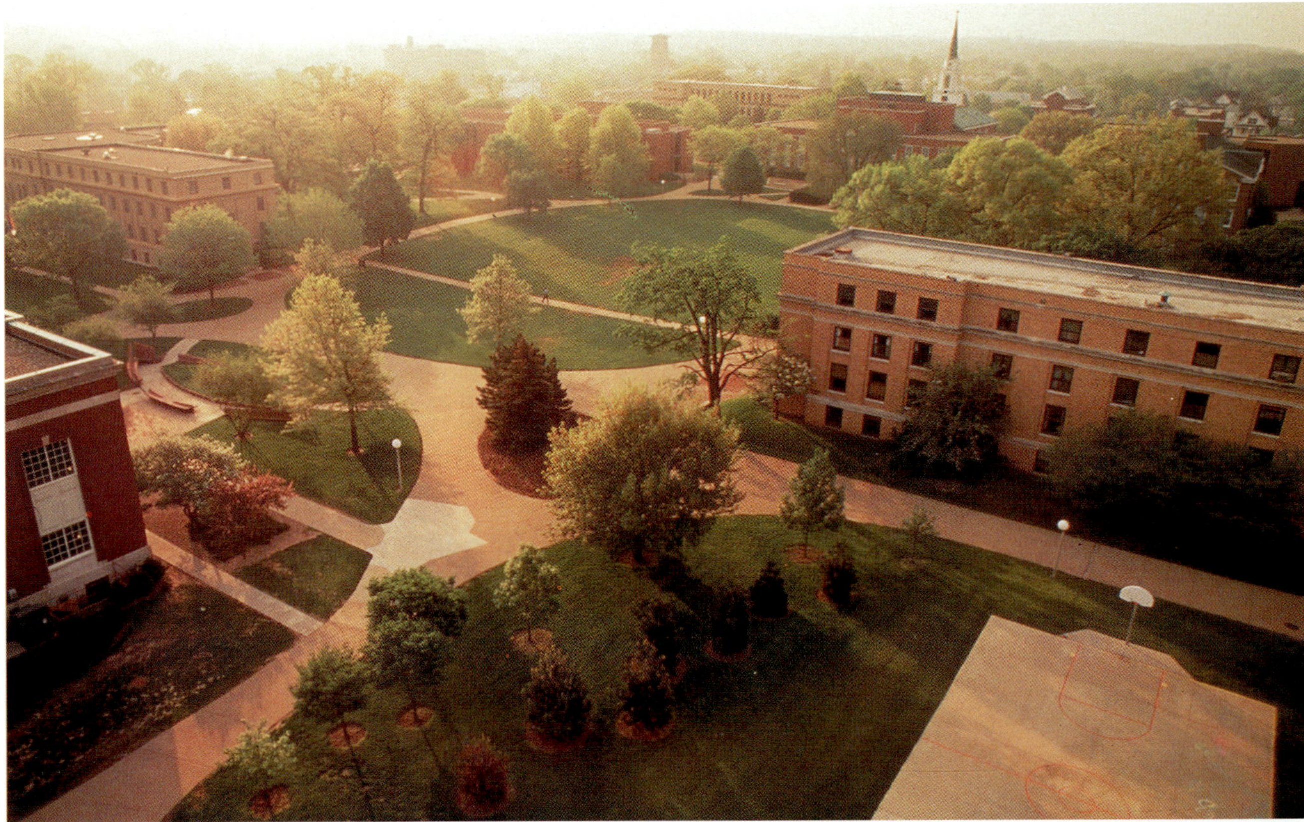

Coe College

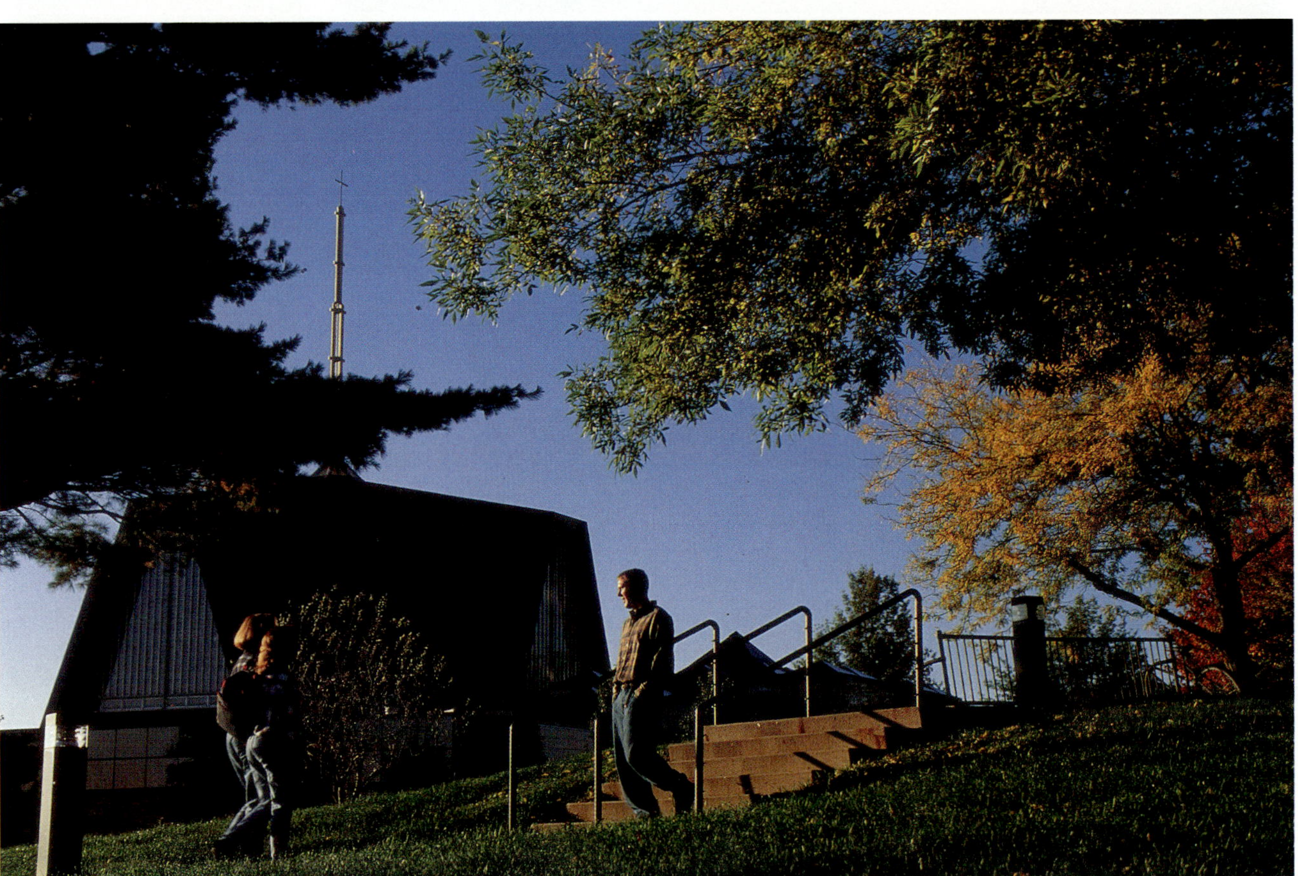

Mount Mercy College

Coe College *(top)* and Mount Mercy College *(bottom)* are both four-year, private, liberal arts colleges.
Coe is located on 21 acres in the heart of Cedar Rapids and Mount Mercy's hilltop campus is in the city's northeast quadrant.

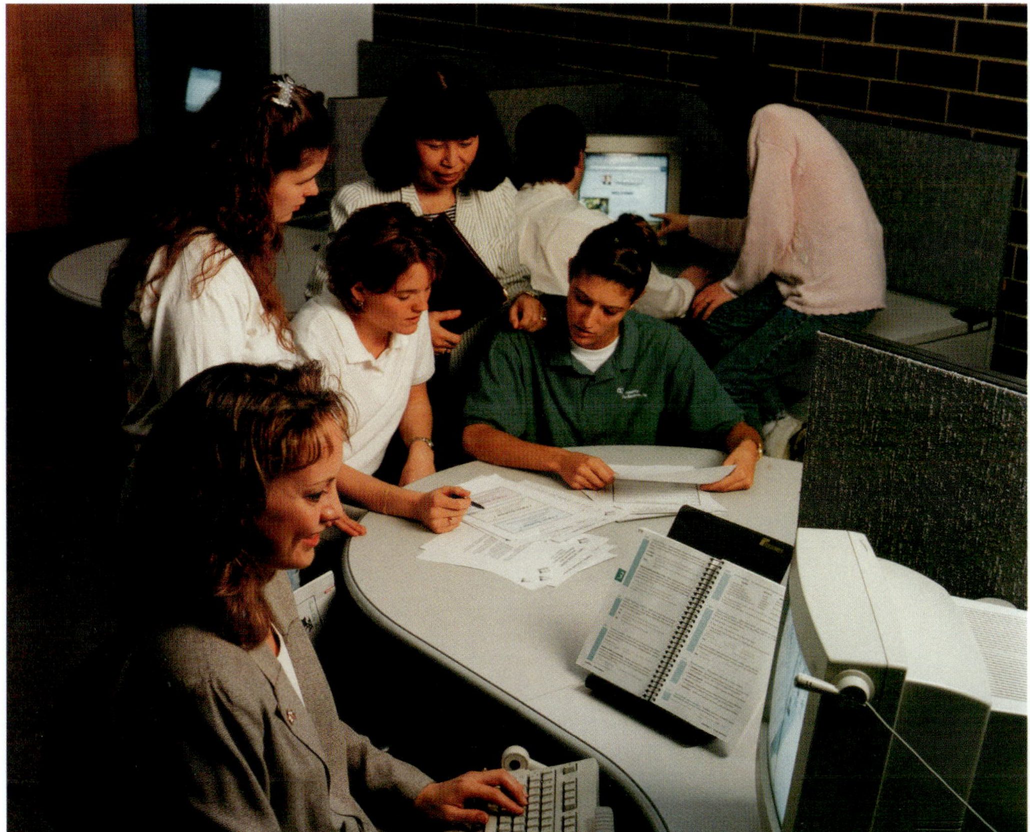

Kirkwood Community College

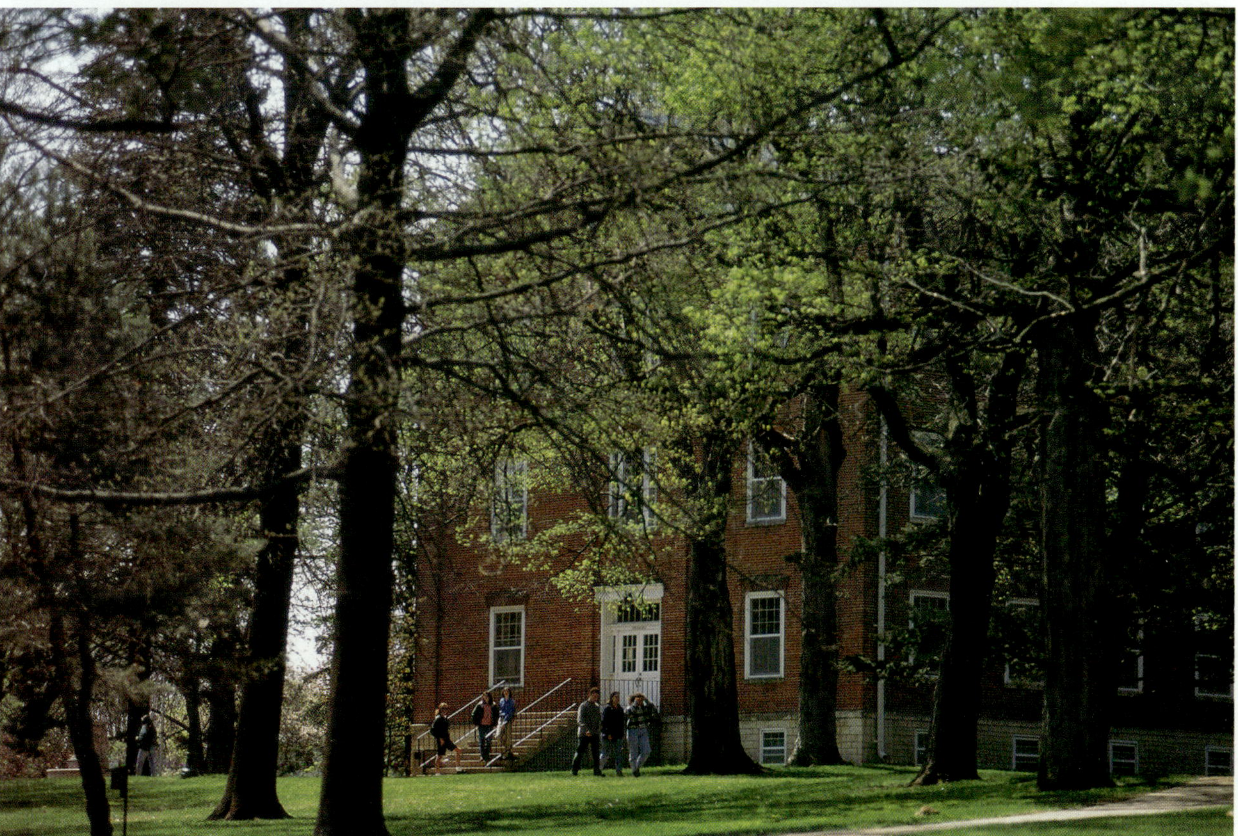

Cornell College

Top: Students in Kirkwood Community College's Business Department learn modern office administration technology through the "virtual office" classroom in Linn Hall. *Bottom:* Much of the Cornell College campus in Mount Vernon is on the National Register of Historic Places.

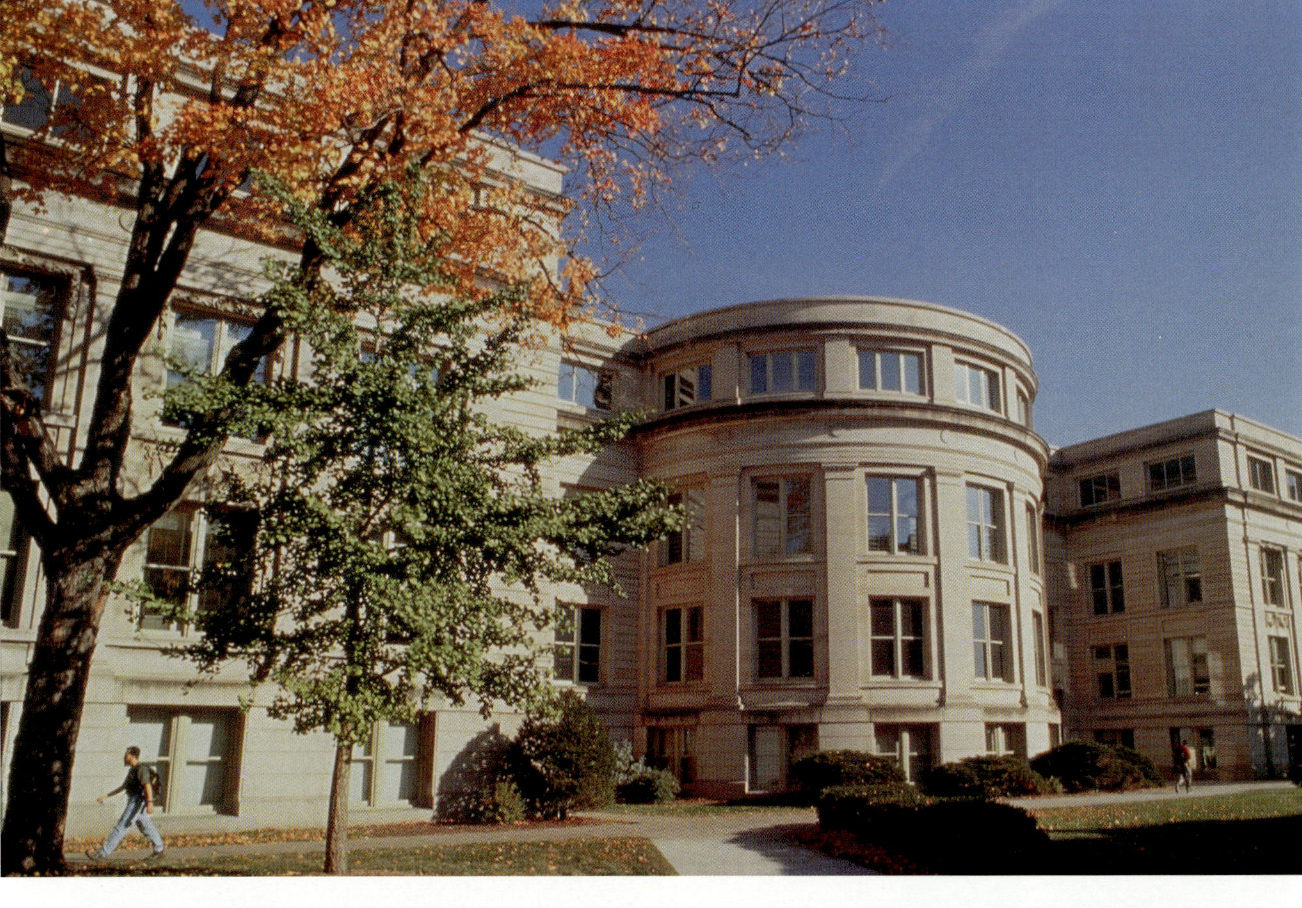

The University of Iowa

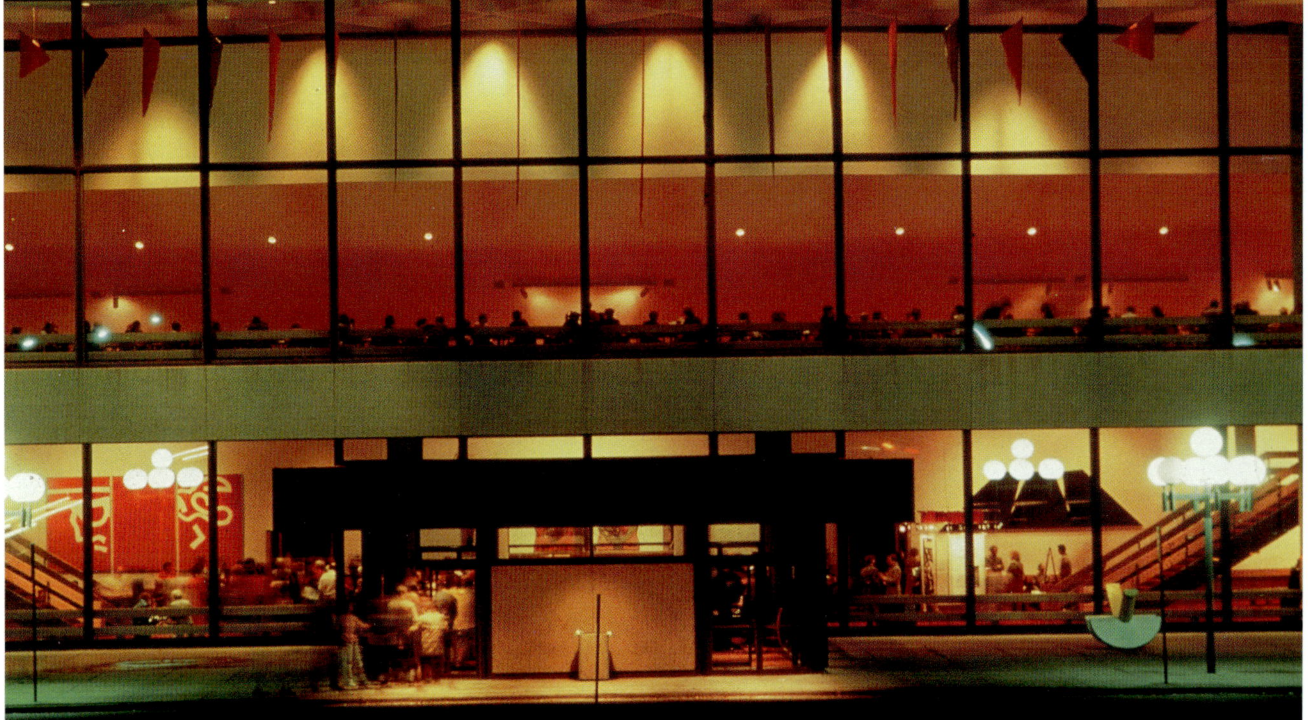

The University of Iowa

The Pentacrest *(top photo)* is the heart of the University of Iowa campus in Iowa City, 28 miles south of Cedar Rapids. Hancher Auditorium *(bottom)* offers Broadway theater, opera, ballet and other top-notch entertainment.

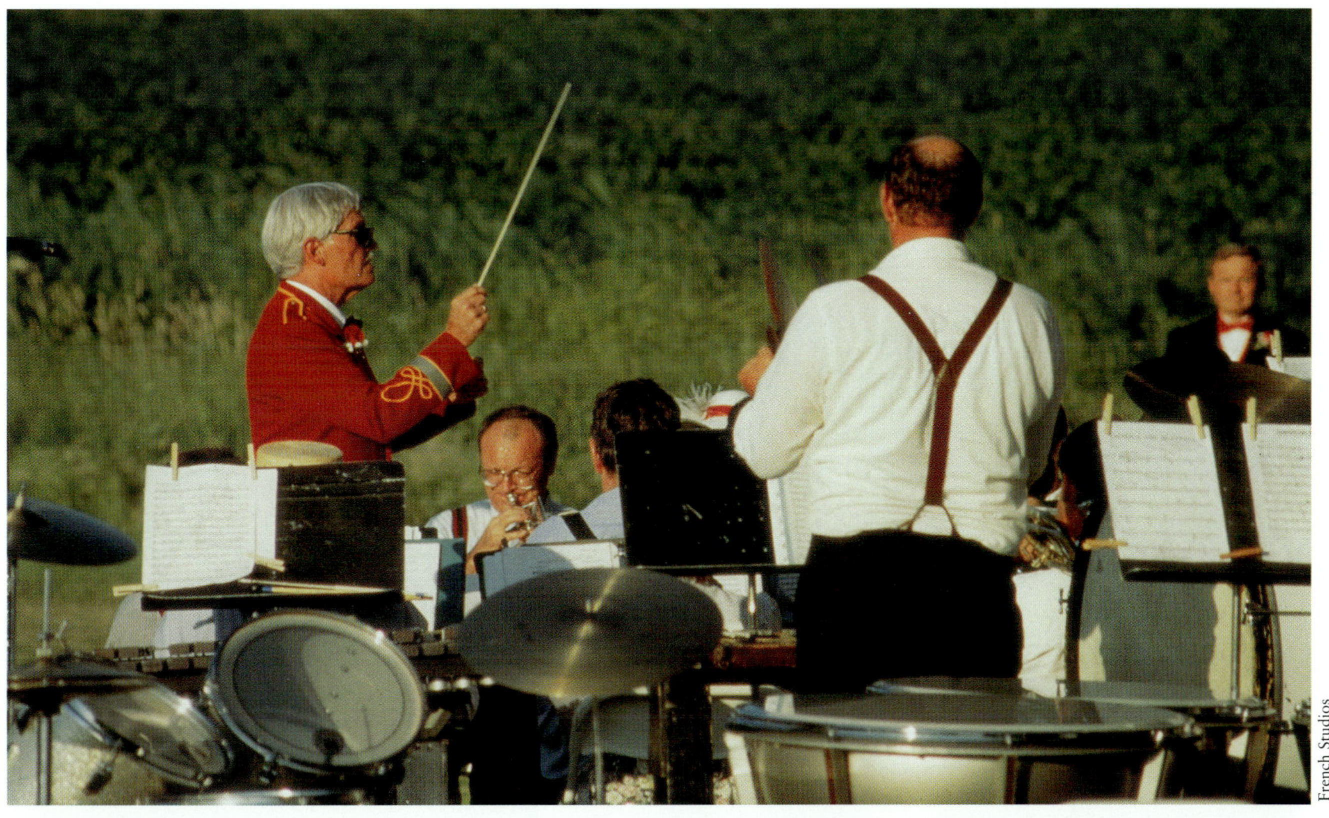

French Studios

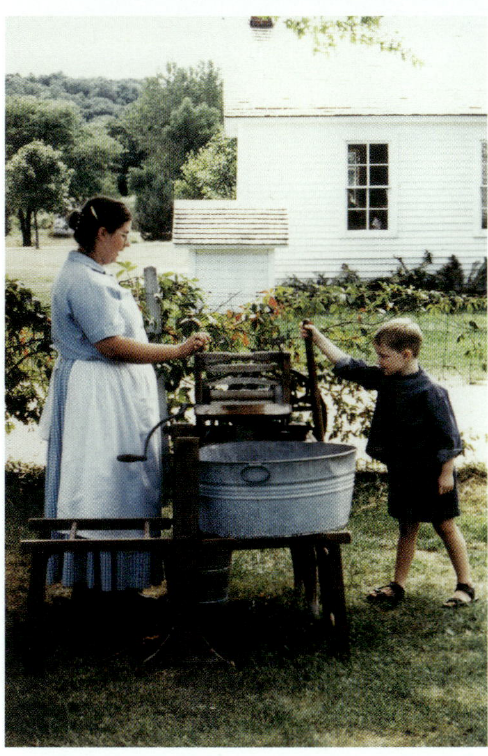

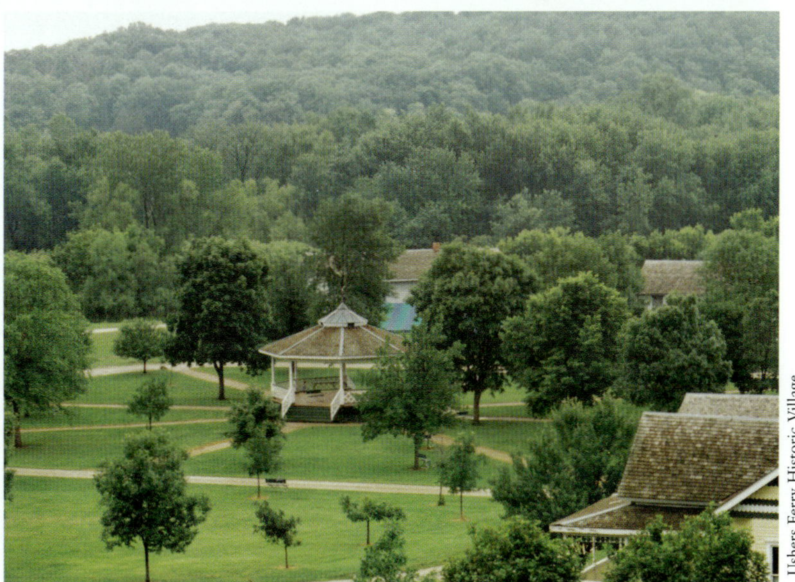

Ushers Ferry Historic Village

The Cedar Rapids Municipal Band *(top photo)* offers musical entertainment at area parks. *Bottom left and right:* Take a step back in time at Ushers Ferry Historic Village. The small Iowa town recreates life of nearly 100 years ago.

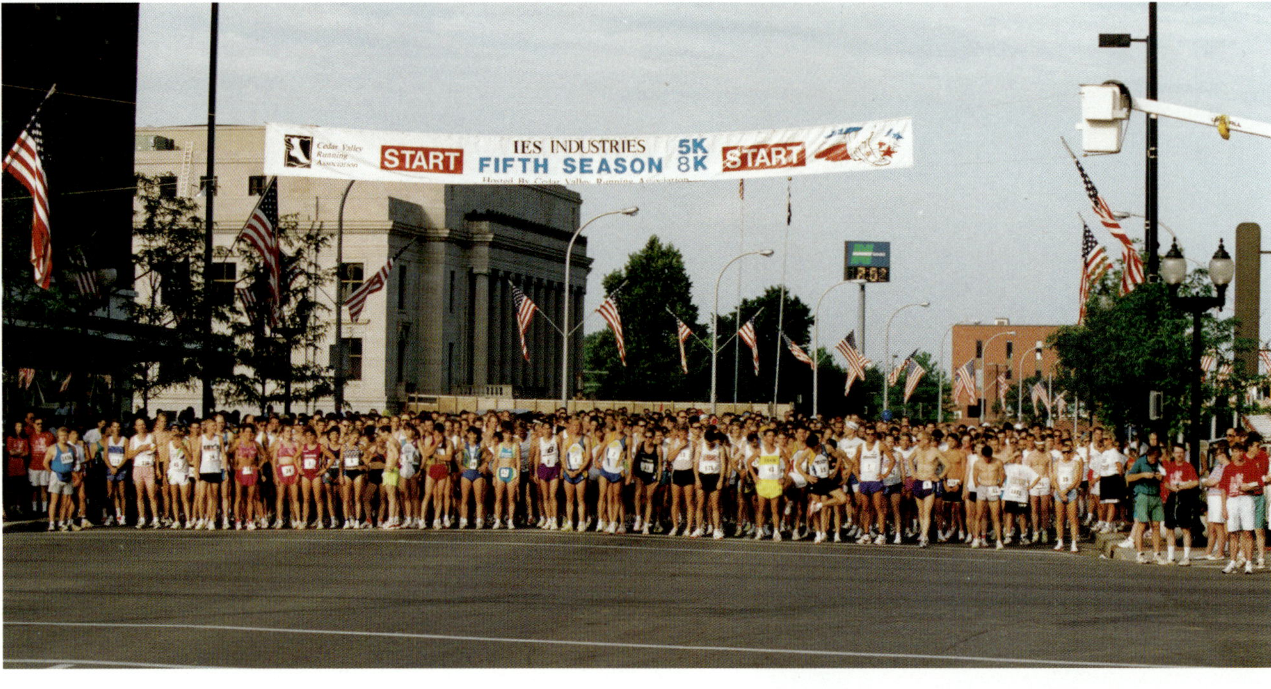

Ron Dreasher

46

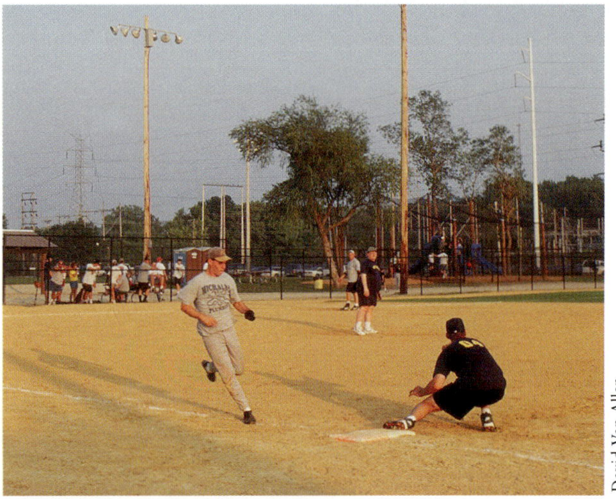

David Van Allen

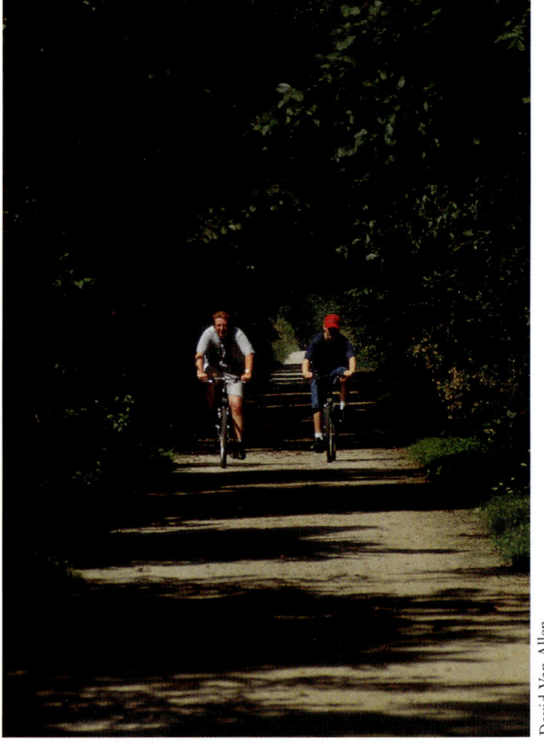

David Van Allen

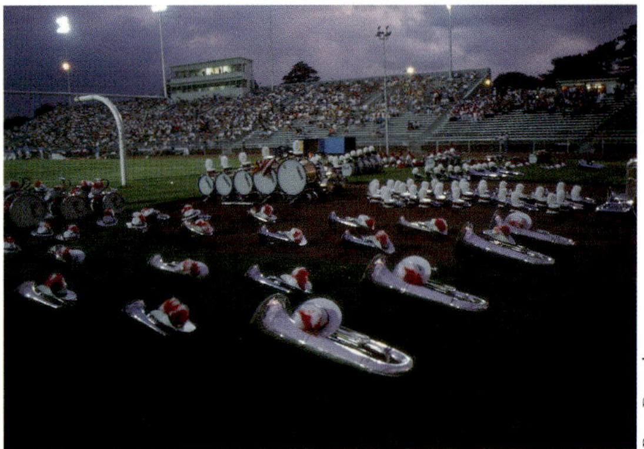

Ron Dreasher

Top: Runners take their mark during the annual Fifth Season race held every Fourth of July. *Middle left:* Softball is a favorite summertime activity, with teams from all over Cedar Rapids participating in organized leagues. *Above:* Bike, hike or cross-country ski on the Cedar Valley Nature Trail, a 52-mile trail connecting Cedar Rapids and Waterloo. *Left:* Drum and bugle corps competition at Kingston Stadium.

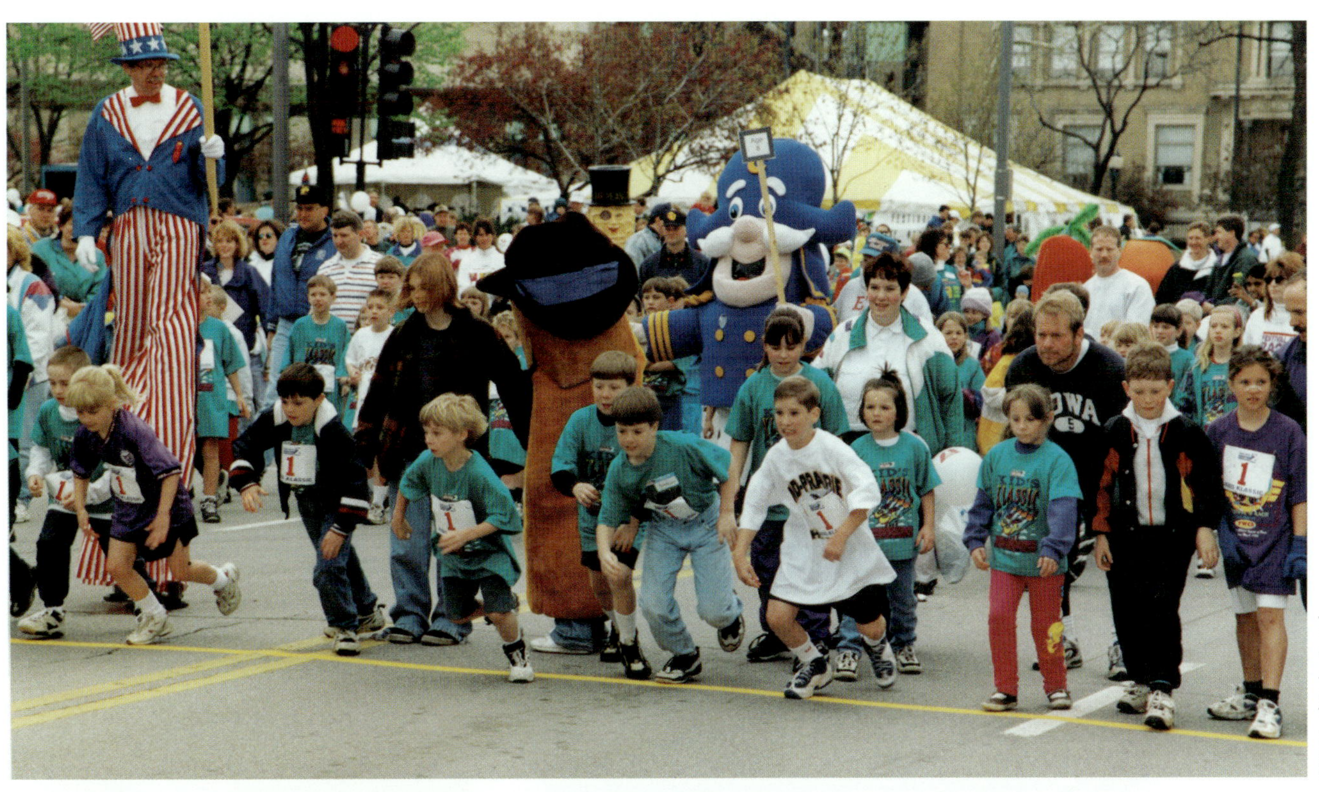

YWCA of Cedar Rapids

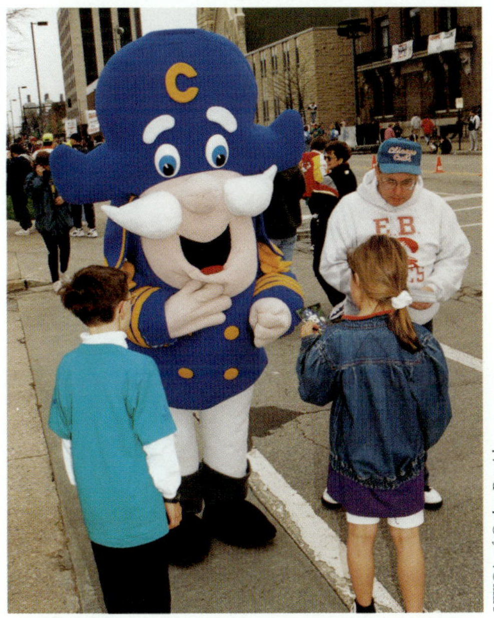

YWCA of Cedar Rapids

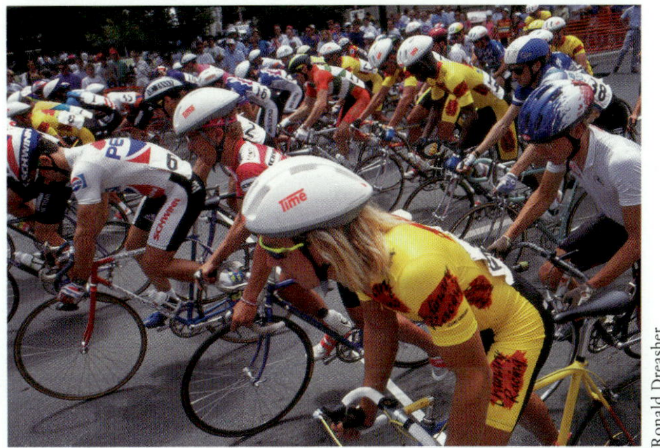

Ronald Dreasher

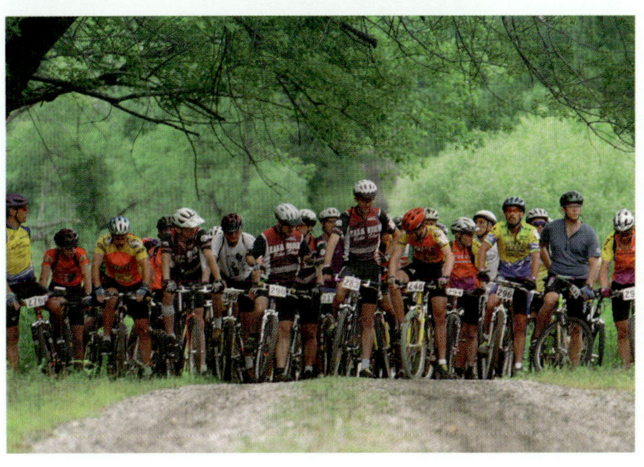

Mark Tade/The Gazette

Top and middle left: Children are active participants in the annual YWCA Festival of Races one-mile fun run. *Middle right and bottom:* Cyclists participate in the Mercy Challenge Criterium, while mountain bikers enjoy off-road cycling events.

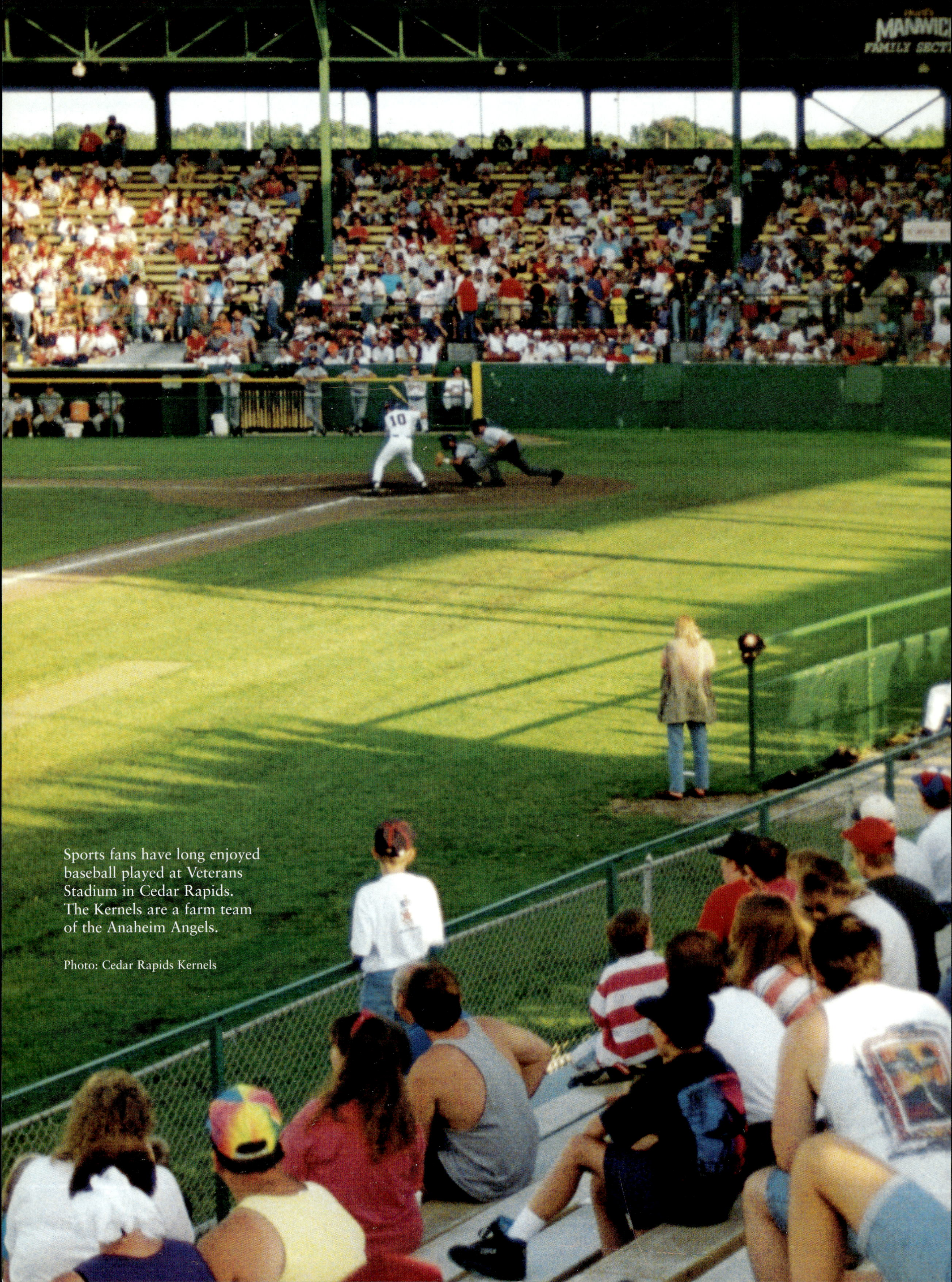

Sports fans have long enjoyed baseball played at Veterans Stadium in Cedar Rapids. The Kernels are a farm team of the Anaheim Angels.

Photo: Cedar Rapids Kernels

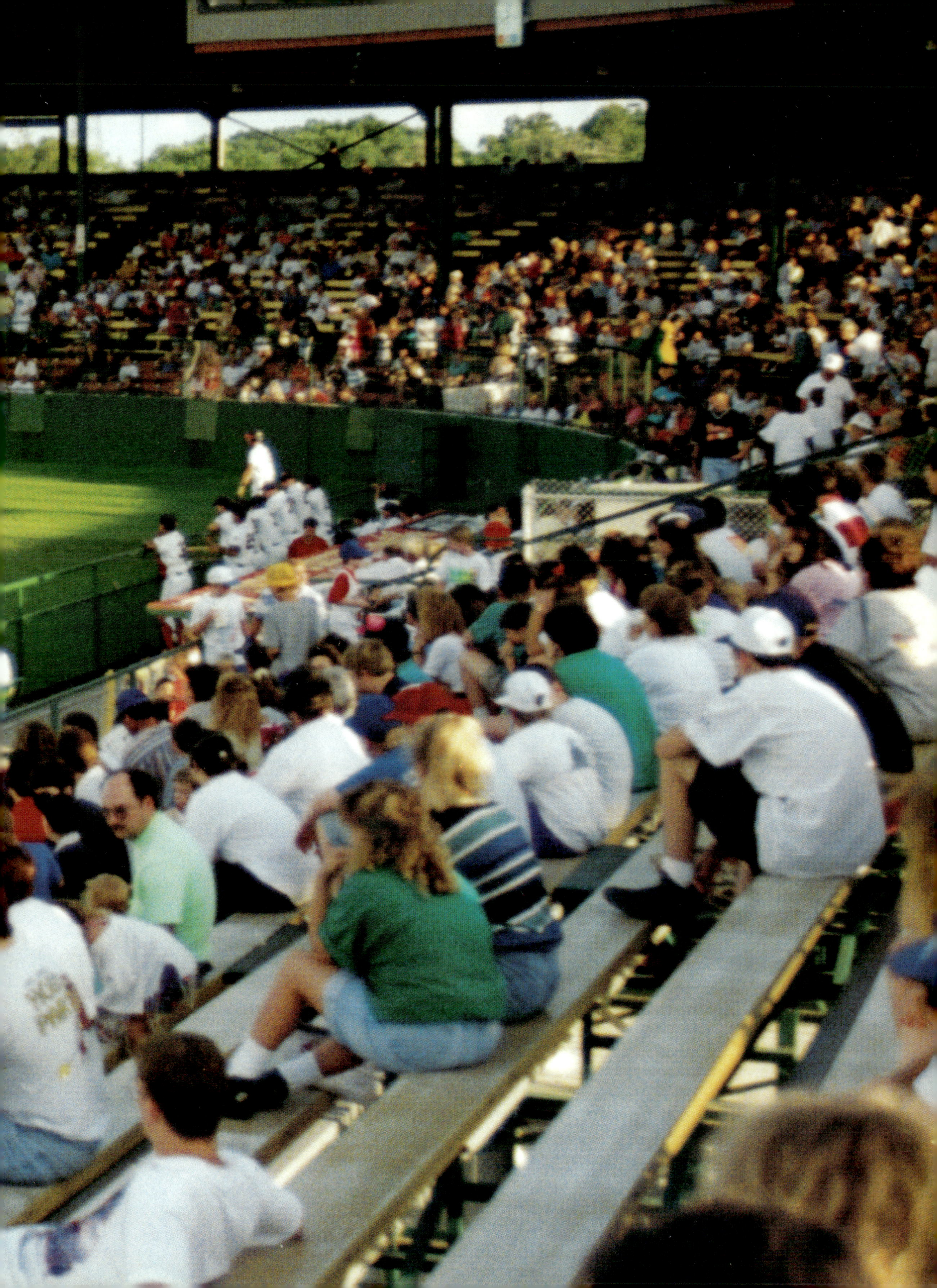

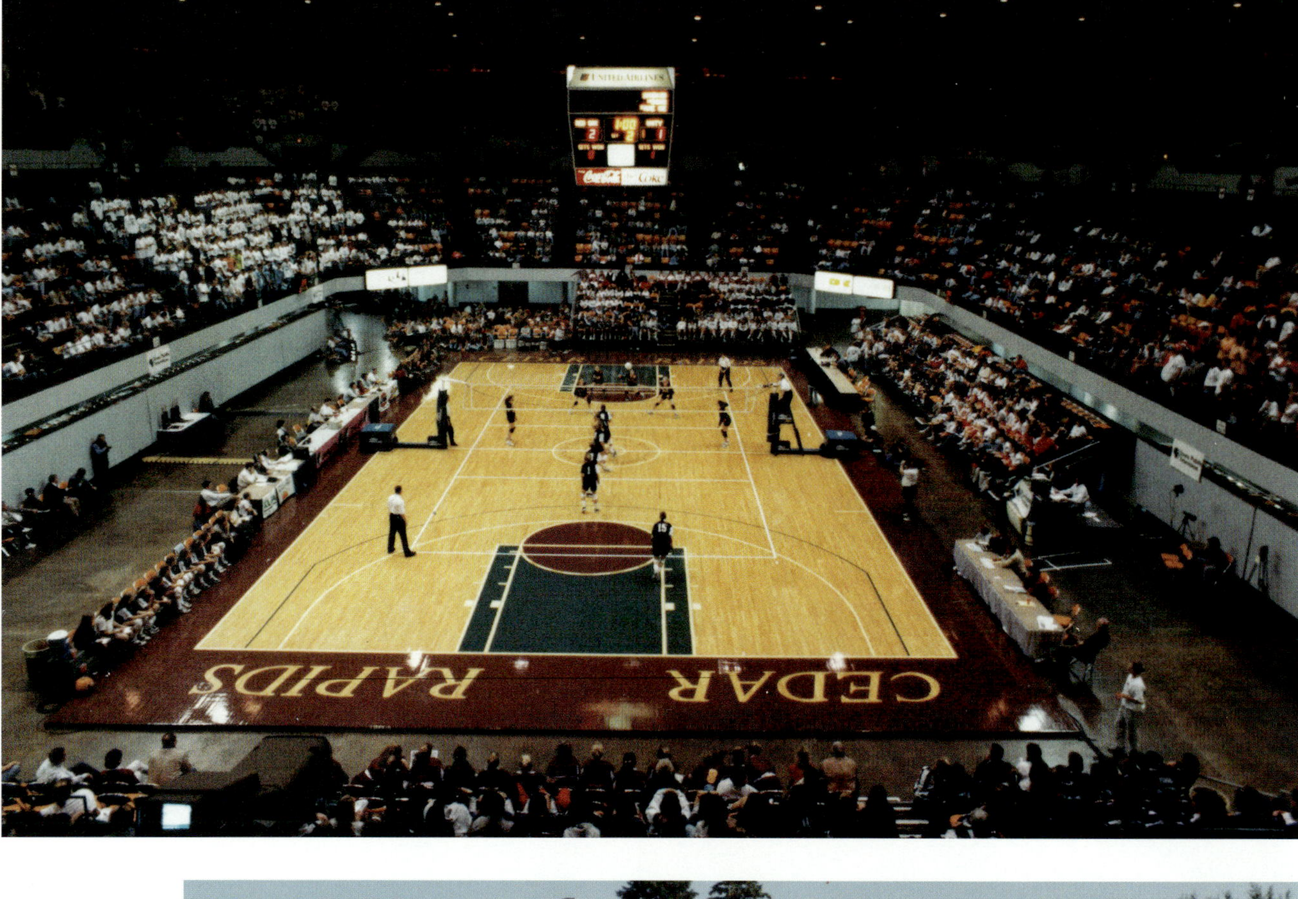

Five Seasons Center/Ogden Entertainment

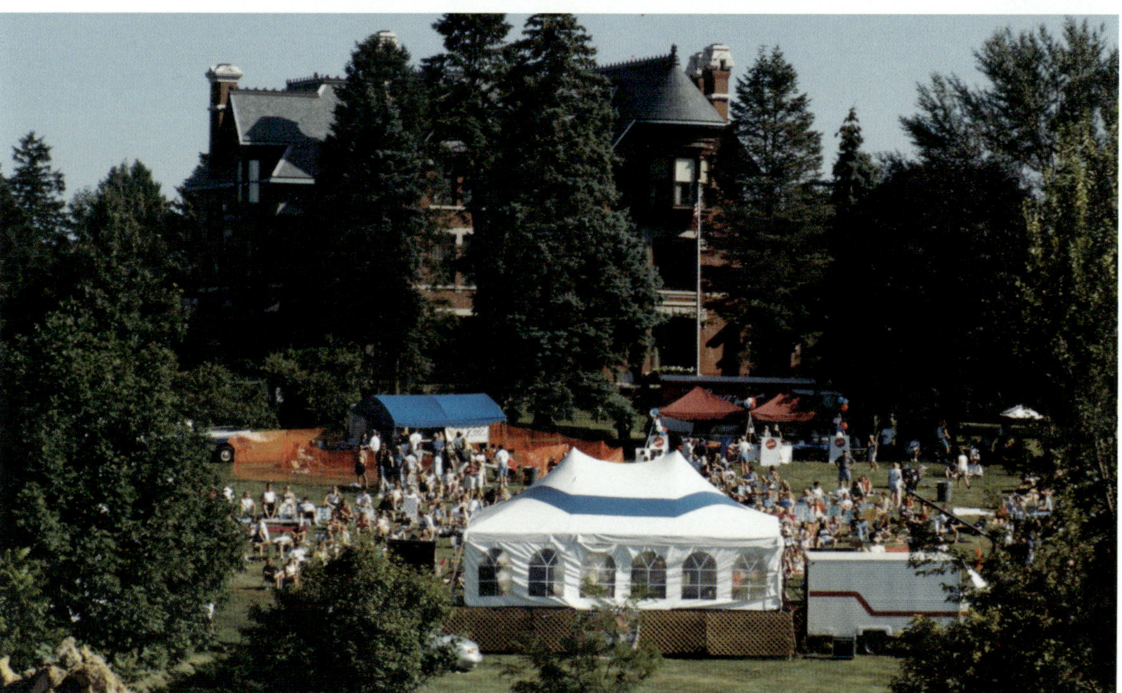

David Van Allen

A multi-purpose venue, the Five Seasons Center *(top)* is used for state girls' high school volleyball tournaments as well as conventions, trade shows and musical events.
Bottom: Bluesmore, a summer music festival, is held on the grounds of historic Brucemore.

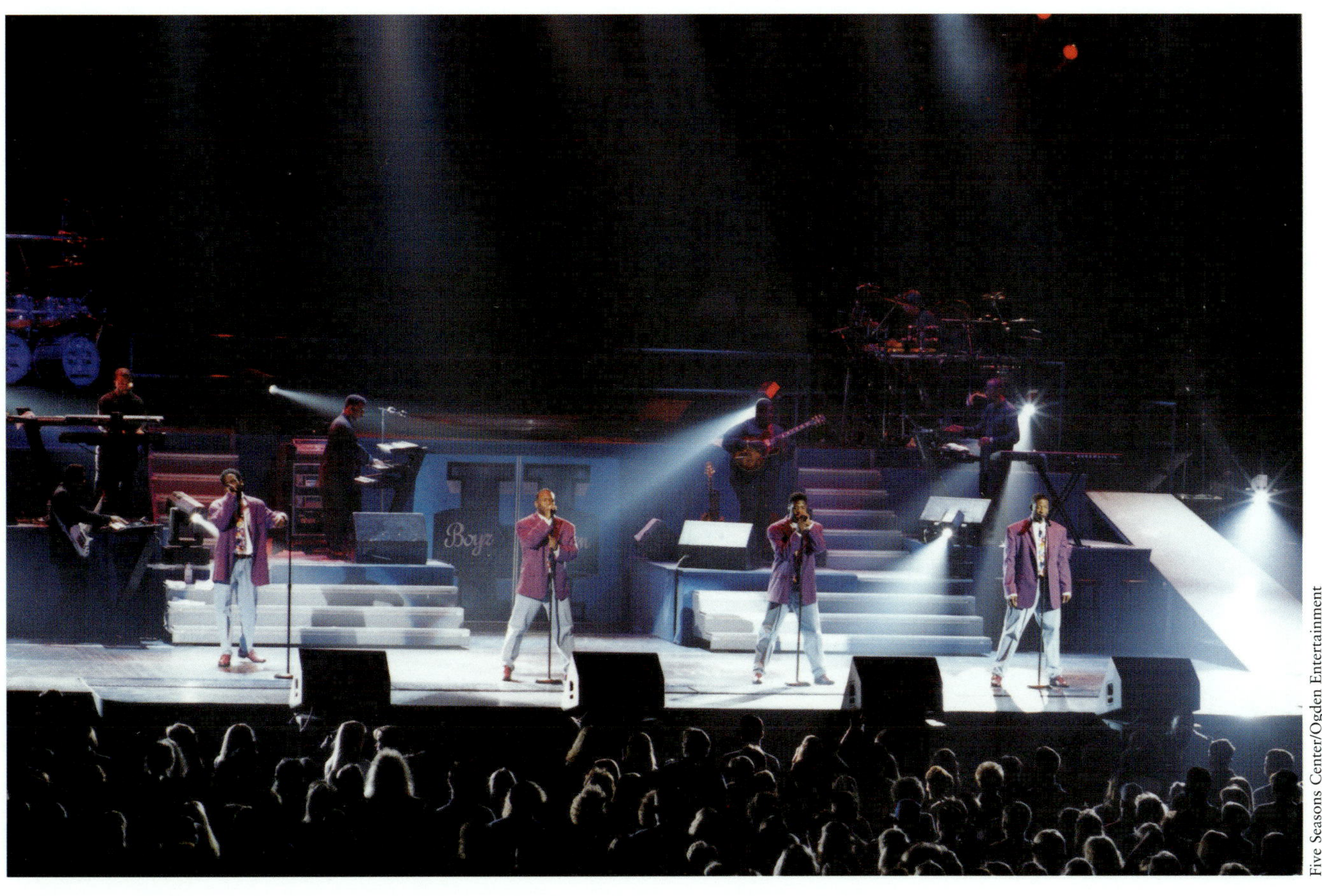

Five Seasons Center/Ogden Entertainment

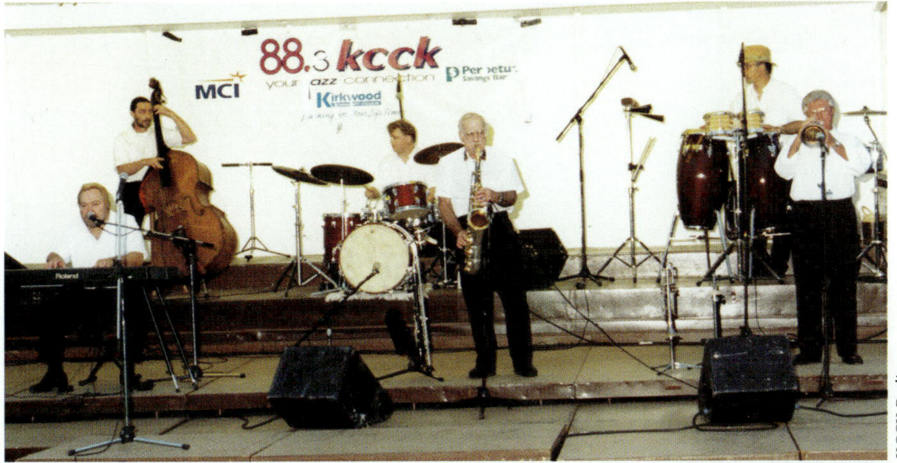

KCCK Radio

The Five Seasons Center draws top groups such as Boyz II Men, while local jazz groups entertain music lovers at Jazz in the Park concerts.

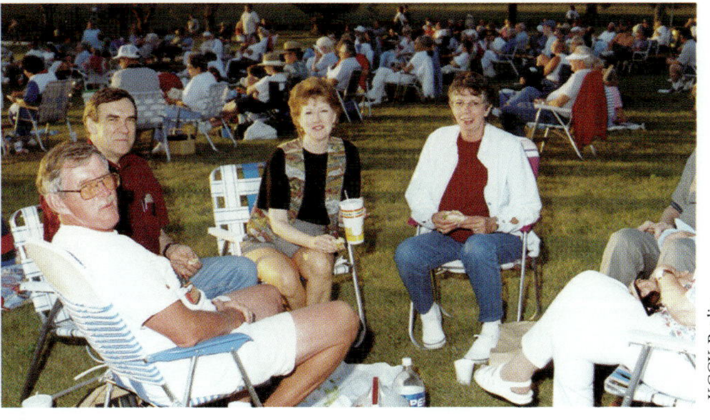

KCCK Radio

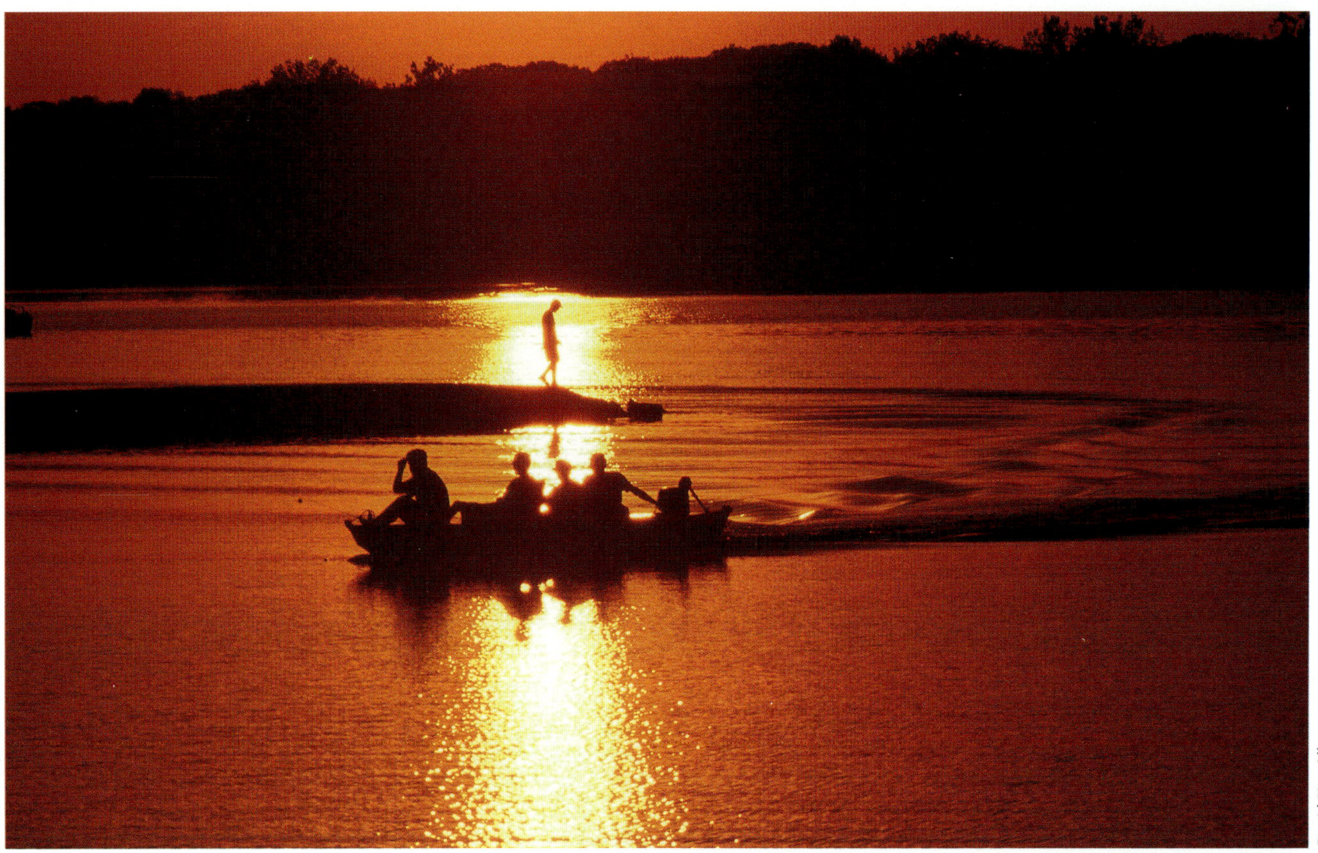

David Van Allen

Lake Macbride State Park

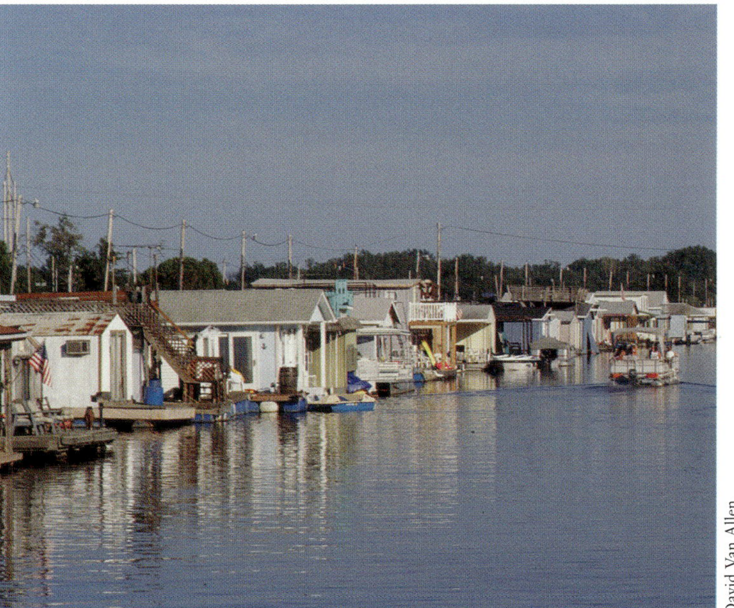

David Van Allen

Cedar River Houseboat Harbor

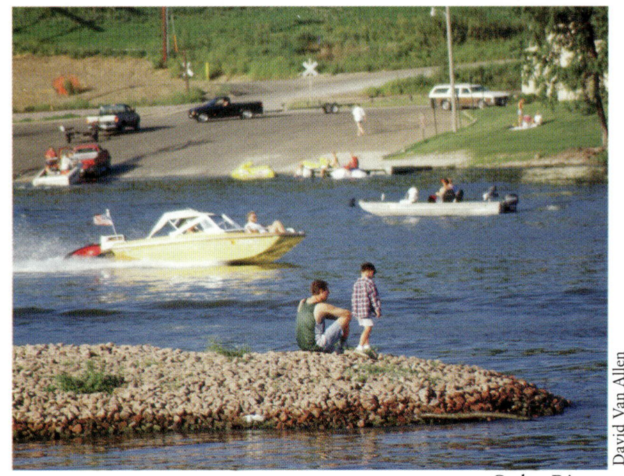

David Van Allen

Cedar River

Boating and fishing enthusiasts take advantage of nearby waterways—the Cedar River, Lake Macbride and the 5,000-acre Coralville Lake.

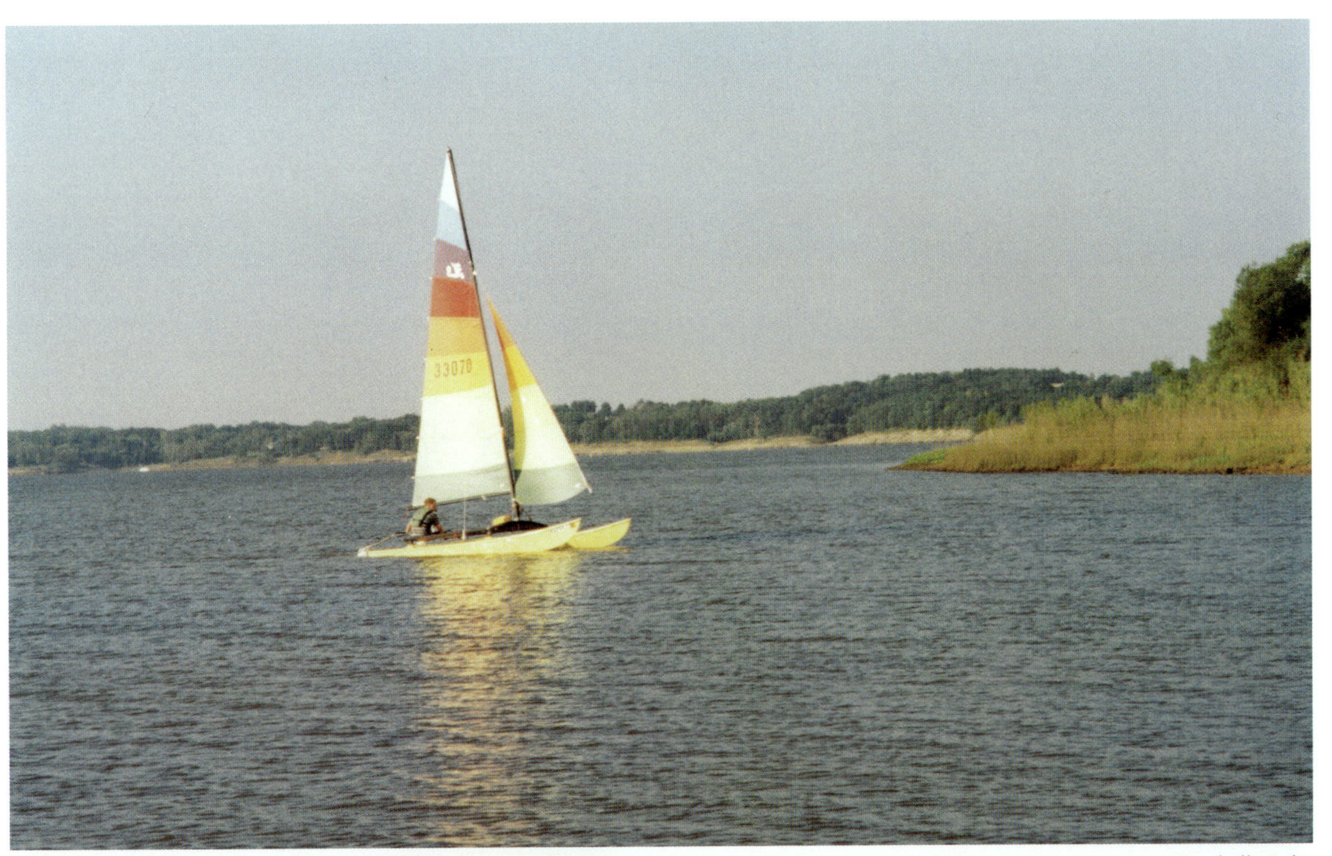

Coralville Lake

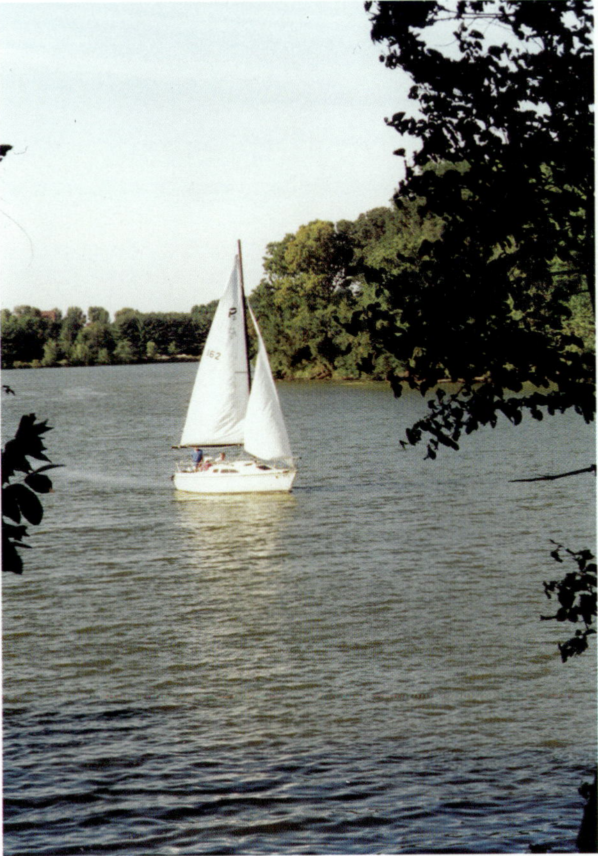

Lake Macbride State Park

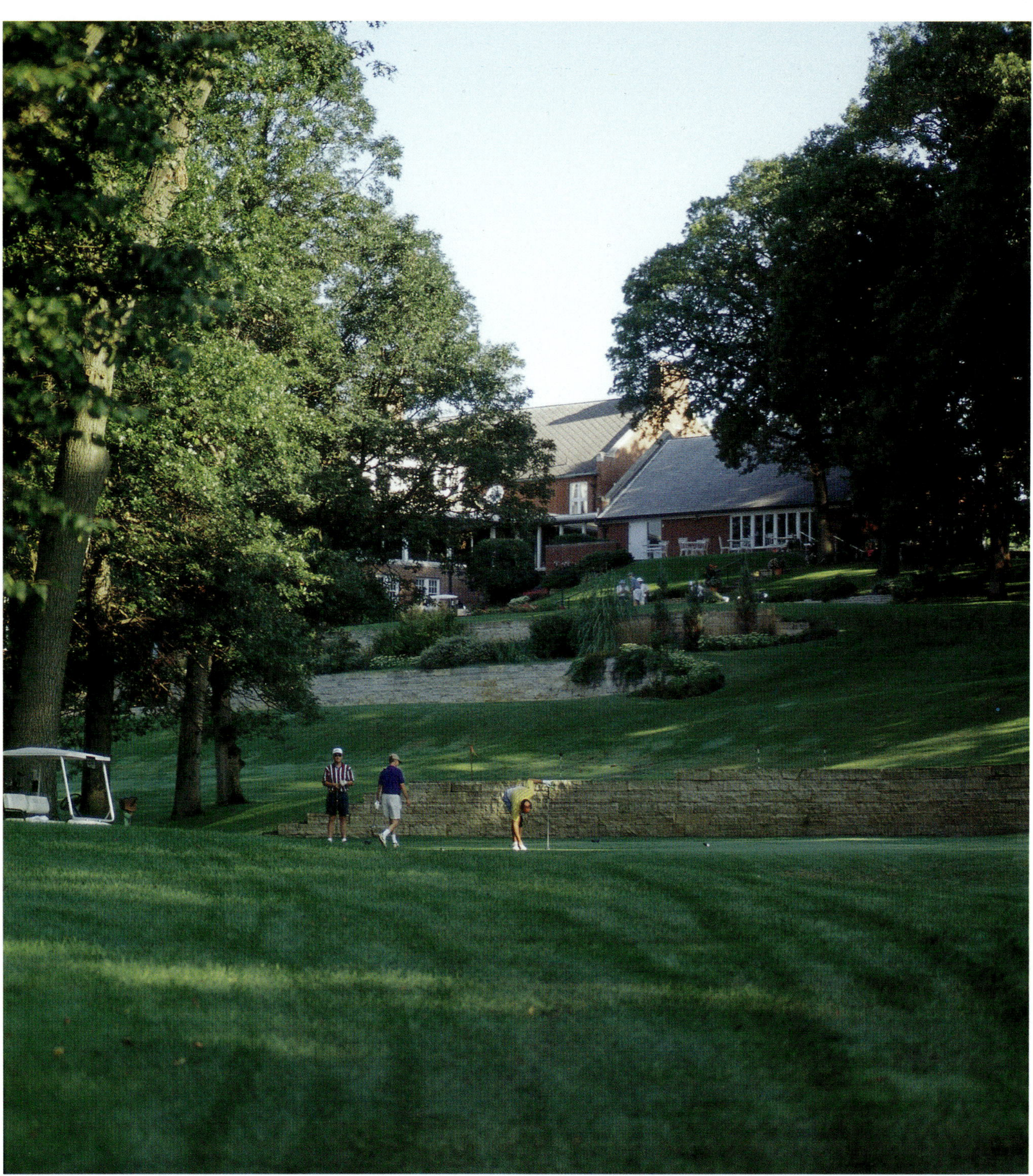

David Van Allen

Golfers at the Cedar Rapids Country Club golf course.

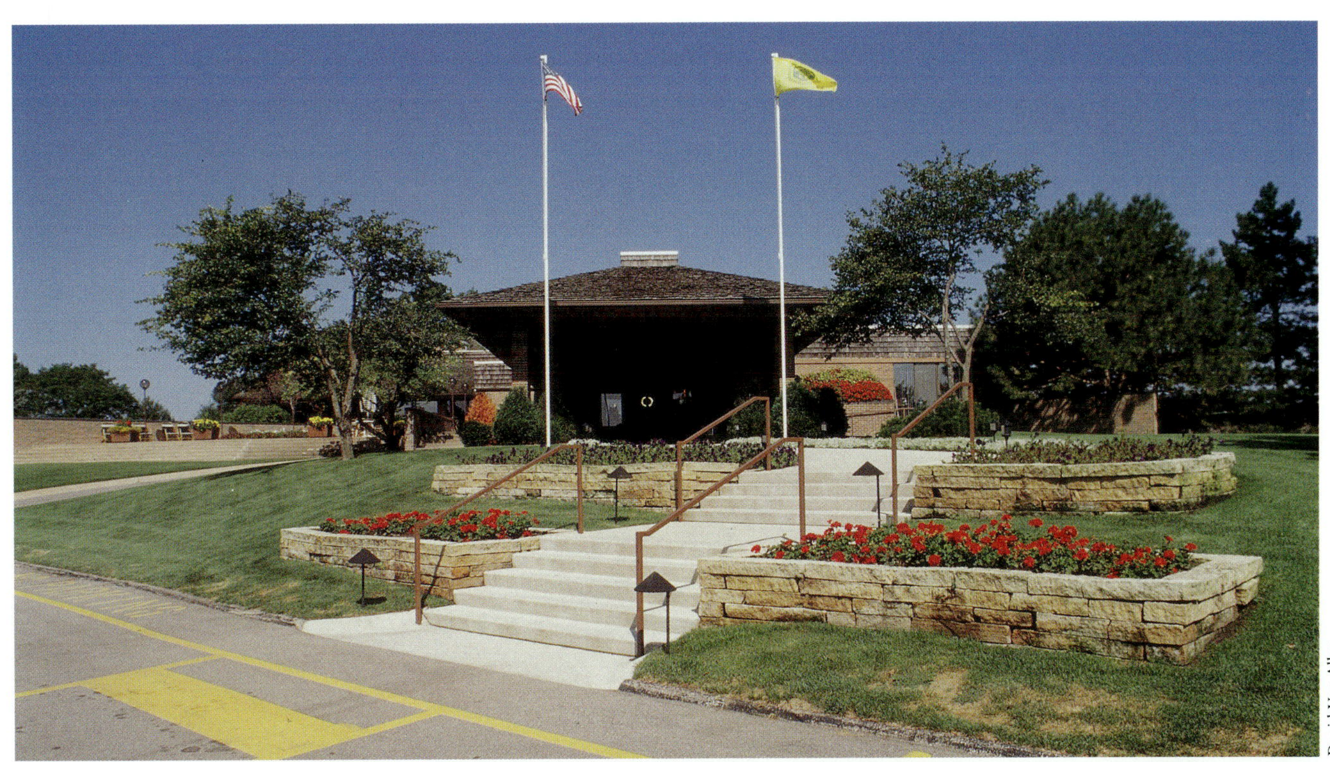
David Van Allen

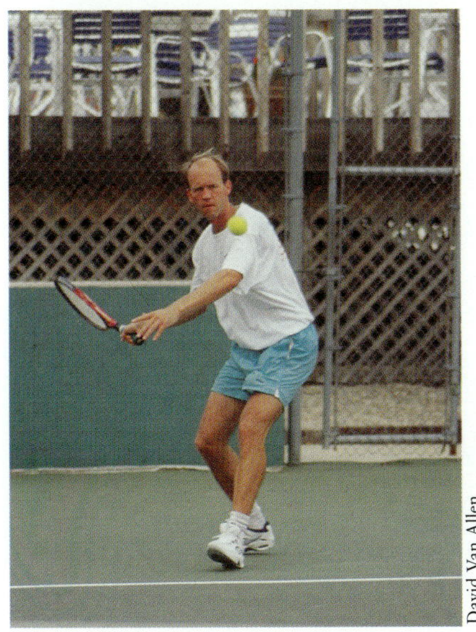
David Van Allen

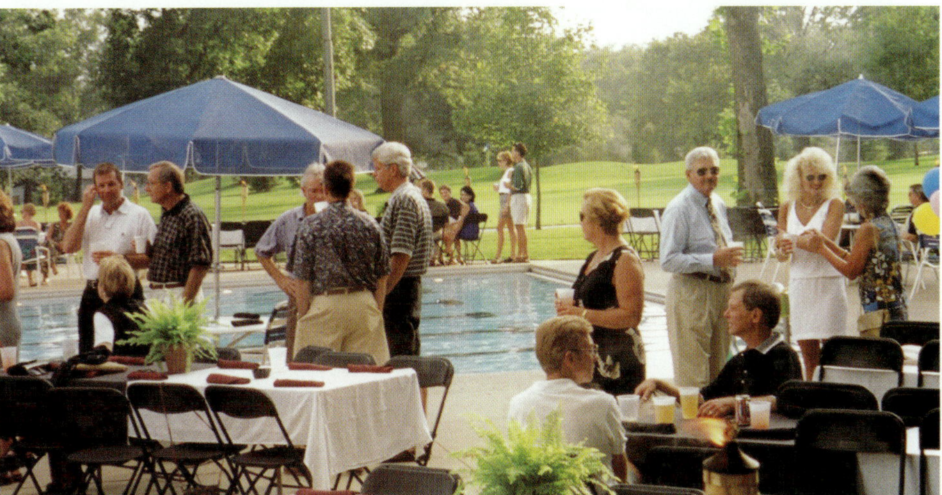
Elmcrest Country Club

Elmcrest Country Club members enjoy *(clockwise from top):* the clubhouse, a pool party, tennis.

Festivals

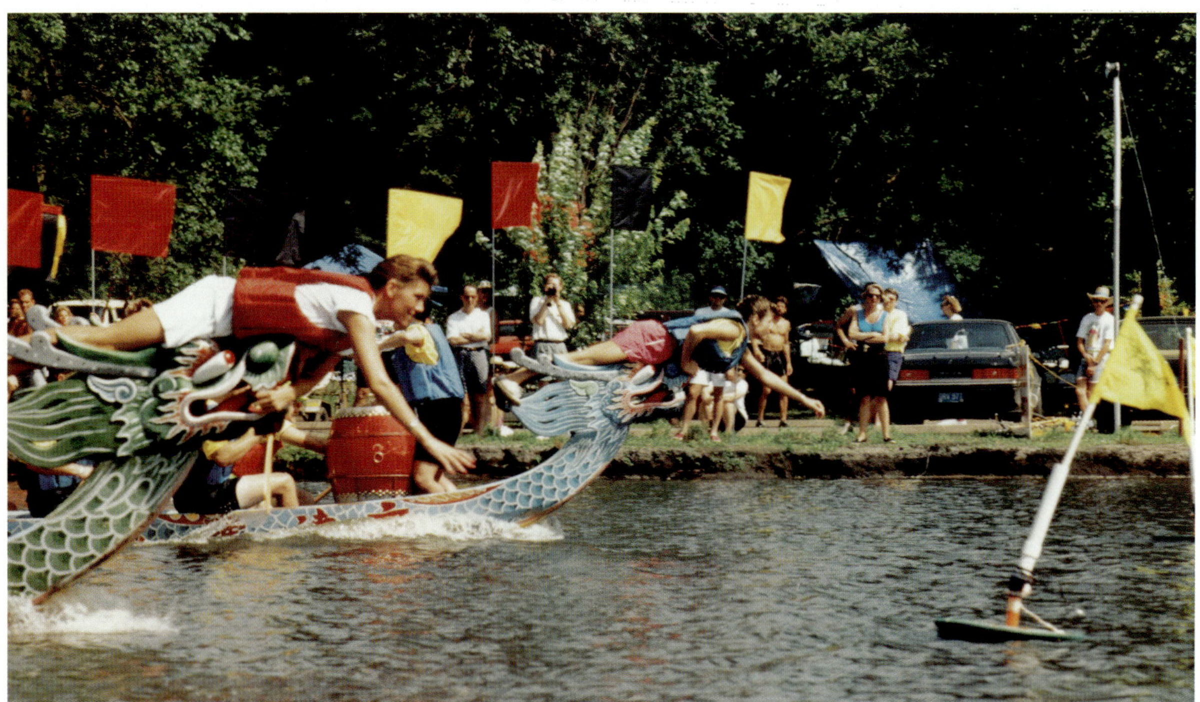
Freedom Festival

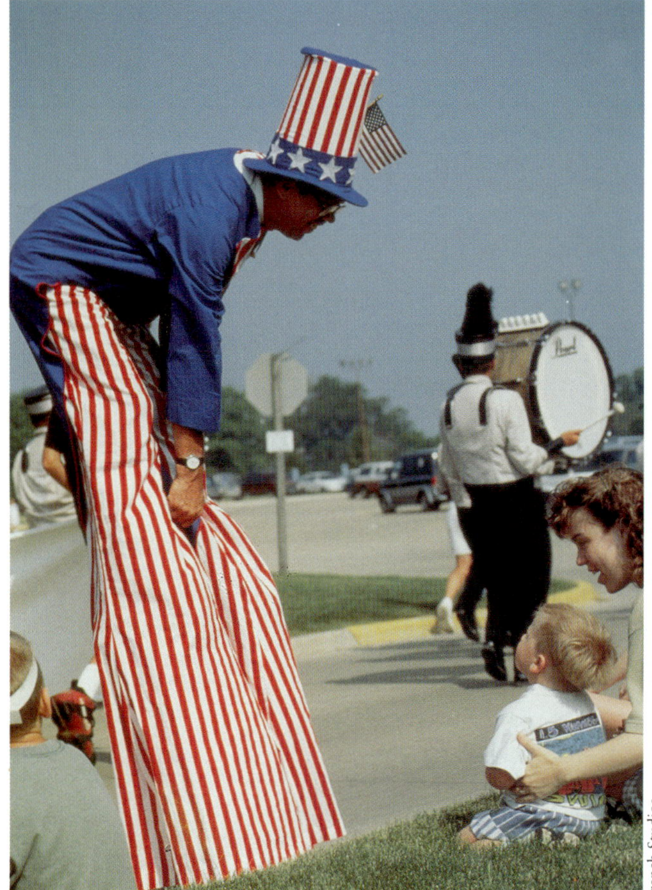
French Studios

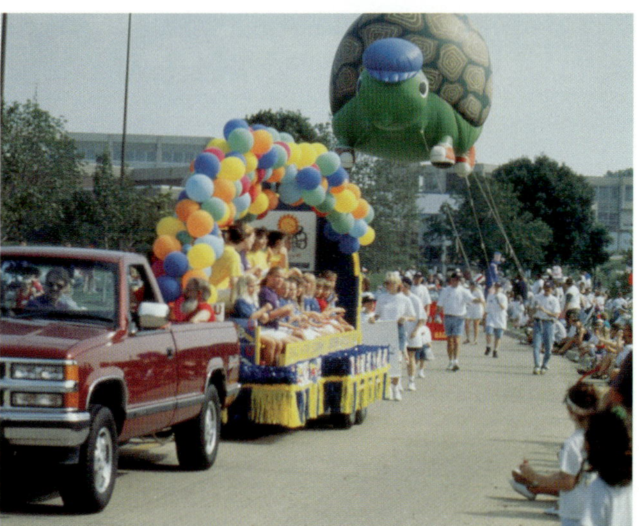
French Studios

One of Cedar Rapids' premier events is the annual Freedom Festival. Activities include dragon boat races, parades and fireworks.

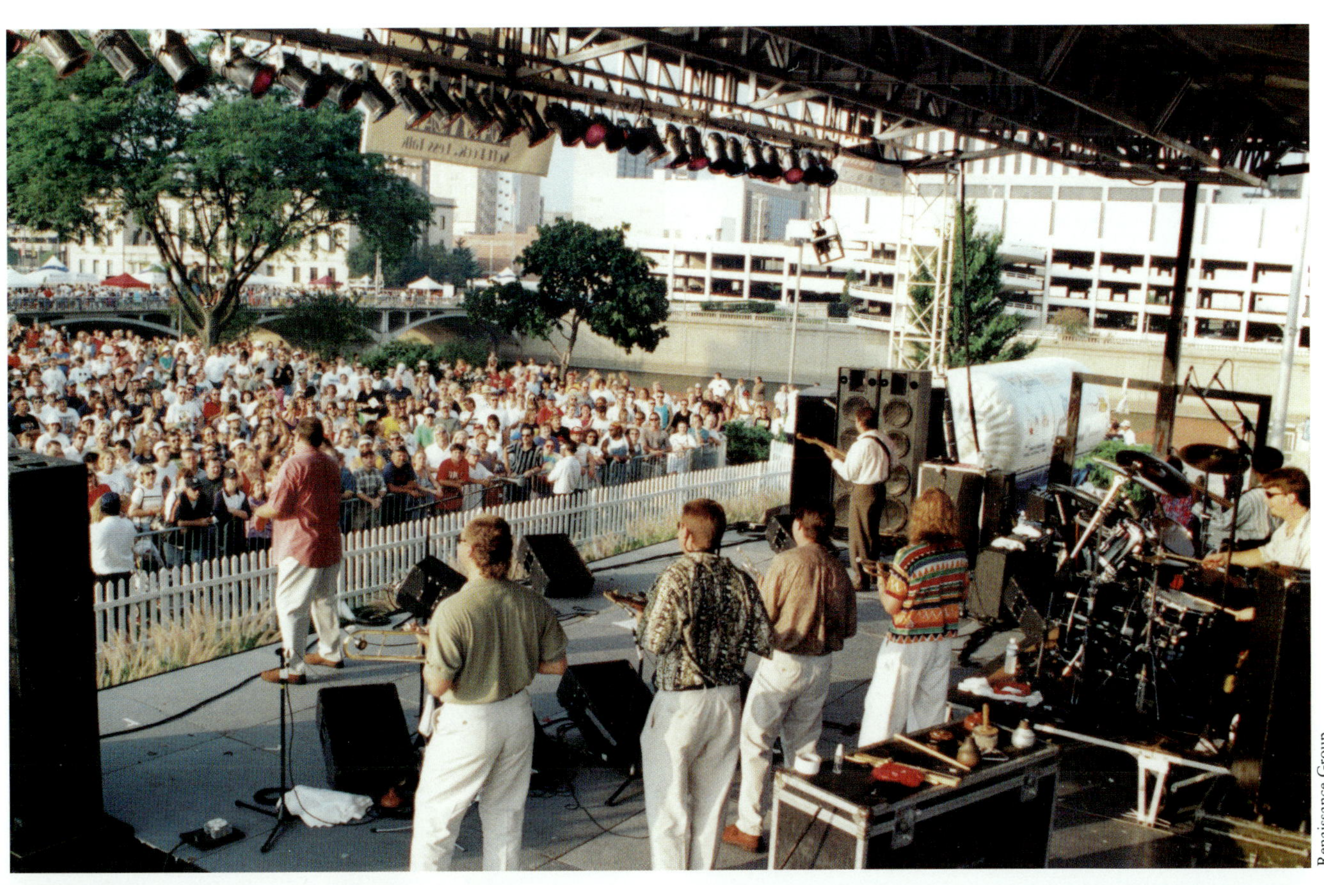
Renaissance Group

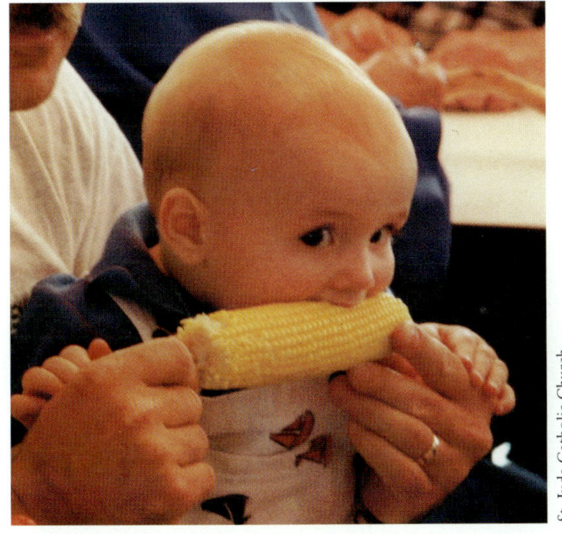
St. Jude Catholic Church

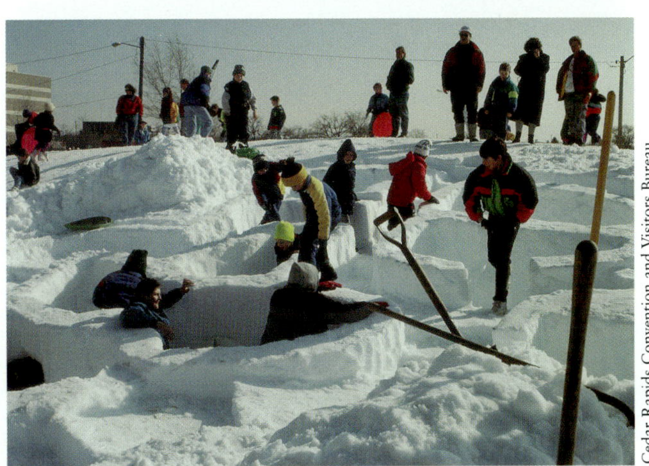
Cedar Rapids Convention and Visitors Bureau

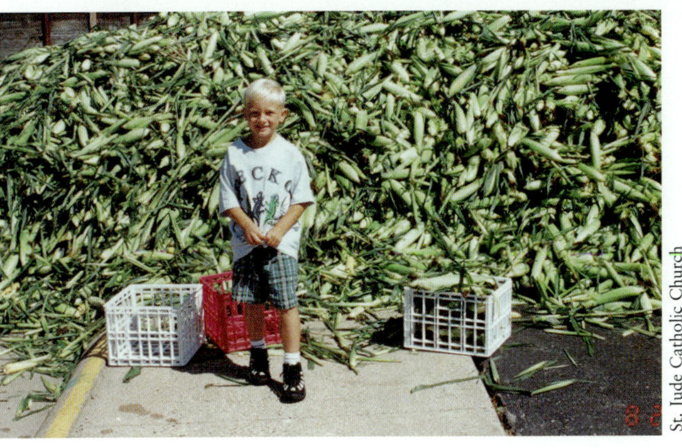
St. Jude Catholic Church

Top: Blood, Sweat and Tears performs during Taste of Iowa, Cedar Rapids' Labor Day festival. *Middle left and bottom:* Tons of sweet corn are enjoyed during St. Jude's annual Sweet Corn Festival. *Middle right:* Snow sculptors create works of art during Winterfest.

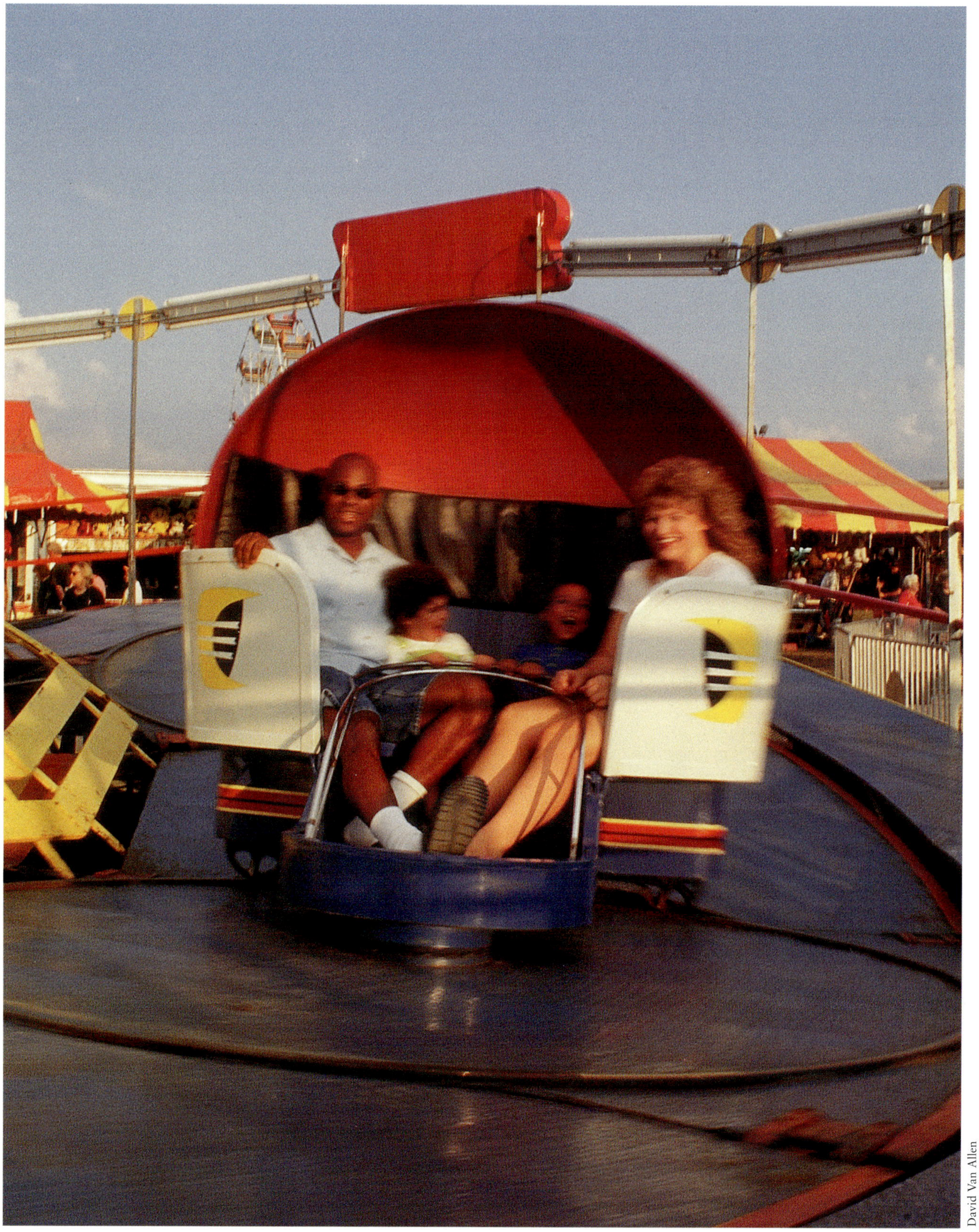

David Van Allen

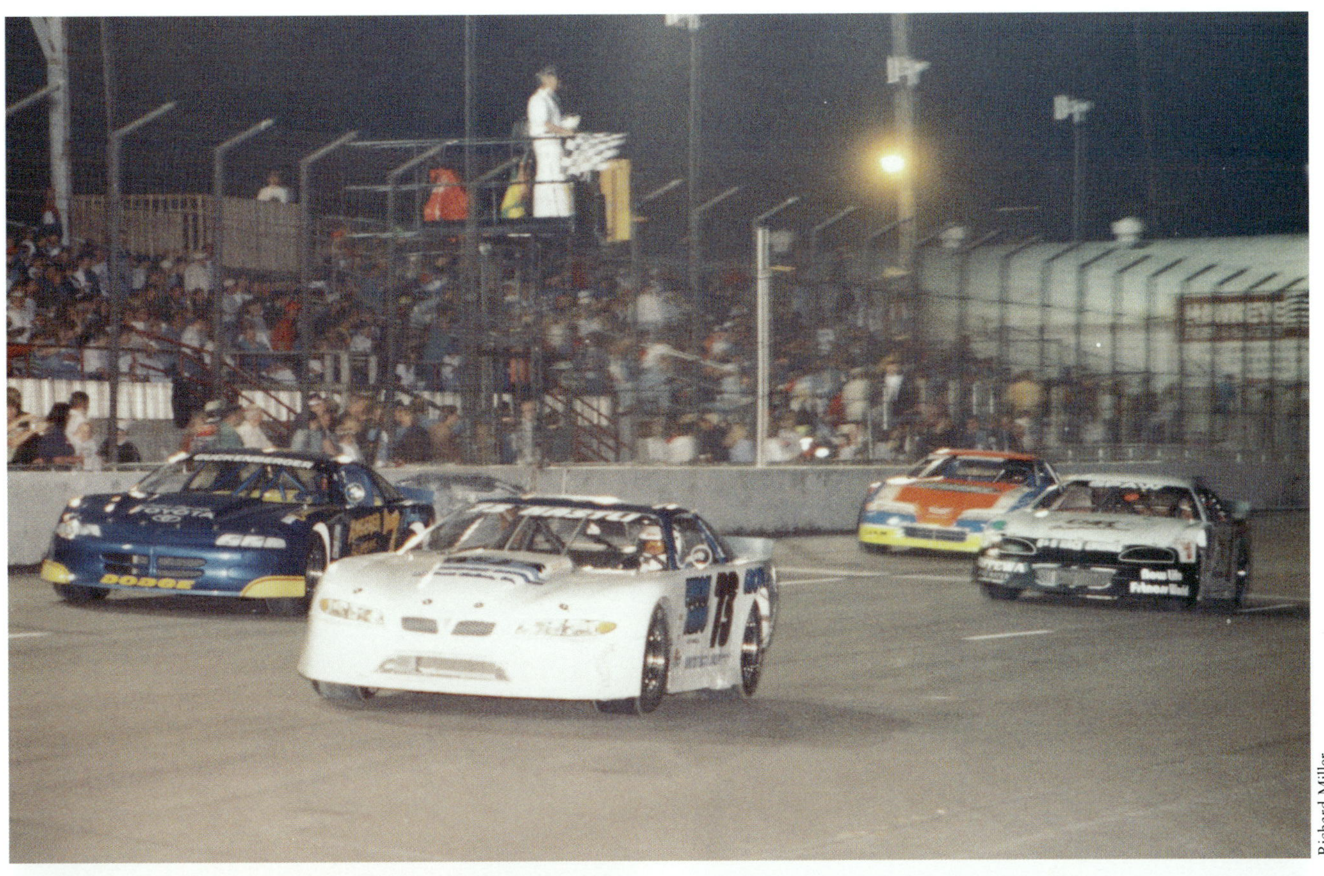

Richard Miller

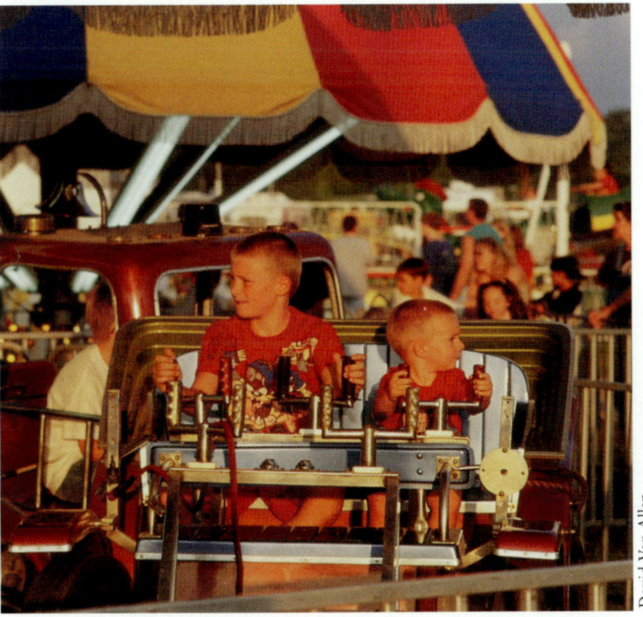

David Van Allen

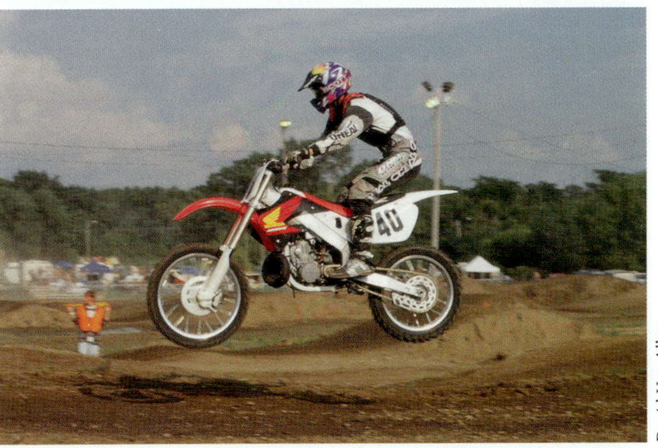

David Van Allen

The All Iowa Fair, held every year at Hawkeye Downs in Cedar Rapids, includes classic midway rides, stock car and motorcycle racing.

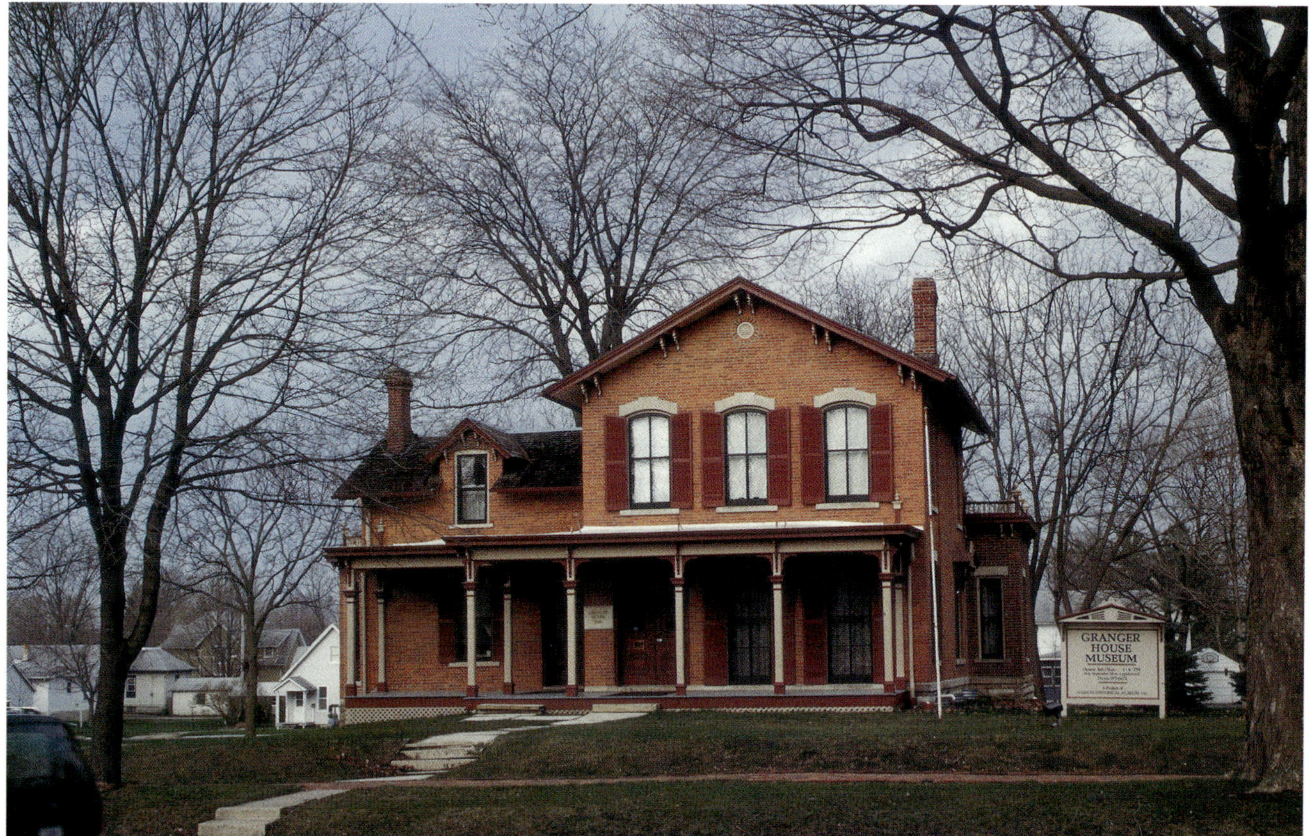

Marion Chamber of Commerce

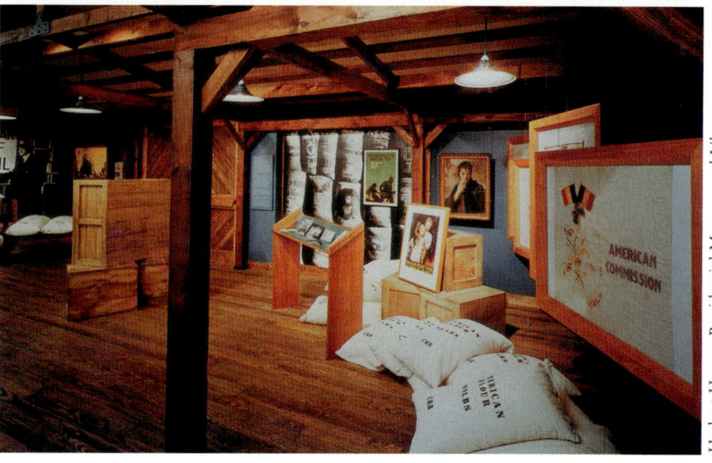

Herbert Hoover Presidential Museum and Library

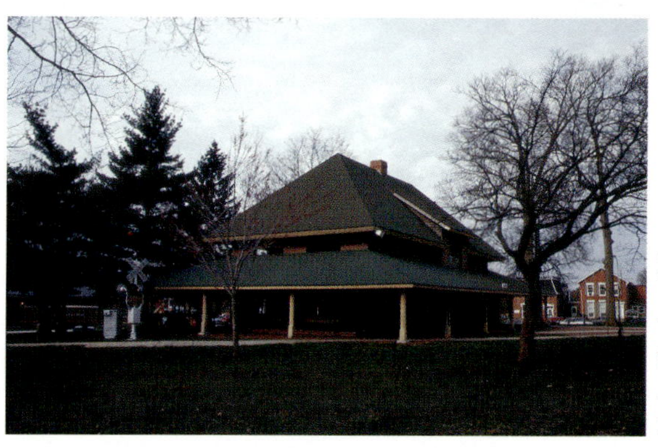

Marion Chamber of Commerce

The Granger House in Marion *(top)* is a restored Victorian home and carriage house open for tours and activities. *Bottom right:* The renovated railroad depot in Marion. *Bottom left:* West Branch is the birthplace of Herbert Hoover, 31st U.S. president. The Herbert Hoover Presidential Museum and Library and National Historic Site includes Hoover's birthplace, blacksmith shop and a museum with changing exhibits.

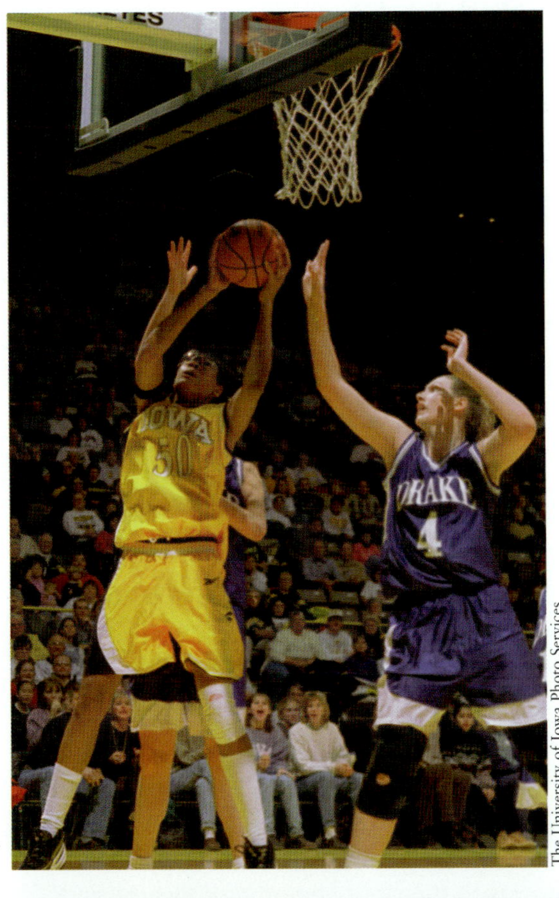

The University of Iowa Photo Services

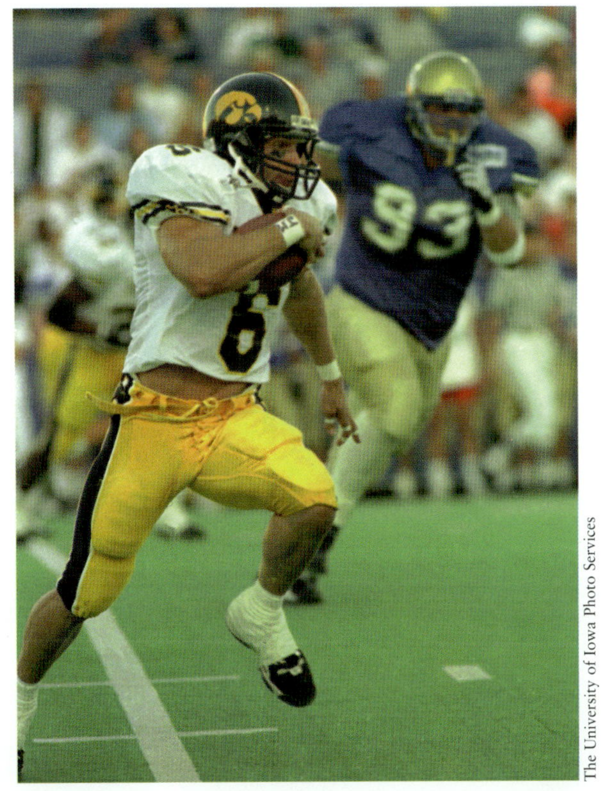

The University of Iowa Photo Services

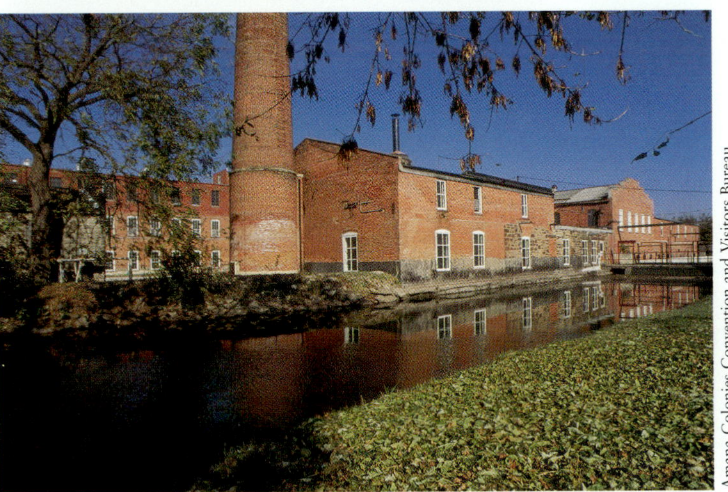

Amana Colonies Convention and Visitors Bureau

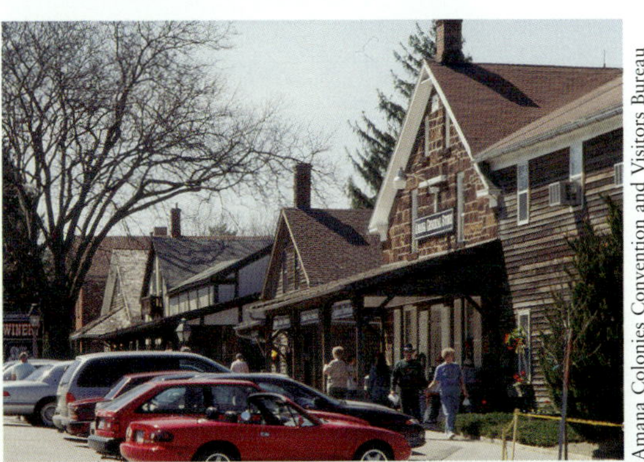

Amana Colonies Convention and Visitors Bureau

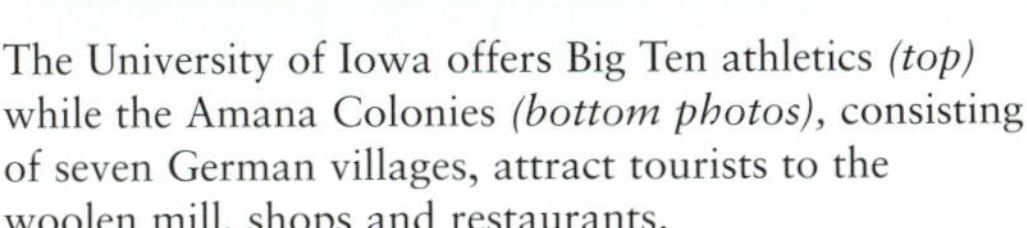

The University of Iowa offers Big Ten athletics *(top)* while the Amana Colonies *(bottom photos)*, consisting of seven German villages, attract tourists to the woolen mill, shops and restaurants.

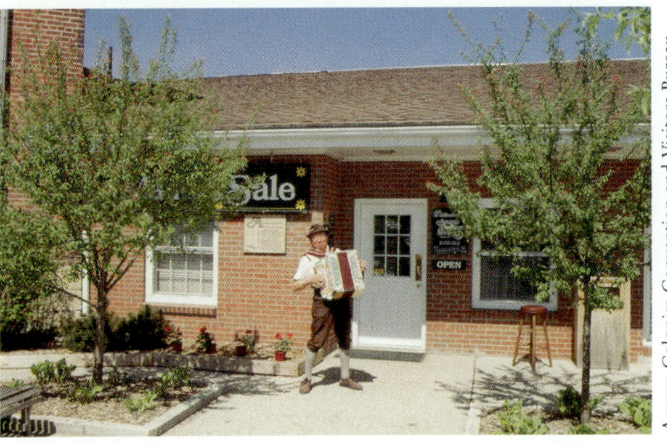

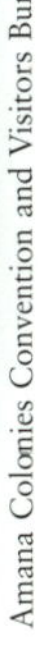

Amana Colonies Convention and Visitors Bureau

Rome on the prairie

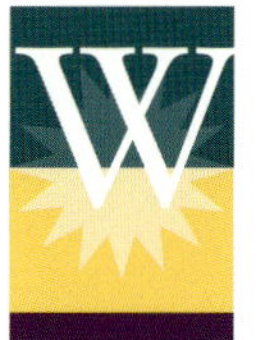

When Nan and Tom Riley donated their collection of Roman busts to the Cedar Rapids Museum of Art in 1997 it created a ripple of change for the oldest fine arts organization in the state.

The Riley collection, given as a way of saying "thank you" to their city, included busts of several Roman emperors, noblemen, women and children. Valued at more than a million dollars, pieces from the collection of 21 busts have been exhibited around the country, including the Metropolitan Museum of Art in New York.

The size and quality of the Riley gift to their hometown museum expanded the identity of the museum in ways its director, Donald Doe, could not have predicted.

"A creative form often defines a city," Doe said nearly a year after the Riley exhibit opened. "When you think of Minneapolis you don't think 3M. You think of the Walker Art Center. We want that to happen here. And in some circles it's already started."

If Doe could give a name to the museum's role in the community, he might borrow the title given to a lecture series on the Roman busts: Rome on the Prairie. The title fits not only the Cedar Rapids Museum of Art as it is positioned now, just before the new century, but also the city's entire arts community.

Traditions in the arts are strong in Cedar Rapids. The names of Grant Wood and Marvin Cone are as embedded in this community as the rolling hills they painted. Families pass on their season tickets to the city's community theater, and the Cedar Rapids Symphony, established in 1922, has achieved a national reputation as a model for the entire country. In good times and bad, the city continues to support the "big three" as the backbone of the community's cultural activities.

But that same sense of tradition, of honoring the past, can sometimes lead to complacency. Art, after all, is about process and change. As the Cedar Rapids Symphony asked its supporters in 1997

Cedar Rapids Museum of Art winter garden.

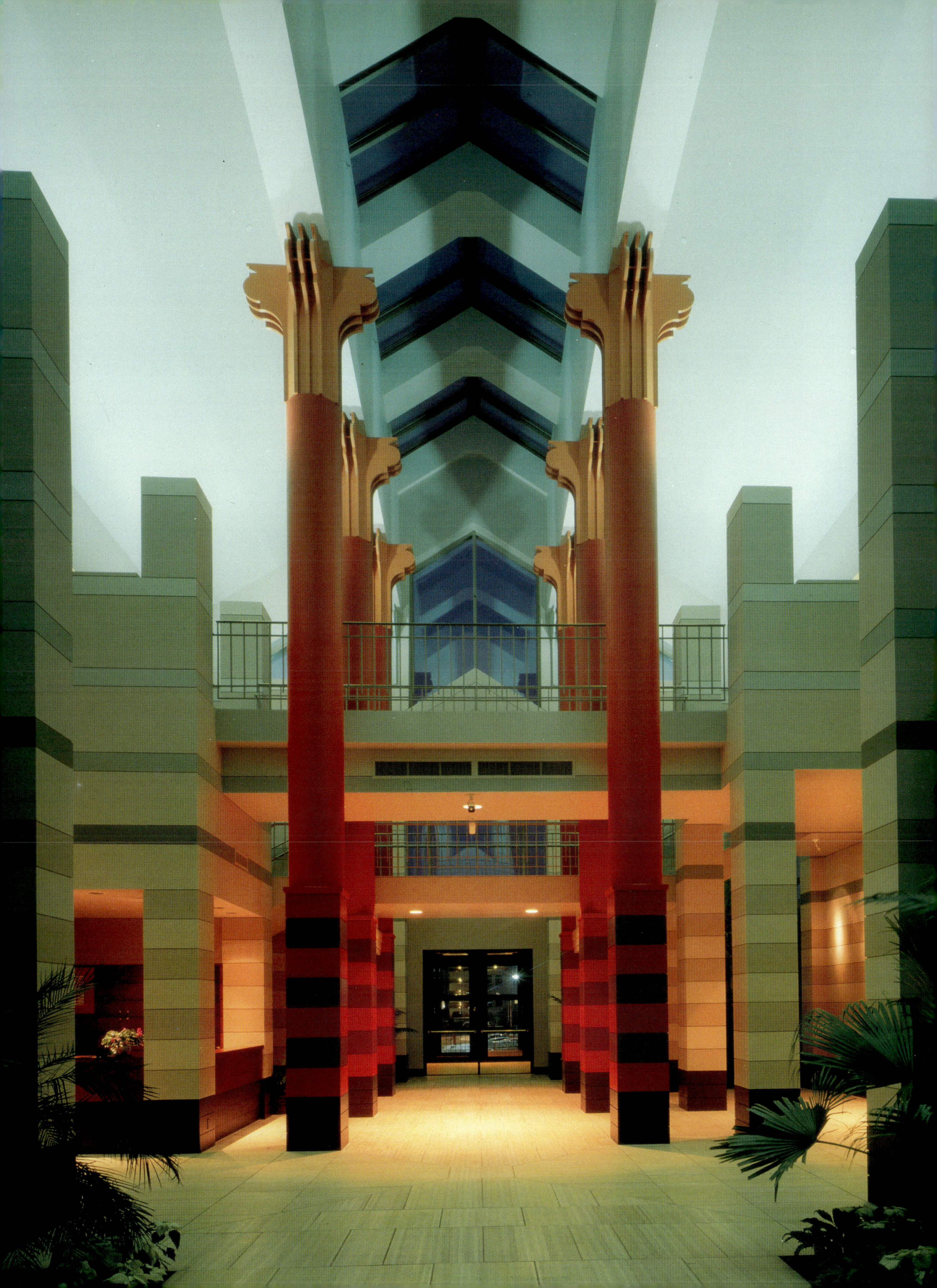

CEDAR RAPIDS
Legends & Leaders

Grant Wood
1891-1942

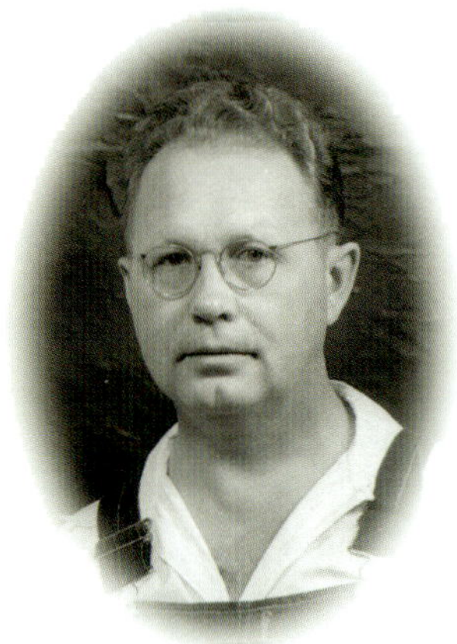

Few other artists captured the Midwestern personality better than Grant Wood. Born on a farm near Anamosa, Wood and his family moved to Cedar Rapids when he was 10 years old. Even when he was a young boy, his artistic talent was evident. His teachers held on to his water colors and drawings, and today nearly a dozen of his boyhood works exist.

Cedar Rapids was home to Wood most of his life. He is best known for his work that portrays simple farm life—"American Gothic" and "Stone City Landscape." In Cedar Rapids, he is also known as the designer of the stained glass window at Veterans Memorial Coliseum. The window commemorates the efforts of American war veterans.

Photo: Cedar Rapids Museum of Art

during its 75th anniversary, "What do you do for an encore?" When it comes to the arts, the answer is you keep growing.

The community built a "big museum," is how Donald Doe refers to the $10 million art museum that opened in 1989. Cedar Rapids has always thought big when it came to the arts.

Inspired by the Chicago World's Fair in 1890, residents brought back to their small town the big idea of creating an arts community. The concept grew into a lively arts association that flourished.

However, it was the city's first professional artists—Grant Wood and Marvin Cone—who established an even stronger tradition in the arts. The two artists lived and worked in the community and they found loyal and devoted patrons. Department stores showcased the artists' works in shop windows; and teachers, who early on saw Wood's talent, held on to his youthful watercolors and drawings.

But it was one of Wood's leading benefactors, John B. Turner II, who, like the Rileys in 1997, changed the focus of the Cedar Rapids Museum of Art. In 1972 Turner and his wife, Happy, donated more than 60 pieces of work, mostly done by Grant Wood, to the Cedar Rapids Art Association, the museum's predecessor. The gift laid the foundation for what has since become a major collection of regional art. Years later, the gift also spawned the idea of creating a big museum.

It is a building that, at first glance, appears out of scale for the size of the community, Doe recalls thinking when he came here in 1996. His rationale: It is about the same size as the art museum in Tucson, Arizona, which in population is four times the size of Cedar Rapids. The fact that the community chose a building of its size says a lot about how Cedar Rapids feels about the arts, Doe acknowledged.

"Ten years ago (in 1988) the museum Cedar Rapids now has didn't exist," he said. "To have built this affords a certain amount of responsibility. Responsibility to use our amazing resources to achieve the potential that's been given to us."

Carrying the torch of bygone eras is a responsibility for each of the main cultural institutions in Cedar Rapids. Whether it is the symphony, Theatre Cedar Rapids or the Museum of Art, none are resting on any laurels. They continue to seek ways to

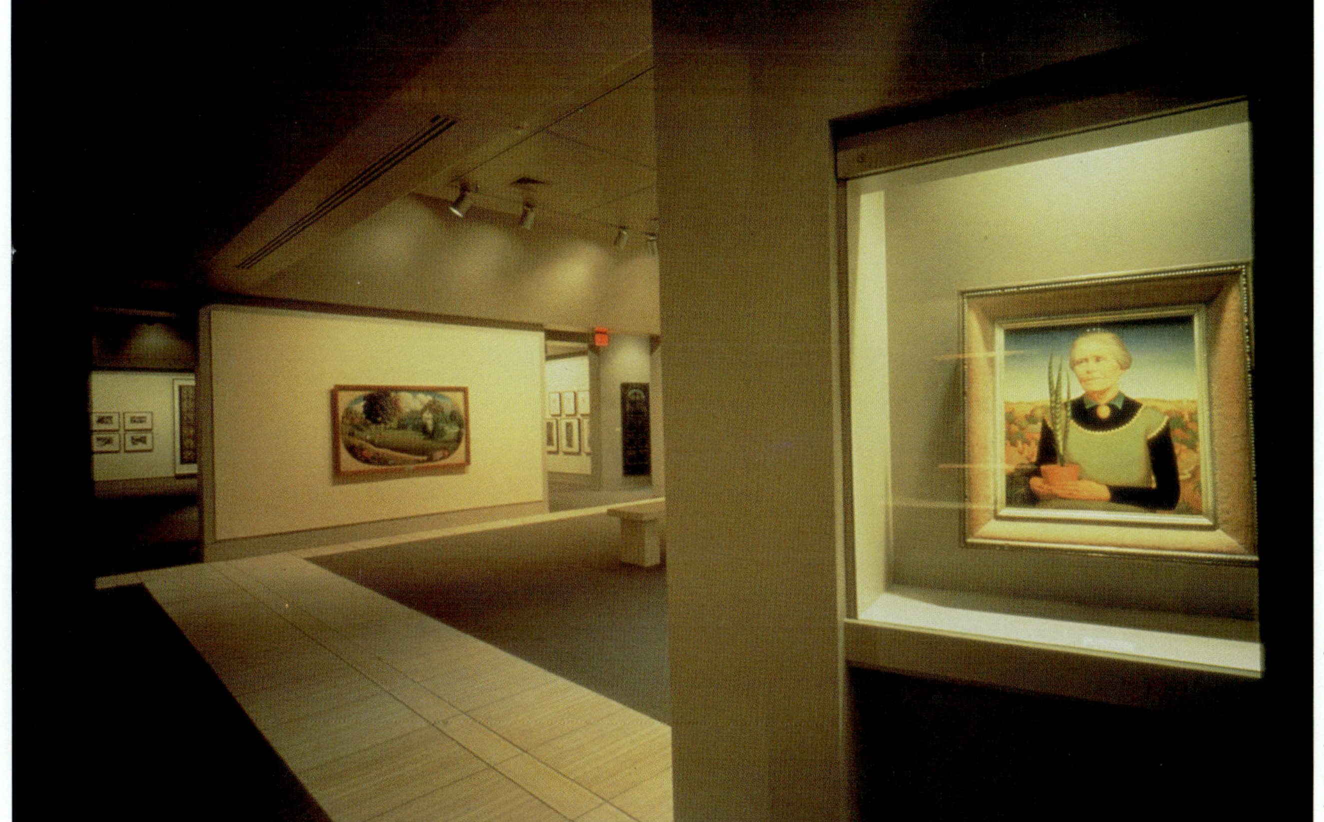

Cedar Rapids Museum of Art

Art works by Grant Wood are part of the museum's permanent collection.

strengthen their base. For most of them, education and a new-found cooperation among the city's old and new artistic guard have been the key to remaining vital.

When Greene's Opera House was the premier theater in Cedar Rapids it attracted top acts of the day. The live entertainment—music, theater—prompted people to ponder and laugh and took them away from their day-to-day existence.

We still need those things, believes TCR executive director Richard Barker. "It is one thing to see 'To Kill a Mockingbird' on TV or at the movies, but it's really something to see it on stage, to listen to it on stage, to listen to the words, to feel the story that you don't get with TV," he said.

Audiences' options for entertainment have changed, bringing new challenges. Opening your doors is no longer enough to get people inside the Paramount or TCR. The strategy for success in the next millennium is a mix of education, of becoming flexible and in some cases trying out new venues, said symphony executive director Kathy Hall.

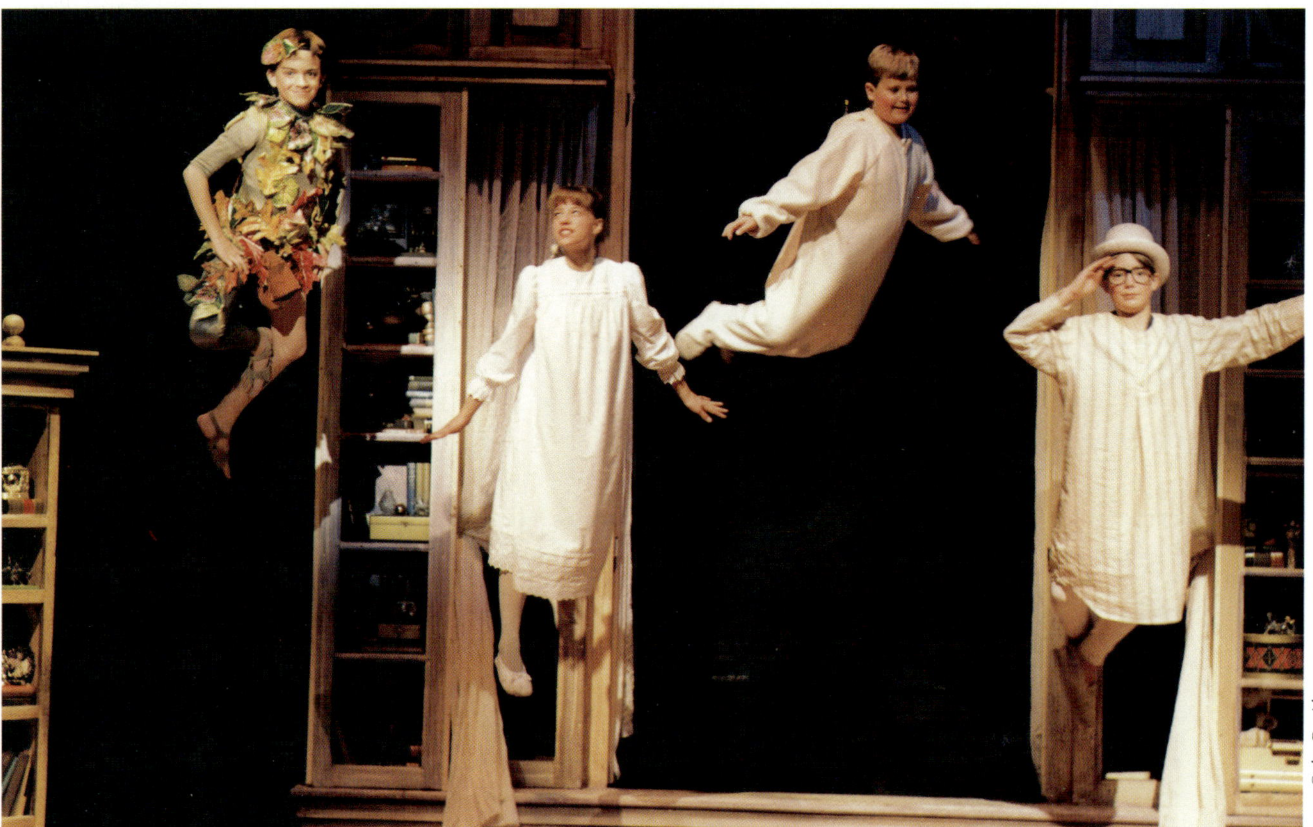

Theatre Cedar Rapids

A Theatre Cedar Rapids production of "Peter Pan." *Facing page:* Red Cedar Chamber Music, Jan Boland and John Dowdall.

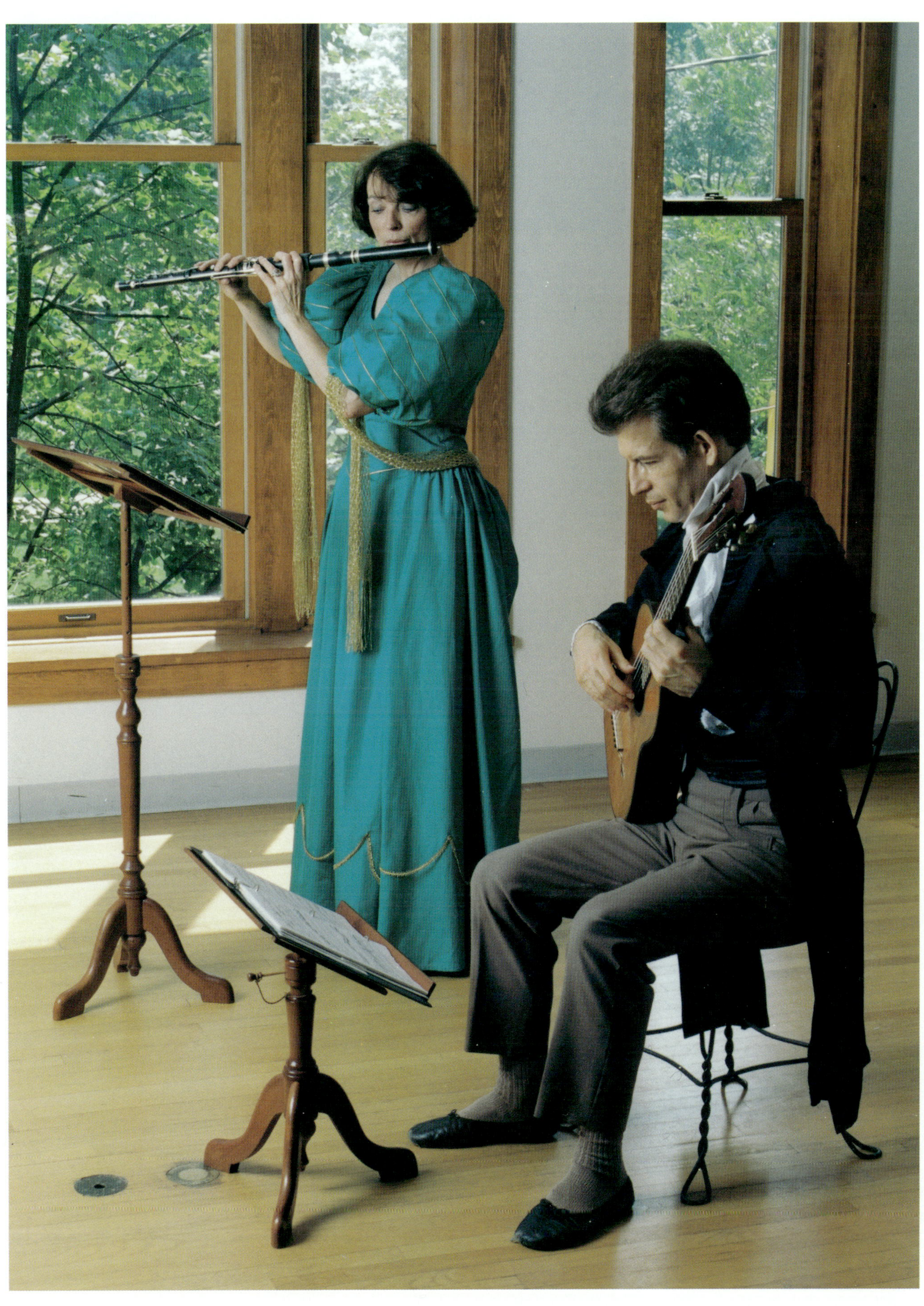

Gordon Photography

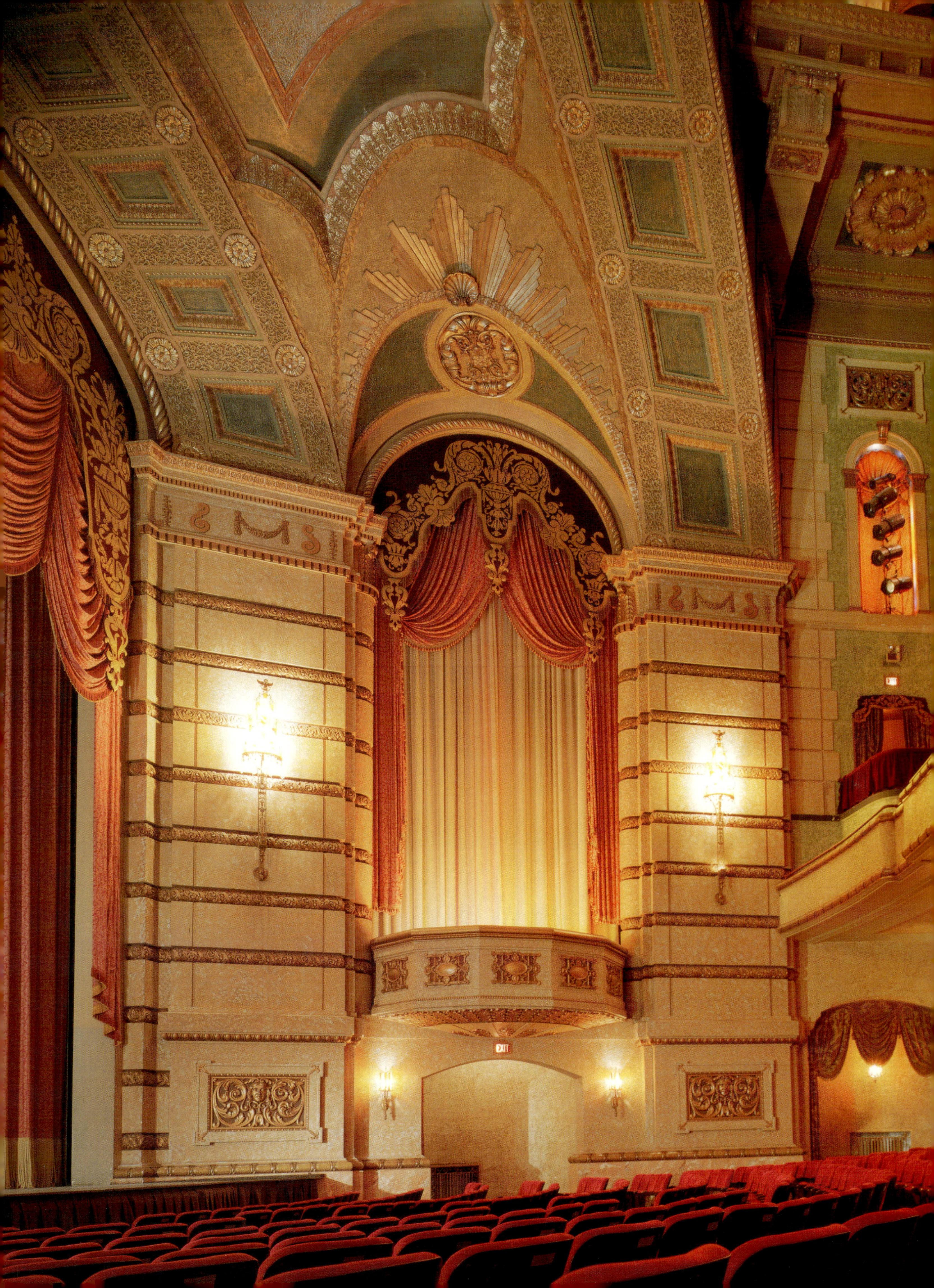

Hall focuses on audience development. In the early '80s the symphony targeted the youth of the community. Youth and Discovery concerts were added to the symphony's lineup. Later, in 1986, a Symphony School opened. A partnership with the Cedar Rapids Community Schools brings a strings program to third-grade students, and city youngsters receive vouchers for concerts.

"We're constantly changing as the community changes," Hall said, looking back at the symphony's past decade. "We seek out partnerships with other organizations...to become more user-friendly."

The saving grace for the city's oldest arts organizations, Barker believes, may be their alliance with some of the youngest arts groups.

Much of this cooperation began through the efforts of a newcomer to the arts scene in Cedar Rapids. In the early 1990s, F. John Herbert moved his non-profit art operation from Iowa City to Cedar Rapids.

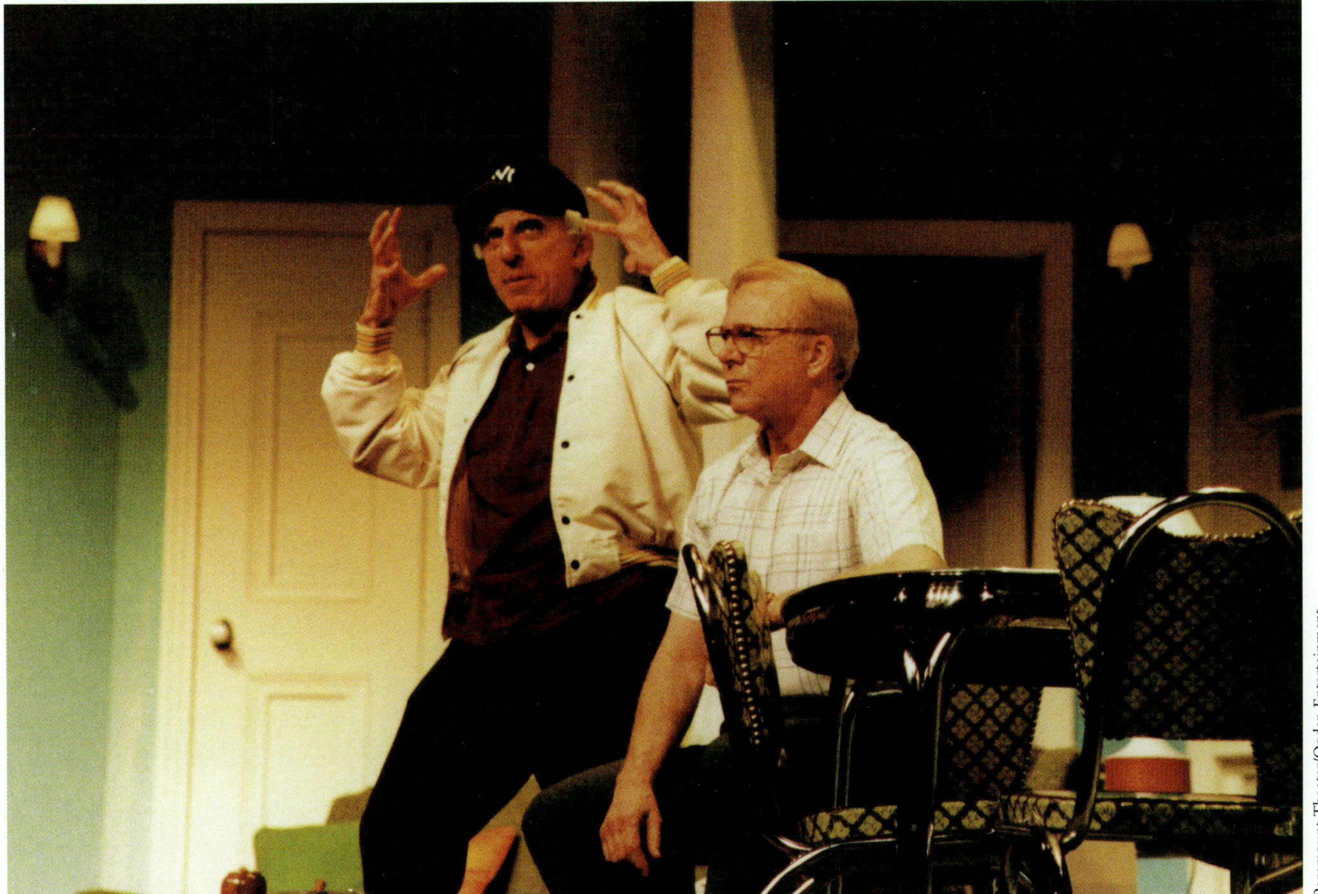

Paramount Theater/Ogden Entertainment

Built in 1928, the Paramount Theatre *(facing page)* is an elegant setting for concerts and plays. Jamie Farr and William Christopher brought "The Odd Couple" to the Paramount Theatre.

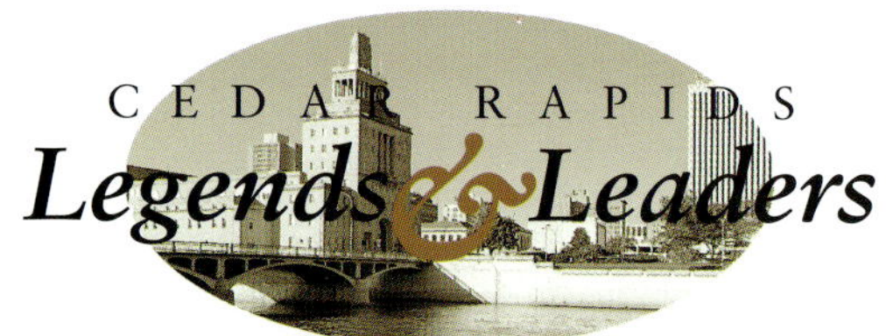

The Cherry Sisters

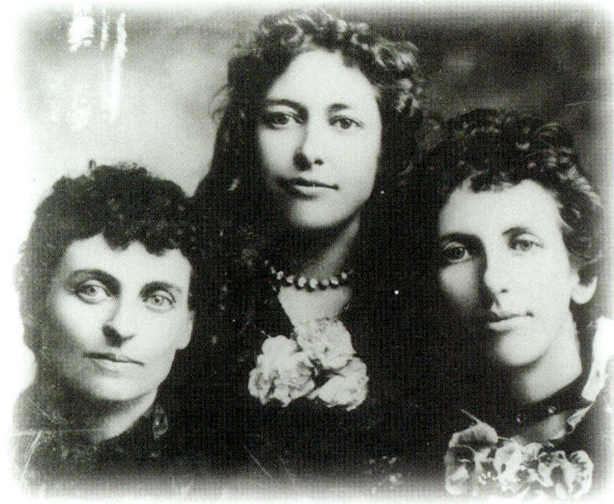

The Cherry sisters, known as the worst act in vaudeville, got their start in Cedar Rapids. They "performed" in leading opera houses throughout America, where audiences pelted them with overshoes and rotten vegetables. Critics announced they were so bad they were good. The New York Times referred to the sisters—Addie, Effie and Jessie—as the Vegetable Girls. Still they packed the house, earning as much as $1,000 a week.

The sisters also made legal history by suing the Des Moines Leader *in 1901 for libel. The newspaper had written a disparaging review of the sisters' act, describing their singing as "the wailing of damned souls." The court ruled against the sisters after witnessing the act in court.*

Eventually, the sisters retired and returned to Cedar Rapids to run a home bakery. Effie continued to make news when she ran for Cedar Rapids mayor in 1923 and 1925. She lost both elections.

Photo: Iowa State Historical Society

He kept hearing people say there wasn't much going on in the arts in Cedar Rapids. Herbert thought differently. In fact, he had an idea. He wanted to create a cultural corridor in Cedar Rapids that included all of the arts groups in the downtown area extending over to Czech Village. Together, Herbert thought, we can do a better job of bringing an awareness of the arts.

Herbert's idea became a proposal and in 1993 the Downtown Cultural Alliance (now known as the Cedar Rapids Area Cultural Alliance) was born. Founding members included the Cedar Rapids Metropolitan Arts Council, the Museum of Art, the symphony, public library, TCR, Science Station, Linn County Historical Museum, the National Czech and Slovak Museum and Library and the Czech Heritage Foundation.

The youngest member of this alliance was the arts organization founded by Herbert and his partner Mel Andringa. Its name, CSPS, came from the name of their building, which is in a long-time Czech neighborhood.

"CSPS means in the Czech-Slovak language a prudential society and in its heyday this building was a meeting hall for Czechs," Andringa said from a gallery in the building.

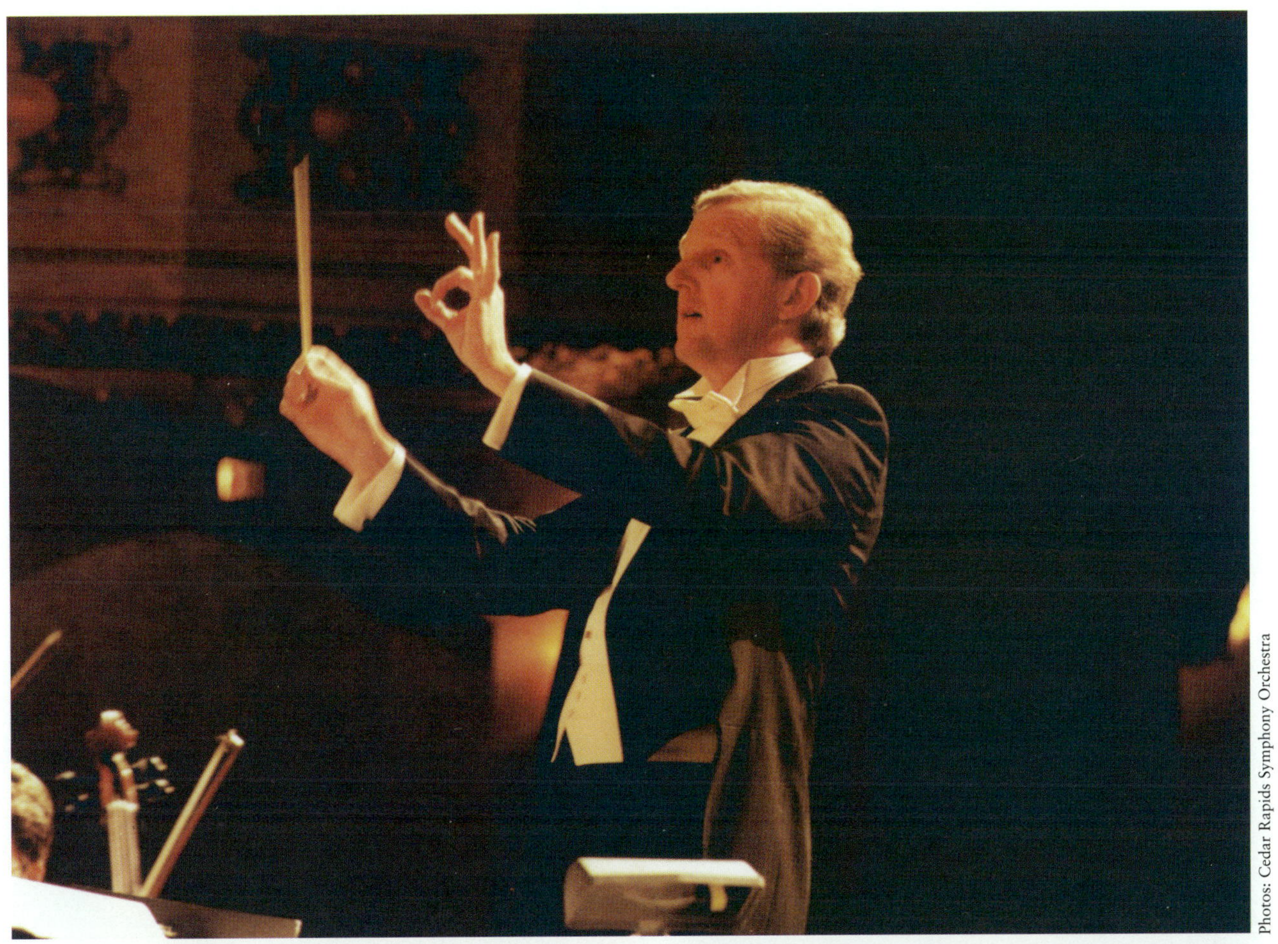

Photos: Cedar Rapids Symphony Orchestra

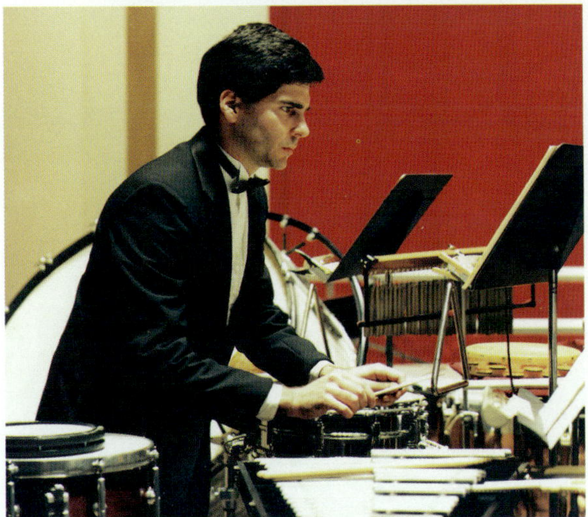

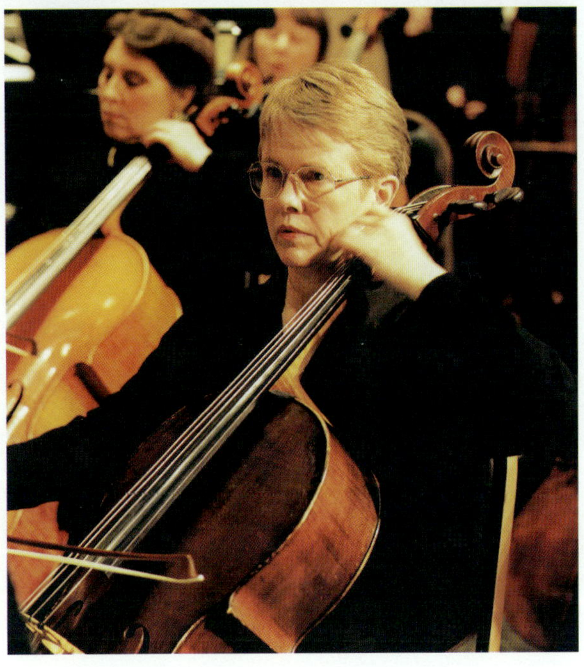

The Cedar Rapids Symphony, under the direction of Christian Tiemeyer, is the largest in Iowa performing classical, pops, chamber, youth and "Discovery" concerts each year.

The concept of art that Herbert and Andringa brought to Cedar Rapids was based on community centers they had seen in their travels to Europe. Unlike museums that "own" the art, these centers would show or display art. "The art there was produced by gypsies—artists who traveled from place to place who were looking for opportunities to do things in out-of-the-way places."

Looking back, Andringa thinks their concept was an awakening for area artists who had been somewhat stuck into thinking about art in one certain way. "We thought if we could get the art community thinking differently we'd change the way the community thinks about art," he said.

CSPS is now considered a station, or a stop, for visual and performing artists who travel the globe much like early performers did in the days of the opera houses. The experiment, as Andringa calls CSPS's early days, is no longer an experiment. Andringa and Herbert's ideas of joint programming and moving art offsite to new venues have been absorbed by the mainstream cultural organizations.

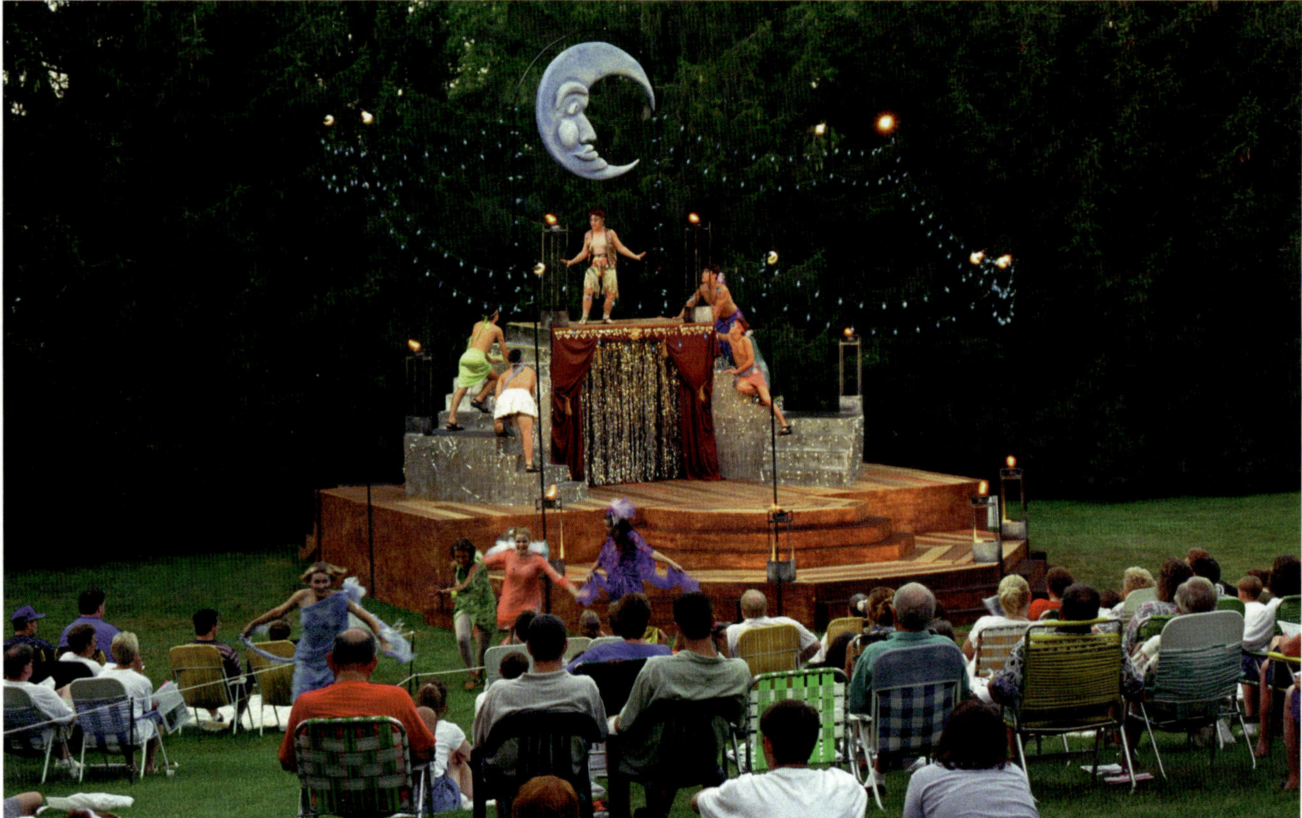

Mark Tade/The Gazette

The Classics at Brucemore, a partnership between Brucemore and Torchlight Theatre, brings Shakespeare to the historic estate. *Above and facing page:* "A Midsummer Night's Dream" at Brucemore.

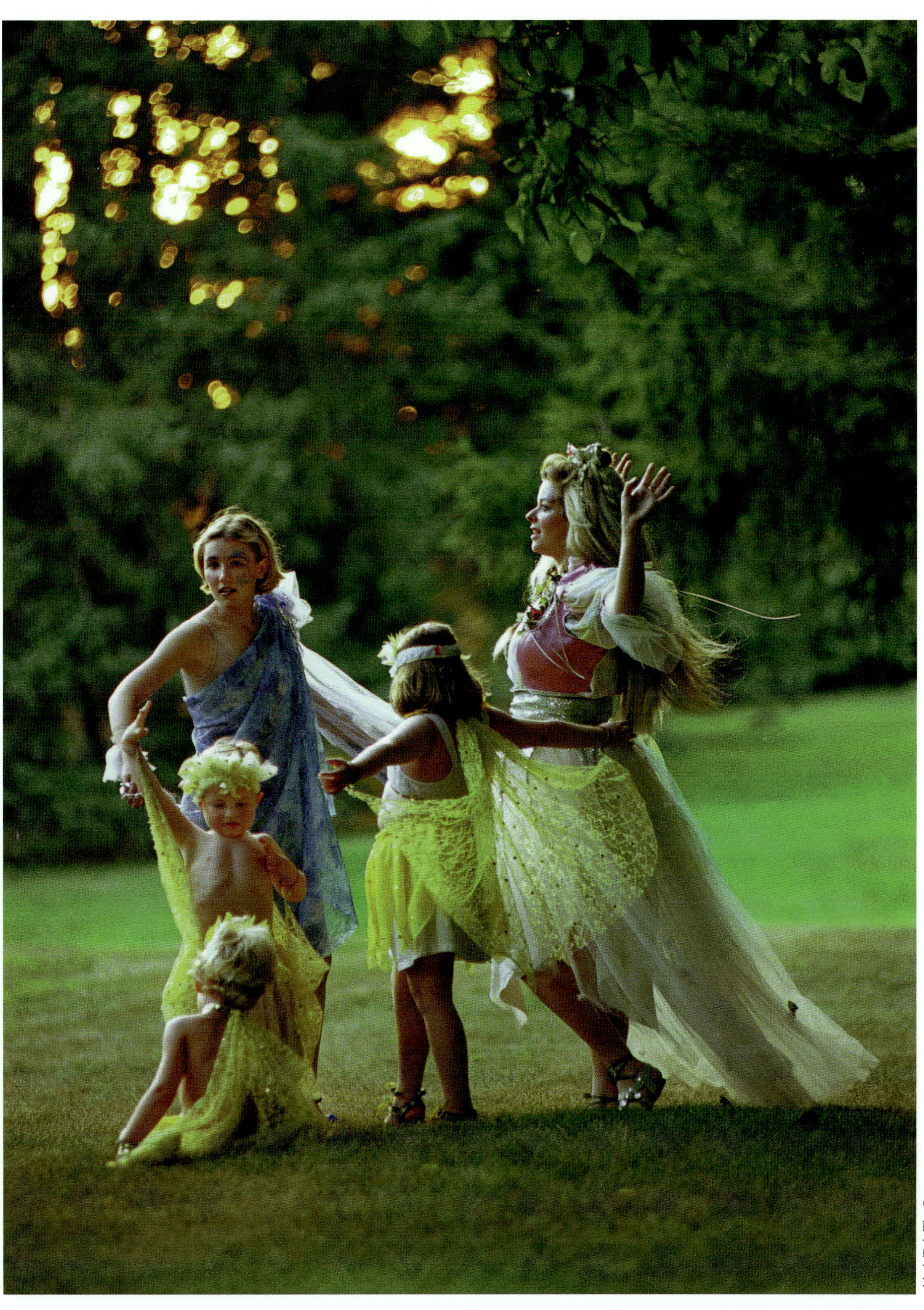

Mark Tade/The Gazette

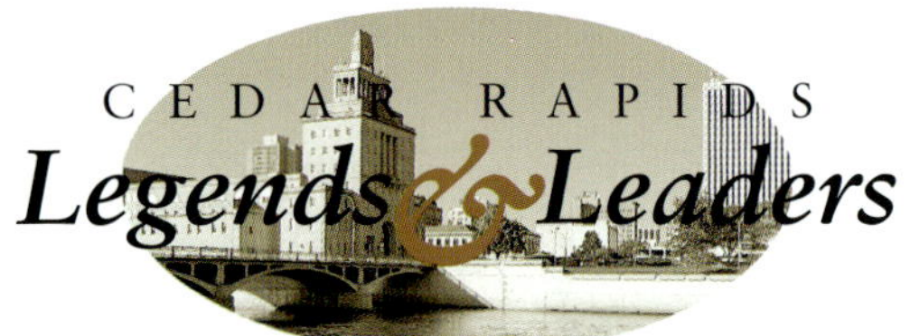

Carl Van Vechten
1880-1964

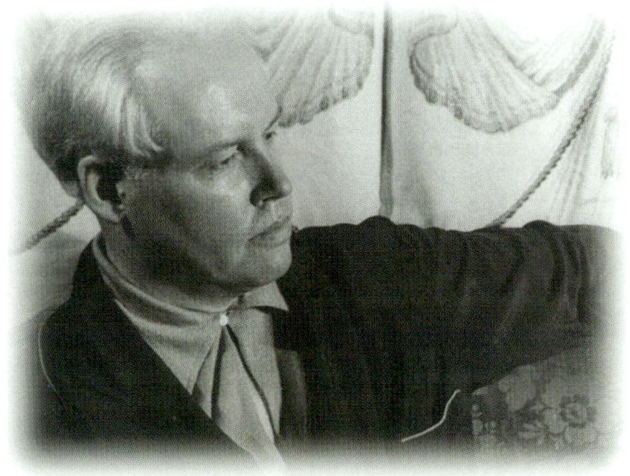

Carl Van Vechten grew up in Cedar Rapids with a reputation as somewhat of an odd duck. His interests in art, photography and music may have set him apart from other children but became the foundation for a diverse and successful career in the arts.

Van Vechten was first a music critic covering the New York music scene and a writer whose book—The Tatooed Countess, *a parody of life in a Midwestern town—was roughly based on his hometown. After 1932, Van Vechten's interest turned to photography, particularly chronicling the thriving African-American culture in Harlem. Among the creative artists he photographed were Billie Holiday, Marilyn Horne, playwright Edward Albee and artist Joan Miro.*

His book, Generations in Black and White, *includes some of the 15,000 photographs Van Vechten took in a career that spanned more than 30 years.*

Photo: Courtesy of Bruce Kellner, representing the Estate of Carl Van Vechten, from the collection of The Cedar Rapids Community School District.

The symphony now plays concerts at TCR. At the Freedom Festival, jazz, blues and chamber music fill the art museum. Artists from CSPS play in the venerable Paramount Theatre.

By their nature, Andringa said, artists are uniquely prepared to deal with change. It's a part of their work gleaned from controlling their materials.

"One of our goals, though, in importing these artists and making changes isn't to change the city. You look at Grant Wood. He allowed his style to change because of his travels. I guess we hope through our work with artists from all over, something catalytic will happen. Possibly that spark will again bring a significant change that will focus attention back to Cedar Rapids."

The consensus is there is room for both the old and the new in the arts. Local artist and one-time art museum director Stan Wiederspan describes Cedar Rapids and its surrounding communities as a cultural smorgasbord. People can pick and choose, but most of the arts, he said, "are magnetic."

Andringa believes we will always have a need to connect with our roots and our history. "You have to be grounded," he said. "But that is only one of two legs. The other leg must always step forward into new situations."

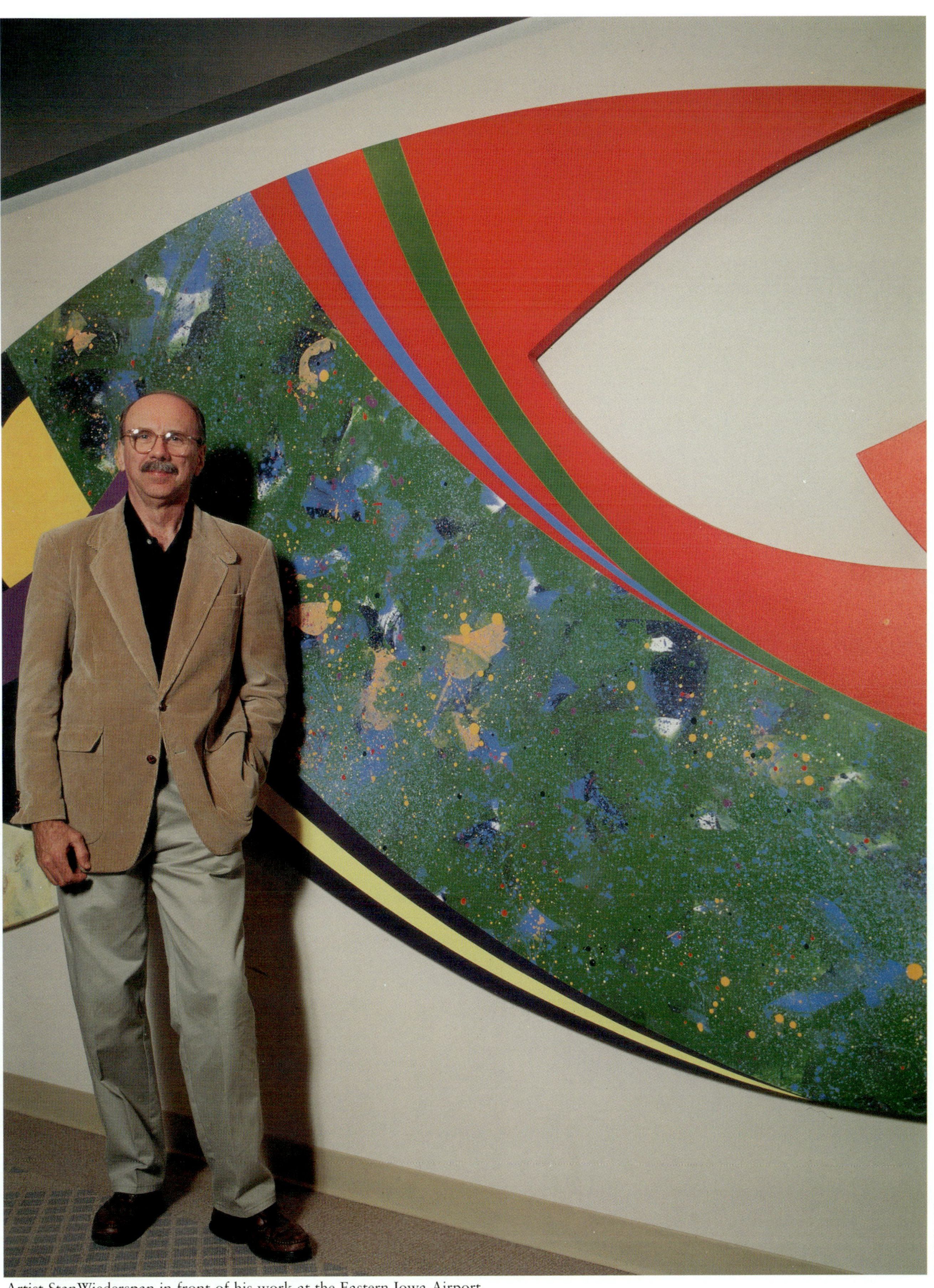

David Van Allen

Artist StanWiederspan in front of his work at the Eastern Iowa Airport.

Sculptures

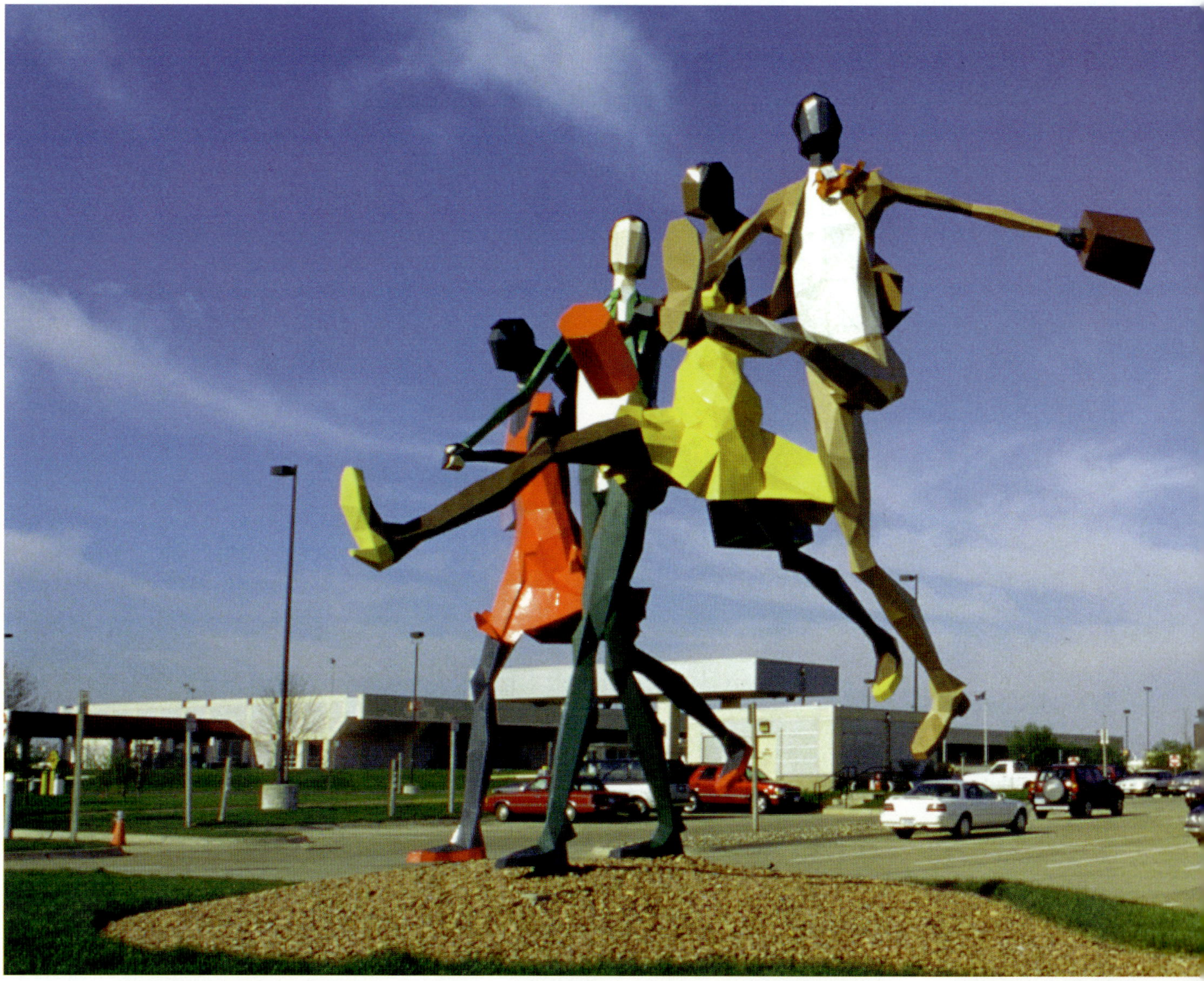

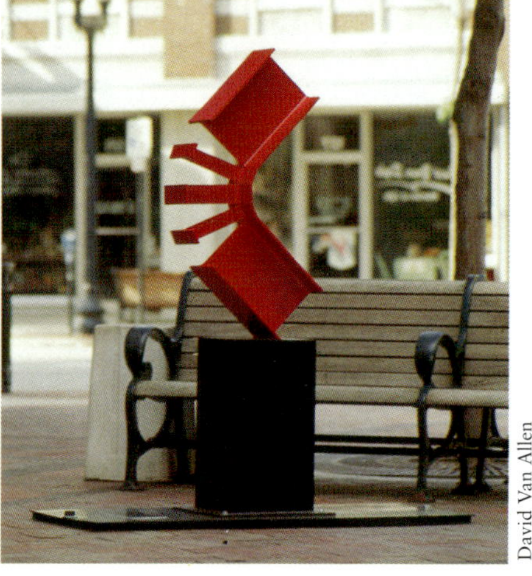

David Van Allen

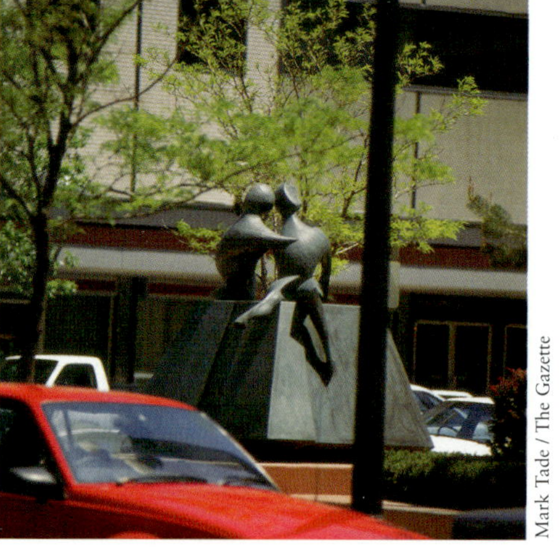

Mark Tade / The Gazette

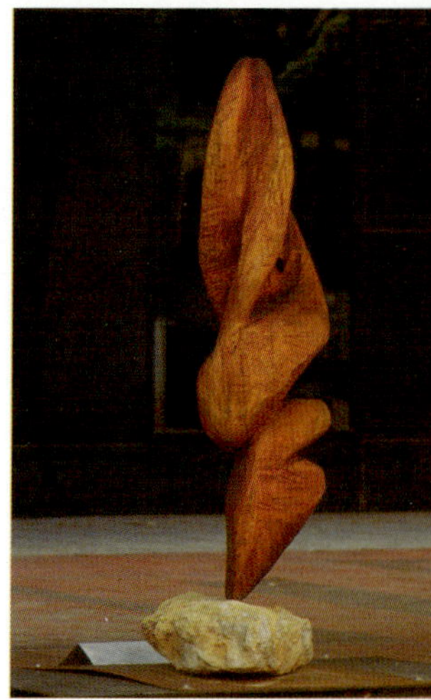

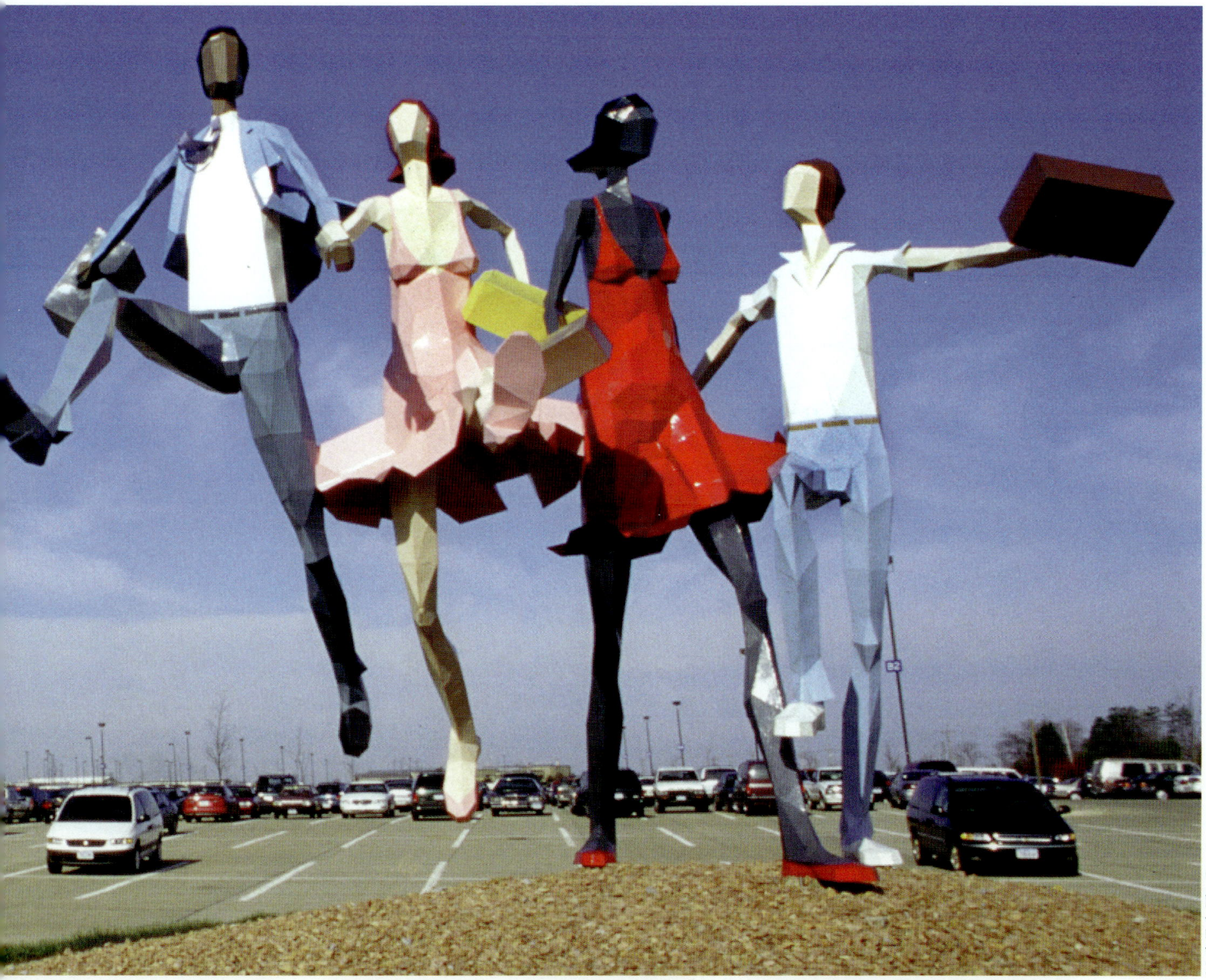

Mark Tade/The Gazette

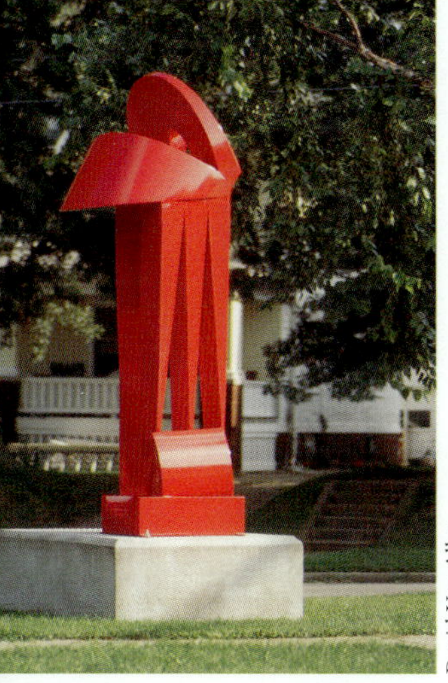

David Van Allen

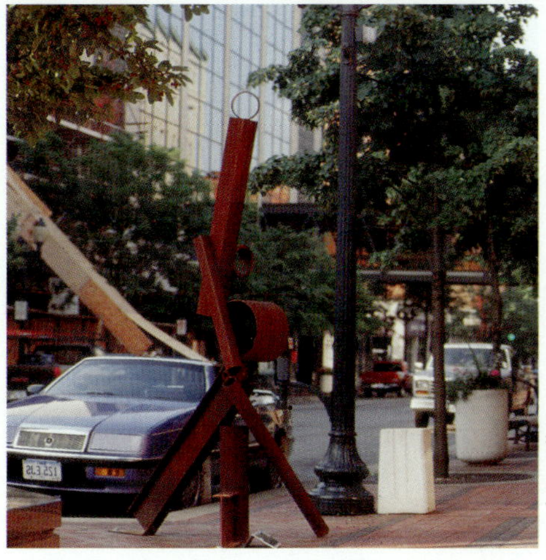

David Van Allen

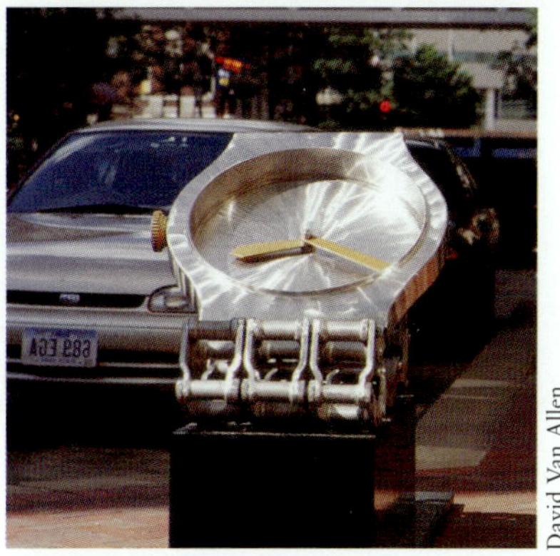

David Van Allen

Art in public places: "In Transit," a larger-than-life outdoor sculpture by Dennis Patton, greets people at the Eastern Iowa Airport *(top)*. Public art is on display throughout the city of Cedar Rapids.

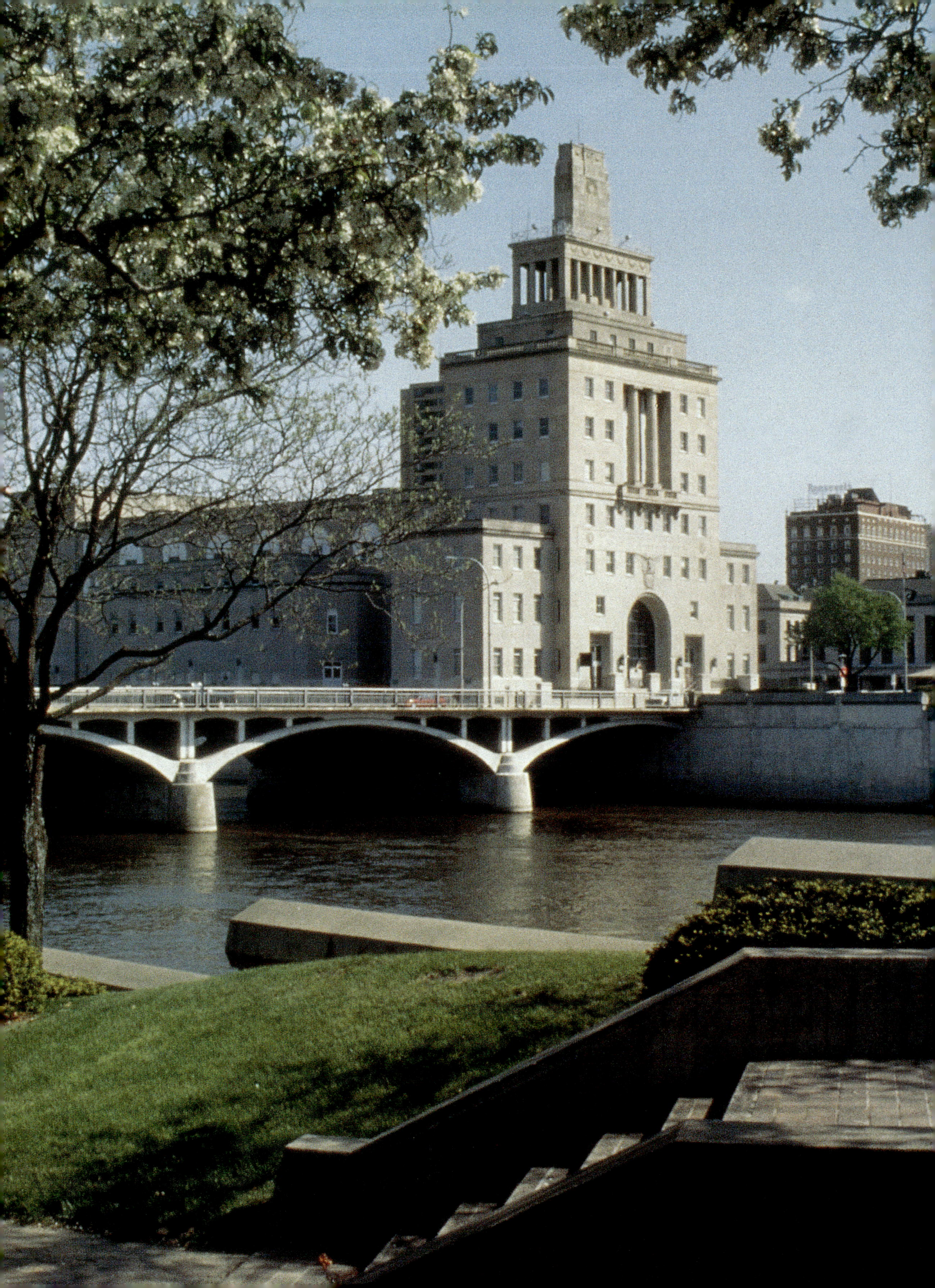

Acts of God and Government

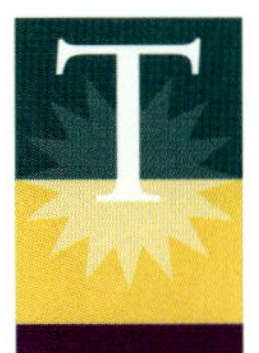o say that an act of God made Cedar Rapids city government what it is today isn't too far from the truth. It actually took two acts of God, along with the usual politicking, public hearings and polling.

Local lore has it that the roots of Cedar Rapids' commission form of government can be traced to the aftermath of a hurricane that devastated Galveston, Texas, in 1900. When Galveston's government infrastructure was destroyed along with many of the city's physical structures, some surviving opportunists rebuilt it in their own image, with friends and cronies in key spots as commissioners.

The hurricane was the second act.

In fact, Galveston's own commission government was inspired by an earlier natural disaster. That one took the form of a yellow fever epidemic that struck Memphis, Tennessee, 12 years earlier. The commission form of government that sprouted to meet the challenges of the time in Memphis was adopted later by Galveston, Cedar Rapids and ultimately many other cities.

Cedar Rapids took on the new form in 1908. Galveston's version lasted from 1900 until 1960. It was thrown aside that year in a noisy election that followed a League of Women Voters drive to adopt a city manager form of government.

Some would say Galveston was quicker than Cedar Rapids to see the error of its ways. Others continue to argue that it ain't broke here, so there's no need to fix it.

Besides, we like it.

Those who actually voted (about 25 percent of those registered) said so resoundingly in March of 1996, voting by a 63 percent majority to keep the commission form intact, leaving Cedar Rapids as one of only a handful of U.S. cities still governed this way.

Bright, attractive people

The 1996 vote followed our own noisy, confusing debate over the merits of various forms of government. It was sparked by perennial council candidate P.T. Larson, who proposed changing to a council and city manager form of government, and a study by the Cedar Rapids Efficiency and Reform Commission. As it did in Galveston, the League of Women Voters became involved, in our case by lobbying—successfully—for establishment of a Charter Commission.

The Charter Commission recommended adoption of a "strong mayor" form of government with a city administrator. When decision time came, the so-called Home Rule Charter netted only 20 percent of the vote and the council-manager form also on the ballot claimed less than 17 percent of the voters' favor. With 63 percent of the vote for the status quo, the commission form stayed in place.

Mayor Lee Clancey, who took office just two months before the vote, says the commission form likely won out simply because there were too many choices on the ballot and they were difficult for people to understand.

"They were given three different choices and I don't think people truly understood each of those forms of government," Clancey said recently. "It was just easier to keep what's known."

Dave Shay, a retired broadcaster who chaired the Charter Commission, said he believes it was Clancey's election as the first woman mayor and the election of Public Safety Commissioner Nancy Evans, also a first, that derailed the move to remake government. The Charter Commission was formed during a period of considerable council dissension under Mayor Larry Serbousek, when J.D. Smith and Lyle Hanson both were campaigning to succeed him.

Cedar Rapids

Legends & Leaders

Martin Barber
Isaac Whittam

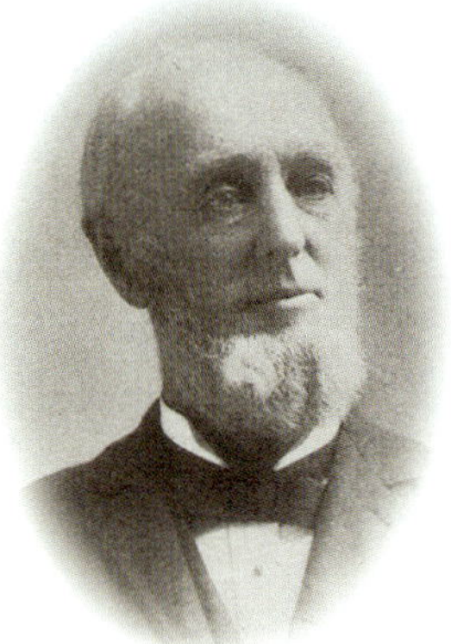

Isaac Whittam

In the first eight years of its official existence, Cedar Rapids was incorporated twice, and thereby claims not one but two individuals as "first mayor."

On January 15, 1849, the State Legislature passed an act of incorporation approving the Cedar Rapids town charter, and Governor Ansel Briggs signed it. The town's first officers were elected that April, including Mayor Martin L. Barber, councilmen Joseph Greene, Stephen L. Pollock and James Leverich, and recorder Homer Kennedy. They held their first council meeting a few weeks later on May 11. Barber was reelected in 1850 to his second and final term.

In April 1856, Isaac Whittam was elected mayor. A few months later, voters adopted a new city charter by a vote of 45 to 2, then reelected Whittam as mayor in August of that same year, making him the first mayor of the City of Cedar Rapids.

Photo: *Pioneer Days in Cedar Rapids*, Laurance

Shay said people tired of the city government squabbles and so were ready to make a change.

To the surprise of many, Clancey succeeded Serbousek, making history by winning the mayor's office in the November 1995 election. Cedar Rapids suddenly had two women on the city council after nearly 150 years of all-male leadership.

"They were bright, attractive people," said Shay, "and I think the voters of Cedar Rapids felt that they had made a big change in city government and figured, 'Well, that's enough change for now. Let's see how well these new people can run this old form of government.'" Clancey, Evans and the rest of the new council took office in January 1996 and the squabbling, for the most part, came to an end.

Clancey agrees that her election had a large effect.

"Between January and March there was a demonstrated difference in the way in which this council was operating and this form of government was operating," she said. "I think that people felt there was, in essence, a change in the government and they thought they could handle what currently existed."

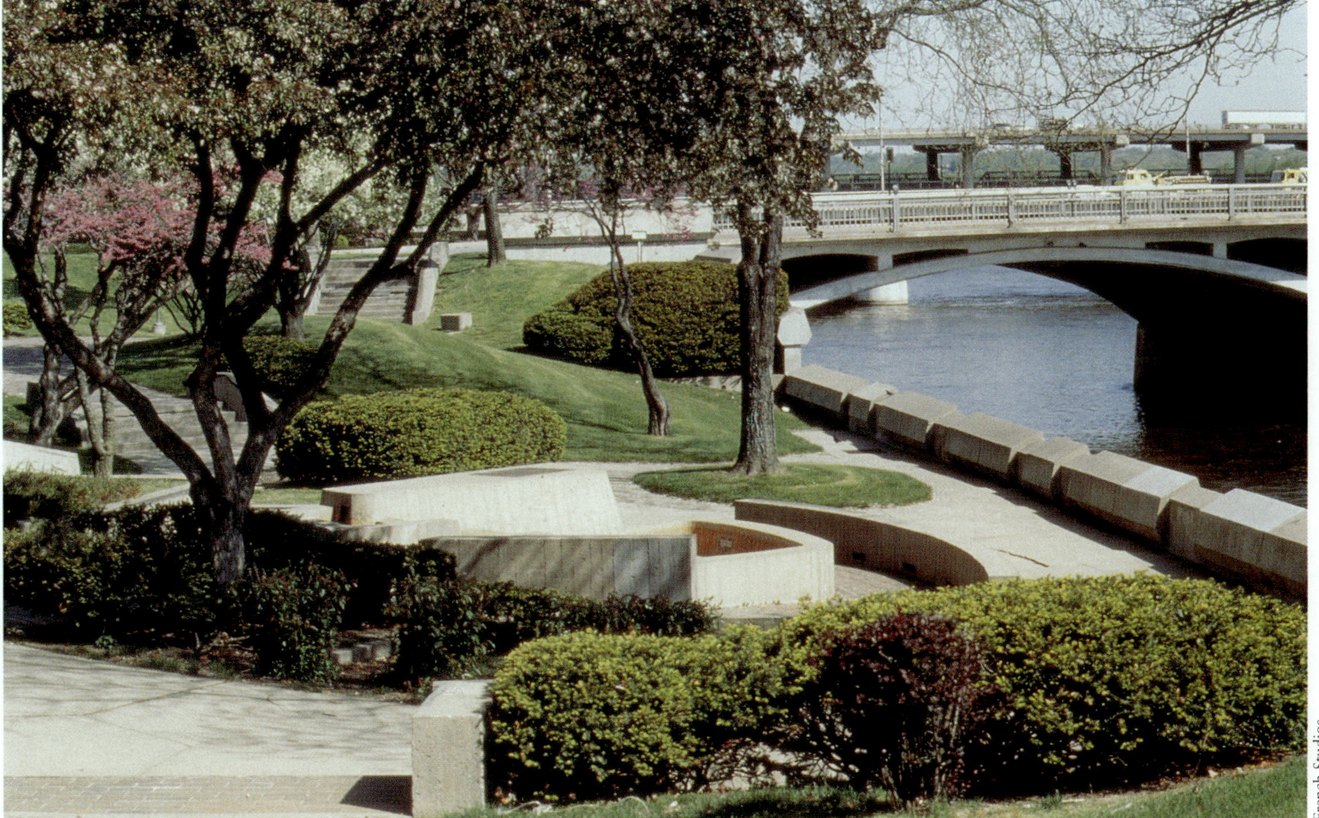

French Studios

Greenery and pathways give the riverfront a park-like feel.

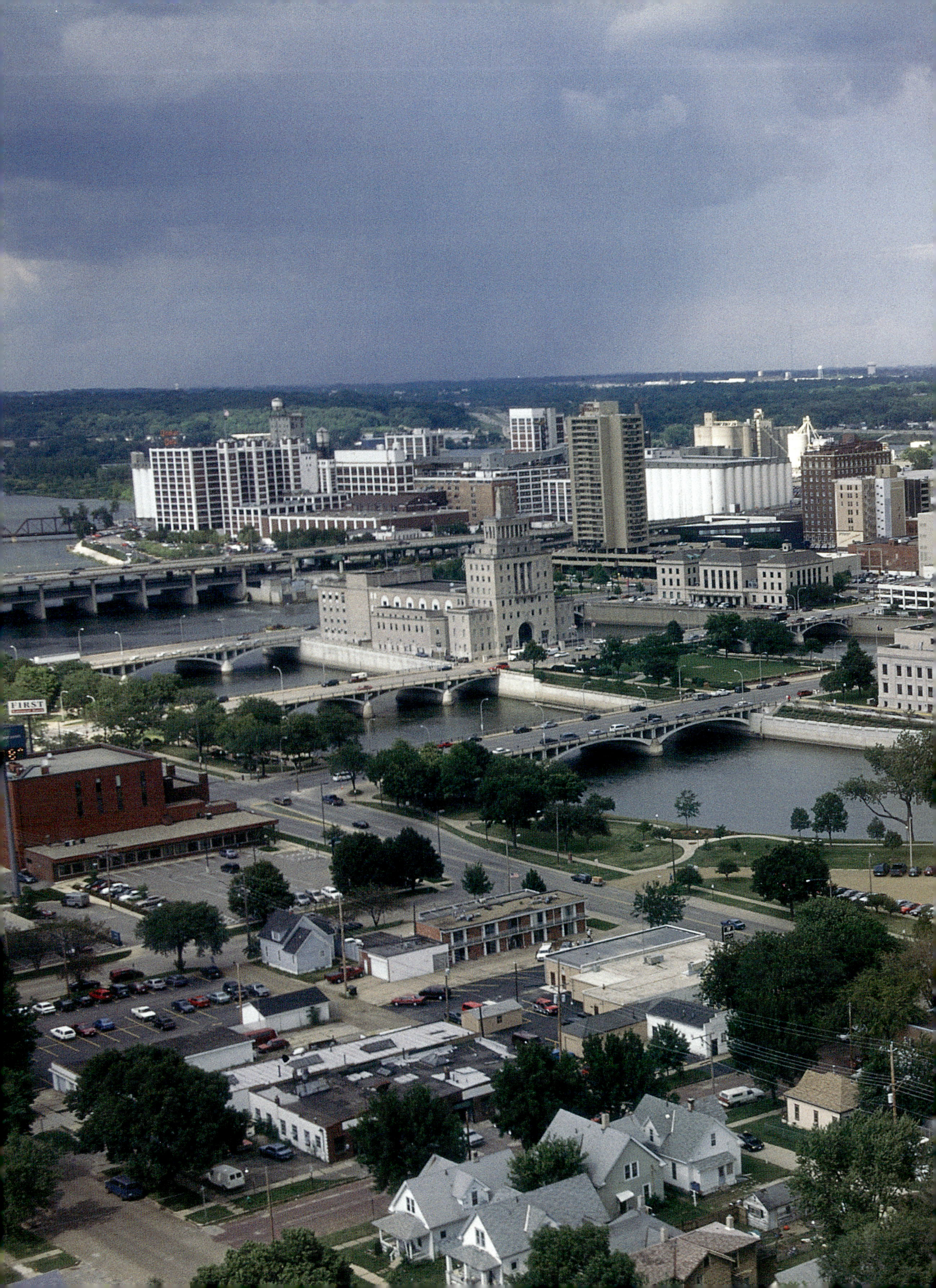
FIRST

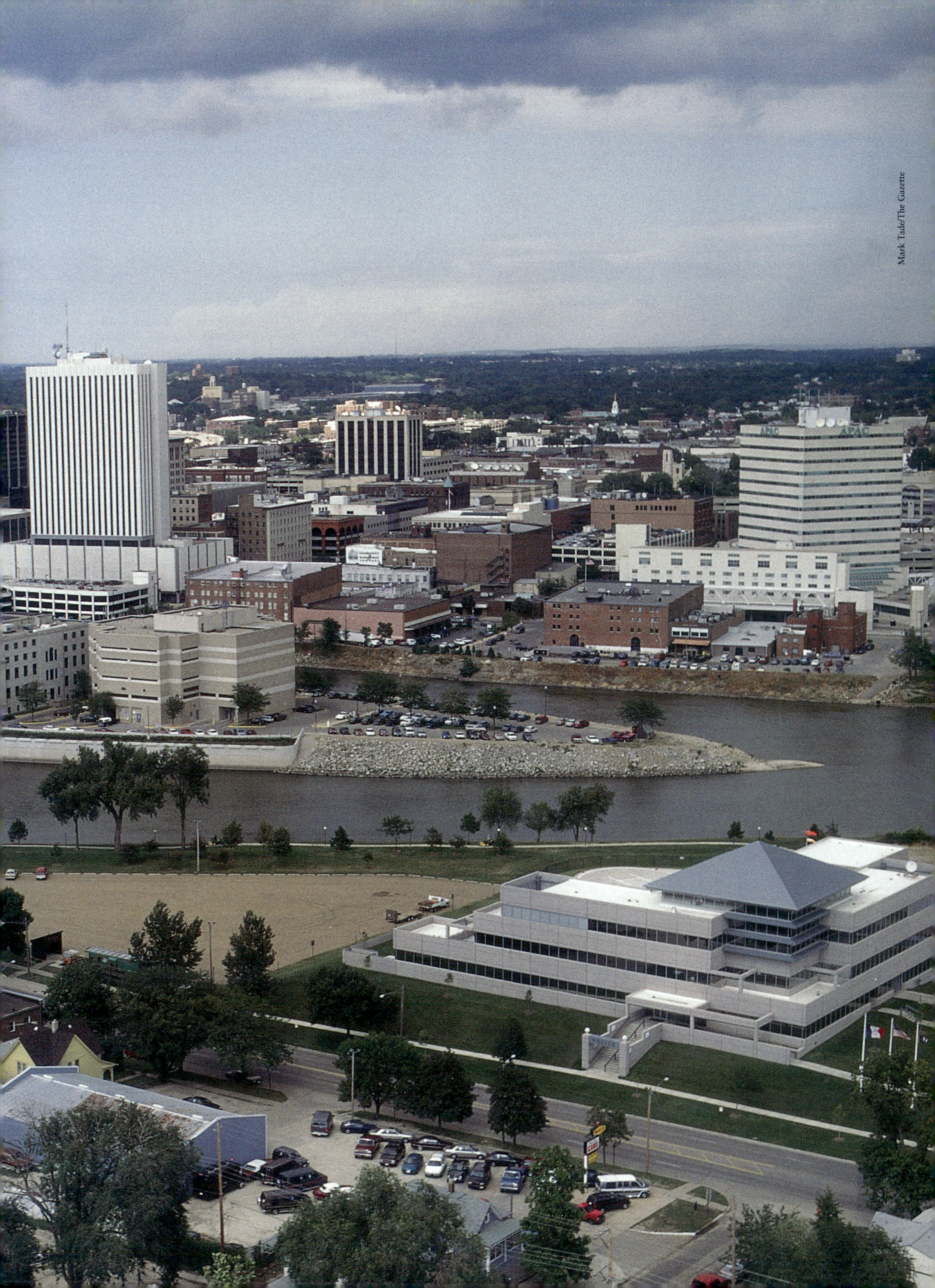

Mark Tade/The Gazette

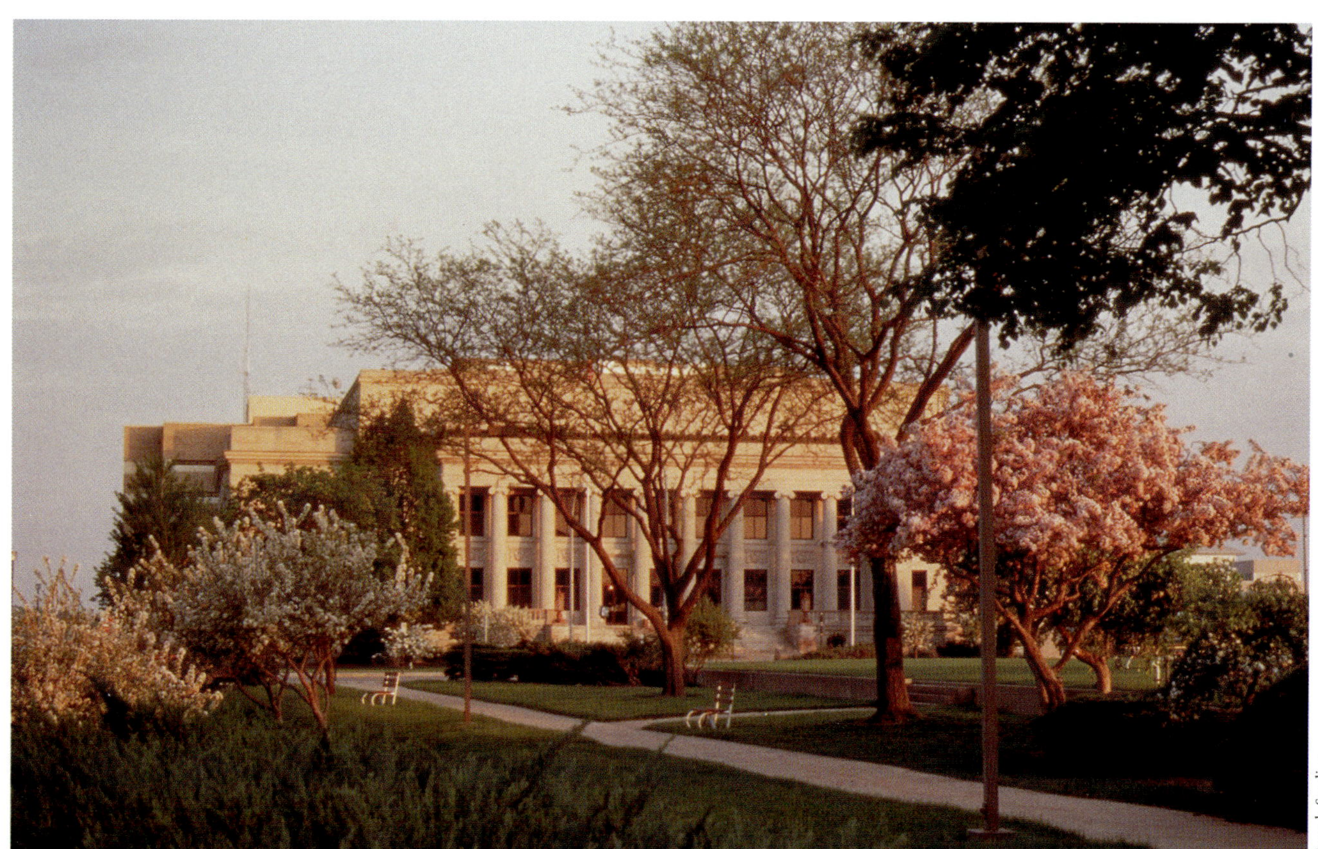

The Linn County Courthouse

Blessed with good people

Clancey and Shay agree that the commission form of government has interesting strengths and weaknesses, and that how well or poorly it works depends almost entirely on the people elected to run it.

Shay, who has lived and worked as a broadcaster in Cedar Rapids since 1959, observed that "any form of government will work if you have good people, and Cedar Rapids, by and large, has been blessed with good people."

Clancey echoed that view, saying, "This is probably the most effective form of government if you have people on the council who are willing to work together. I think this is the worst form of government you can have if you have a council that doesn't want to work together, so my goal on coming into office was to try to create a more team-oriented atmosphere."

The very nature of the commission form of government may have contributed to the notable absence of women from the council throughout most of its history. Few women had the opportunity to develop the hands-on skills needed to run a parks department, streets department, public safety department or finance department. That, obviously, has changed.

The emphasis on candidates with specialized areas of expertise makes the commission government uniquely strong when qualified candidates fill those posts, but uniquely vulnerable when that doesn't happen. It's what has killed this form of government in many communities, and what may eventually kill it here.

"You elect somebody to head the finance department. Well, if that person doesn't know the first thing about finance and decides to run it hands on, you have chaos," said Shay. "That is what happened in most cities. That will probably happen here some day, I suppose, and there will be discontent and people will get upset."

In the meantime, city government no doubt will continue to change while it stays the same—as individual mayors and commissioners come and go, leaving their own unique impressions or none at all, depending on strength of personality, conviction and persuasive powers.

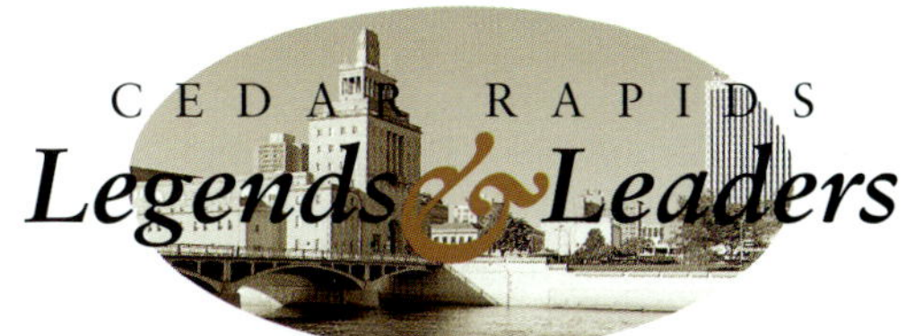

Bourke B. Hickenlooper 1896-1971

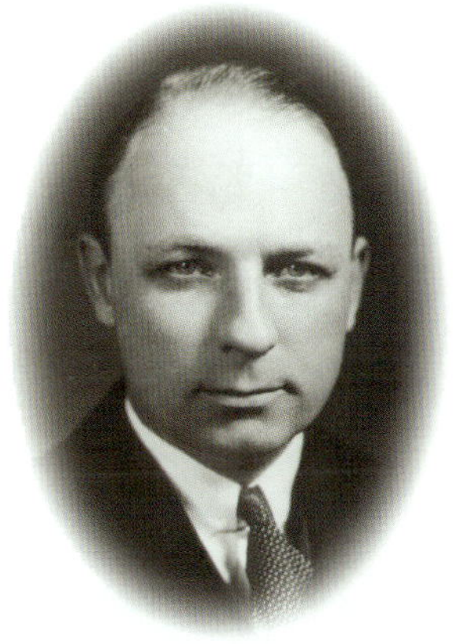

A graduate of the University of Iowa School of Law, this native of Blockton in southwestern Iowa became one of Cedar Rapids' best known and most influential citizens as he served in top state government posts and the U.S. Senate.

In 1922, shortly after earning his law degree, Bourke Blakemore Hickenlooper moved to Cedar Rapids to practice law. He was elected lieutenant governor in 1938 and served in that office from 1939 to 1943. He was inaugurated as governor in January 1943 and served as the state's chief executive until 1945, when he was sworn in as a member of the U.S. Senate.

His career in the Senate spanned the darkest days of the Cold War, and he served on the Senate Agriculture Committee from 1949 until 1965. His last Senate term ended in 1969.

Photo: Iowa State Historical Society

One politician who left a definite and distinctive mark on our recent history is Donald Canney, mayor from 1969 to 1992. While Canney served as mayor of a commission government, many believe his style of leadership made it operate much more like a strong mayor form of government.

One hell of a city

Canney is remembered as a mayor who got things done, and a visionary of infrastructure. During his tenure, Cedar Rapids established much of the groundwork that made it possible to attract new manufacturing and high-tech businesses to the city in the '80s and '90s. Public and private investment, lobbying and other politicking through the '60s, '70s and '80s led to expansions of wastewater treatment capacity and sewer systems and new airport facilities, downtown buildings, roads and highways.

Jim Hoffman, Priority One chairman, marvels at the record of achievement and infrastructure growth during the Canney years, saying, "These guys were

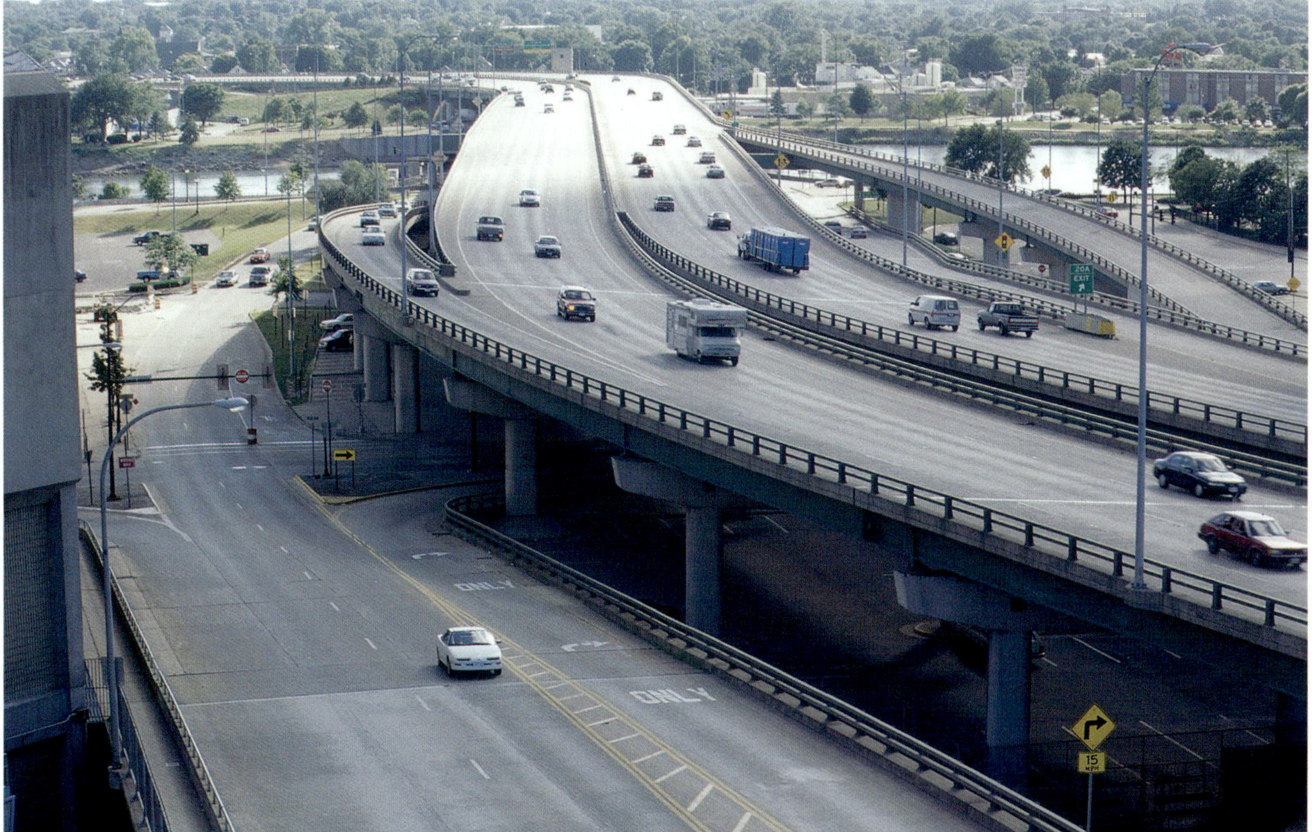

David Van Allen

Interstate 380 gave Cedar Rapids a much-needed north-south expressway.

really thinking, and they weren't thinking small."

Canney, a Cedar Rapids resident since 1954, was elected Public Improvements Commissioner in 1965 before becoming mayor at the end of the decade. Urban renewal was a federal priority at the time, and Cedar Rapids was badly in need of rejuvenation. Retailers had begun disappearing from the downtown area, a trend that accelerated as more and more mobile shoppers were attracted outward to new shopping centers and malls.

"Essentially the core of the city and the central business district and the surrounding areas were almost totally bombed out," Canney said. "It looked like Berlin after the war. Everything had been torn down but nothing had really been going up. I always said it would be one hell of a city if we ever got it put back together again."

As it went back together, it went together differently from what it had been for decades. What was once a thriving retail center evolved into what is now a thriving office and financial center.

In the same period, city and state officials successfully lobbied for an addition to the interstate highway system that led to construction of Interstate 380 through the central business district. It took an

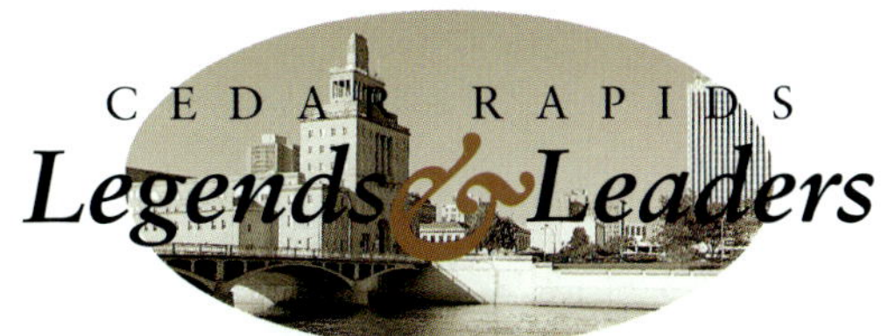

Sen. Billy Haskell
1857-1927

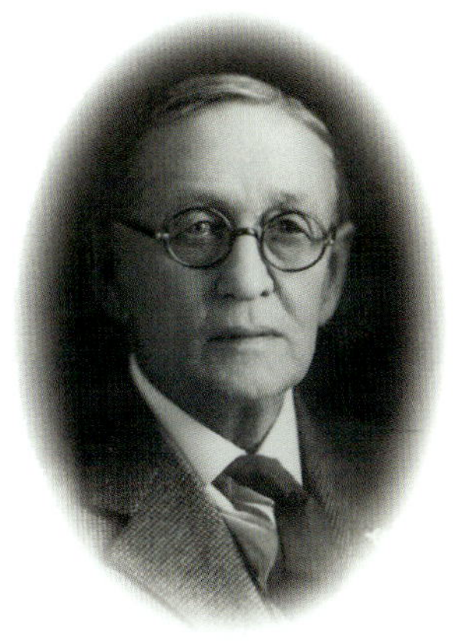

As a state senator, Haskell was known as a friend and advocate of children and as an early supporter of providing health care to the indigent. Evidence of his devotion was seen in his efforts to obtain funds to build a children's hospital at the University of Iowa.

Haskell was also a successful Cedar Rapids businessman. He ran a thriving business, served as the city's postmaster and founded Johnson Gas Appliance. In 1897 Haskell purchased the first horseless carriage in Cedar Rapids, a steam-driven vehicle called a locomobile. He took school children for rides and was arrested several times for scaring horses. The Cedar Rapids city council even seriously considered an ordinance against Haskell's vehicle. Perhaps because of his interest in automobiles, Haskell is considered one of the state's earliest boosters for better highways and streets.

Photo: Iowa State Historical Society

act of Congress, but it gave Cedar Rapids a badly needed north-south expressway and solved some local transportation problems while connecting the city to the larger interstate system.

Planning for growth also required expansion of the sewage treatment plant, which is being expanded yet again to accommodate growing industrial needs, and land acquisition to ensure room for growth at the Eastern Iowa Airport.

"There's all kinds of room to grow at our airport," Canney said. "One of my first priorities when I became mayor was to buy land around the airport so there was room to expand."

Canney said it is inevitable that Cedar Rapids will grow, and that how it continues to plan for growth is critical.

"If cities become large at the expense of rundown areas and blighted areas, that's not going to attract many jobs for the people that do end up in the urban areas," Canney said. "If the city center ever loses its ability to enhance its taxes, if it loses that tax base, that city is doomed to blight and decay."

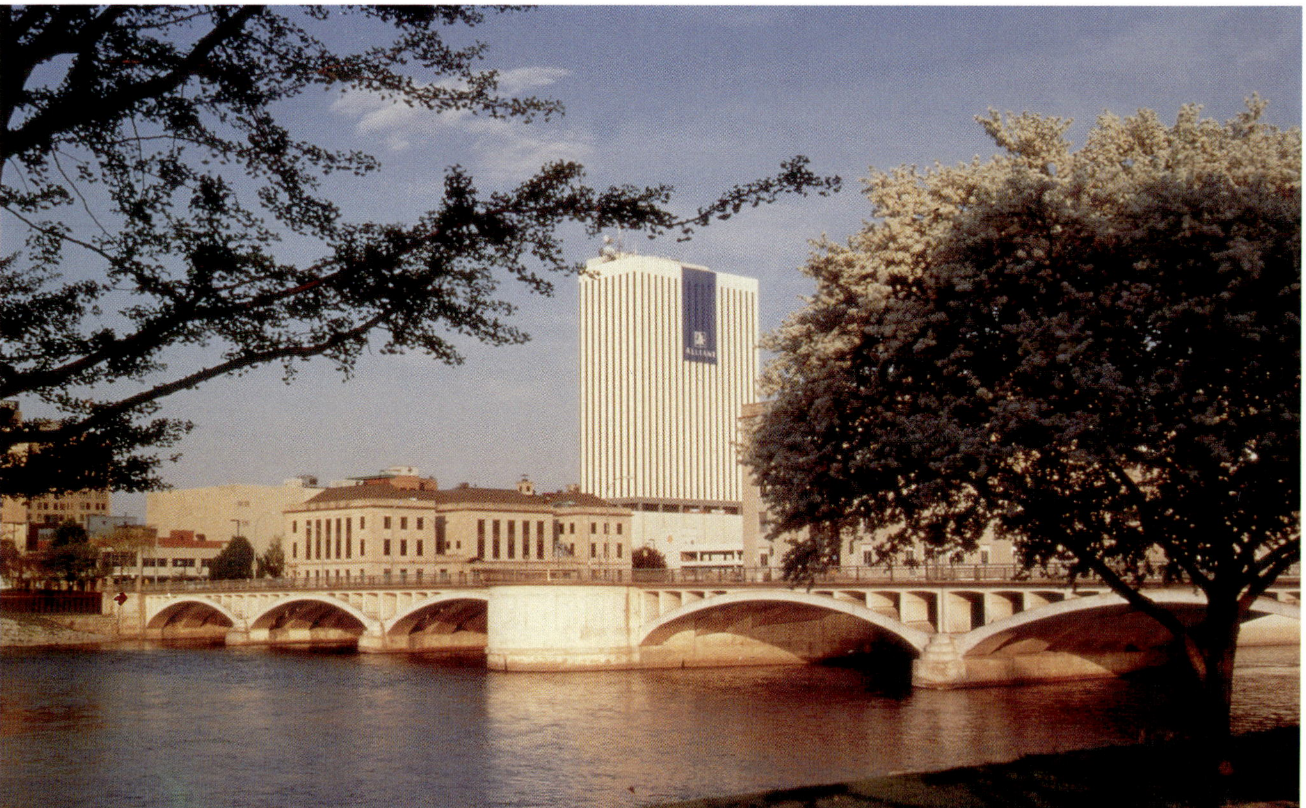

French Studios

A riverside view of downtown Cedar Rapids.

Mayor Lee Clancey agrees that standing still is a recipe for failure, and cites projects such as the Neighborhood Living Initiative and an ambitious riverfront development plan as examples of what it takes to keep growing in positive ways.

The Neighborhood Living Initiative, a fledgling program implemented in the fall of 1997, is intended to help the city's neighborhood associations identify properties that need rejuvenation and to connect them with corporate volunteer help and sources of financing.

The riverfront development plan may ultimately give Cedar Rapids border-to-border pedestrian access to the riverfront, and greatly expanded recreational opportunities and greenspace along the river, an asset that so far has been underutilized.

"It's the old adage that you can never stay static, you've got to be constantly changing," Clancey said. "People's expectations continue to rise. If you can't meet those expectations, you're going to be perceived as losing ground. We have to keep trying to meet people's expectations."

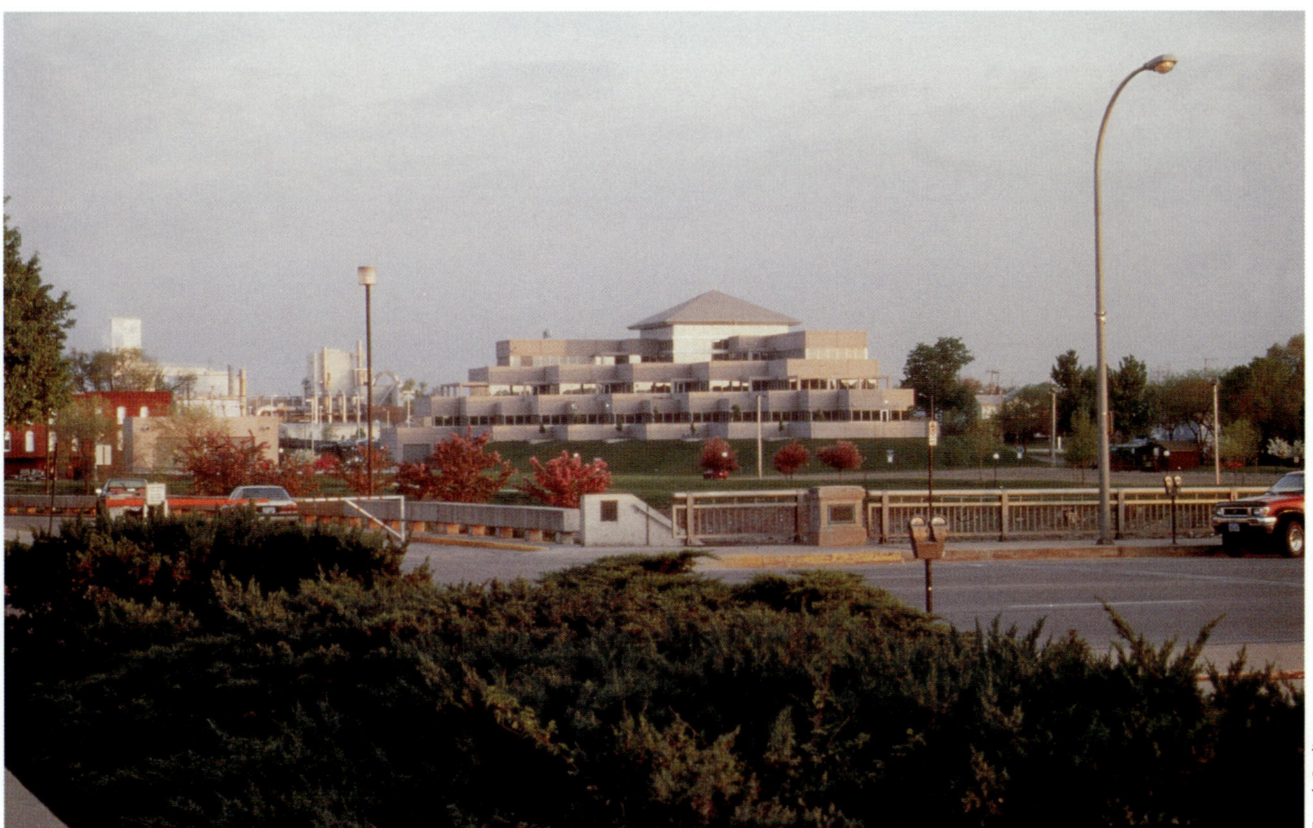

French Studios

The Cedar Rapids Police Department moved to this modern facility in 1997.

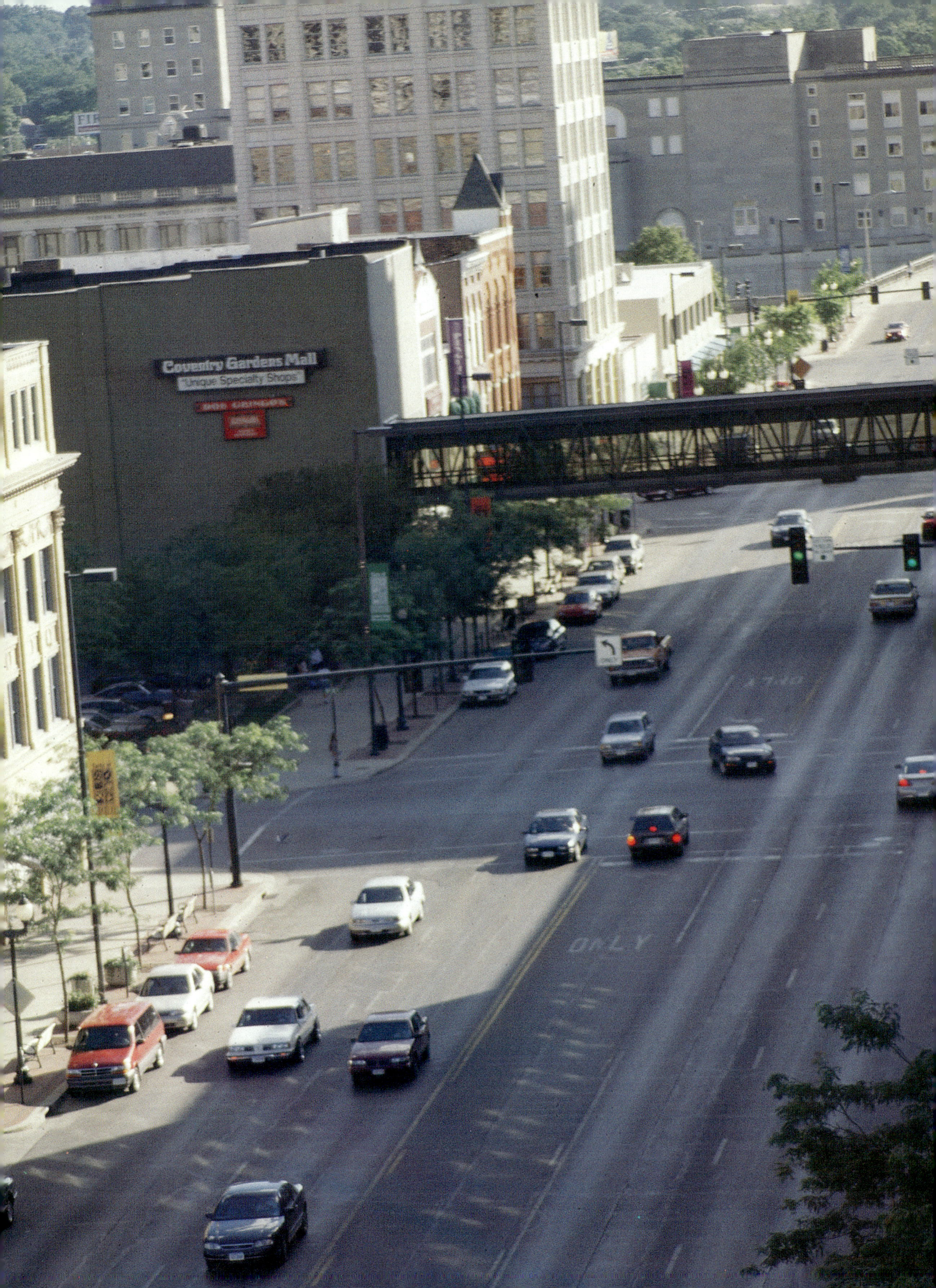
Coventry Gardens Mall
"Unique Specialty Shops"
ONLY

Ginseng and gall bladder

Jack Evans tells the story with relish, which is fitting. It's a story about a dinner, after all. About wining and dining. About a courtship. As with many good courtships, much was accomplished over dinner.

Leading up to the dinner were numerous trips between Korea and Cedar Rapids, as Poongsan Corporation and city and state leaders worked on a deal to bring the PMX Industries copper and brass milling plant to Cedar Rapids. The arrangement still had not been finalized when the Korean visitors were toasted during a dinner at the historic Brucemore mansion on Cedar Rapids' southeast side.

Dr. Yang Ahn, a local Korean physician invited to the dinner, presented Poongsan Chairman Chung Ryu first with a ginseng root, for which he was politely thanked. But the second gift from Dr. Ahn proved to be the clincher, said Evans, president of the Hall-Perrine Foundation.

"He pulled out this long, black, disgusting thing," said Evans. "None of us knew what it was."

The chairman obviously knew. His eyes lit up, he thanked Dr. Ahn profusely, and he put the gift in his pocket. It was the gall bladder of a bear, believed by the Koreans to be an even more powerful aphrodisiac than ginseng root.

The seduction was complete. PMX Industries opened its Cedar Rapids manufacturing operation in 1991.

The courtship of PMX Industries is but one of a growing number of successful business development efforts carried out in the 1980s and '90s by Cedar Rapids' latest generation of movers and shakers, who have done much to turn the city into what it is as it celebrates its 150th year.

Our earlier history is sprinkled with men who were the heavyweights of their time, individuals like Howard Hall who used their own considerable influence and wealth to recruit businesses to help boost the local economy and create new jobs. It is only recently, however, that city and business leaders have developed the team approach that has proven so successful in luring businesses like PMX, Genencor, Toyota Motor Insurance Services, the Nordstrom Fulfillment Center and others.

Bubbles bursting

Cedar Rapids used to think of itself as largely recession-proof, on the theory that people always

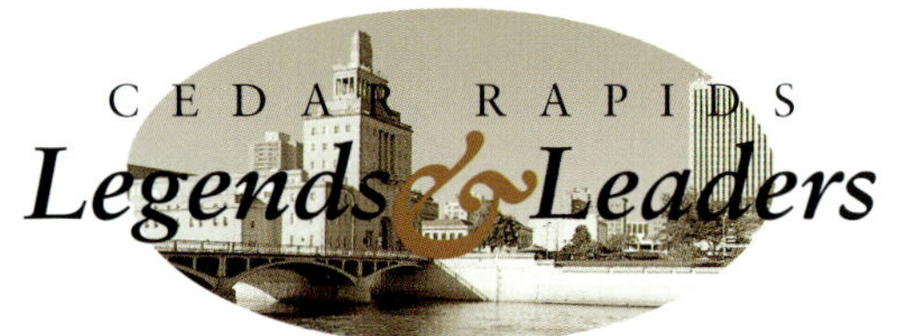

Arthur Collins
1909-1987

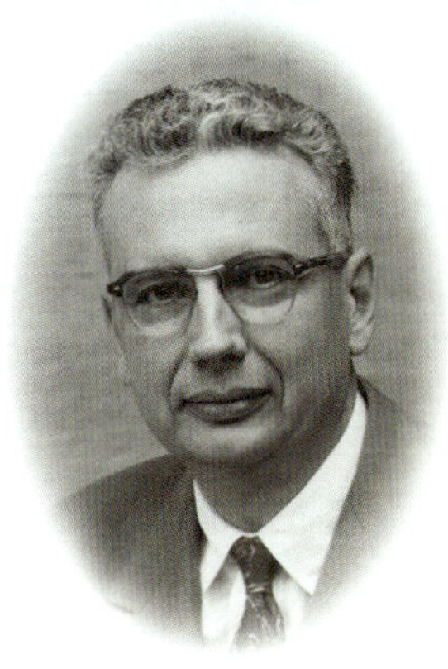

The founder of Collins Radio Company built his first crystal receiver at the age of 9 at the home of a friend who was also a radio enthusiast. When the antenna was struck by lightning, the friend's father asked the boys to find another place to explore their hobby. They moved to the Collins home.

Collins received his radio operator license at the age of 14. By 1931, he was building and selling amateur radio equipment from the basement of his home. Two years later, Richard E. Byrd's expedition to the South Pole used Collins Radio equipment to stay in touch with the rest of the world. Collins built the company into one of Cedar Rapids' largest employers.

Collins Radio is now known as Rockwell Collins, one of the world's premier manufacturers of aviation communications equipment and electronic controls.

Photo: Rockwell Collins

need to eat and much of the economy was tied in some way to agriculture. There is some truth to the theory, of course. It's why Cedar Rapids fared better than many communities during the Great Depression, according to Harold Becker, chairman of Guaranty Bank.

Becker's grandfather, Abraham, left Russia in 1900 to escape religious persecution, and was naturalized in 1906. The Becker family were grocers for the next 50 years. While banks and many other local businesses were falling victim to the Great Depression, the Becker grocery stores stayed open.

"We would dole out what we called 'relief foods' from the government," Becker said. "We had people on relief, we had people getting subsidies from the county, but it wasn't like the big cities where you saw breadlines and beggars and people on the streets selling apples. We weren't a bonanza, but we weren't nearly as bad as hundreds of communities across the country."

Other food-related businesses—Penick & Ford, National Oats, Quaker Oats, T.M. Sinclair & Co.—were able to maintain their employment levels better than other manufacturing companies and thus helped Cedar Rapids weather the storm.

When the 1970s and '80s arrived, however, the community found it was no longer so well insulated from economic ups and downs. That particular bubble burst in a big way, beginning in 1969.

Radio communications pioneer Arthur Collins had built Collins Radio into an industrial and technological powerhouse and the largest single employer in the city. After expanding into avionics for the airline industry in the 1960s, however, Collins Radio's fortunes fell along with those of the airlines, resulting in major layoffs that traumatized the community.

"From 1969 to 1971 we went from almost 14,000 people to 5,800 in a little over a year," said Jack Cosgrove, Rockwell Collins president. "That's how dire it was." Cosgrove, with the company for 42 years, said Collins' expansion into the airline business was both good news and bad news.

"The good news was that it opened up whole new vistas of products and systems," he said. "The bad news was that in the latter part of the '60s when the airlines business went down, that brought down the Collins Radio Company. We were very close to

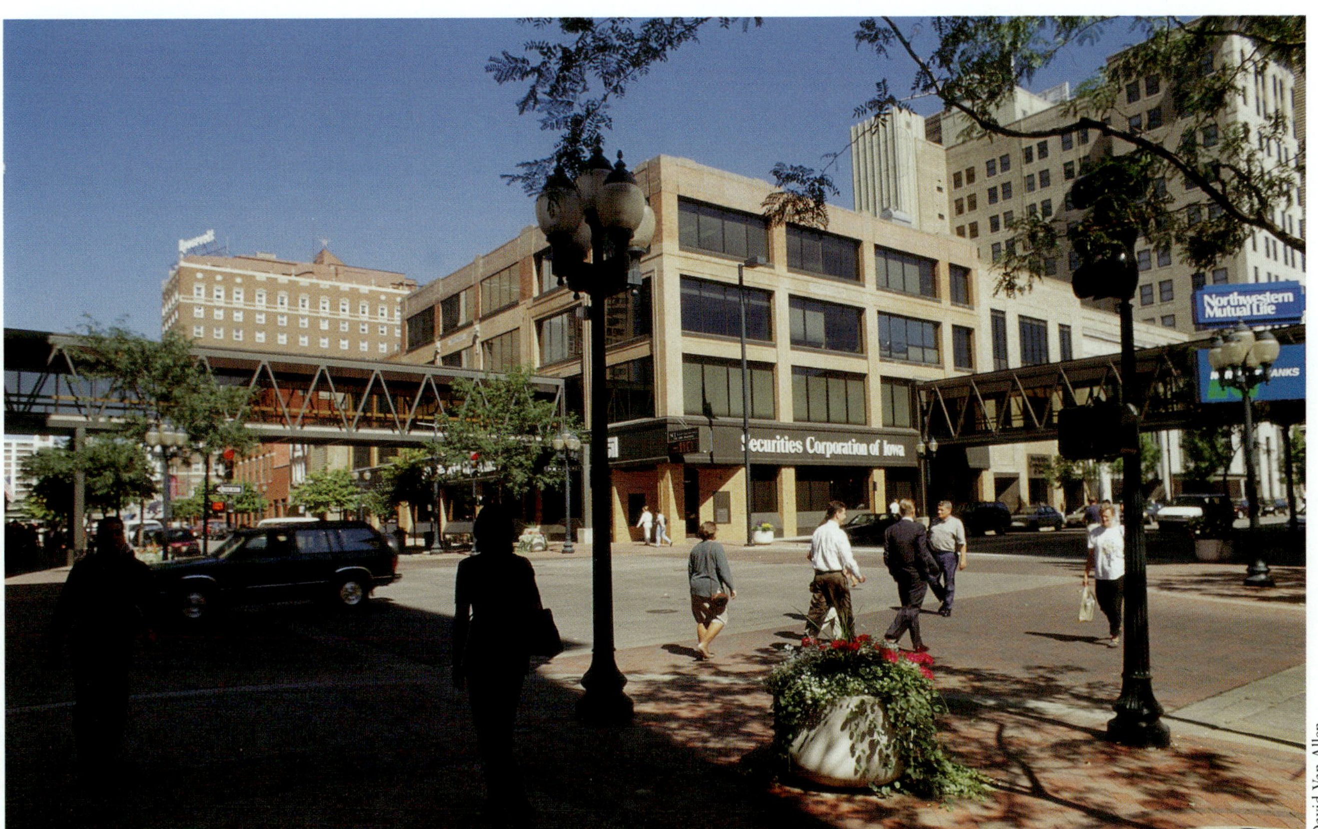

David Van Allen

Downtown Cedar Rapids has evolved into an "urban office park."

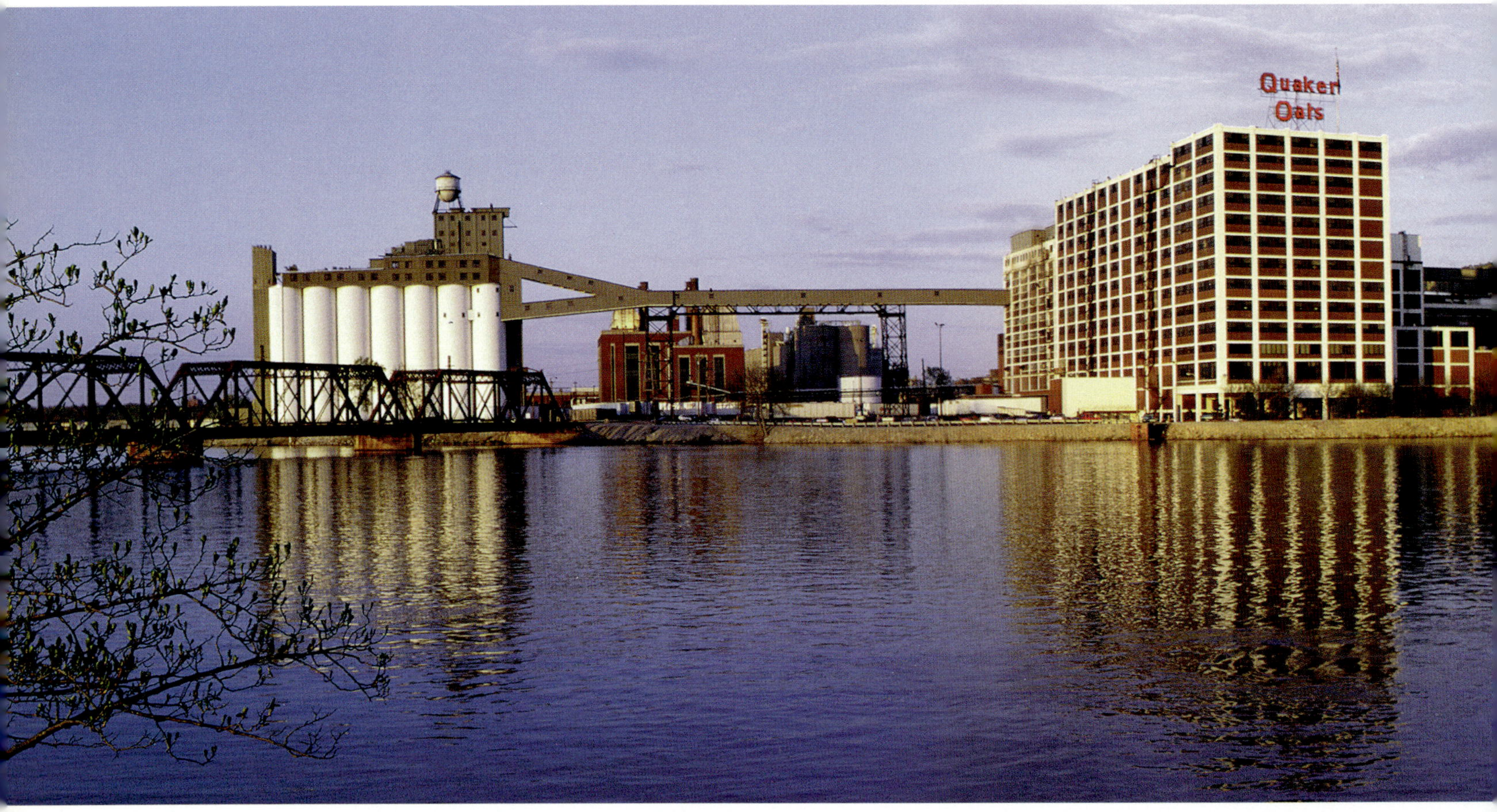

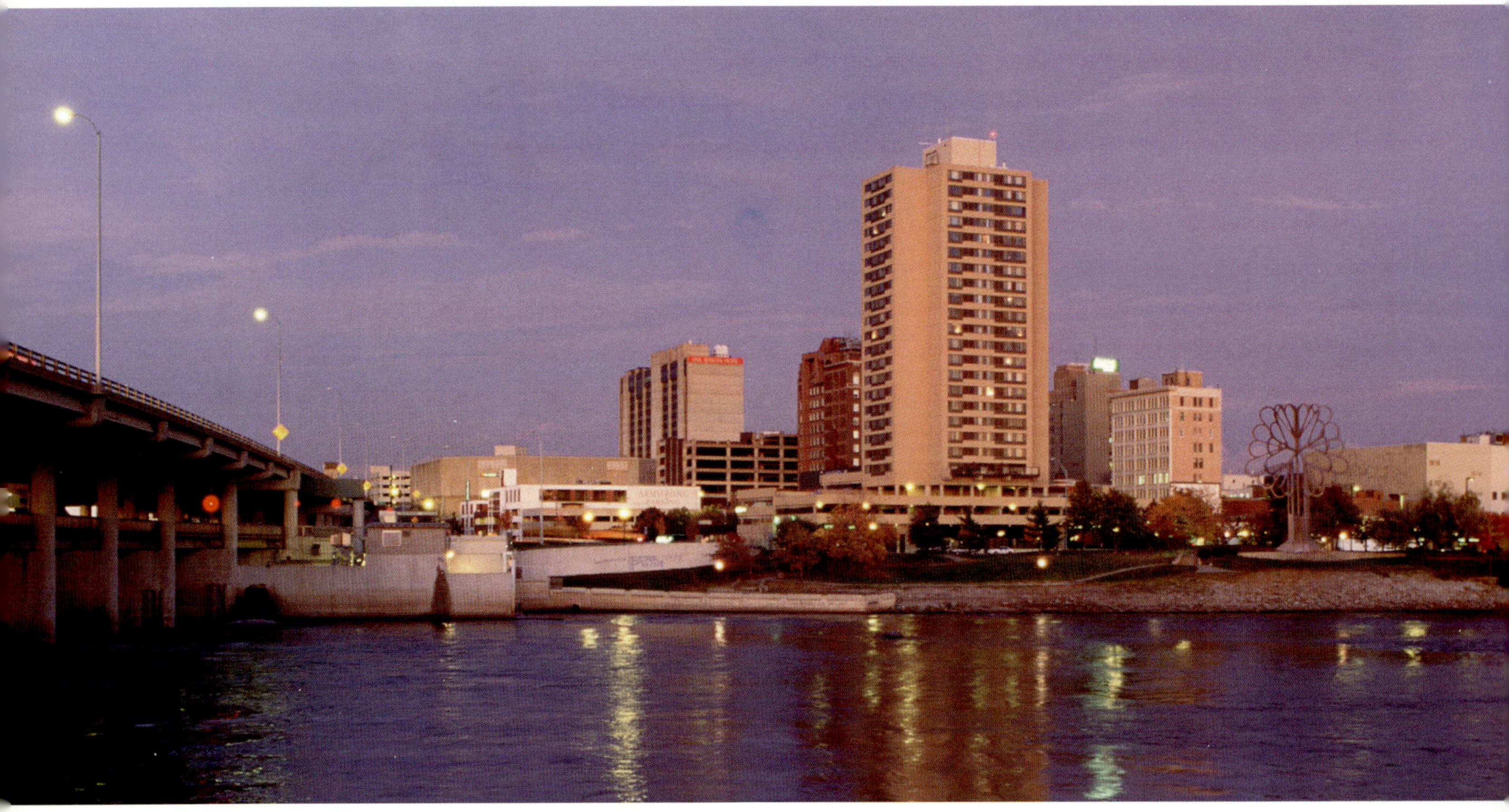

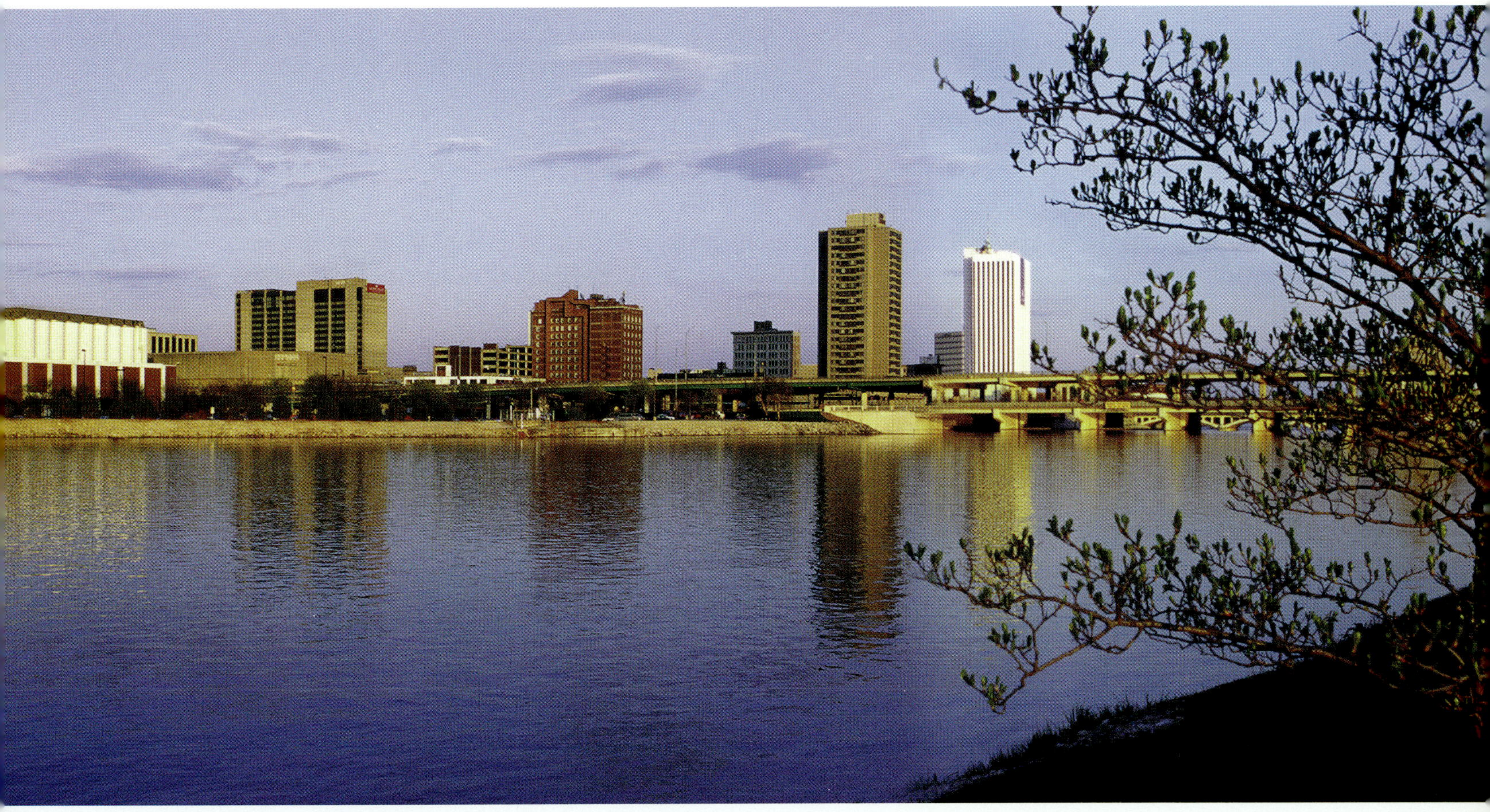

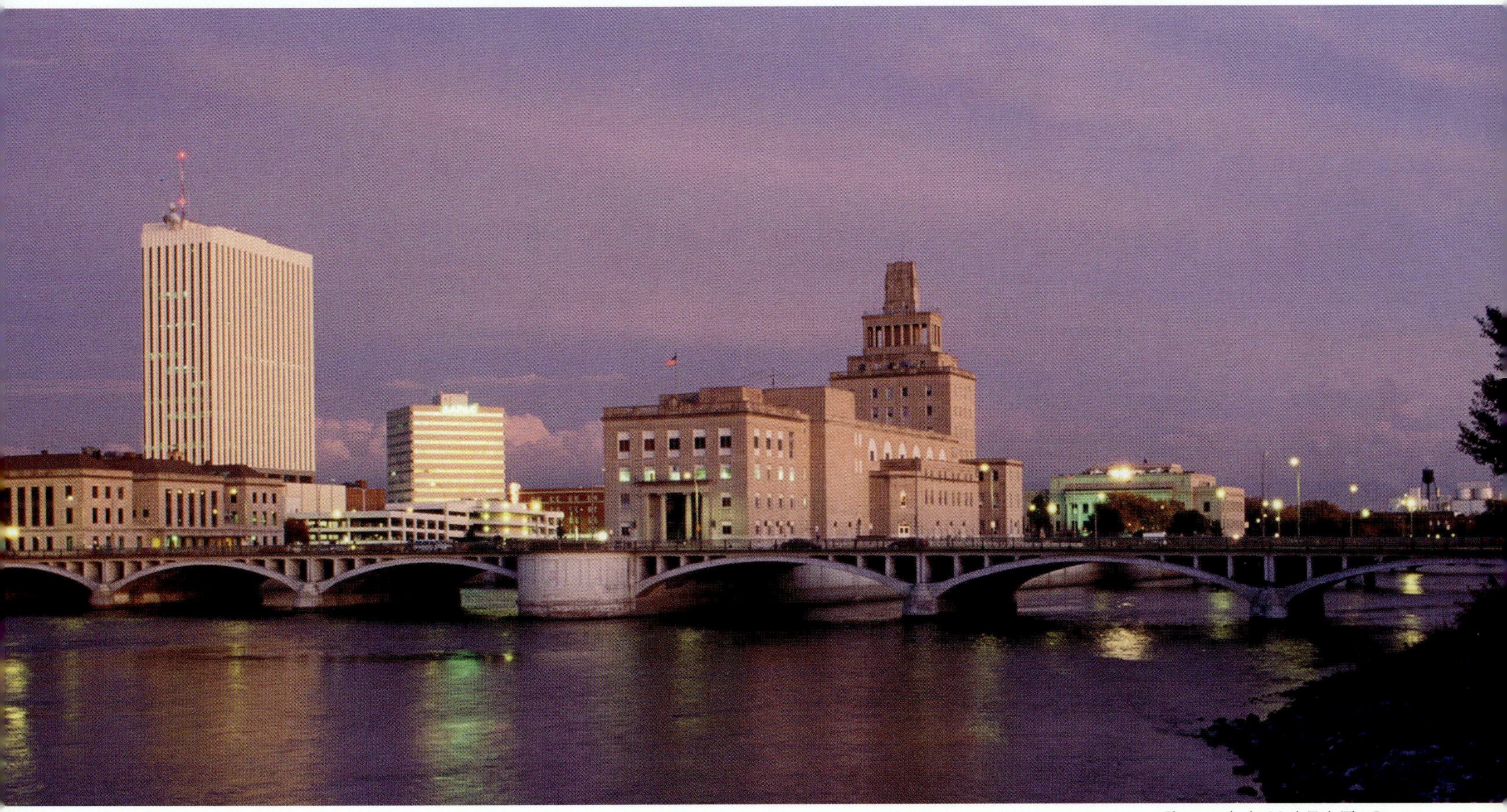

Photography by Mark Tade/The Gazette

the verge of bankruptcy."

That massive job loss was followed a decade later by still more economic battering, as climbing interest rates, a slowing national economy and increased international competition hit Cedar Rapids hard. Indeed, the Farm Crisis years of the early to mid-1980s could be considered a major passage in our economic life, with effects that will last well into the 21st Century.

It was then that Cedar Rapids lost several major employers and turned, perhaps forever, from the heavily unionized, manufacturing- and agriculture-oriented community it had become. It was a passage from a largely nuts and bolts mechanical and agricultural world into a digital age of fiber-optic connectivity, and an age of cooperation.

Spirit of cooperation

"In about 18 months, we lost that whole sector of the economy," said Tom Aller, who was executive assistant to the mayor and city council for much of the 1970s and '80s. Now executive vice president of 2001 Development Corporation, Aller said the

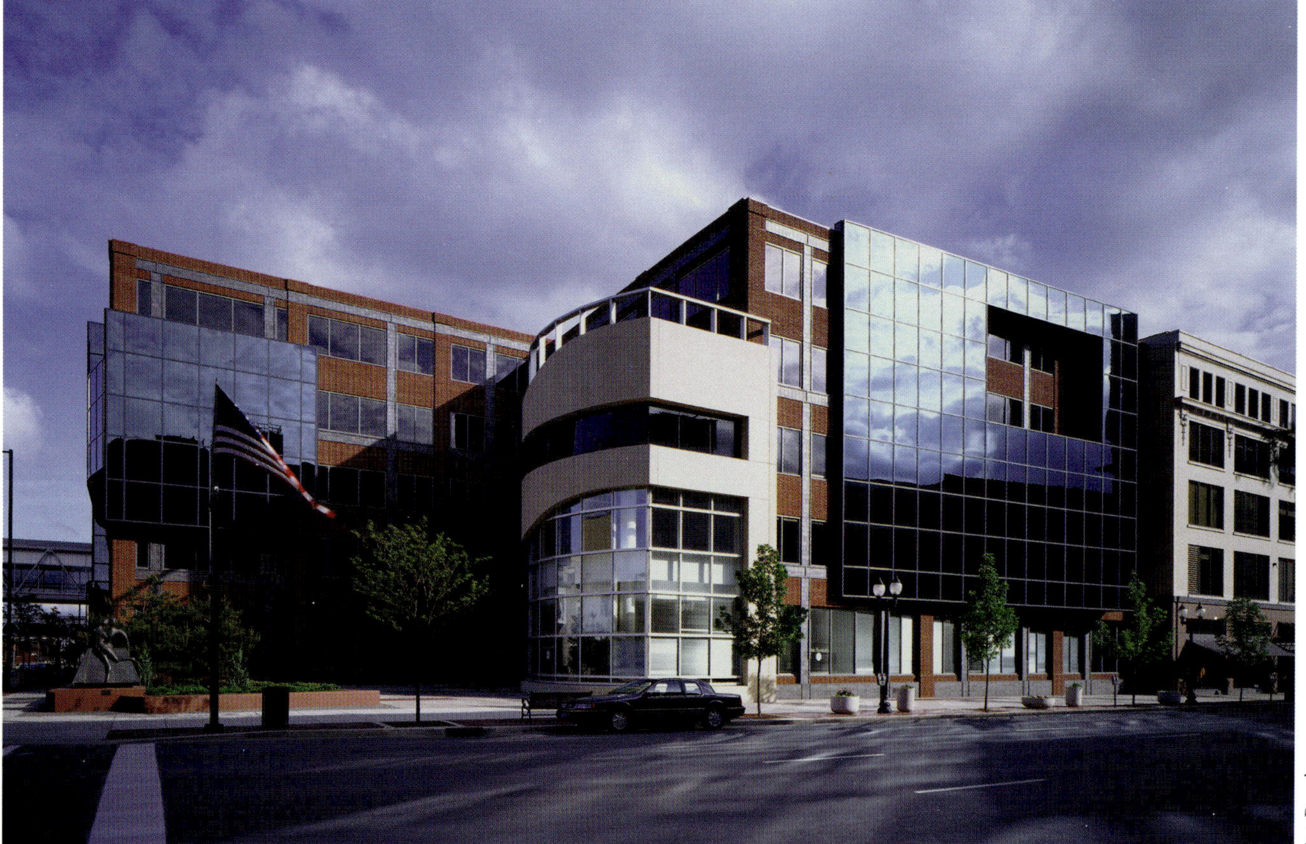

Ron Dreasher

Town Centre office complex is an example of downtown revitalization.

trauma of the economic downturn sparked a new spirit of cooperation and community involvement that continues today.

"I think everybody got together and rolled up their sleeves," Aller said. Spearheaded by then-mayor Donald Canney and Lee Liu, chairman of IES Industries and now Alliant chairman, a group of community leaders formed the Committee of 100, which evolved into a division of the Chamber of Commerce now known as Priority One.

Motivated in part by a desire to help the community and in part by "enlightened self-interest" —new businesses consume more power and bring new people who buy new houses and consume other goods and services—members of Priority One pool their resources and work with city and community leaders to actively pursue new business.

Priority One board chairman and Alliant executive Jim Hoffman said one initial impediment to new development at the time was Iowa's image, or rather the perception that it didn't even have an image. Then, just as a combination of circumstances had led to hard times for many in the early '80s, other circumstances and developments made new growth and rejuvenation possible. Hoffman credits heavy

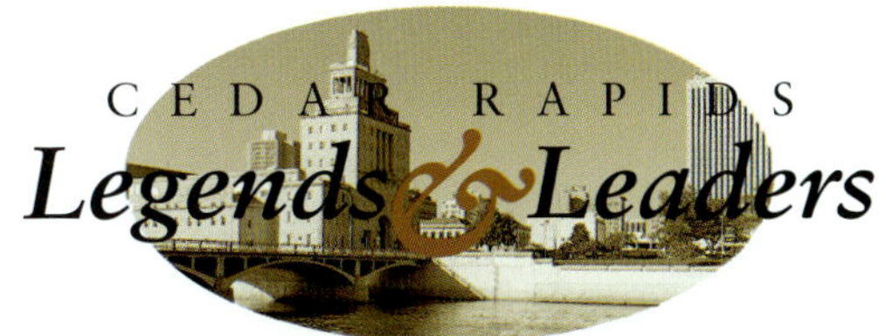

Howard Hall
1894-1971

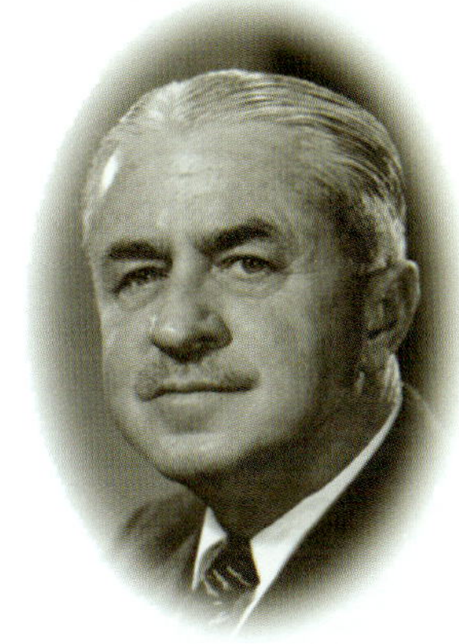

Industrialist, philanthropist and animal lover Howard Hall and his friend and fellow soldier John Jay acquired a controlling interest in the Carmody Foundry shortly after the end of World War I. It soon became Iowa Steel and Iron Works and Hall became its president. The two founded Iowa Manufacturing Co. in 1923.

Hall married Margaret Douglas of the prominent Douglas family in 1924. Hall became president of Iowa Manufacturing in 1929, served on the boards of several major corporations, and is legendary for his charity and loyalty to friends and employees as well as to the community.

Dedicated to the development of Cedar Rapids and to providing jobs for its citizens, Hall frequently acted behind the scenes to attract new businesses and jobs to the area. He gave money freely to local causes, churches and synagogues, and the Hall Foundation—now the Hall-Perrine Foundation—has given millions more since its founding in 1953.

Photo: Brucemore

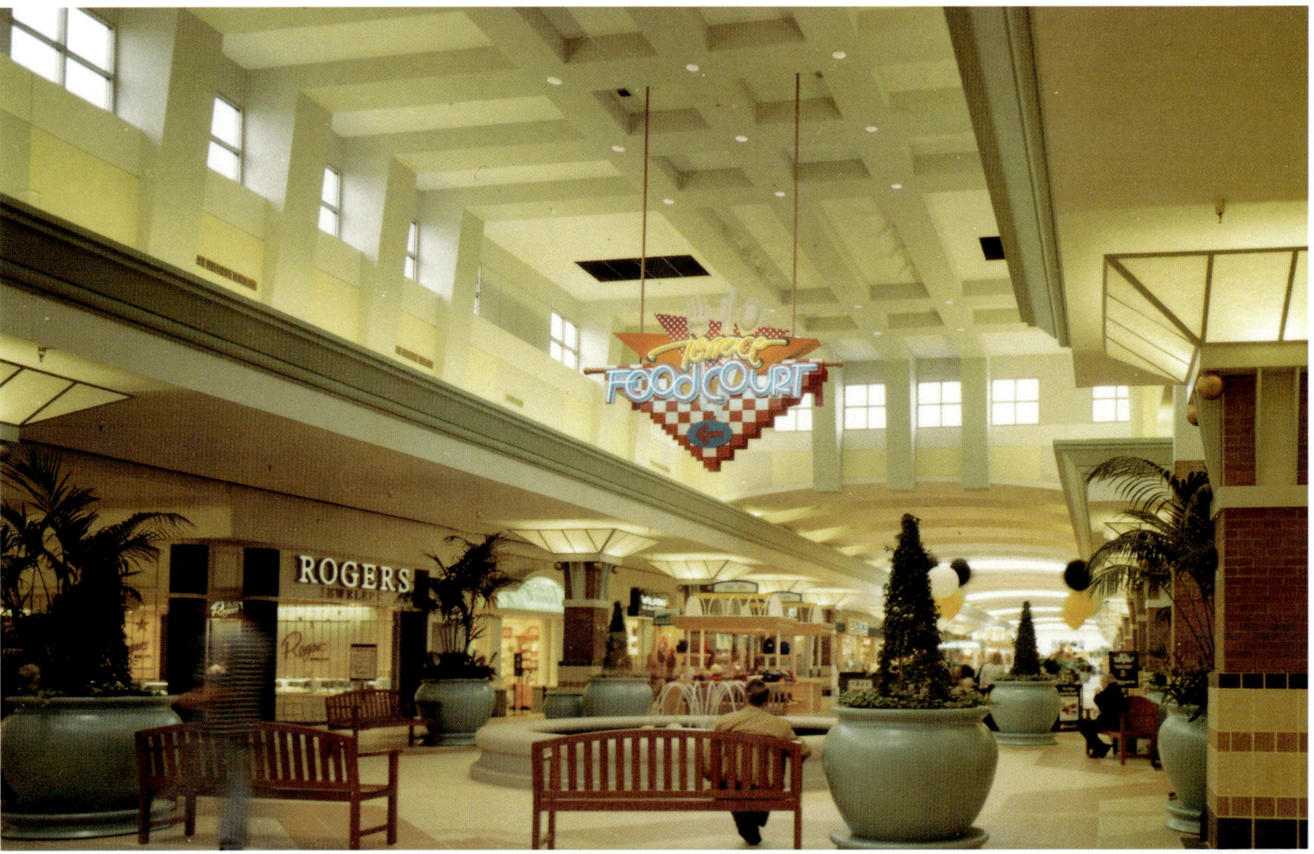

Lindale Mall

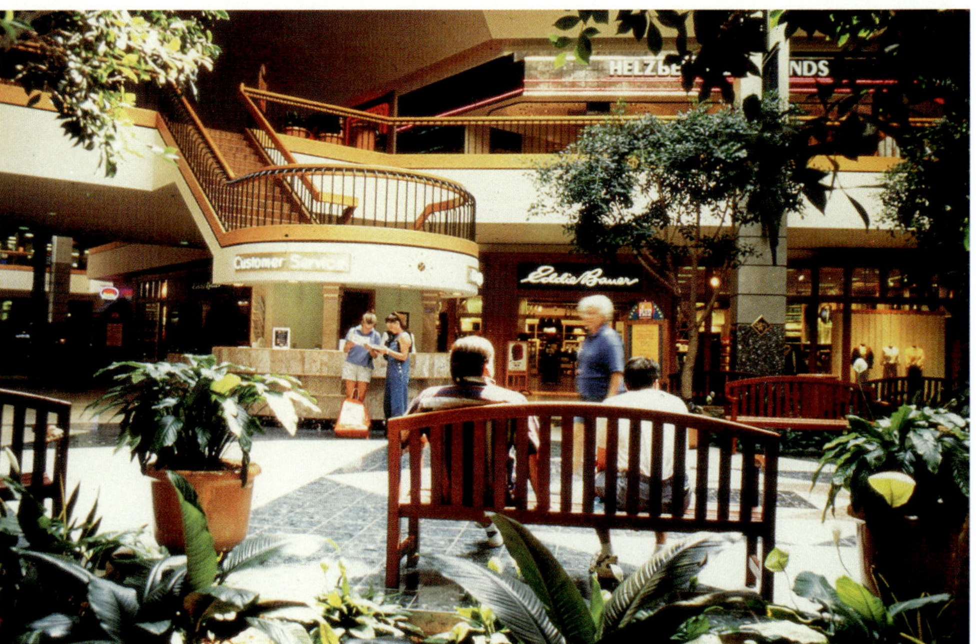

Westdale Mall

A new look for Lindale Mall *(top)*; a garden-like setting at Westdale Mall *(bottom)*.

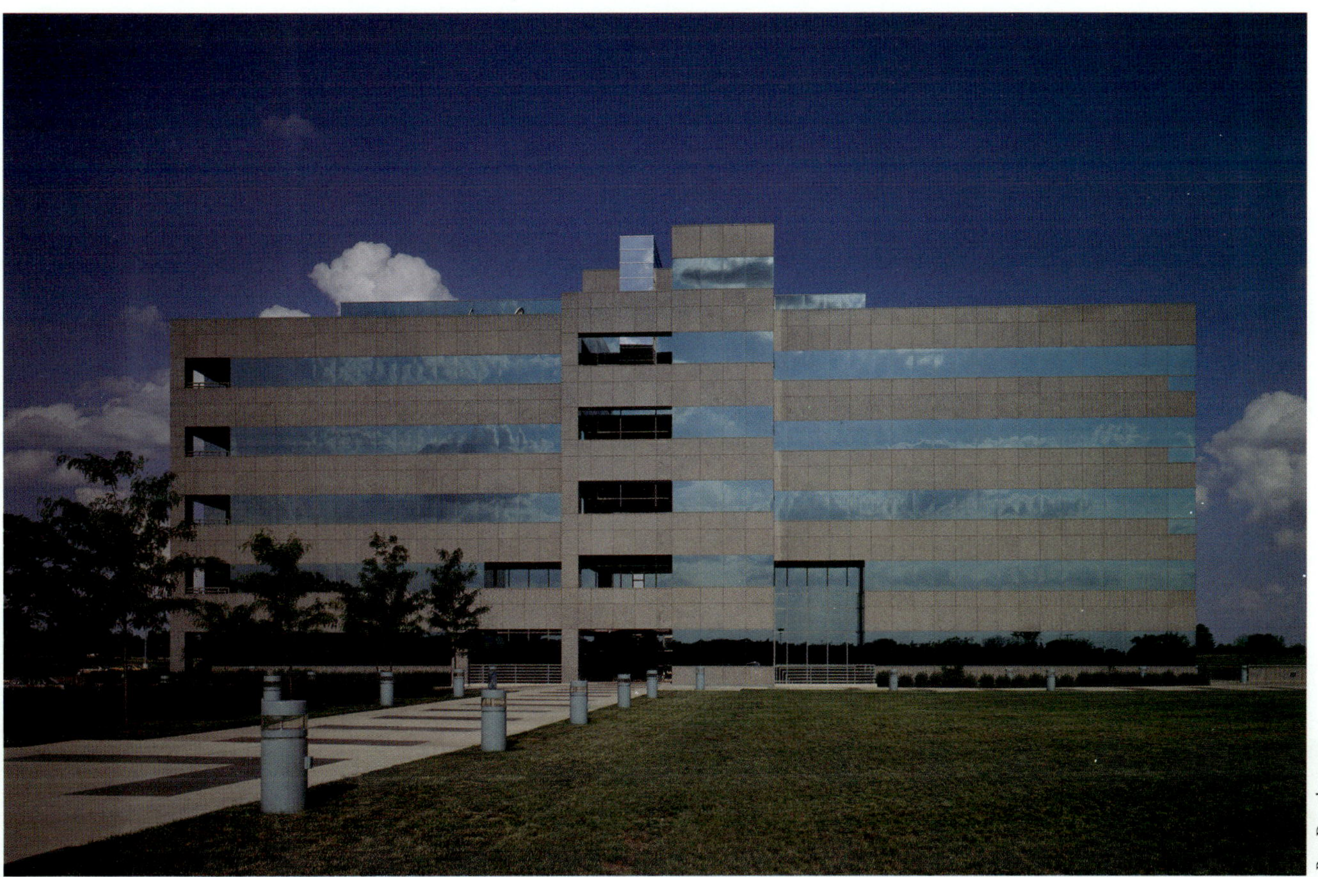

Ron Dreasher

The Aegon headquarters in northeast Cedar Rapids.

investment in infrastructure, the state's active image advertising program, and cooperation among "the three legs on the stool of economic development"—government, business and financial institutions.

"Other communities have factions that fight like cats and dogs," Hoffman said. "In Cedar Rapids, we seem to be able to get together." Another key, of course, is what many like Hoffman describe as a uniquely literate, productive workforce.

Learning new skills, making new fortunes

While some mainstays of the old economy were crumbling or leaving the city in the '80s, and even into the early '90s with the closing of Farmstead Foods, the first signs of our digital future were cropping up. That productive workforce was changing, as factory hands moved away or were retrained to work in the budding telecommunications industry.

We'll never know how successful, or unsuccessful, Clark McLeod's first business venture might have been had he chosen differently for the first Teleconnect location. The choice was between a building owned by a local doctor and a mortuary building that belonged to Cedar Memorial.

Attention to Details

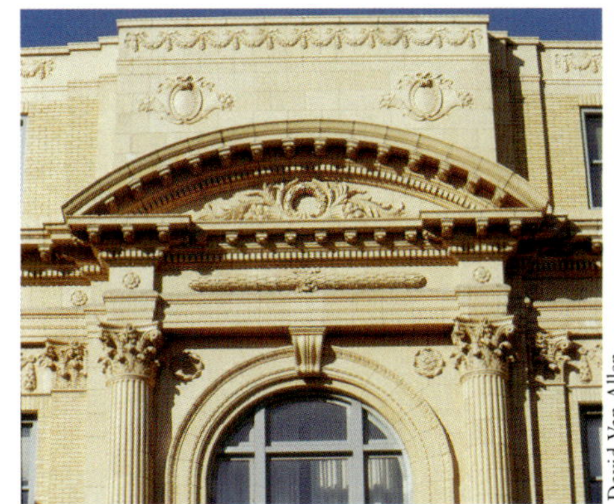
David Van Allen

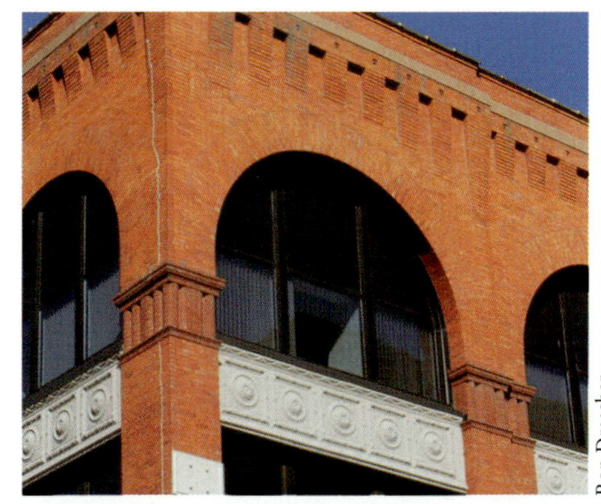
Ron Dreasher

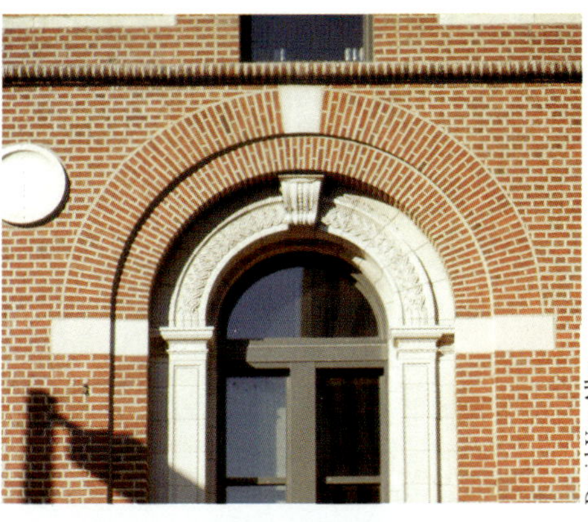
David Van Allen

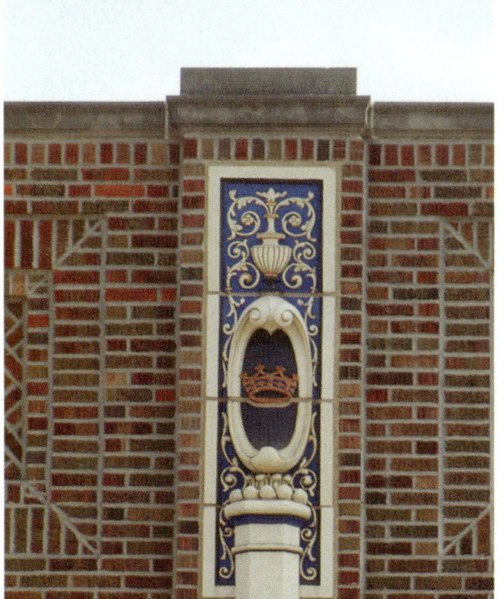
David Van Allen

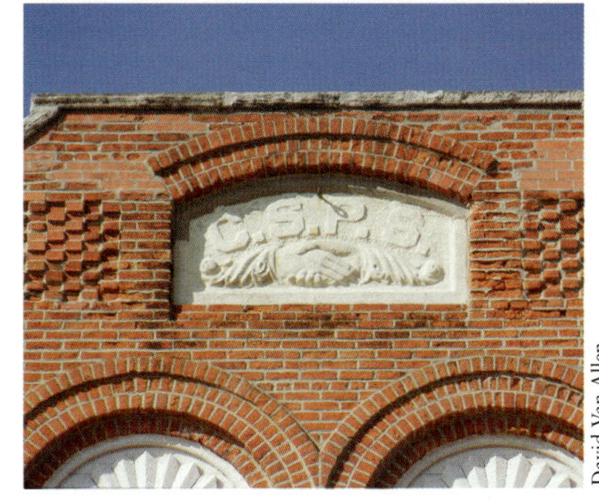

David Van Allen

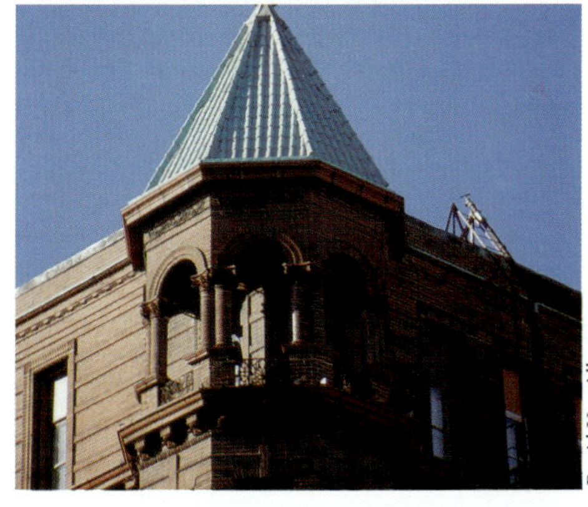
David Van Allen

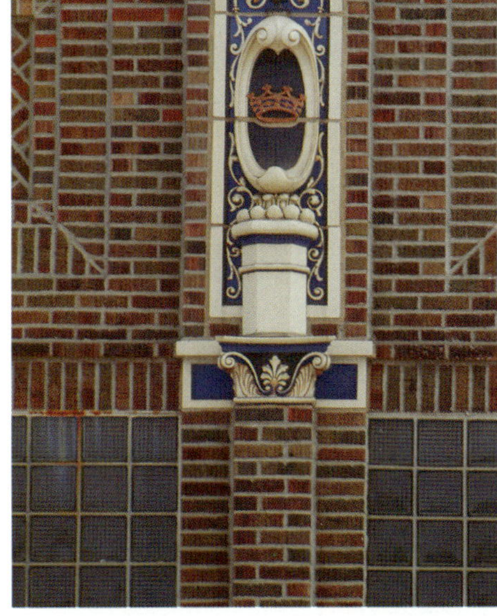

David Van Allen

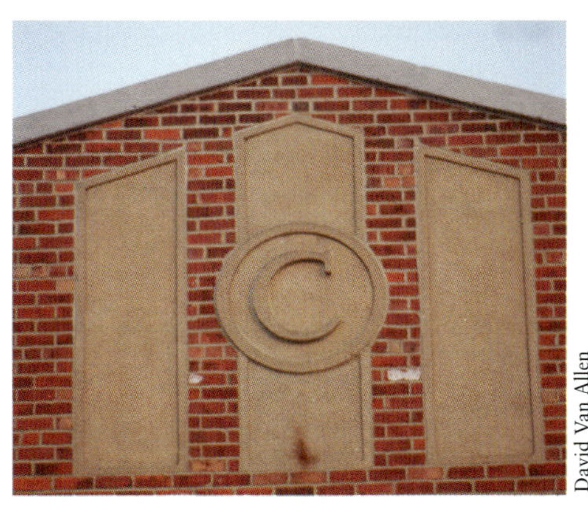
David Van Allen

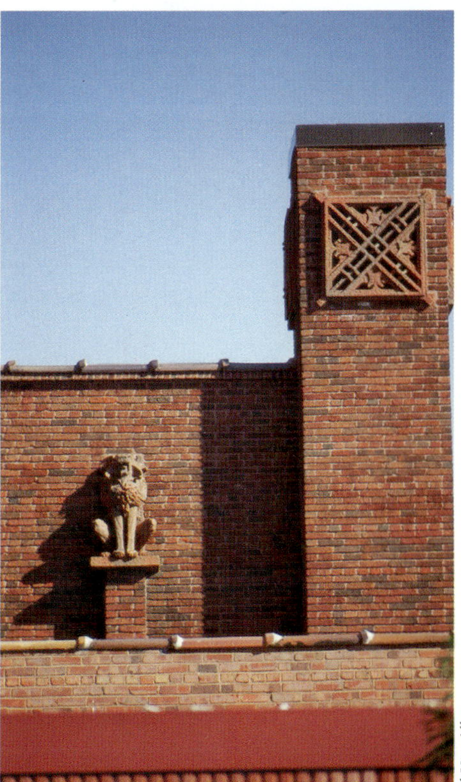
David Van Allen

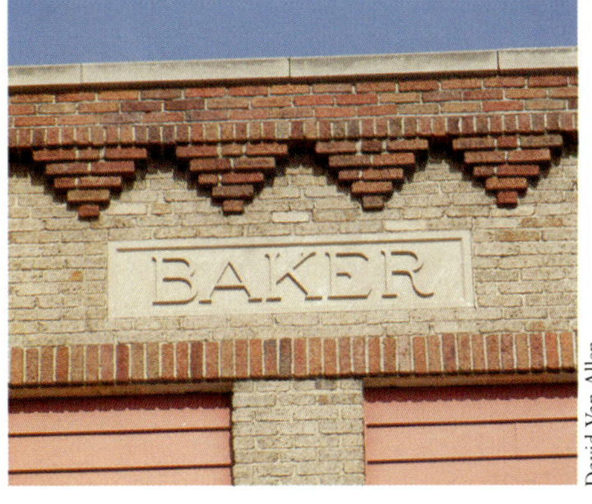

David Van Allen

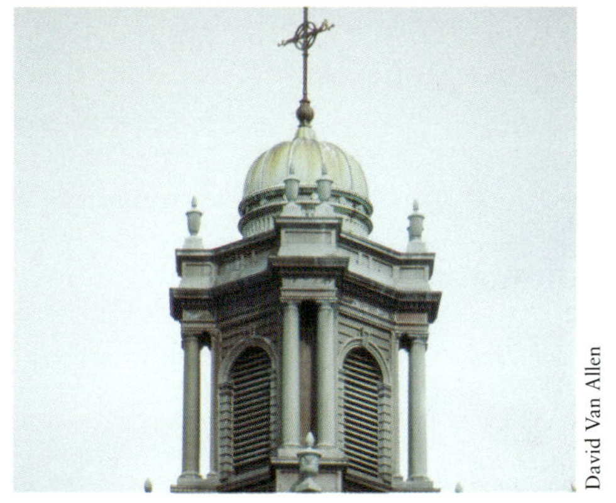
David Van Allen

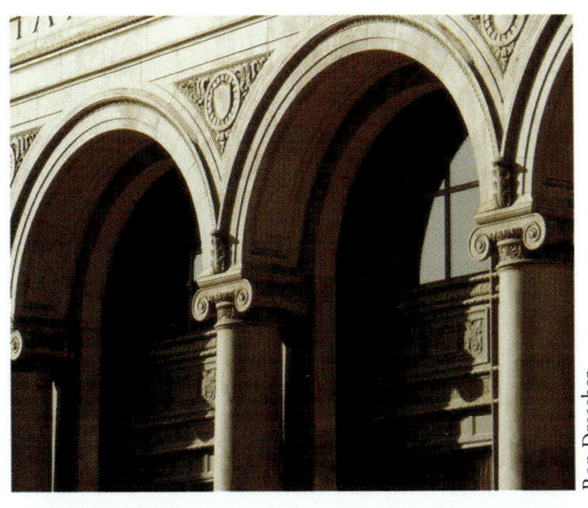
Ron Dreasher

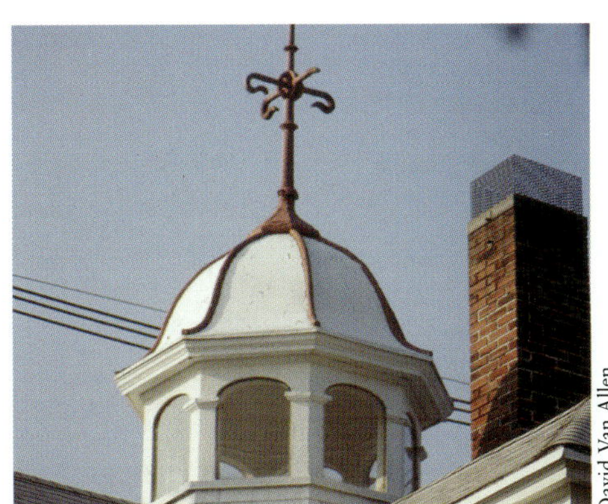
David Van Allen

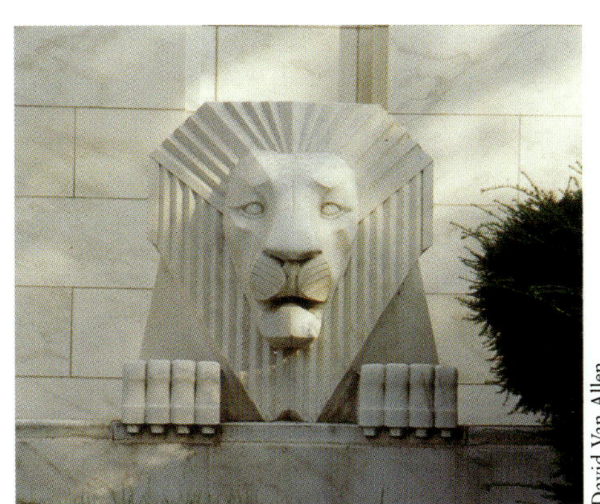
David Van Allen

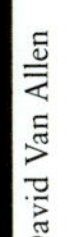

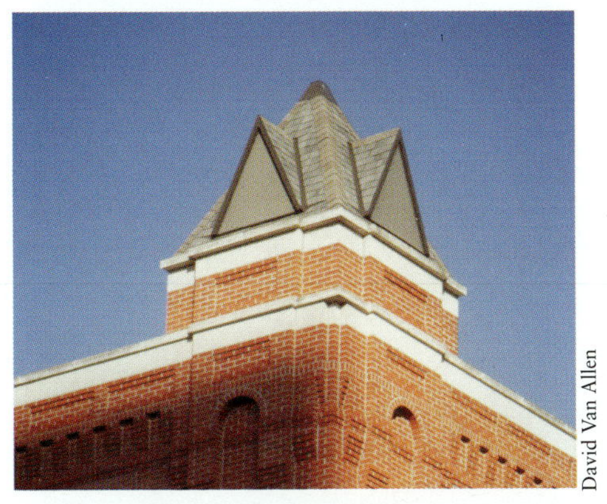
David Van Allen

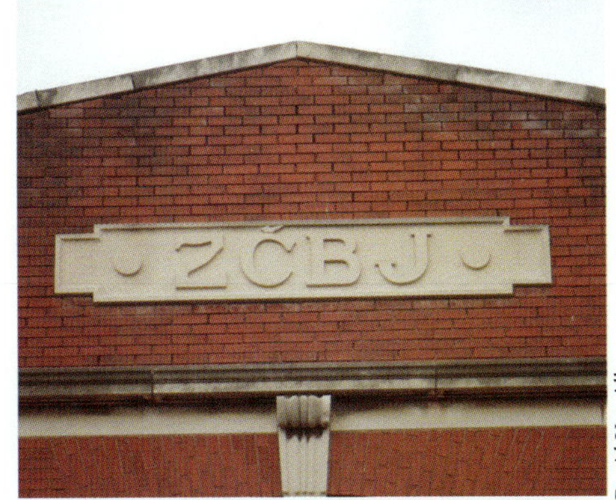

David Van Allen

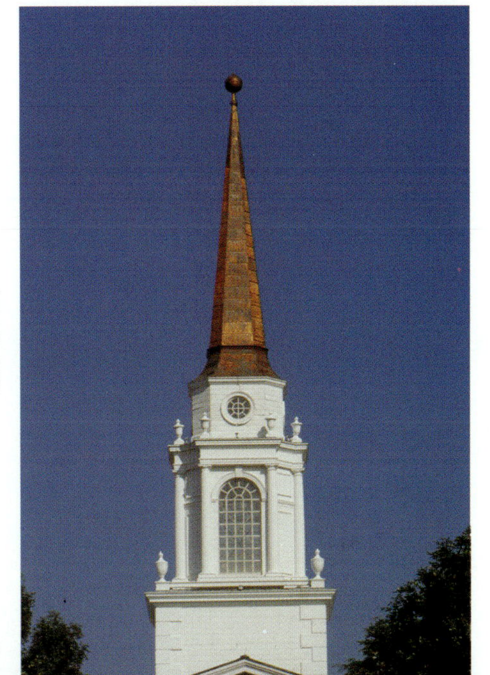
David Van Allen

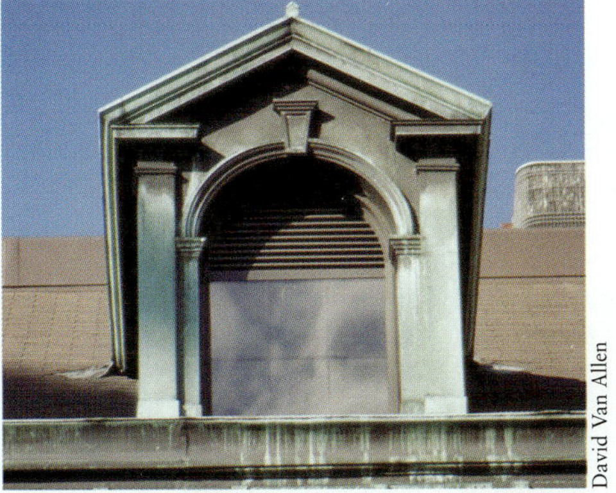
David Van Allen

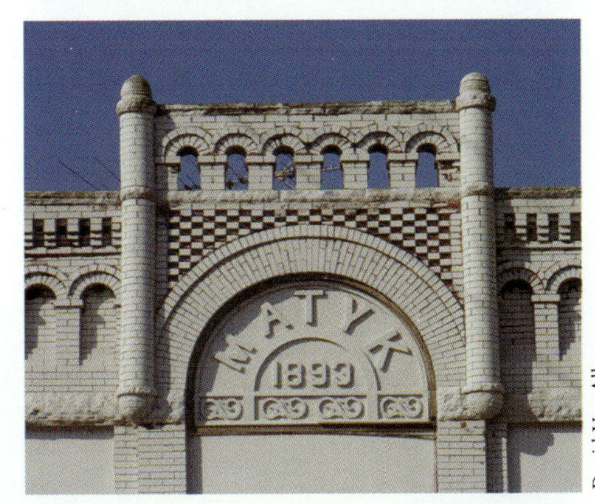

David Van Allen

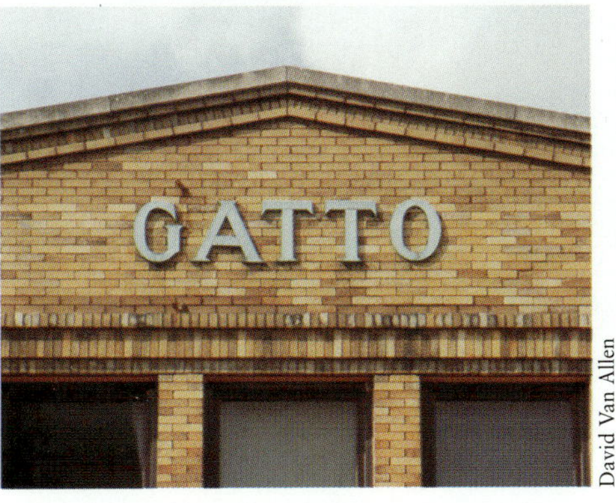

David Van Allen

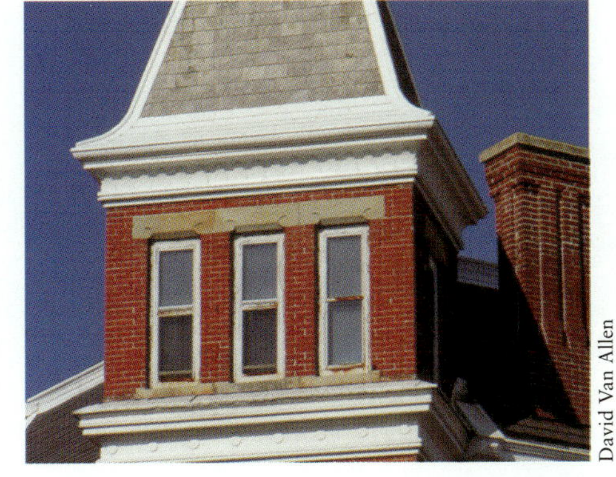
David Van Allen

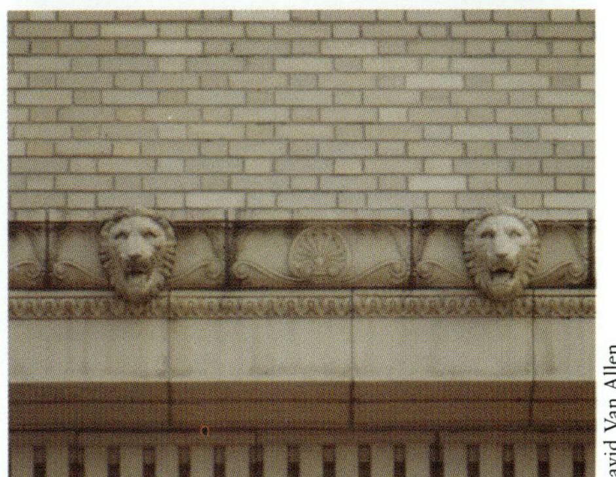
David Van Allen

"I figured I'd better not start a business in a place for the dead," McLeod said. "We decided it would have been difficult to bring business customers in. As we were walking through, we went right by an embalming machine, and that did it for me."

He picked the doctor's office on Center Point Road instead, and the business he founded in 1980 to sell and install telephone equipment ended up doing much to heal Cedar Rapids' wounds from the loss of jobs in other industries.

Teleconnect entered the long-distance reselling business in 1982 and had net sales of $4.3 million, which grew to nearly $168 million by 1987. After a 1988 merger with SouthernNet, Inc., and a name change to Telecom*USA, the company grew to become the nation's fourth-largest long distance company and had nearly 6,000 employees. In 1990, it was sold to MCI, another long-distance reselling pioneer based in Washington, D.C. The price tag: $1.25 billion.

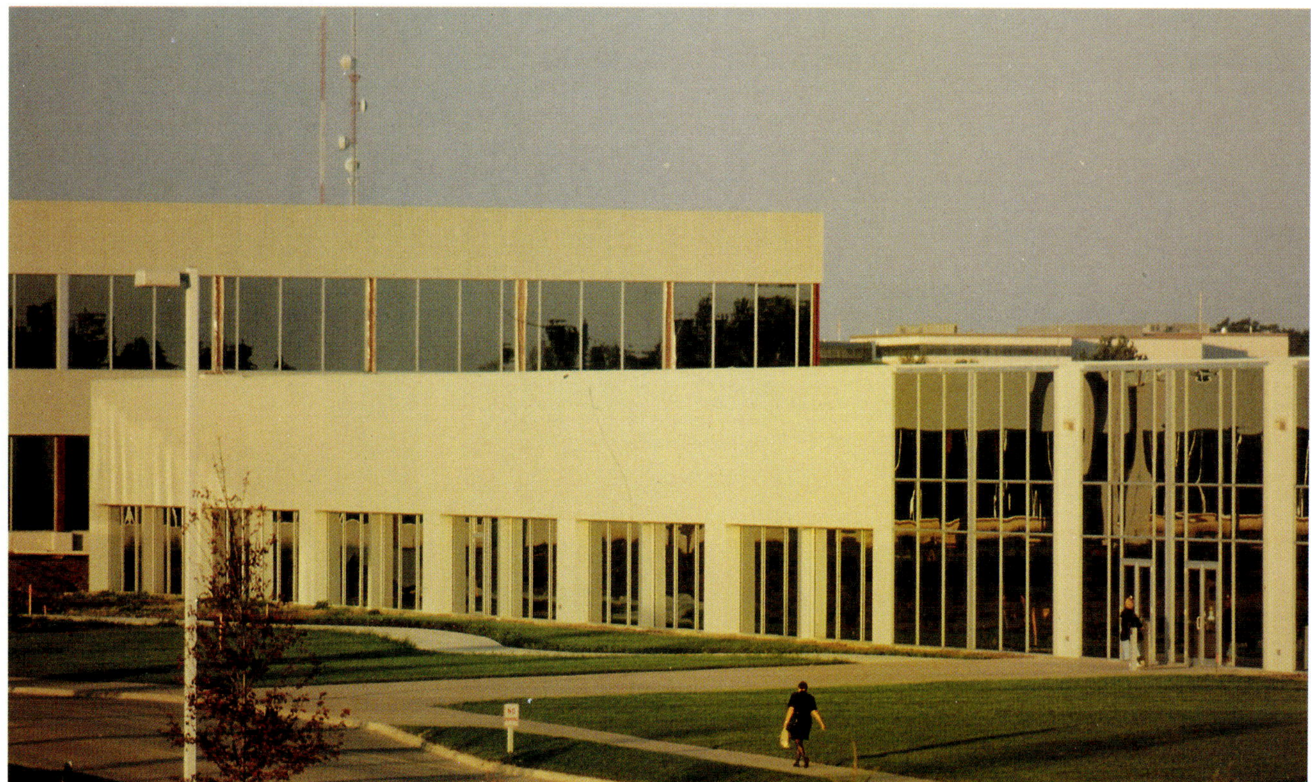

David Van Allen

McLeod Technology Park.

A non-compete agreement kept McLeod out of the long distance business until 1993, but his second telecommunications company, now known as McLeodUSA, also has grown to become a major industry competitor and employs nearly 5,000. It also owns Ruffalo Cody and Associates, the Cedar Rapids direct marketing and telemarketing company, as well as McLeodUSA Publishing, a corporate descendant of Telecom*USA Publishing.

MCI and McLeodUSA both continue to be major Cedar Rapids employers. As the city's reputation for being telecommunications-friendly spread, it has since attracted others in similar fields, including APAC Teleservices. A ready supply of people who speak English very plainly and an ideal central-U.S. location are seen as big advantages for businesses that sell coast-to-coast by telephone.

Reaching out

While the time was right for the telecommunications industry to take root here, it was also time for business to go a'courting, looking for other business to help rejuvenate the city and surrounding area.

The first substantial joint effort in pursuit of a major business was the attempt in 1985 to lure the Saturn automobile assembly plant to Eastern Iowa.

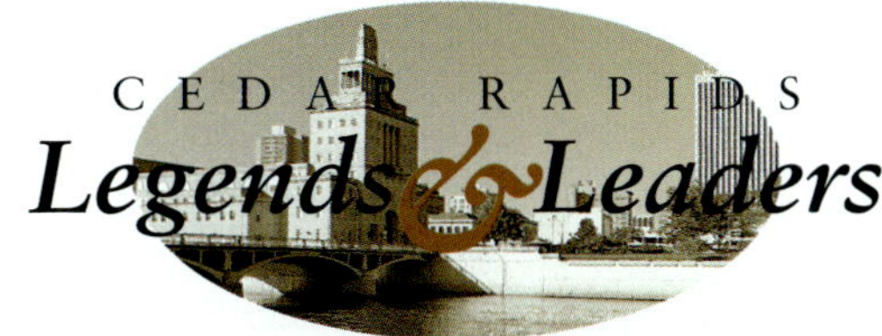

Irene Hall Perrine
1901-1994

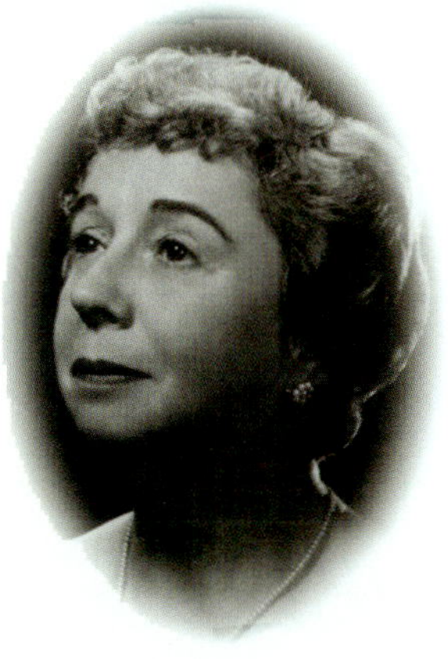

The sister of philanthropist and manufacturer Howard Hall, Irene Perrine attended Coe College and taught sixth graders in Lisbon, Iowa, for two years early in her life. She is remembered today as a kind and generous philanthropist; her close friends also knew her as an astute businesswoman and excellent judge of character.

Irene Perrine most enjoyed giving when she could do it anonymously. It wasn't until after her death that the Hall Foundation was renamed the Hall-Perrine Foundation in recognition of her philanthropic support and that of her husband, Beahl T. Perrine. Among their many other charitable causes, the Perrines inspired and funded a cancer education program that became known as the Mercy Cancer Center.

Photo: Brucemore

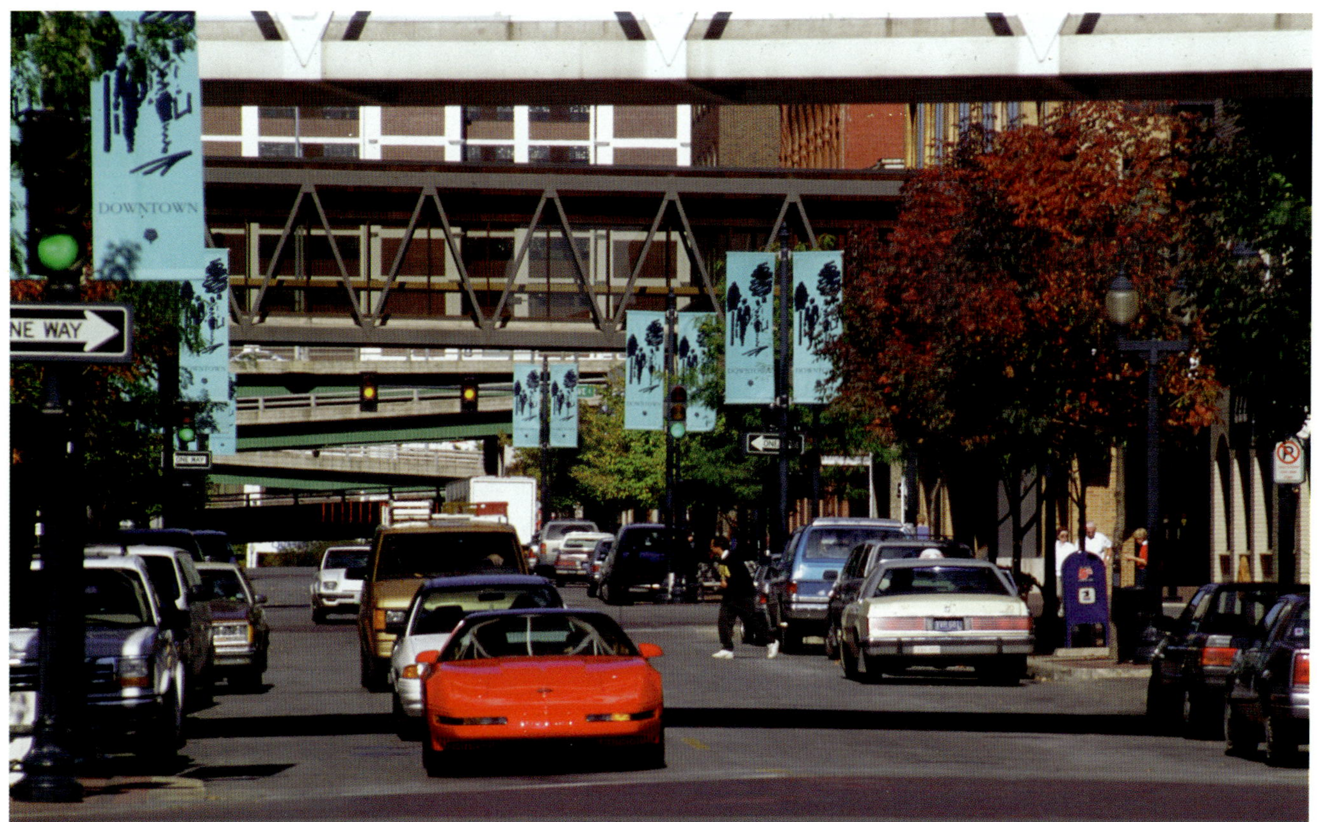

Mark Tade/The Gazette

A busy downtown street.

The effort ultimately was unsuccessful, but it reflected a new way of thinking and a new way of marketing the community. Efforts were no longer simply Cedar Rapids-focused, but began to promote the "corridor" concept, encompassing the larger Cedar Rapids and Iowa City area as a single entity that offers many attractive business, recreational, cultural and educational opportunities.

Gary Streit, co-chairman of Foresight 2020 and executive vice president of the law firm of Shuttleworth & Ingersoll, described the Saturn effort as "the birth of a regional perspective" that continues to pay dividends.

"This community has an amazing capacity to try new and interesting ways to solve problems," Streit said. "It's been very gratifying. There seems to be more common purpose in this community than there is in a lot of others. There's a broad base of people willing to take leadership roles."

Such growing diversity of leadership in the business community is perhaps one of the most significant if less obvious developments in Cedar Rapids history. It's an enormous change from that more paternalistic time not too awfully long ago, when a few of the wealthiest men devoted themselves to community betterment and job creation. Their efforts led to magnificent successes as well as spectacular failures as the economy ebbed and flowed.

The economy, too, is more diverse than ever. Agriculture continues to be a major source of well-being, as it probably always will in this heart of the country. Rockwell Collins has a new name and new corporate colors to reflect changes in its business. Financial service providers, new computer-related businesses and other high-tech and biotech companies now populate our industrial landscape.

Challenges loom large, community ready

So successful has been the Cedar Rapids economic development effort of the late 20th Century that it has spawned the need for yet another new development initiative. Many business leaders say we've become victims of our own success, luring so much in the way of new business that luring workers to fill new positions has now become a top priority and a daunting challenge.

"It's really hard to find people," said Steve Junge, president of P.M. Lattner Manufacturing Company, a century-old Cedar Rapids family

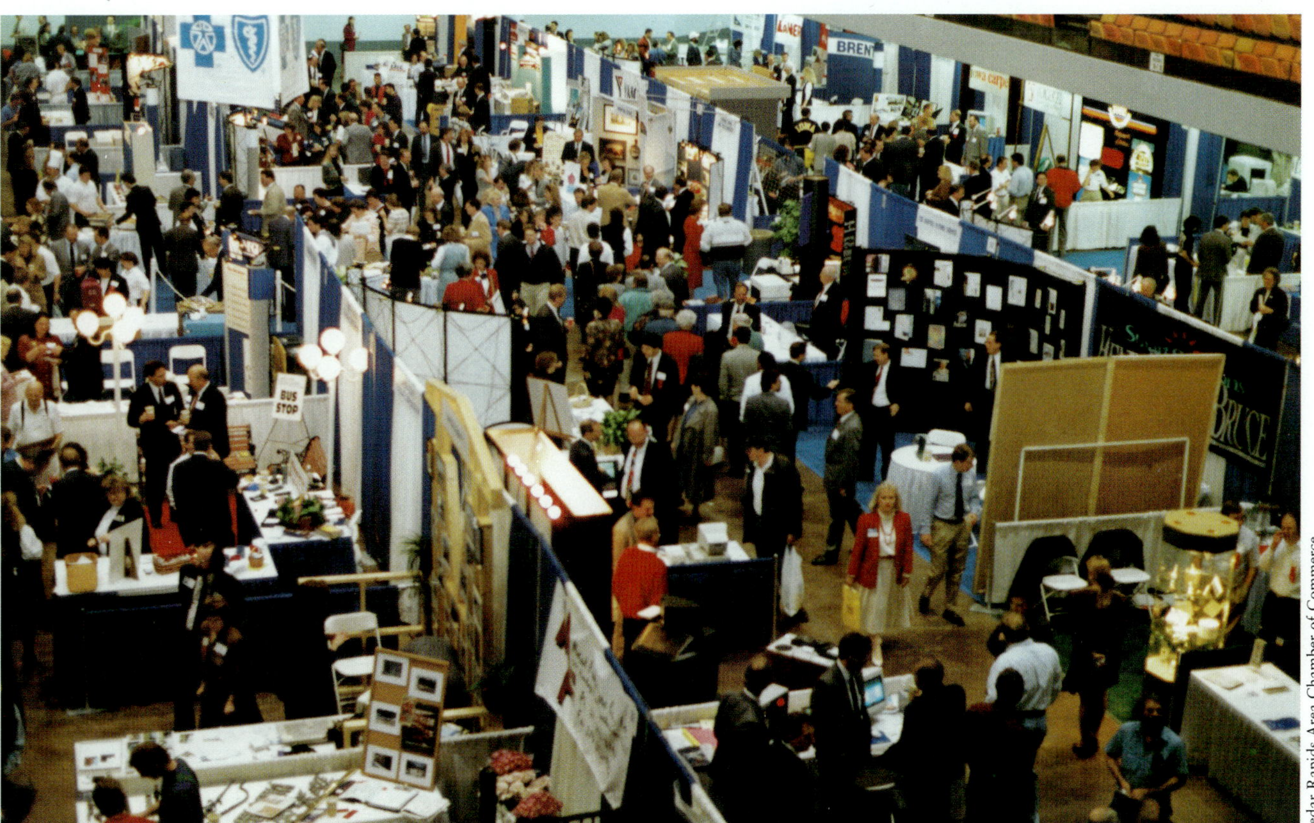

Cedar Rapids Area Chamber of Commerce

Cedar Rapids is a regional center for conventions and trade shows like this one at the Five Seasons Center.

business that makes steam boilers for use throughout the United States and for export to many foreign countries. Junge used to see four or five job applicants in a single day. Now, he may see only four or five in two months. Large employers like Rockwell Collins report literally hundreds of positions unfilled because not enough qualified people are willing to stay here or move here.

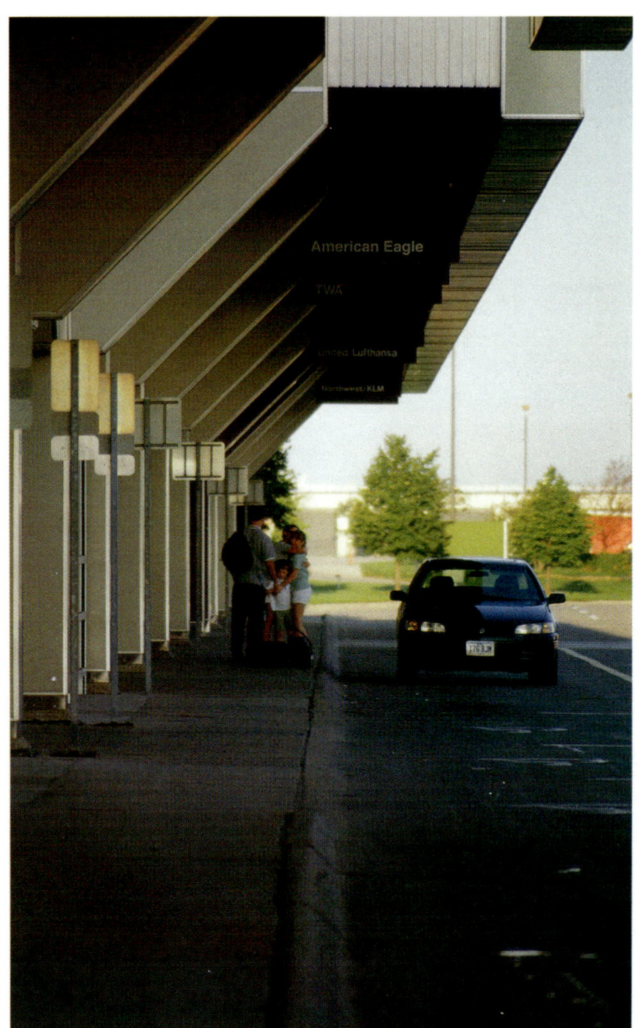

Saying goodbye at the Eastern Iowa Airport.

Junge and others say too many Eastern Iowa young people leave the area right after college, and retaining and attracting new workers will continue to be a major challenge for the foreseeable future. Already, a new workforce development initiative by the Chamber of Commerce is beginning to pay dividends, luring former residents and former area students back from positions in other states.

But while there is anecdotal evidence that the initiative is working, there is much left to do, and business leaders are rightly wary of resting on their laurels.

Largely gone are the days when people followed jobs; companies now go where people want to live. As a result, making Cedar Rapids a place where more people want to live—and spreading the word about the assets that make life here so attractive—is perhaps our biggest challenge as a community.

With new diversity in leadership, an energetic and imaginative group of citizens dedicated to community involvement and improvement, and a mix of businesses and industries that is more diverse than ever, Cedar Rapids appears ready to meet that challenge. We're better prepared than ever, it seems, to weather whatever storms the new century might bring, and better prepared to handle the prosperous times, as well.

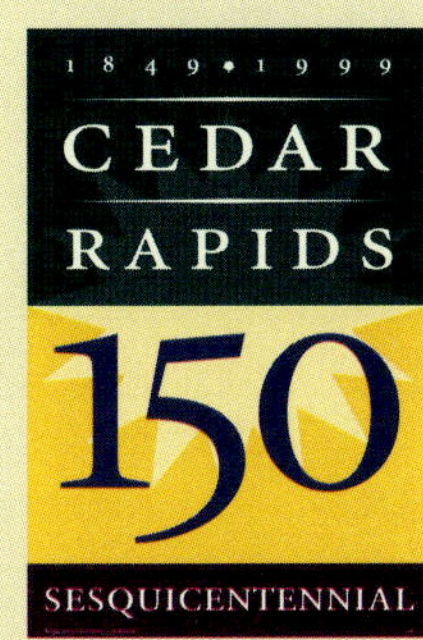

The following pages take a look at the Cedar Rapids area businesses and institutions whose support made this volume possible. They are presented in sections reflecting the years of their founding.

By Neil R. Baumhover

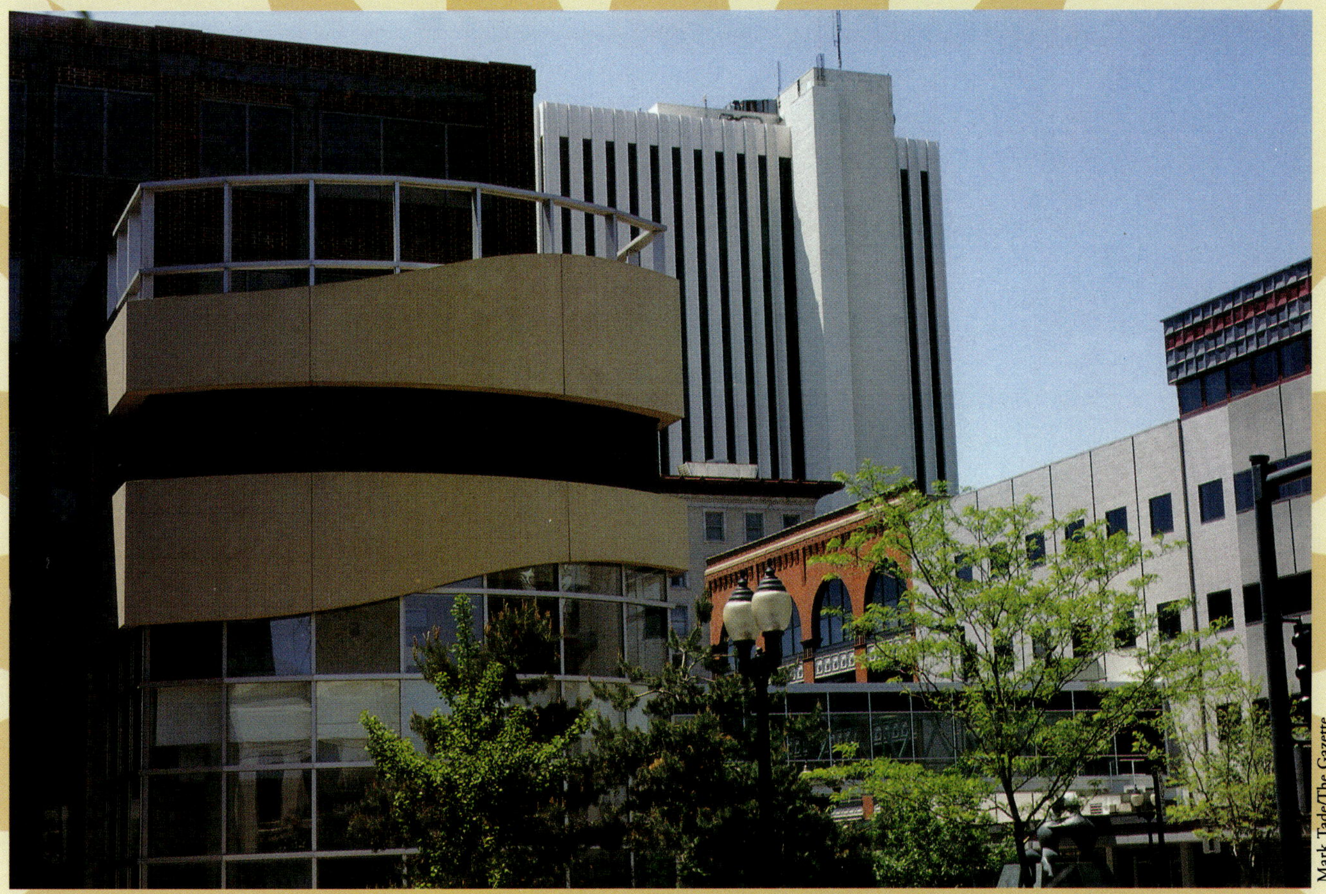

Mark Tade/The Gazette

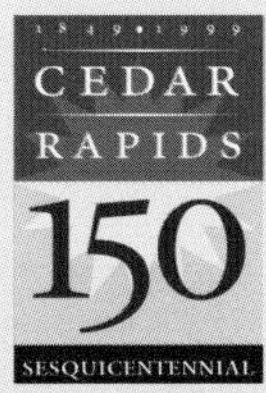

1840 1860

Coe College – 1851

Cedar Rapids Area Chamber of Commerce – 1850s

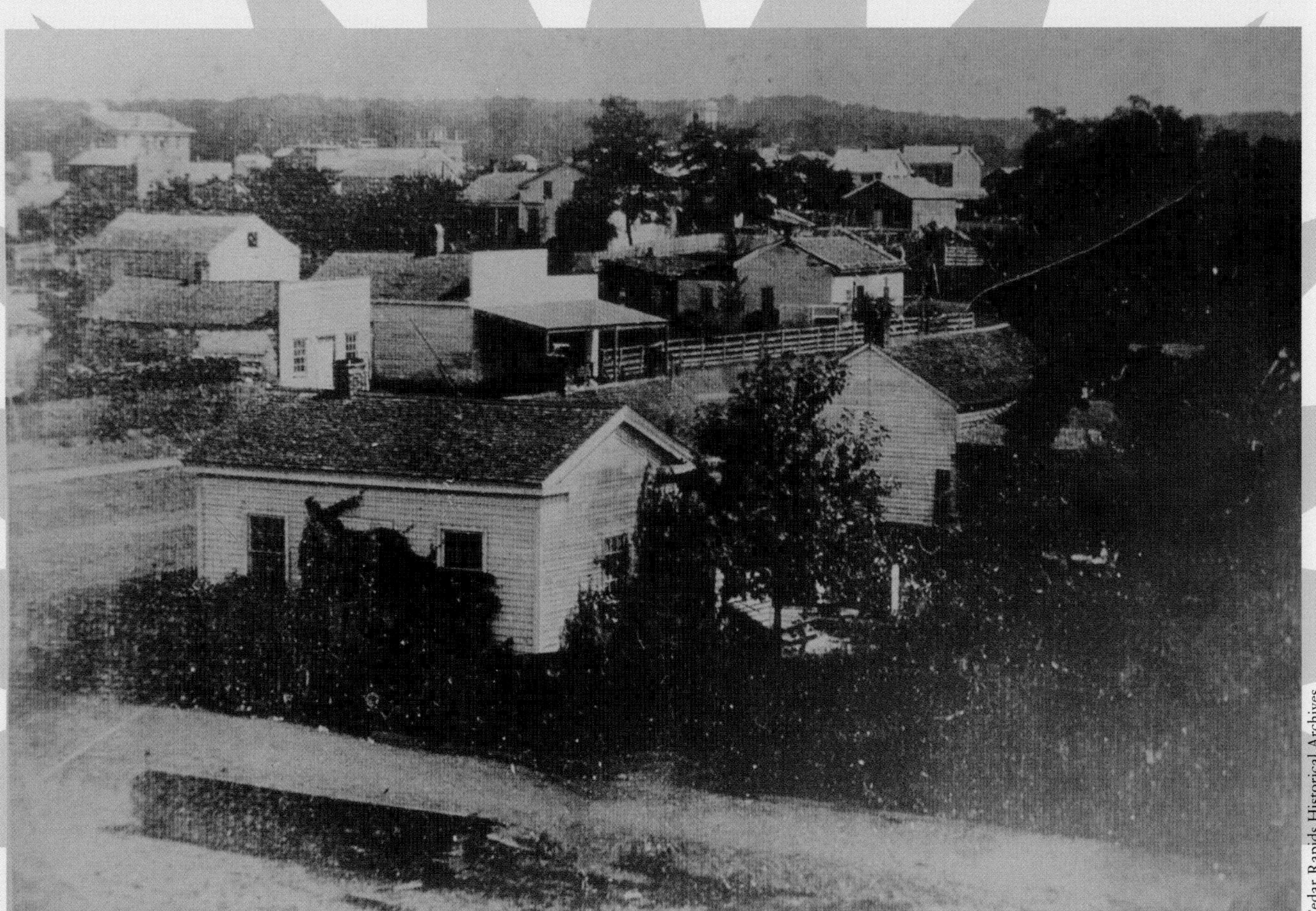

Cedar Rapids Historical Archives

The intersection of what is now First Avenue and Second Street SE as it appeared in 1856.

Coe College

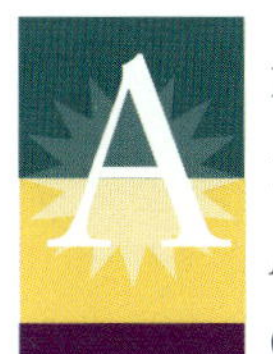

A LEGACY OF EDUCATIONAL EXCELLENCE THAT BEGAN NEARLY 150 YEARS AGO CONTINUES TODAY AT COE COLLEGE. WITH AN INNOVATIVE CURRICULUM ROOTED IN THE LIBERAL ARTS, COE OFFERS OPPORTUNITIES RARELY FOUND IN PRIVATE colleges of similar size. Not only does the college educate young people, but it also enriches the lives of area residents. Coe alumni have provided a core of leadership for Cedar Rapids since its earliest days.

New York Farmer

The institution of higher education that came to be known as Coe College was born in the parlor of the Rev. Williston Jones, pastor of what is now First Presbyterian Church. He opened it as the School for Prophets in 1851 to instruct young men for the ministry.

Two years later, Jones canvassed the East for capital. Daniel Coe, a farmer from Durham, N.Y., donated $1,500, provided the school would be open to both women and men. The money bought three lots and 80 acres of land, where Coe College now stands.

Today, the campus is a mixture of vintage and modern buildings, reflecting an appreciation for the past and a desire to provide the most up-to-date facilities.

A Plan for Achievement

The Coe Plan, an innovative curriculum grounded in the liberal arts, is designed to ensure that Coe students make an effective transition from college to career. It combines leadership development opportunities, a required practicum experience, and activities focused on ensuring competencies in written and oral communication, teamwork, and computer skills, as well as growth in the areas of independent and critical thinking, creativity, ethical decision-making, and aesthetic appreciation.

A selective, four-year, residential college of 1,200 students, Coe has been widely recognized for the accomplishments of its alumni, faculty and students. The college offers more than 35 majors leading to degrees in a broad spectrum of fields, granting Bachelor of Arts, Bachelor of Science in Nursing, and Bachelor of Music degrees, as well as the Master of Arts in Teaching.

Community Connections

Since 1979, Coe students have performed hundreds of full- and part-time internships in Cedar Rapids and Marion businesses and organizations. Coe also contributes to the Cedar Rapids community through a variety of partnerships with community schools and cooperative relationships in areas such as teacher education and nursing.

Through a vast array of high-quality lecture programs, music and theater events, art exhibits, and continuing education offerings, the college enriches the academic and cultural life of the Cedar Rapids community as well as the lives of its students.

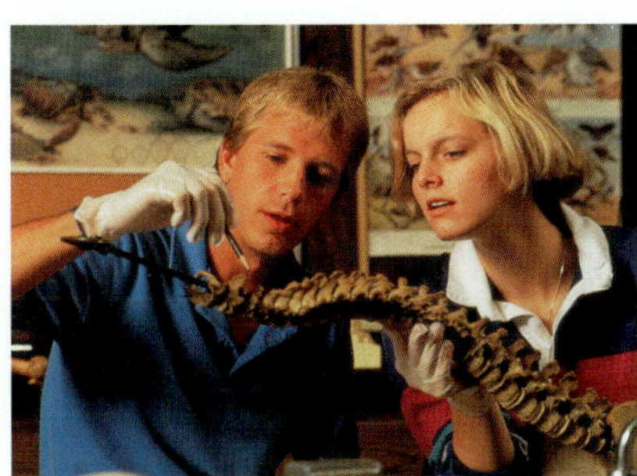

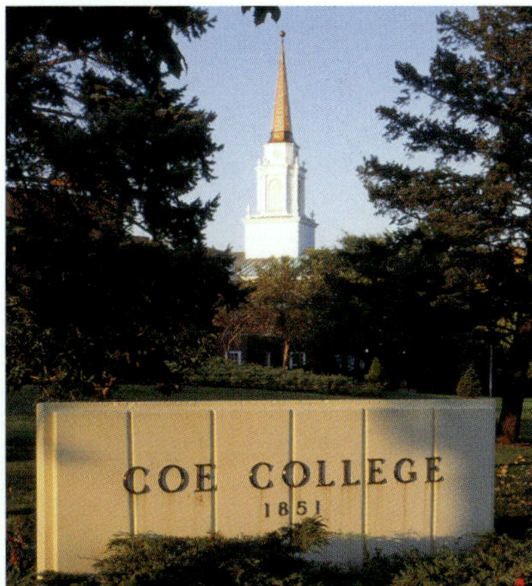

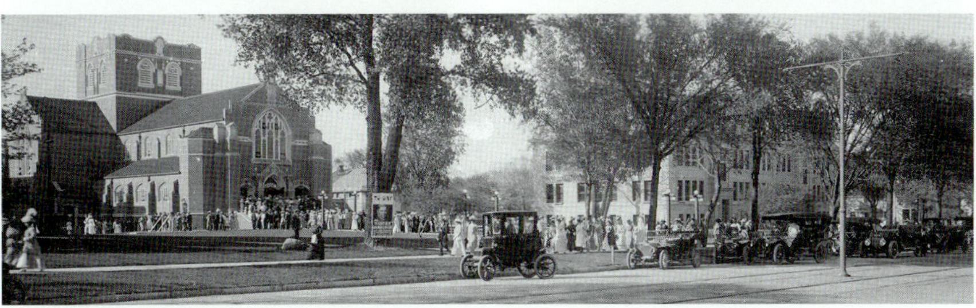

Coe students have exceptional opportunities for conducting advanced research at the undergraduate level, working with highly regarded faculty and state-of-the-art equipment (top left). A 1912 photo captures members of the Coe and Cedar Rapids communities leaving a performance by the New York Symphony Orchestra at Sinclair Chapel.

Cedar Rapids Area Chamber of Commerce

The history of the Cedar Rapids Area Chamber of Commerce reflects the history of business trends in the community. This mirroring stems from a progressive spirit that started as early as the 1850s.

Over the years, as businesses were faced with challenges, the chamber responded in ways that spurred growth. Growth occurred in the areas of business, community and economic development.

The historically relentless spirit to improve Cedar Rapids and surrounding communities continues today.

Even in the current time of prosperity, the Cedar Rapids Area Chamber of Commerce does not rest in its mission to build on the established momentum of growth.

Evolution of Success

The chamber evolved from business and civic organizations during the 1850s. Several of the founding members of the community met to discuss city betterment. The early efforts had little long-term importance because they were single-issue goals.

After the Civil War, an economic boom occurred. The 1880s brought more manufacturing and railroad improvements to the area.

In 1881, the importance of industry and commerce was formally recognized when the Cedar Rapids Board of Trade was established, along with an auxiliary group, the Manufacturers and Jobbers Association.

The Cedar Rapids Board of Trade was responsible for starting a long tradition of having state and national conventions held in the city.

About sixteen years later, the board was dissolved and the Cedar Rapids Commercial Club took over. Among the accomplishments of the club was the establishment of the 16th St. NE industrial area.

Reflecting a national trend, the Commercial Club was renamed in 1918 to the Cedar Rapids Chamber of Commerce.

Through its efforts, the industrial and commercial base of the city was continually expanded before and after World War II. The Eastern Iowa Airport of today was originally a community development concern of the chamber.

As the marketplace became truly global, neighboring chambers combined forces in 1970 to create an *area* chamber that was united in effort. By sharing leadership and resources, economic and industrial progress would continue.

Rallying Point

Community resources and citizen spirit combined into one chamber to reverse the 1970s trend of closing manufacturing plants.

A national model known as the Committee of 100 was established by the chamber. Money was raised from businesses to create a grassroots organization: Priority One.

As the Recession of the 1980s hit home, Priority One brought together people from Belle Plaine to Anamosa and from North Liberty to northern Linn County.

With a small staff and a multiyear budget of well over a million dollars, the retention and expansion of existing business was the major focus.

Offices were even set up in Europe and Asia to attract overseas businesses to the Cedar Rapids area. Companies that had a piece of the United States market but no manufacturing facility here were entreated.

Foreign and domestic companies alike were attracted to the quality of people in the Cedar Rapids area. The people were dedicated, had a strong work ethic and took tremendous pride in their work.

The infrastructure was strong, too. There was an abundance of good roads, water, sewer, electricity and natural gas.

Unstoppable

Coming back from a loss of more than 10,000 in population, there are currently over 100 new businesses in the area.

Today, not only have the 10,000 in number returned, but 10,000 more have come to Linn County. The surrounding counties as a whole have also added 10,000 in number.

Having attracted more businesses, the goal is now to attract former Iowans back to the area and build on the record growth.

The chamber and area businesses will work to continue the momentum of growth established by Priority One. With teamwork, the future will produce a destiny of prosperity for all.

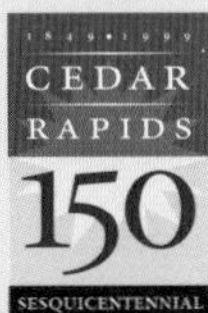

1860
1880

Quaker Oats – 1873

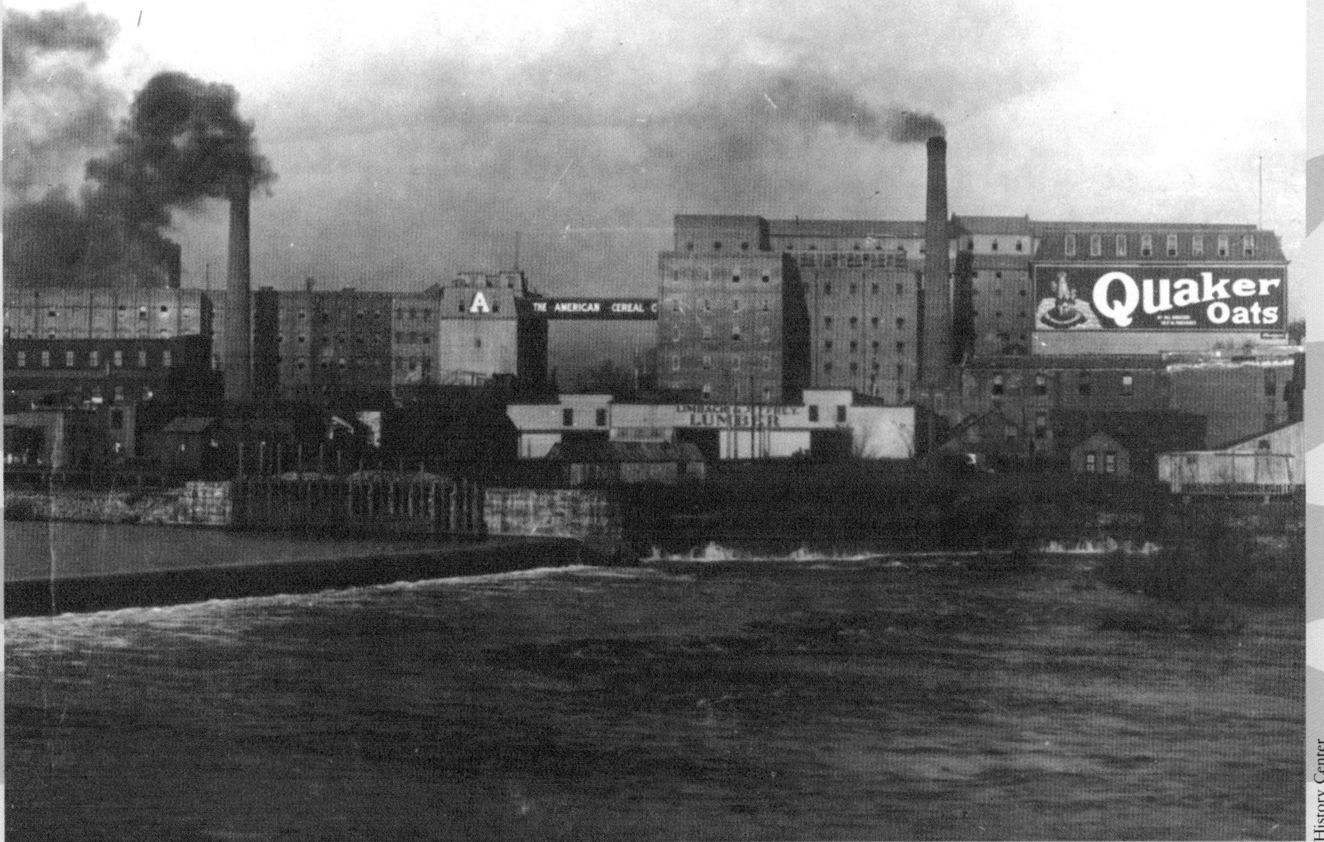

History Center

The Quaker Oats plant, circa 1900.

The Quaker Oats Company

EVERY MORNING, CEDAR RAPIDS CITIZENS AWAKE TO ENJOY QUAKER OATMEAL, CEREAL AND HEALTH BARS. BUT, DO THEY KNOW THAT THE COMPANY THAT PRODUCED THEIR FOOD ORIGINATED RIGHT DOWNTOWN? WITH AN EVER-EXPANDING line of products, The Quaker Oats Company is making nutritional foods and thirst-quenching beverages for all to enjoy—morning, noon and night.

The first trademark for a breakfast cereal, the Quaker Oats Man (below). The original mill (far below) of Robert Stuart, situated along the swift flowing Cedar River.

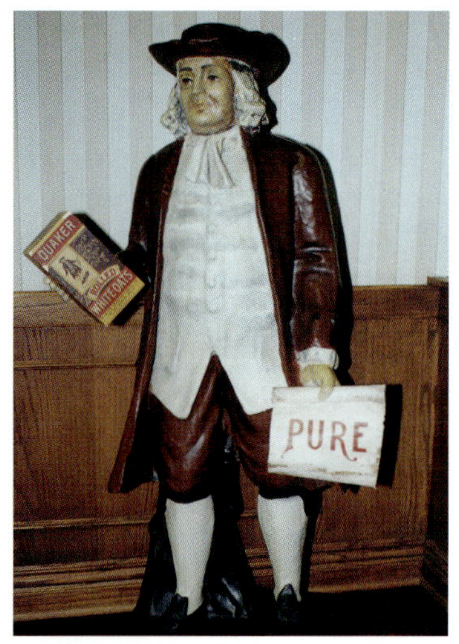

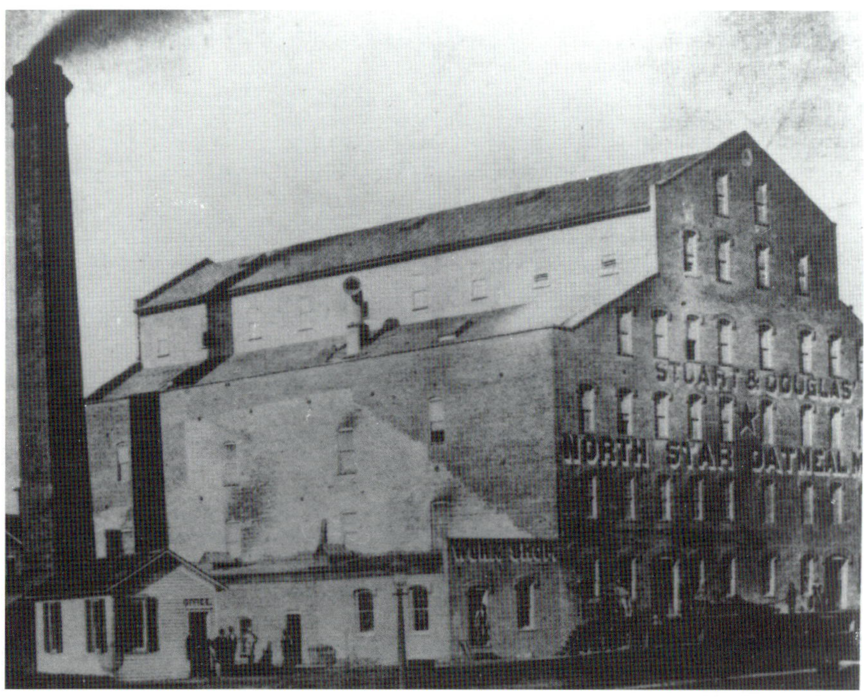

The Scottish Invasion

Twenty-year-old Robert Stuart persuaded his father, John, to move their failing North Star Mills from Ontario to the magnificent oat fields of Cedar Rapids, Iowa, in 1873. During the construction of the new mill, John fell and fractured a leg. He returned to Ontario, leaving Robert to operate the business.

George Douglas, a Cedar Rapids businessman, introduced young Stuart to his attractive niece, Maggie. By 1879, they married. The mill was renamed Douglas and Stuart, with George as a member of the plant's management.

America's Cereal

Over the next several years, Stuart ambitiously laid the groundwork for a future giant. In 1888, the oat empires of Henry Crowell of Ohio, Ferdinand Schumacher, also of Ohio, and Stuart of Iowa, combined. They formed the American Cereal Co., one of the many new, licit and popular conglomerations of the age.

Crowell, who loved the limelight, was elected president; Stuart, who sidestepped publicity, was made vice president, and Schumacher, who liked to run everything in which he was involved, was made treasurer.

As a compulsive entrepreneur, Crowell continued to push his own, pre-merger Quaker Oats as a product of American Cereal.

The name "Quaker" was devised as a virtuous identity that would instill buyer confidence. As America's first breakfast cereal trademark in 1877, Crowell made the label famous. Calendars, cooking books, short-course cooking schools, free sample boxes, booths at fairs, colorful postcards and prizes in boxes were some of the innovative methods. In fact, the paper cartons themselves were innovative. Cereal was previously retailed in bulk and freshness could not be guaranteed.

With the overwhelming popularity of the Quaker Oats name, the American Cereal Co. naturally changed its name in 1901 to the name everyone knows today: The Quaker Oats Company.

Fire and the Roaring Twenties

In 1905, a disastrous fire totally destroyed the Cedar Rapids mill. Restoration immediately began and two years later, a new mill was completed.

Expansion continued through the years and daily production of rolled oats steadily increased. To keep up with the escalating demand for Quaker products, major facility expansions were undertaken in the 1920s. Elevator G, still the major grain storage facility, was completed in 1926. The Package Building, which constitutes the main part of the current plant, was constructed in 1927.

Famous Names

The 1930s and 1940s saw expanding product lines as the Cedar Rapids plant became the leading producer of Quaker's cornmeal, grits, flours and corn oil.

As the largest cereal mill in the world today, the Cedar Rapids plant is also the primary producer of many nationally famous foods.

Life cereal was first produced in 1958, followed by Cap'n Crunch in 1964. That same year, the plant started production of convenient Instant Oatmeal. The plant began manufacturing Aunt Jemima Syrup in 1966.

As more women entered the work force in the 1970s, less time for meal preparation fueled interest in snacks and convenience foods. The fitness craze also created a demand for nutritional products.

To accommodate this changing market, the company introduced Quaker 100% Natural cereal and Quaker Corn Bran. The decade also brought Life cereal commercials featuring "Mikey," which became one of the longest running campaigns in the company's history.

In 1996, the company introduced Quaker Bagged Cereals. As a more economical method of packaging, the line quickly became a hit with consumers.

While not manufactured at the Cedar Rapids facility, other famous names now under the Quaker banner include Rice-A-Roni, Noodle-Roni and Gatorade.

Cap'n of Industry

Strong brands that compete in the beverage and grain-based food markets continue to be the lifeblood of The Quaker Oats Company. Ninety percent of the company's retail brands hold the number one or two position in their relevant product categories.

With wonderful standings in the marketplace, Quaker Oats looks forward to a bright future of even greater growth and progress in Cedar Rapids and worldwide.

A banner (right) displaying Quaker's commitment to its unions. The Cedar Rapids plant is the largest in the Quaker Oats family (below).

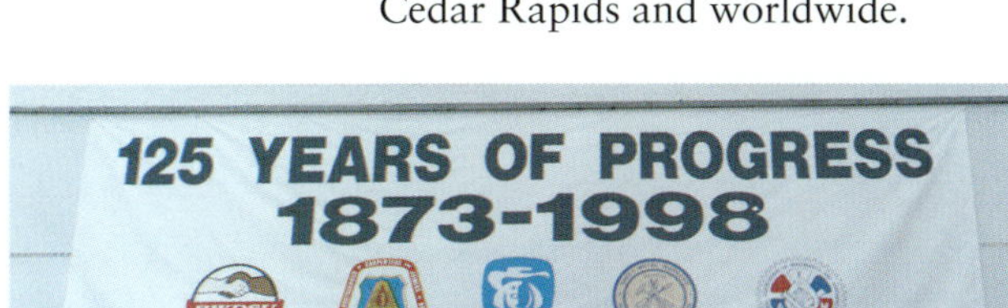

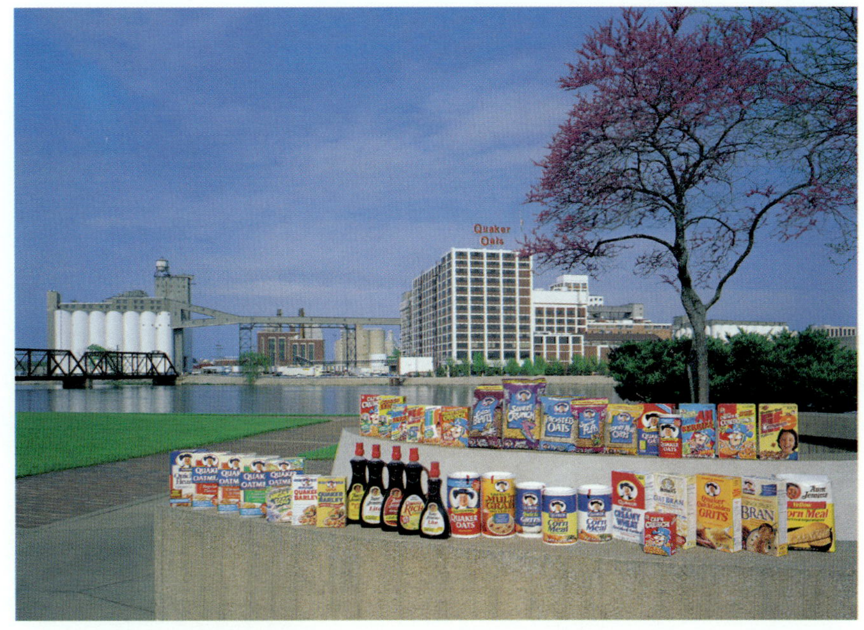

CEDAR RAPIDS 150 SESQUICENTENNIAL

1880 1900

Evergreen Packaging Equipment – 1880

Rinderknecht Associates, Inc. – 1880

Alliant Utilities – 1882

King's Material, Inc. – 1882

The Gazette Family of Companies – 1883

St. Luke's Hospital – 1885

Penford Products Co. – 1895

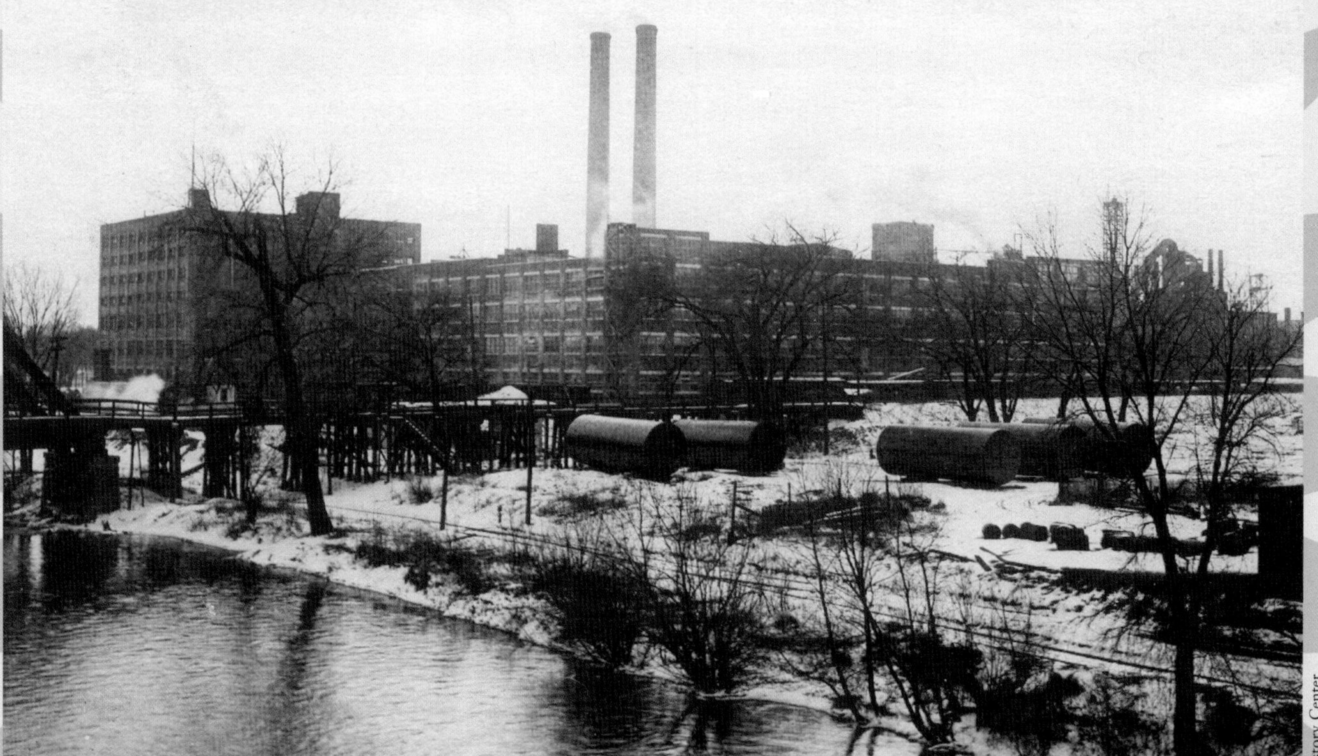

History Center

An early view of Douglas Starch Works, predecessor to Penford Products Co., with the Eighth Avenue Bridge at left.

Evergreen Packaging Equipment

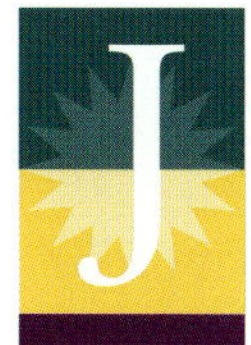

UICES AND MILK ARE FRESHER, EASIER TO TRANSPORT AND MORE CONVENIENT TO DRINK THANKS TO THE INNOVATIONS BY EVERGREEN PACKAGING EQUIPMENT. WITH A LEGACY OF OVER 100 YEARS OF BETTER PACKAGING, THE COMPANY helps businesses around the world provide wholesome products to their customers.

Imaginative Buttermaker

In 1879, John G. Cherry left Walker, Iowa, and brought his family to Cedar Rapids, where he started as "chief buttermaker" for a large creamery.

While working at the company, Cherry became concerned with the unsanitary way cream was delivered from the farm to the creamery.

Cherry's inventive genius prompted him to begin working on an idea for a jacketed cream can that would insulate the product from extreme heat or cold, and thereby preserve its quality until delivery.

With his idea perfected and patented, Cherry resigned as chief buttermaker to establish the J.G. Cherry Co. in 1880, a company that would forever change the world's perception of "freshness."

Continued Freshness

The J.G. Cherry Co. merged with the D.H. Burrell Co., a stainless steel equipment manufacturer from upstate New York, and five other companies to form Cherry-Burrell Corp. in 1928.

The packaging division of Cherry-Burrell was purchased by International Paper in 1991. Known today as Evergreen Packaging Equipment, it is a part of International Paper's liquid packaging division.

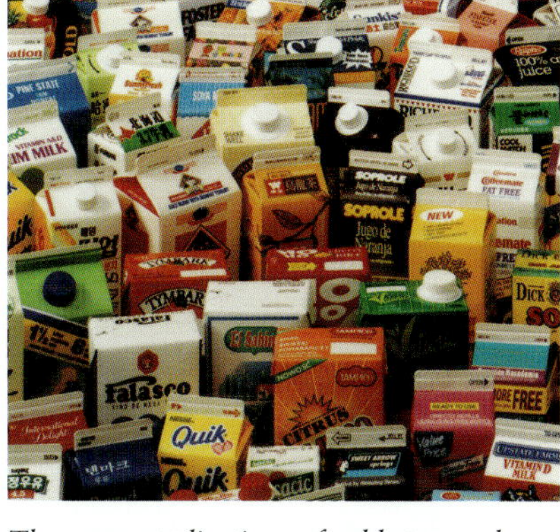

The many applications of gable top and aseptic packaging systems. Spouts are a shared feature of the two systems.

Evergreen Packaging Equipment carries on the spirit of J.G. Cherry by manufacturing gable top carton and aseptic packaging systems for the preservation of freshness.

Packages of the Future

Gable top carton equipment was being made in Cedar Rapids as early as the 1960s. By the early 1980s, gable top packages had swept the globe.

Spouts, a popular convenience that originated as an option with gable top packages, is a feature of new machines or a retrofitted capability on earlier machines.

In 1994, production of aseptic packaging systems started in Cedar Rapids. Aseptic packaging, such as the little drink boxes with a straw, is beneficial because it does not require refrigeration.

Today, Evergreen Packaging Equipment is exporting over 50 percent of its gable top machines. Rapid growth is occurring in aseptic packaging as well.

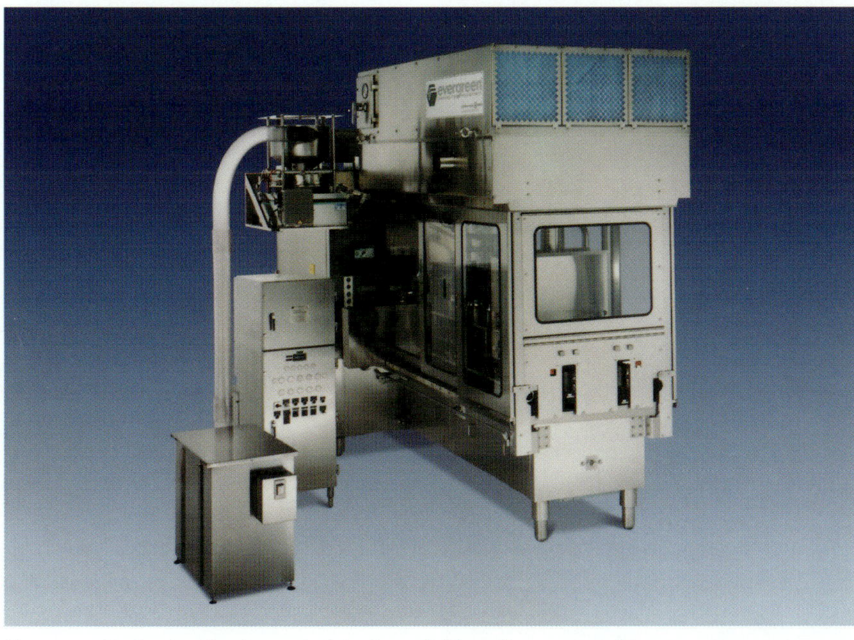

Evergreen Packaging Equipment's fast, dependable and accurate gable top carton equipment features the addition of spouts to the packages.

Alliant Utilities

A LITTLE MORE THAN 100 YEARS AGO, ELECTRICITY WAS A CURIOSITY WHOSE USES MOST PEOPLE COULD NOT FATHOM. THIS WAS NOT THE CASE, HOWEVER, FOR THE PEOPLE OF CEDAR RAPIDS. WHILE THE EARLY CITIZENS WOULD NEVER know laser surgery, e-mail and electronic scoreboards, they knew that the power of electricity could improve the quality of life.

Today, Alliant embodies that pioneering spirit. As a partner with the community, the company brings a range of resources and technical skills to help its customers be more productive and profitable.

One of the first combined power and light units of 1896 (below). This unit was capable of producing 400 kilowatts. Training at the DAEC simulator is one factor that influenced the nuclear plant's licensed reactor operator 100 percent pass rate in 1996 and the plant's overall outstanding performance.

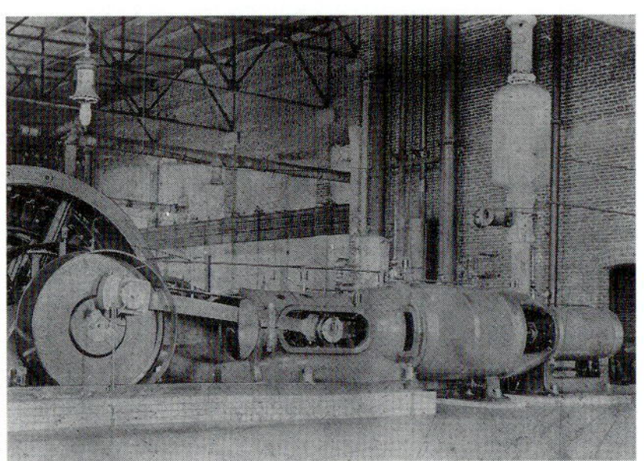

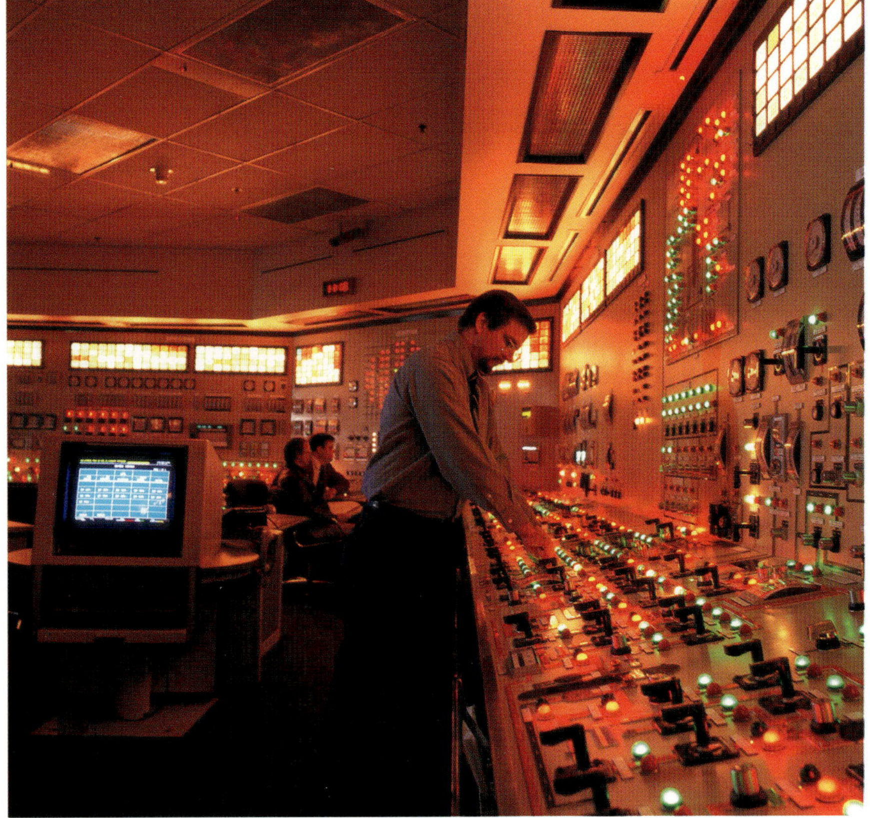

Electricity Is the Greatest Show

At first there was darkness. Then came the "Greatest Show on Earth."

Early in June 1882, the Barnum and Bailey circus brought to Cedar Rapids not only their show, but also their electric arc lamps and a small generating unit.

The combined luminescence of the lamps gave so much light that people sat up all night claiming it had been "as light as noonday."

Struck by the power of this new type of lighting, many public meetings were held to discuss the ways and means of securing electric lights.

On August 18, 1882, the Cedar Rapids Light and Power Co. was founded. The initial investment of the company was $12,000. The outlay provided for a generator, an old barn, wiring and a payroll of two.

More Power

At first, Cedar Rapids Light and Power sold lighting for large rooms, store fronts and street illumination.

As electric lines proliferated, appliances of all kinds were introduced. In 1932, after a long succession of name changes, the company changed to Iowa Electric Light and Power Co., also known as IE.

Before long, electricity was interwoven into the fabric of everyone's life, leading to a continual public demand for more energy.

IE sought to satisfy its customers' energy needs with the construction of the Duane Arnold Energy Center (DAEC) in Palo, Iowa.

Since its launch more than 20 years ago, DAEC has earned consistently high ratings from the Nuclear Regulatory Commission and is listed among the best performing nuclear plants in the United States.

The Advent of Alliant

In 1992, IE acquired the southern Iowa territory of Union Electric Co. to help better serve customers. Two years later, IE and Iowa Southern Utilities joined to form IES Utilities, a wholly-owned subsidiary of IES Industries Inc.

In 1998, Alliant was formed from the proud traditions of three energy service providers: IES Industries Inc., Interstate Power Co., and WPL Holdings, Inc.

Alliant is guided by the leadership of Lee Liu, chairman of the board of Alliant and former CEO of IES Industries. A 1953 graduate from Iowa State University in electrical engineering, Liu joined IE in 1957. He led IES Industries' successful completion of the three-way merger.

More Than a Name

The origins of the name Alliant convey a commitment. It is an "ally" for its customers, communities, investors and employees. The company is "reliable" and it will be "all" it can be for those who work with it and for it.

Homes and Businesses

Alliant offers customers an ever-expanding array of products and services designed to enhance the comfort and security of their homes and the productivity of their businesses.

More than a million residential and business customers in Iowa, Wisconsin, Minnesota and Illinois count on Alliant for service. They look to the company for reliable, competitively-priced electric and natural gas energy.

Business customers, both within and outside Alliant's utility service territory, turn to the company for total energy solutions.

These may include comprehensive business-process improvements designed to drive down production costs while driving up product quality. Answers can also be found in backup energy supplies, which ensure uninterrupted production for businesses and manufacturing plants.

Four Business Units

Alliant is organized into strategic business units: Alliant Utilities, Alliant Power and Alliant Industries. Internal support comes from a separate centralized Alliant Corporate Services unit. Together, these four business units help the company keep its promise to all customers.

Two of the units, Alliant Utilities and Alliant Industries, are headquartered in Cedar Rapids.

Alliant Utilities carries on the operational excellence of the three merged utility companies under one banner. This unit offers reliable, competitively priced supplies of electricity, natural gas, water and steam. It also provides responsive, round-the-clock service.

Alliant Industries is the umbrella under which Alliant markets energy and other products and services to industrial, commercial and residential customers outside the regulated utility sector. This unit also pursues energy-related partnerships in marketplaces around the globe.

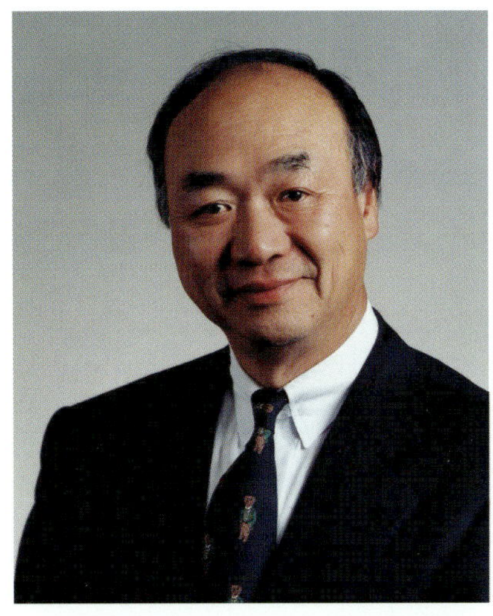

Lee Liu joined the former Iowa Electric Light and Power Co. in 1957 as an engineer and advanced through numerous engineering, management and executive positions prior to being named chairman of IES Industries, Inc. in 1991. IES merged with two other companies to form today's Alliant.

Allies Forever

Alliant is well positioned to meet the ever-changing needs of customers in America's heartland and around the world. It is backed by $5 billion in assets, an energized work force, a commitment to the future, and a promise to solve customer problems.

In a world where all customers soon will have a choice of energy suppliers, Alliant is finding new ways to meet customer needs by developing an array of products and services that no other provider can surpass.

Rinderknecht Associates, Inc.

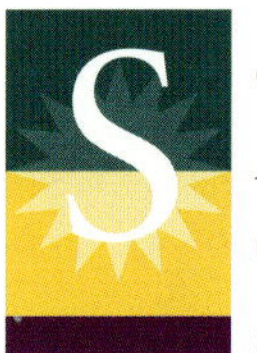

SOME OF THE MOST IMPORTANT BUILDINGS IN THE CITY ARE ONES BUILT BY RINDERKNECHT ASSOCIATES, INC. COMMERCIAL, INDUSTRIAL AND INSTITUTIONAL CONSTRUCTION IS THE PRIMARY BUSINESS OF THE COMPANY. But, having been responsible for so many structures in the community, it could be said that Rinderknecht is also in the business of building lives.

Cabinets to Buildings

Theodore Stark was a cabinet maker in the "old country" of Germany. Emigrating, he settled in Cedar Rapids, and began carpentry jobs in 1880. Ten years later, he was joined by his brother, Robert.

Working together as the Theodore Stark Construction Co., the brothers used their quality craftsmanship in early projects such as the Paramount Theatre, St. Paul's Methodist Church, and McKinley, Roosevelt and Franklin schools.

Rinderknecht Revolution

Richard Rinderknecht worked for the Starks as a youth. In 1933, at the age of 26, he teamed with the sons of the original Stark brothers to form the Stark Building Co.

Rinderknecht bought out the remaining interests of the Stark family and organized the R.W. Rinderknecht Co. in 1941. After the war, Darrell Schumacher joined the company. E.G. Branstetter, an army buddy of Schumacher's, joined in 1950.

During the late 1940s, when veterans returned home, there were few construction companies building residential housing. The company went temporarily outside its realm of larger building construction to create sixty houses within one year.

In 1968, Rinderknecht retired and Schumacher became president. Three years later, Rinderknecht Associates, Inc. was formed to allow increased ownership by key employees.

Today, the company is completely employee owned and there are no Rinderknechts in the company.

"He said we could use the name, so long as we didn't embarrass it," said LaVerne Flagel, a longtime executive who is now company president.

Structures of Life

The emphasis of quality through craftsmanship that began in 1880 remains the company standard today.

With enduring structures, the firm has impacted the lives of Cedar Rapids residents.

Health care buildings have been constructed at Mercy Medical Center and St. Luke's Hospital. Educational needs have been met with structures at the grade schools, the high schools, and at Mount Mercy College, Coe College and Kirkwood Community College. Many churches in the city have been company projects as well.

"We've taken care of people from birth to death," said Flagel, "and I think we will continue to play a role in all the parts of human history."

The pride employees take in their work demonstrates their dedication to the growth of Cedar Rapids. It is a hearty growth that will continue well into the next century.

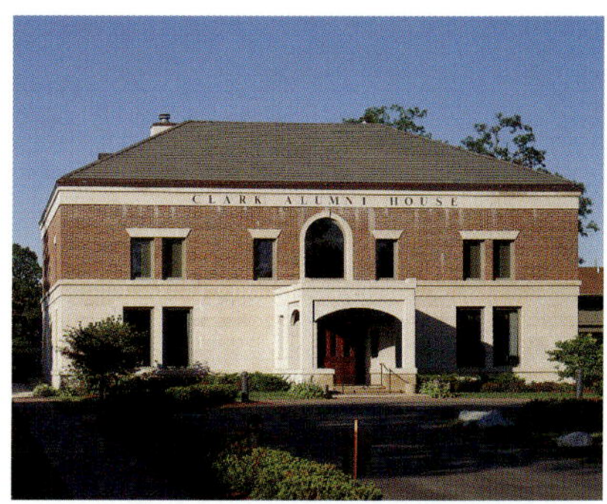

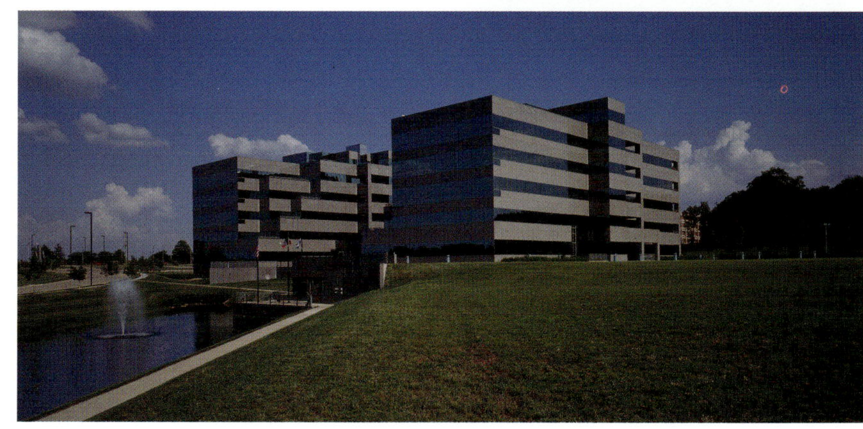

The Coe College Clark Alumni House (top) was built by Rinderknecht Associates. The North Point Plaza buildings (above) are Class "A" office developments, the caliber of buildings typically found in areas like Chicago and New York City.

King's Material, Inc.

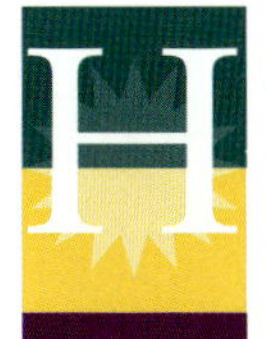

HAVING SUPPLIED THE CONCRETE FOR NEARLY THREE OUT OF EVERY FOUR HOUSES IN CEDAR RAPIDS, KING'S MATERIAL, INC. HAS LITERALLY HELPED BUILD THE CITY. IN ADDITION TO RESIDENTIAL CONSTRUCTION, THE COMPANY HAS ALSO provided the material for industrial, commercial and institutional projects.

Company Crowning

Founded in 1882 by William King, King's Crown Plaster Co. originally sold plaster and sand. It wasn't until 50 years later that the company got involved with concrete.

In the 1930s, ready-mix concrete evolved and the company became the first such business in Cedar Rapids. Four three-quarter cubic-yard mixers were mounted onto Model A Ford chassis and the first "ready mix" concrete was delivered to Quaker Oats.

Concrete Technology

Today, King's Material is highly automated. Computers and electronic scales take the place of springs, dials, and counterweights.

With a central, wet-mix concrete plant, the concrete is premixed before it is loaded into the trucks. The computer technology in the plant creates tremendous accuracy in the concrete mixture.

"On a mix that has 40,000 pounds of cement, sand and stone, we are accurate within 10 pounds," said Charles A. Rohde, president of King's Material.

Applications of concrete have also become extremely precise. Factory or warehouse floors that require super flatness need laser screeds to level the concrete. Versus traditional screeding methods, a laser beam shoots across the form and guides the screed. Laser screeds and concrete pumps are just some of the many advanced tools in concrete mechanics.

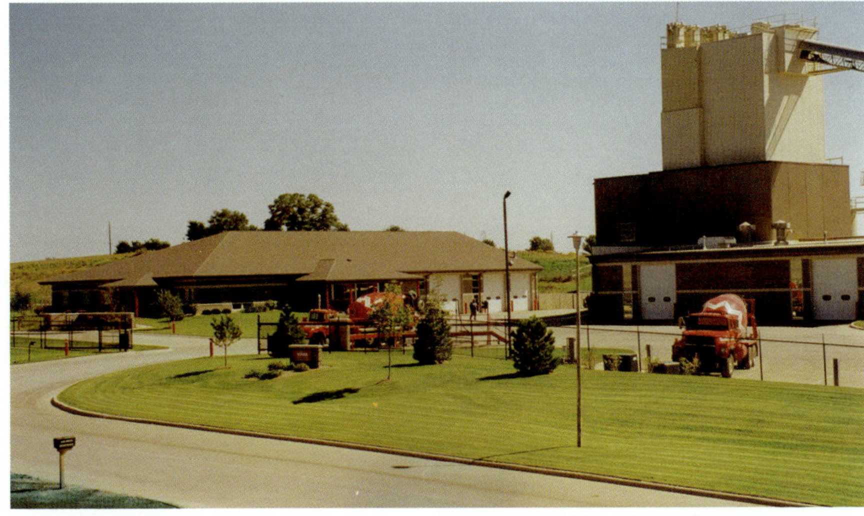

King's Material central mix concrete plant, in 1995, at 355 50th Ave. Dr. SW, Cedar Rapids.

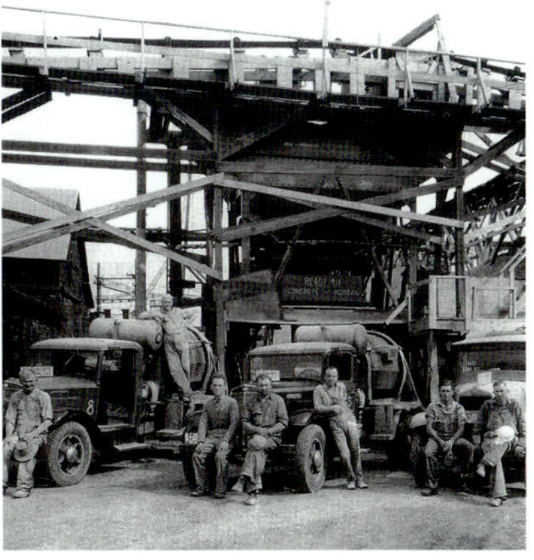

King's ready-mix plant in 1936.

Material for a King

With successful projects such as the award-winning staircase in the Cedar Rapids Public Library and the gigantic concrete dome over the ADM power terminal, King's is looking forward to providing the material for future projects.

Beyond poured, pumped and sprayed concrete, King's Material manufactures and sells architectural masonry, segmental concrete retaining walls, custom stone and sells over 1500 different types of brick. The company also sells concrete reinforcement, insulation, caulking, waterproofing products, and concrete and masonry tools.

The company's core will remain with permanent building material in the future.

Building trends are favoring the low maintenance material.

"People are again putting more brick and more stone in their houses, and commercial and industrial owners are using more permanent concrete paving," said Rohde. "I see this trend continuing."

The Gazette Family of Companies

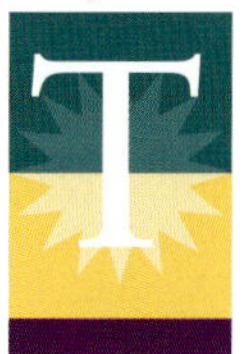

THE MISSION OF THE GAZETTE FAMILY OF COMPANIES IS LITTLE CHANGED FROM WHAT IT WAS MORE THAN A CENTURY AGO WHEN THE FIRST FOUR-PAGE NEWSPAPER WAS SOLD BY NEWSBOYS ON STREET CORNERS FOR 3 CENTS A COPY.

Simply put, President Joe Hladky says, it is to maintain the company's position as the information provider of choice for our market.

But, oh, how things have changed since that initial paper came out January 10, 1883. As head of the locally owned, independent company, Hladky says continual growth and diversity have allowed The Gazette Company to become a media force of the future.

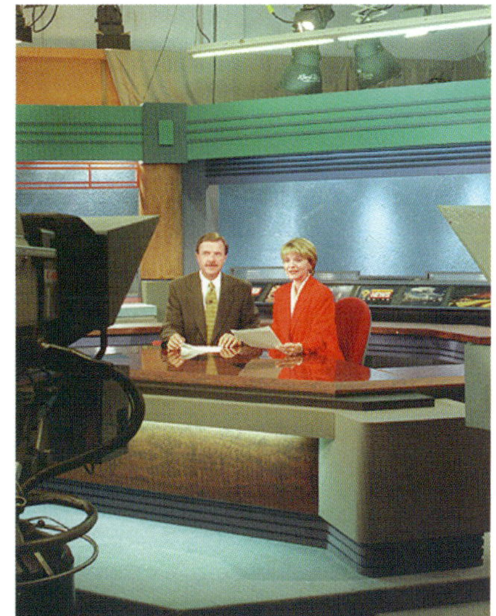

The company's flagship newspaper, *The Gazette,* now reaches 192,000 readers and 216,000 readers on Sundays throughout its 16-county circulation area. "That's a tremendous number of customers to satisfy," notes Dale Larson, vice president and general manager of The Gazette.

Producing and delivering 84,100 copies of The Gazette on Sunday (and 68,458 copies weekdays) is accomplished through the efforts of 361 full-time and 171 part-time employees, in addition to free-lance correspondents and nearly 1,000 independent distributors, carriers and drivers. In addition to publishing the second largest daily newspaper in the state of Iowa, The Gazette Company offers a wide range of other communications products.

Branching into new media

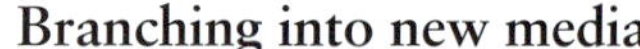

The company's first offshoot into a new medium for the traditional newspaper operation came in 1947 with the sign-on of KCRG-AM and KCRK-FM radio. A television station, KCRG-TV Channel 9, followed six years later.

The formation of *Iowa Farmer Today,* a weekly controlled-circulation newspaper sent to farm operators throughout the state, was a new venture started in 1984. Utilizing an expensive press that previously sat idle for much of the day proved so successful that a commercial printing division, Color Web Printers, Inc., was formed in 1987.

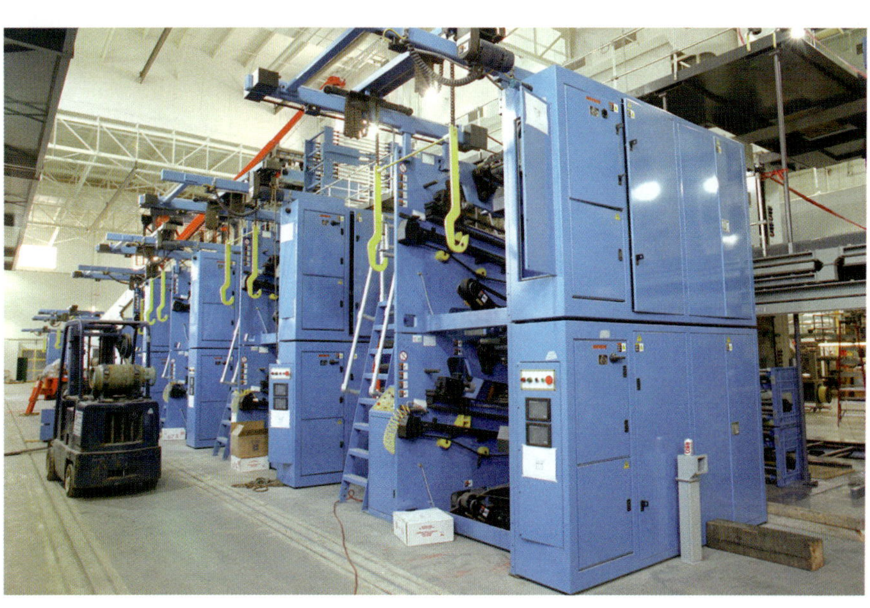

Above left: KCRG-TV9 anchors Bruce Aune and Liz Mathis.

Left: A state-of-the-art Universal 70 printing press installed at The Gazette Company's new facility in southwest Cedar Rapids.

The Gazette Family of Companies

In order to take advantage of yet another segment of the advertising market, The Gazette Company purchased the *Penny Saver,* a shopper based in Marion, in 1988. *The Advertiser* in Johnson County was purchased a year later.

In 1992, Gazette Direct Marketing Services was formed to produce market information and products for the company's subsidiaries and to provide direct marketing services to outside customers. The principle of adding value to existing assets led to the introduction of CITYLINE, a telephone-accessed information service, in 1987. Along with operating CITYLINE, Interactive Media, Inc., creates Internet web sites for Eastern Iowa customers and operates FYIowa.com and desmoines.com.

The next corporate move, buying control of Decisionmark Corp. in 1993, marks one more example of building on company strengths. Using customer databases already on hand, the new high-tech company develops a range of marketing and data analysis software for a number of industries.

In 1995, Gazette Technologies was formed to develop data warehousing software that would help The Gazette Company and other newspapers manage their internal databases.

Most recently, The Gazette Company purchased *The Iowan*, a 46-year-old, award-winning magazine featuring articles and high-quality color photographs of people and places from across the state.

Even though the company continues to evolve and add new media products, overall stability has always been a standard. In fact, several members of the company's board of directors are descendants of the two partners who started the business in 1883. In an effort to further secure the company's stability, an Employees Stock Ownership Plan (ESOP) was formed in 1986 to provide retirement benefits to employees. Hladky points out that the ESOP gives employees a stake in the company's growth performance.

New location, new opportunities

In the most massive undertaking in company history, all Gazette Company subsidiaries and operations will move to a new location in southwest Cedar Rapids over the next few years. When complete, the facility at 4700 Bowling Street SW will have nearly 900 employees from the different entities under one roof. Installation of a new press with extensive color capabilities and a high-tech packaging and finishing center are being completed.

Located on 42 acres just north of Highway 30, the new site will have 150,000 square feet of existing plant space for production purposes. Renovation and new construction will add approximately 150,000 square feet for the company's print, broadcast, marketing and software businesses.

"We're designing a media workplace of the future," Hladky points out. "We're approaching this as though we are starting from scratch." Through corporate-wide committees and meetings, employees have been given the opportunity to help develop the reinvented company.

Changing our location may change how we do things, Hladky says, but it won't change what we do. "By combining forces, we can do a much better job of being an information provider. That's how we'll remain a strong company in Cedar Rapids well into the future."

St. Luke's Hospital

Part of a system with a goal that no Iowan is more than 30 miles away from an affiliated healthcare provider, St. Luke's Hospital provides comprehensive care to people in the northeast quarter of the state.

A historically strong organization, St. Luke's Hospital is open to new approaches that maintain the high quality of healthcare, while making it both accessible and affordable.

"I Was Sick and You Visited Me"

On a night in 1882, a tramp who had been hopping a freight train fell and was badly injured. A blizzard howled.

Taken to the fire station, the dying man asked to speak to an Episcopal minister. Shortly after the Rev. Samuel Ringgold finished administering the sacraments, the man died.

Ringgold felt the man might not have died had there been an adequate care facility available.

The following Sunday he quoted Jesus on the need for humans to minister to each other. Cedar Rapids, as a Christian community, needed a real hospital so that people could be cared for, as Jesus had requested.

With the congregation singularly moved, a collection was taken for the building of a hospital. The response exceeded even the Reverend's hopes.

With donations of money and lots from the townspeople, the Rev. Ringgold's dream was realized on May 7, 1884. The cornerstone was laid for a hospital to be known as St. Luke's.

The first cornerstone for St. Luke's Hospital was laid on May 7, 1884, and the hospital began with 15 beds. St. Luke's has since become a regional center serving health needs of people throughout eastern Iowa.

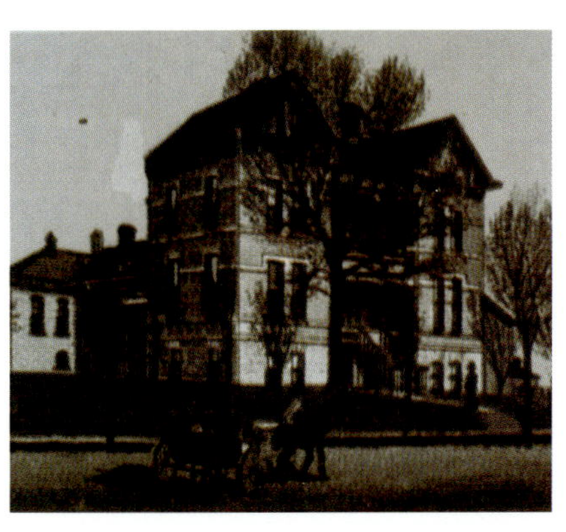

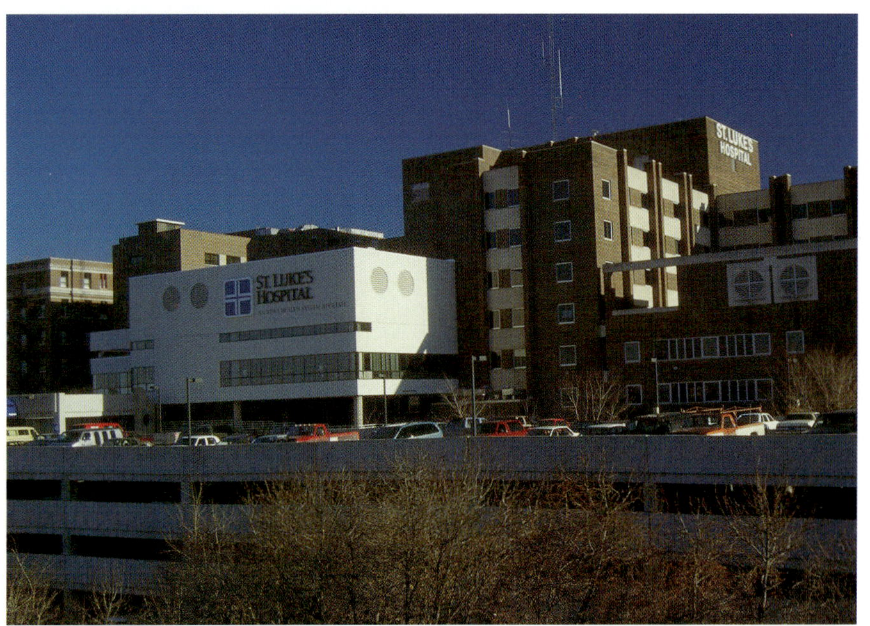

One of the Finest

Today, St. Luke's Hospital continues its tradition as one of the nation's finest hospitals.

A 560-bed healthcare facility, St. Luke's offers comprehensive health services to the people of northeast Iowa. The diverse services include cardiac care, emergency/trauma services, obstetrics, orthopedics, psychiatric/mental healthcare, rehabilitation, surgical services and wellness services.

Healthy Babies, Healthy Hearts

St. Luke's has been particularly innovative in obstetrics and cardiac care.

In 1973, St. Luke's joined a select group of Iowa hospitals and the state Department of Public Health to lay the foundation for a network providing advanced, regional care for premature babies born in Iowa. Following on this commitment, in 1977 St. Luke's opened the first advanced intensive care nursery in the Cedar Rapids area. Supported by local philanthropy, including funds from the Variety Club of Iowa, St. Luke's neonatal intensive care unit has preserved the lives of hundreds of tiny infants, some weighing little more than a pound. Still the most advanced NICU in the Cedar Rapids area, the St. Luke's nursery is an important part of an entire birth care center that focuses on family-centered and developmentally appropriate care. St. Luke's also has a renowned heart care center. In a 1996 report from Iowa's Health Management Information Center, St. Luke's was ranked as the best among Iowa hospitals for quality in cardiac bypass surgery and cardiac valve procedures. During the 20 years following the opening of the St. Luke's heart center in 1978, more than 7,000 cardiac procedures were performed. In partnership with area physicians, St. Luke's has continued to introduce to eastern Iowa advanced heart care procedures that have improved patients' lives, cut lengths of hospital stays and recovery time, and helped reduce costs.

Computers and You

At St. Luke's Hospital, the use of technology has grown to facilitate patient diagnosis, improve patient care and increase operational efficiencies.

Teleradiology, a system that digitizes and sends X-rays via telephone wires, was expanded to speed

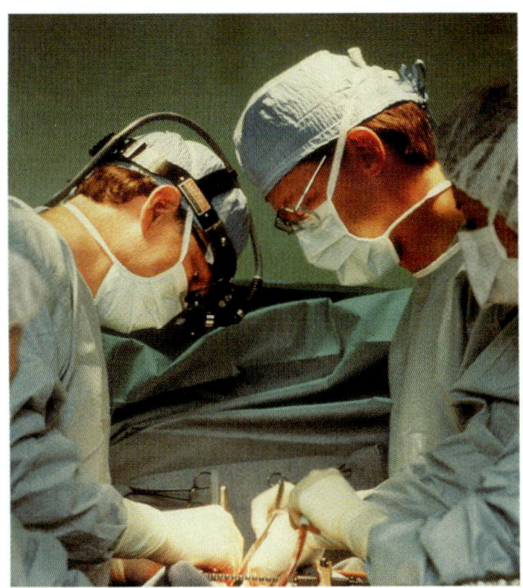

Early Cedar Rapidians boasted that "St. Luke's has the best-equipped operating room west of New York City." The hospital has continued to provide both advanced inpatient and outpatient surgery capabilities.

diagnosis of patients being cared for in the neonatal intensive care unit, coronary care unit, intensive care unit and radiology department.

Thanks to an automated perioperative documentation system that St. Luke's helped develop, nurses in all operating rooms log patient information on-line. This reduces duplication of information and enhances reporting capabilities.

The system is integrated into the Information System Enterprise, which links all Iowa Health System hospitals with a single, clinically-based information system.

Holistic Healing

St. Luke's Center for Health and Well Being is one of only two such centers in the Midwest offering hospital-based holistic services.

Complementing traditional medical treatment, therapy is administered by trained professionals, many of whom are registered nurses.

All the therapies offered at the center share the concept of life energy flowing through the body. When the flow of energy becomes blocked, an illness may result. Hatha yoga, reflexology, tai chi, massage therapy and meditation are some of the services that help restore energy balance. Patients gain an awareness of the inseparability of the body, the mind and the spirit.

The therapy can counter conditions such as chronic pain, insomnia, depression, anxiety, muscle contraction headaches and phobias.

A Health System for Iowans

In January 1995, St. Luke's Hospital helped pioneer the creation of the Iowa Health System, a community-based partnership with physicians, hospitals, civic leaders and local volunteers across the state. Affiliates of this innovative system have worked together to develop the state's most comprehensive integrated healthcare delivery network, designed to improve the health of all Iowans.

As a result of the system's community commitment and state-wide vision, St. Luke's and the other Iowa Health System affiliates are able to draw on a substantial pool of clinical, operational and financial resources to better offer Iowans access to sophisticated, effective healthcare services. St. Luke's and its Iowa Health System partners have proven that they are leaders in providing beneficial and patient-oriented change.

Penford Products Co.

As a full-line supplier of specialty carbohydrate-based products for the paper industry, Penford Products Co. is highly respected and recognized within the industry. Penford Products has a great advantage in the marketplace because it is able to offer a wide variety of well-tailored products and solutions.

As the paper industry's needs change in the future, Penford Products will develop new product technology to help its customers succeed in global competition.

Five Generations

In 1895, two brothers, George B. Douglas and Walter D. Douglas, amended the name of a linseed milling business they started in Cedar Rapids just one year earlier.

Changing the name from Iowa Mill and Elevator Co. to Douglas and Co., they began a legacy that would eventually become today's Penford Products.

By 1914, the brothers had sold their linseed milling interest and had become, instead, the largest independent starch works in the world.

Five years later, a major explosion leveled the facility and Penick & Ford Ltd. purchased what was left.

By 1921, Penick & Ford, the second generation of the company, began operating the reconstructed plant. In 1950, they developed and patented some highly modified starches known as the Penford Gum line.

Penick & Ford sold to the third generation, R.J. Reynolds, in 1965. R.J. Reynolds bought the company to use the starch in cigarette paper.

Because of a federal antitrust suit, they were forced to spin off to generation number four, VWR United Corp., which held the company from 1971 to 1984.

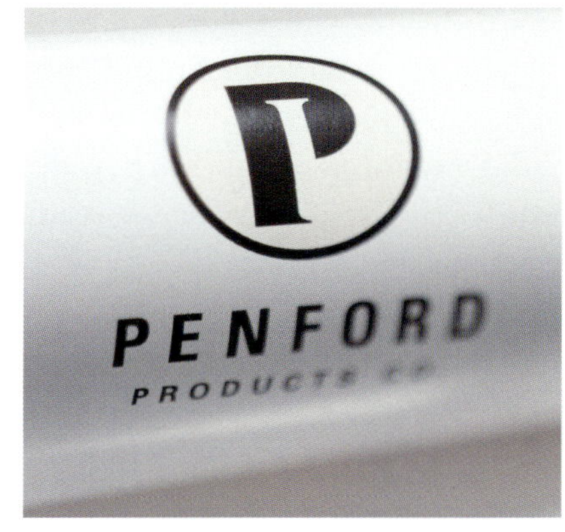

In 1984, the fifth generation spun off as a company known as Penford Products Co. with PENWEST as the parent company.

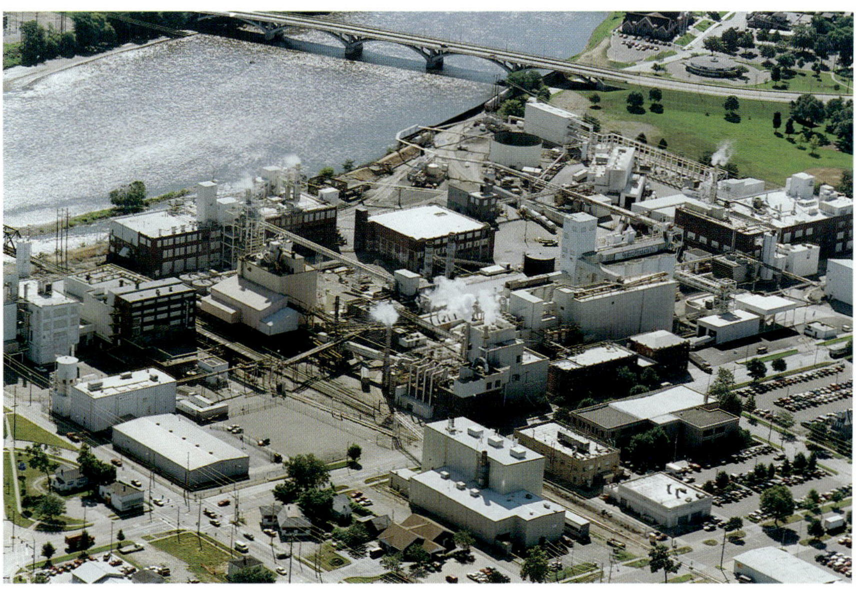

Penford Products' logo (upper right) replaced the familiar "mountain peak" symbol that was introduced in 1984. The company's 29-acre complex, (above), located along the Cedar River at 1001 First Street SW, grinds 65,000 bushels of corn each day.

Best Seller

Today the company is the Penford Corp. and it has two divisions, a food group and Penford Products.

Penford Products represents a majority of total Penford sales. Its success can be attributed to innovative technologies in carbohydrate-based chemistry for the paper and textile industries.

High-tech Starch

Special starches make papermakers' high-speed machines perform better. The starches act as binders and sizers within the papermaking process.

Penford Products has a long-term commitment to researching and developing solutions for the paper and textile industry.

With a fully computerized paper testing laboratory, Penford Products will continue to tailor value-added products to specific customer needs well into the future.

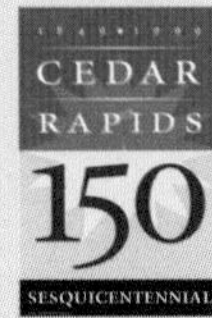

1900 1920

Mercy Medical Center – 1900

Brown Healey Stone & Sauer Architects – 1910

Broulik Painting, Inc. – 1913

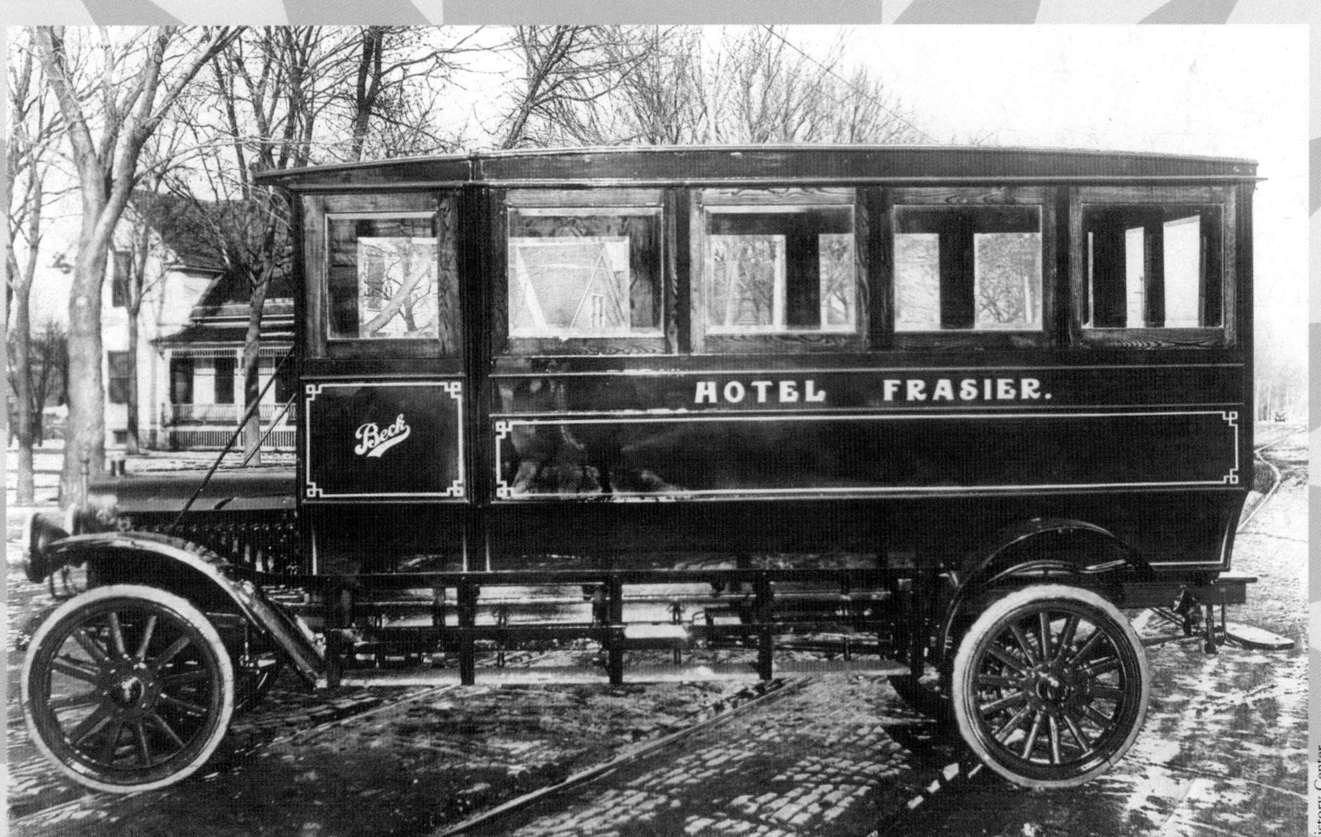

History Center

Motor coach for the Hotel Frasier, with body built by Beck Motor Works, Cedar Rapids, circa 1918.

Mercy Medical Center

THE MERCY TOUCH CONTINUES TODAY, NEARLY 100 YEARS SINCE THE FOUNDING OF MERCY MEDICAL CENTER. MERCY IS COMMITTED TO THE GOOD HEALTH AND COMPASSIONATE CARE OF THE PEOPLE IN EASTERN IOWA.

The first hospital building (below) was amazingly well-equipped for its day. It was here that The Mercy Touch began. The hospital featured private and general wards for men and women, a dining room and a surgery. Mercy Medical Center (far below) as it appears today.

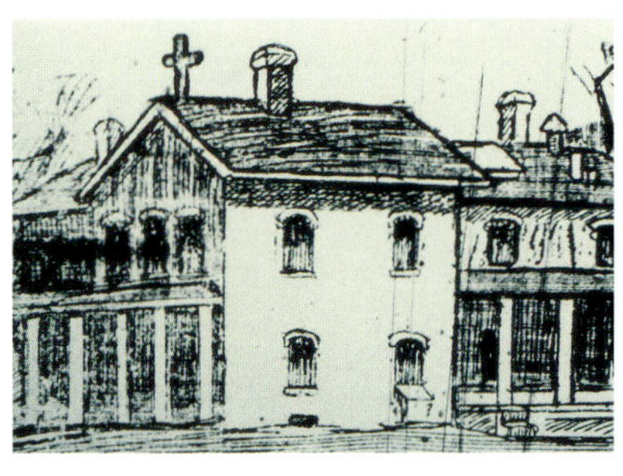

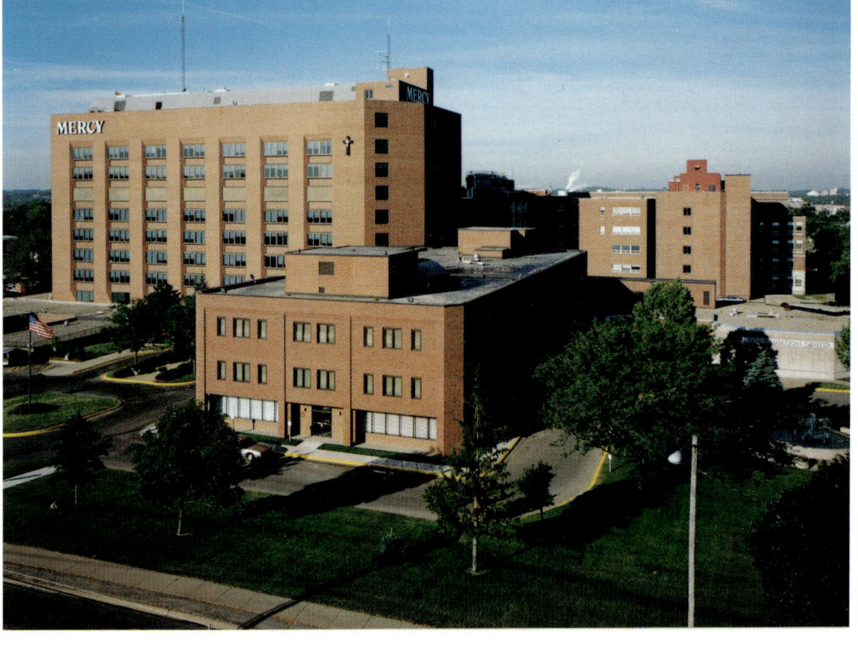

A Century of Caring

In 1899, after nearly 25 years in Cedar Rapids, the Sisters of Mercy began to plan the opening of a hospital. The hospital would continue in a more formal way their visitation of the sick, a characteristic work of the Sisters.

Six years earlier, they had purchased a lot and house. In 1899, they began transforming the house into a hospital.

On November 14, 1900, the healthcare organization later known as Mercy Medical Center, welcomed the people of Cedar Rapids to an open house.

Though technological advances this century would be almost unrecognizable to the founding Sisters, the legacy of bringing The Mercy Touch and the most advanced care available to the people of Cedar Rapids began that day.

The Dedication Continues

Mercy Medical Center is proud to continue its unique blend of technology, competence and compassion.

Mercy is a fully accredited not-for-profit healthcare organization that offers acute, residential and skilled nursing care. It also provides a variety of outreach and home-based services to residents of Eastern Iowa.

In addition to the main campus near downtown Cedar Rapids, Mercy has satellite clinics and physician offices throughout the area.

As a leader in the areas of greatest need, Mercy Medical Center has developed several distinguished Centers of Excellence: Mercy Cancer Center, Mercy Neuroscience Center, Mercy Orthopedic Services, the Sedlacek Treatment Center, Mercy Women's Center, the Birthplace and Special Care NICU.

The Mercy Touch

For nearly a century, Mercy Medical Center has been the place where The Mercy Touch comes to life every day.

The Mercy Touch is unique and takes many forms, including the staff of skilled professionals, working with the latest advances in medical technology. The Touch is the extra measure of understanding and genuine compassion the medical center provides, along with superb medical care. It is also the quick, lifesaving response of the specially trained trauma center physicians and staff members.

Mercy Cancer Center

Leading-edge diagnostic and treatment technology is used at Mercy's Cancer Center. It is affiliated with the Mayo Clinic's North Central Cancer Treatment Group.

As early as 1955, a feature of Mercy's Cancer Center has been the Hall Radiation Center. Originally funded by Howard and Margaret Hall, Mercy became the first cancer care center in Iowa and one of just six in the country equipped for cobalt therapy.

Since that time, Mercy has continued to maintain the most up-to-date technology for the treatment of cancer.

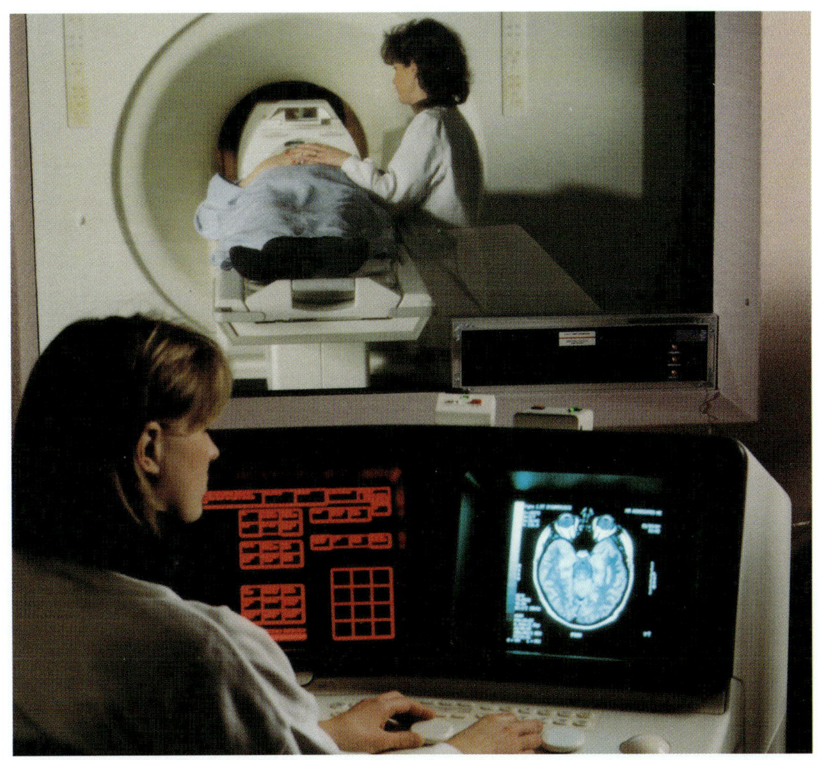

A Mercy Medical Center patient receives the diagnostic benefits of leading edge technology; Magnetic Resonance Imaging (MRI), a non-invasive procedure.

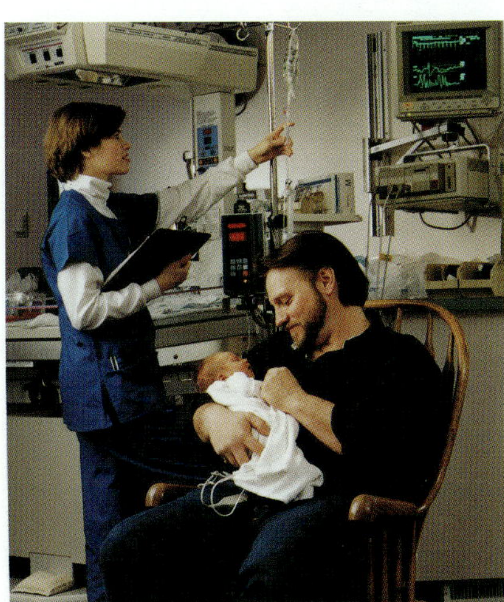

Expert care at the Level II Special Care Neonatal Intensive Care Unit, Mercy Medical Center, is provided by an interdisciplinary team which includes the newborn's family

In 1998, Mercy broke ground for a $4.9 million renovation and expansion to further improve and update the Hall Radiation Center.

The addition of a Varian 2100 computerized, digital, dual-energy linear accelerator will provide significant advances in radiation therapy for Eastern Iowa cancer patients.

Birthplace

Single-room maternity care is a Birthplace feature. Each homelike, relaxing room is fully equipped for labor, delivery and postpartum care. Every BirthSuite has a whirlpool bath for mother and sleeping arrangements for father.

Mercy was the first area hospital to offer a central fetal-monitoring system linked to physician offices. The system tracks and analyzes uterine activity and the baby's heart rate, alerting the staff to any changes.

Approximately one in 10 births need some form of special care. Mercy's Level II Special Care Neonatal Intensive Care Unit provides for new-borns with critical care needs. Located in the Birthplace, this nursery is staffed 24 hours a day with specially trained nurses.

Experience The Mercy Touch

Words and pictures can only suggest advanced technologies, dedicated staff and compassionate philosophy. To be truly understood, the Mercy Touch must be experienced.

Since 1900, thousands of Mercy patients have received personalized health services and medical care.

Today, more than 1,600 employees carry on the Mercy Medical Center tradition – offering patients and their families the highest quality of care.

Brown Healey Stone & Sauer Architects

BROWN HEALEY STONE & SAUER IS DEVELOPING A NATIONAL REPUTATION FOR EXCELLENCE. AS A GENERAL PRACTICE FIRM, THEY ARE KNOWN FOR INNOVATIVE DESIGN AND A HANDS-ON APPROACH IN TEAM BUILDING WITH EACH CLIENT.

Long known for distinction in the design of public and academic libraries, museums, theaters, and college and university projects, the architects, interior designers and planners work collaboratively to solve new and unique challenges.

New York Architect

William J. Brown came to Cedar Rapids from New York in 1910 to form an architectural practice with his brother. The partnership was short lived because the elder Brown died a year later.

Fond of Cedar Rapids and recognizing the potential for growth, William Brown stayed, practicing alone for 40 years and then taking on a partner, Ted Healey.

Achievements

The firm, known today as Brown Healey Stone & Sauer, has designed dozens of well-known buildings and homes in Cedar Rapids and surrounding communities.

Early projects include the Memorial Building (Cedar Rapids City Hall), the original Cedar Rapids Country Club, several elementary schools and three historically significant schools: McKinley Middle School, Franklin Middle School, and Roosevelt Middle School.

The firm continued to gain prominence with more recent accomplishments, including the Cedar Rapids Public Library, The Eastern Iowa Airport terminal building, the Marion Public Library, the State of Iowa Historical Building, the new History Center on First Avenue and the OSADA housing project as well as the majority of the buildings on the Kirkwood Community College campus.

Collaboration

Brown Healey Stone & Sauer, a multi-disciplinary firm, approaches projects in a comprehensive manner.

The stages of development include testing the capacity of a site with principles of good planning, producing building design to solve the programmatic requirements and finally, the interior implementation of a project with appropriate colors, textures, and surfaces.

The Brown Healey Stone & Sauer team believes that what defines them as a first class firm is their willingness to involve their clients in the design process itself. They listen carefully to their client's goals and work together fully on the development of the design concept. This approach involves the client in a collaborative dialogue to insure that their particular goals are fulfilled.

Designing the Future

Brown Healey Stone & Sauer's future is extremely bright. The company is well established and highly respected. At the same time, it employs several new, young architects who constantly keep the focus fresh.

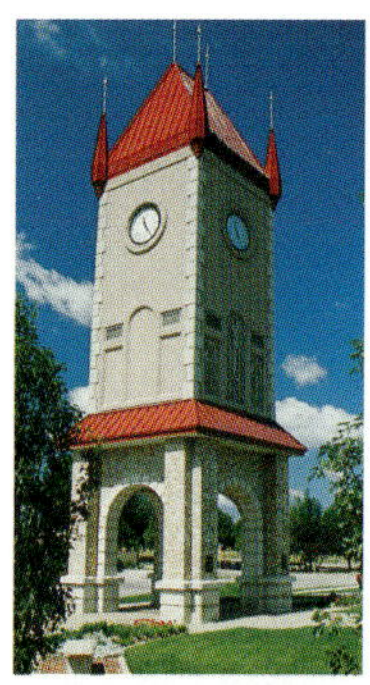

The Carillon Tower at the National Czech and Slovak Museum and Library

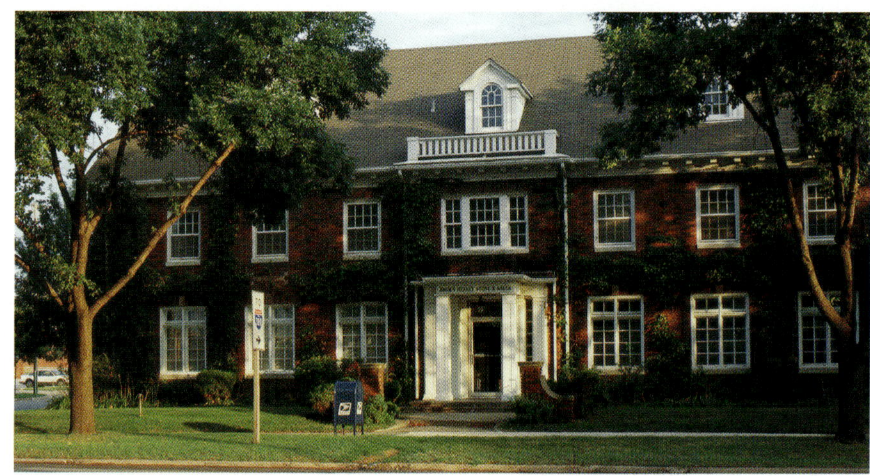

The firm's office is in a historical building that was originally built in 1908 as a funeral home.

Broulik Painting, Inc.

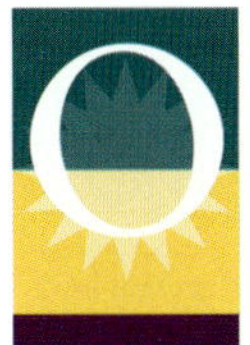

OVER HALF THE COMMERCIAL, INDUSTRIAL AND RETAIL BUILDINGS IN CEDAR RAPIDS ARE SPORTING COLORS APPLIED BY BROULIK PAINTING, INC. THE VARIETY OF CLIENTS PROVES THAT THE COMPANY CAN COMPLETE any project, including high structural painting.

Requests for Broulik Painting's quality workmanship come from as far as 100 miles away. However, the company acknowledges the community's patronage and plans to continue working mostly in Cedar Rapids.

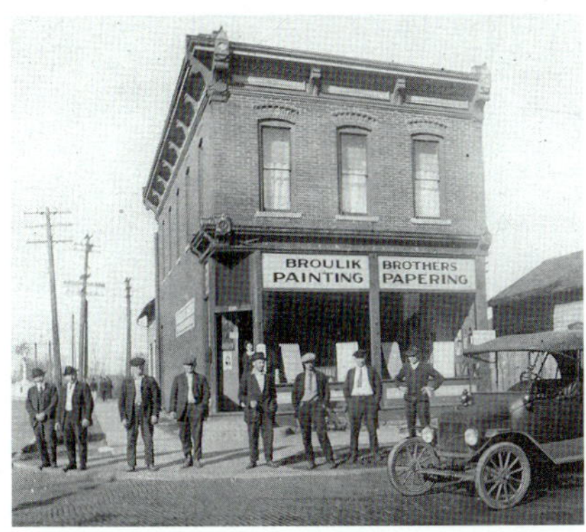

Forming a Legacy

Two brothers, William Broulik and Louis Broulik, formed a painting business in 1913. Before long, Broulik Bros. was one of Eastern Iowa's leading paint and wallpaper contractors.

When the business started, the ambitious Broulik brothers themselves and one man were the crew.

The adherence to dependable standards of workmanship resulted in the enjoyment of steady growth for Broulik Bros. They were employed on some of the area's largest painting jobs of the day.

Early interior and exterior projects included the Memorial building, Collins Radio, Killian's, St. Luke's hospital and the Dows building.

As Time Goes By

In the 1940s, William purchased Louis' share in the company. After 20 years, William turned the business over to his son, Don.

Don Broulik greatly expanded the commercial and industrial segments of the business. Clients ranged from Cargill to FMC Link-Belt. He ran the company until his death in 1979.

Bernie Erenberger, an employee since 1950, continued the business and is now the owner and manager of Broulik Painting Inc.

Recent Broulik accomplishments include the Eastern Iowa Airport, the Aegon buildings, Guaranty Bank building, the Ground Transportation Center, the Alliant Tower and Genencor.

Quality Continues

As ownership changed over the years, the high quality of work remained a constant.

Since its beginnings, Broulik Painting has employed union members of Painter's Local #447. From brushes 85 years ago to rollers and spray guns today, Broulik's crews have always been knowledgeable and professional.

All the workers go through a four-year apprenticeship program. They learn everything from safety to techniques of application.

Looking Ahead

The longevity of Broulik Painting can be attributed to the loyalty of community businesses.

The company plans to continue far into the future the exceptional quality of work to which area businesses have become accustomed.

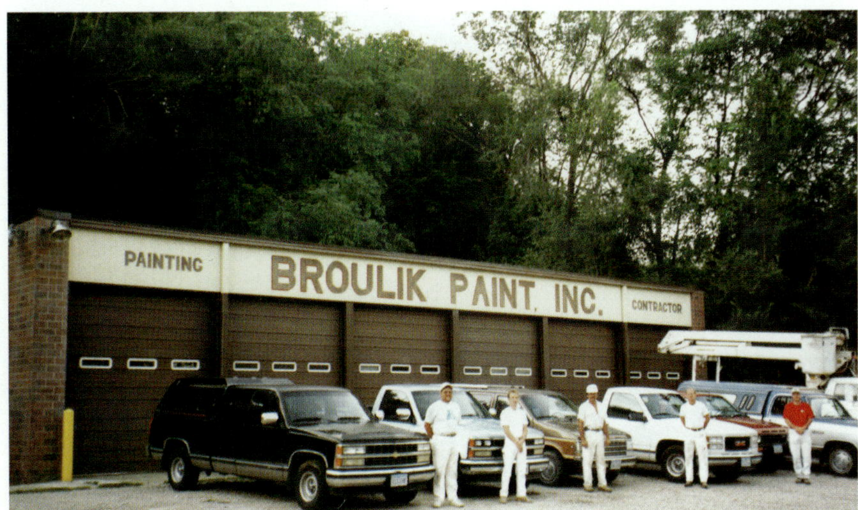

The building occupied by Broulik Painting, Inc. until 1967 (above left) was erected in 1896. The present building and crew are pictured above.

CEDAR RAPIDS 150 SESQUICENTENNIAL

1920 1940

Cedarapids, Inc. – 1923

Pioneer Office Products – 1924

Nesper Sign Advertising, Inc. – 1925

McGladrey & Pullen, LLP – 1926

Farmers State Bank – 1927

Mount Mercy College – 1928

Rockwell Collins – 1933

SCI Financial Group, Inc. – 1938

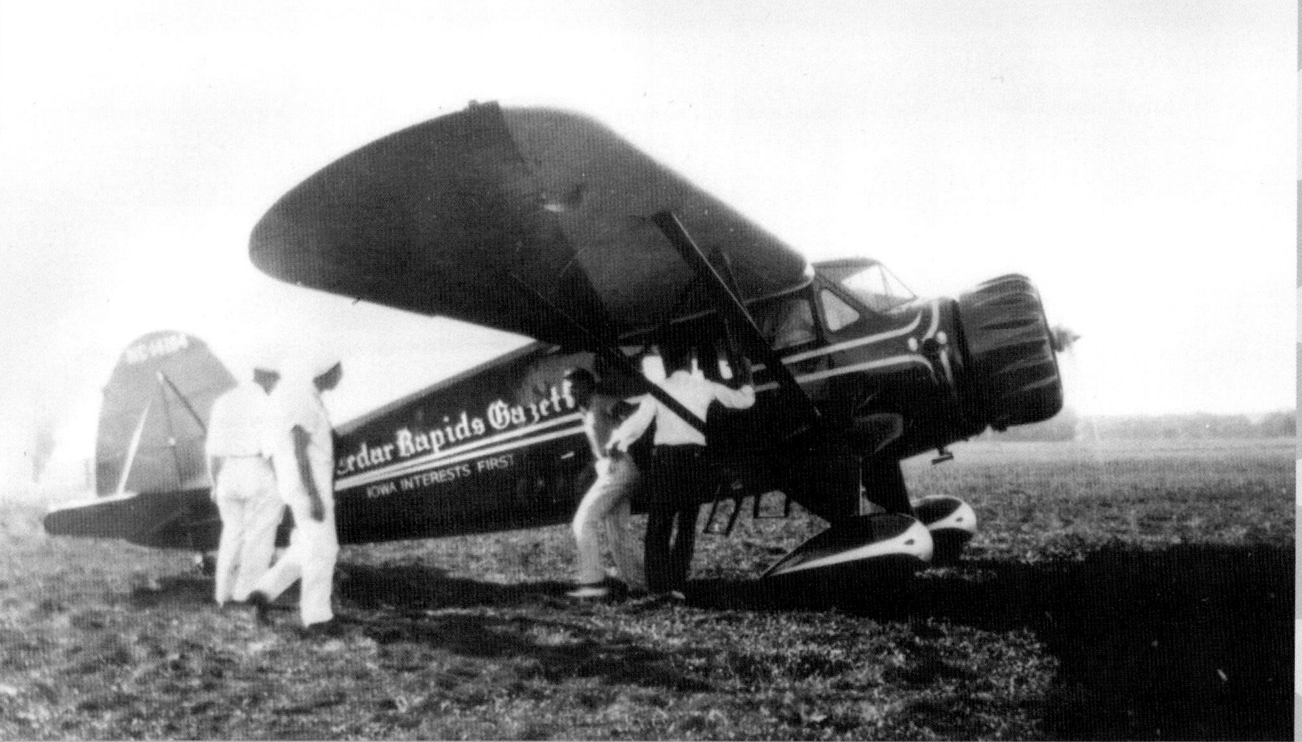

The Cedar Rapids Gazette Stinson Reliant Detroiter aircraft photographed at Hunter Airfield in Cedar Rapids in 1939.

Pioneer Office Products

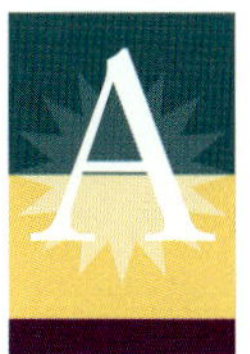

ALWAYS ANTICIPATING THE CHANGING NEEDS OF CLIENTS, PIONEER OFFICE PRODUCTS HAS A HISTORY OF INNOVATION. THE COMPANY HAS PROVIDED THE PROPER BUSINESS SETTINGS AND SUPPLIES TO LOCAL BUSINESSES FOR 75 YEARS.

With this experience, the company is looking forward to supplying the high-performance office of the future.

Absolutely Beeming

Dr. C.A. Beems spun off Pioneer Litho Co. from his Metropolitan Supply Co. in 1924.

Within a year, Erwin Wasta came to work at Pioneer Litho. Traveling the state, he took printing job orders from businesses and schools. In 1936, he purchased the company from Beems and eventually expanded it to include office furniture and supplies.

It has remained a family-owned business ever since.

Erwin's son, James, became president in 1966. Erwin's grandson, John, has been president since 1991.

While the Wasta name has been a constant over the years, business needs have not. Pioneer Office Products has the knowledge to provide expert business solutions, thanks to their history of innovation.

Pioneer Style

Rows and rows of desks all facing the same direction, known as the "open bullpen," had been the way to arrange a business.

The 1960s brought a great infusion of functionality. In 1963, Pioneer Office Products was the first company in eastern Iowa to hire a staff interior designer for the layout of office space.

The showroom area was arranged with small, idealized settings to mimic offices. Customers could pick from a variety of styles and colors. They could see, feel and understand the qualities of each product.

Today, the showroom space is almost gone. Yet, customers can still experience the work setting. The office space of Pioneer Office Products is now the showroom.

By using what they sell in a "working showroom," Pioneer staff members make it possible for customers to view the products in use and see how they function in a live, business setting.

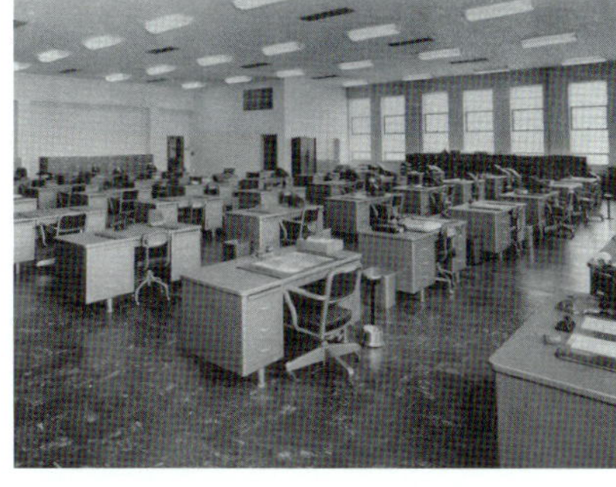

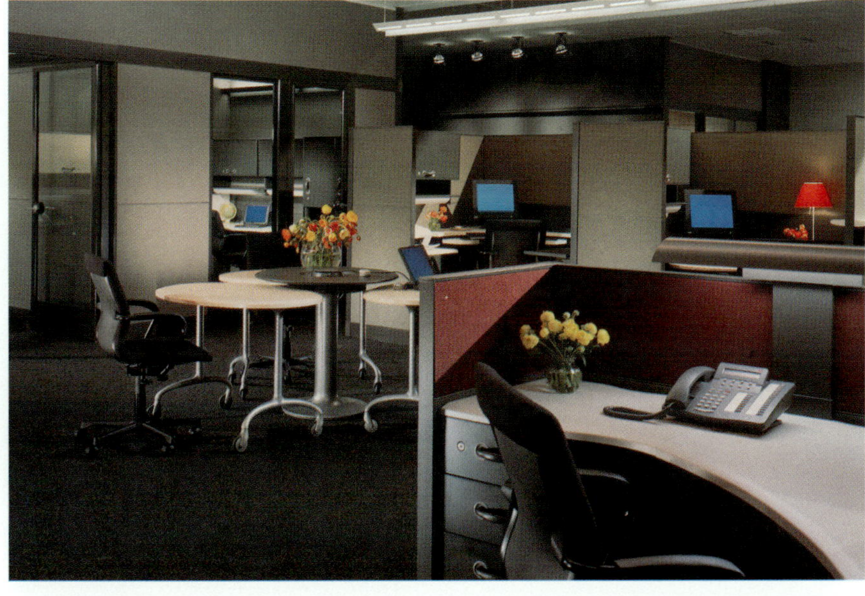

The open bullpen used to be the ideal office environment (above, right). Unifying interior architecture and furniture brings results in the futuristic Pathways product offering (above).

Office of the Future

In 1982, Pioneer Office Products began carrying Steelcase. Today, it is the company's main line.

Going way beyond filing cabinets, Steelcase will soon be providing the entire office area with an innovative product offering called Pathways.

Pathways brings together interior walls, ceilings, floors and furniture to form transportable, modular offices.

Businesses looking for this turnkey office environment solution will turn to Pioneer Office Products. Pioneer will provide the office of the future to Cedar Rapids.

Mount Mercy College

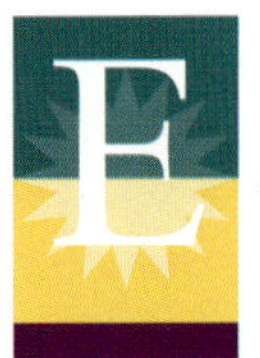

ESTABLISHED ON LINN COUNTY'S HIGHEST POINT 70 YEARS AGO, MOUNT MERCY COLLEGE PROVIDES STUDENTS WITH UNIQUE EDUCATIONAL PERSPECTIVES. THROUGH THE COLLEGE'S LIBERAL ARTS CURRICULUM, STUDENTS BROADEN their understanding of the world. Mount Mercy's emphasis on career preparation and service helps students gain a new outlook on learning and leading.

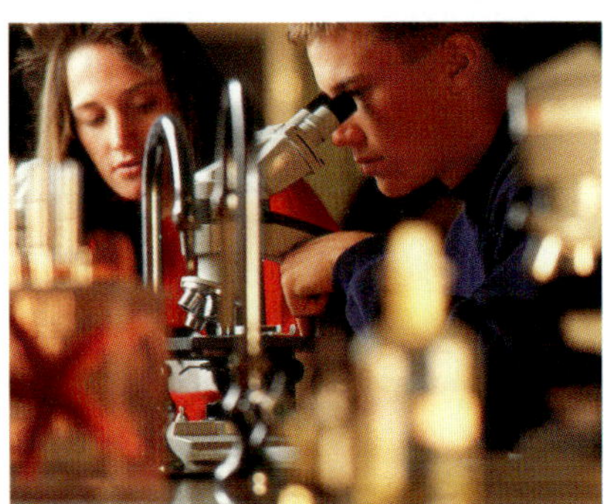

Mound Builders

In 1906, the Sisters of Mercy bought an abandoned rural mansion and land to establish Sacred Heart Academy, a Catholic boarding school for girls. It soon became overcrowded.

The Sisters built Mount Mercy Academy, (later known as Warde Hall) in 1924 as an all-girl high school.

Yet, the Sisters wanted a junior college to educate their own members. The two-year college would defray the costs of four years of teacher education at an outside college or university.

Sharing the building with the academy, a college was established.

With Sister Mary Ildephonse Holland as president, Mount Mercy Junior College opened in 1928.

Seventy years later, Mount Mercy College is an independent, four-year coeducational institution that welcomes all faiths. More than 30 majors are offered, including biology, business administration, computer science, criminal justice studies, education, mathematics, nursing, psychology and social work.

Learning Partners

The college's innovative Partnership Program is designed to help freshmen understand how all the components of their lives contribute to learning.

The program's general education courses are highly interactive, offering concentrated instruction in writing, speaking, reading and critical thinking.

Partnership makes learning a relevant part of everyday life for the students.

Future Leaders

Leadership is an ever-growing, ever-evolving process. Mount Mercy's Emerging Leaders program recognizes, values, nurtures and rewards future service and community leaders.

Students take part in the program's service opportunities and personal growth and development training.

Career Opportunities

Searching for internships or ready to start successful careers, students find at Mount Mercy's career development services a vast career library, job bulletins, career search assistance and a resumé referral program.

The college's nationally recognized professors have developed strong connections with professionals in the area, making them excellent resources as well.

Continuing to Enrich

Mount Mercy provides educational and cultural opportunities to the Cedar Rapids community.

The college offers evening and weekend courses for busy adults, including "Advance," an accelerated business degree program, offered in cooperation with Kirkwood Community College.

Mount Mercy provides resources such as the Busse Library, intercollegiate athletic events in the Hennessey Recreation Center, and a full calendar of art exhibits, readings, lectures and concerts.

Mount Mercy College continues to enrich the life of the community.

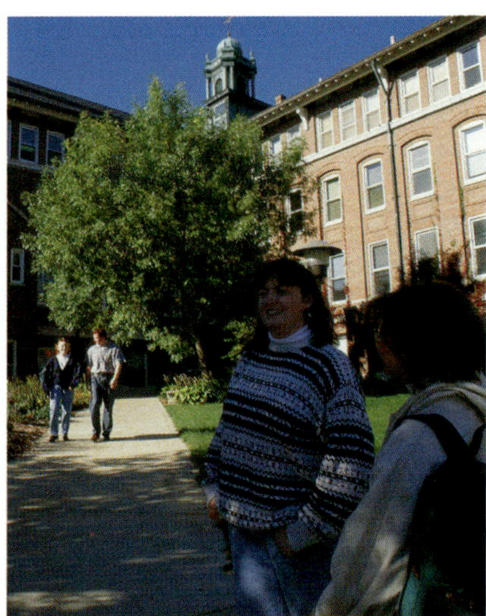

Students have excellent opportunities for learning and leading at Mount Mercy College (above left). The beautiful campus creates an ideal atmosphere for growth. Above, students converse outside Warde Hall.

McGladrey & Pullen, LLP

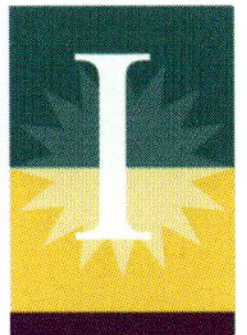

IOWA GROWN AND IOWA RAISED, MCGLADREY & PULLEN, LLP IS ONE OF THE NATION'S LARGEST ACCOUNTING AND CONSULTING FIRMS. MCGLADREY & PULLEN'S KEY TO HELPING CLIENTS SUCCEED IS ITS COMMITMENT TO provide a broad range of value-added management consulting services, in addition to traditional accounting, audit and tax services.

Simple Success Formula

"The key to our success is our ability to draw upon our best resources and to acquire those we don't have, so that we can continue to meet and exceed those needs," stated Larry Bildstein, executive partner-office of national marketing located in Cedar Rapids. "If they succeed, we succeed. It's that simple."

One of the firm's key business strategies is to focus on increasing its expertise in key industry and functional areas. Industry specialty areas include manufacturing, wholesale distribution, and financial institutions. Functional specialty areas include tax, audit, and consulting services, which include human resources, information technology, business and strategic planning, operations and marketing.

"Our professionals have the ability to meet a wide range of client needs, most of which can be handled by our local offices," explained Dean Price, partner-in-charge. "But we have also developed national resources, placing people in key specialty areas. These individuals are available to assist local offices and clients as needed."

Bildstein also emphasized M&P's size advantage in Iowa, noting that of the firm's nearly 3,000 partners and employees, more than 700 are in Iowa. The firm's devotion to its Iowa client base is also evident by the number of offices located within the state. Nationwide, the firm has 63 offices in 16 states. Of these, eight are in Iowa: Burlington, Cedar Rapids, Davenport, Des Moines, Dubuque, Iowa City, Mason City, and Waterloo.

As a result, M&P understands its Midwestern clients. While its client roster is as diverse as Iowa's economy, the firm focuses its efforts on serving owner-managed and closely held businesses. McGladrey & Pullen is committed to helping Iowa businesses grow.

Cedar Rapids partner Ken DeKock (left) discusses a proposal with one of McGladrey & Pullen's many Iowa-based clients.

Partners for the Future

M&P is also helping Iowa business by partnering with the state's colleges and universities to develop beneficial business education programs. The firm worked with the University of Iowa to start the I.B. McGladrey Institute in 1980. The Institute continues to enhance the University's Department of Accounting's research and educational programs.

M&P also partners with Iowa State University and the Iowa Small Business Development Center to sponsor a conference, "Shaping The Future." Now in its seventh year, the conference teaches strategic planning skills to CEOs of small and medium sized companies who work closely with a mentor from M&P to experience the process and value of strategic planning.

Contributions from M&P and the University of Northern Iowa alumni provide support for the McGladrey & Pullen Center for Accounting Education at UNI, which helps the Department of Accounting maintain and strengthen its efforts to provide excellence in accounting education.

Reaching Out

Beyond Iowa's borders, the firm is meeting today's global economic needs. Through the firm's affiliation with RSM International, M&P offices are linked with nearly 400 offices in more than 75 countries worldwide.

Partner-in-charge, Dean Price, commented, "I read that a proactive accountant brings one or two ideas a year into a client meeting, something that will improve that bottom line or the client's competitive position. I think that's what our firm does better than our competition."

Cedarapids, Inc.

IN THE CONSTRUCTION EQUIPMENT INDUSTRY, THE TRADE NAME "CEDARAPIDS" IS SYNONYMOUS WITH DEPENDABLE, QUALITY PRODUCTS. TO THE PEOPLE WHO MAKE THESE PRODUCTS, IT SYMBOLIZES PRIDE IN WORKMANSHIP AND generations of excellence. The company founded as Iowa Manufacturing Co. shares a heritage of proud tradition with the city of its birth.

In 1985, in honor of the high reputation the trade name had come to represent, the company officially became Cedarapids, Inc.

Today, Cedarapids continues its pioneering lead, offering its customers a wide array of technologically advanced products.

The One Piece Outfit of the 1920s (top), and the state-of-the-art portable plant of the 1990s (middle). The main building of Cedarapids Inc. (bottom).

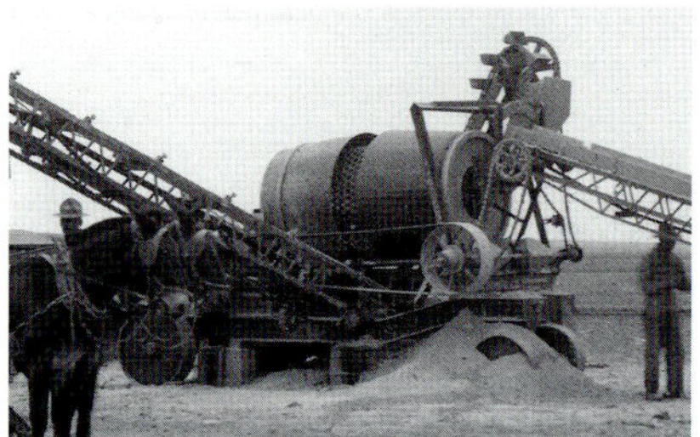

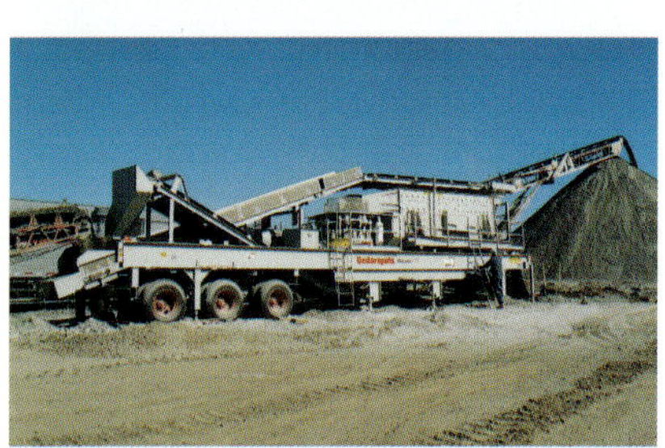

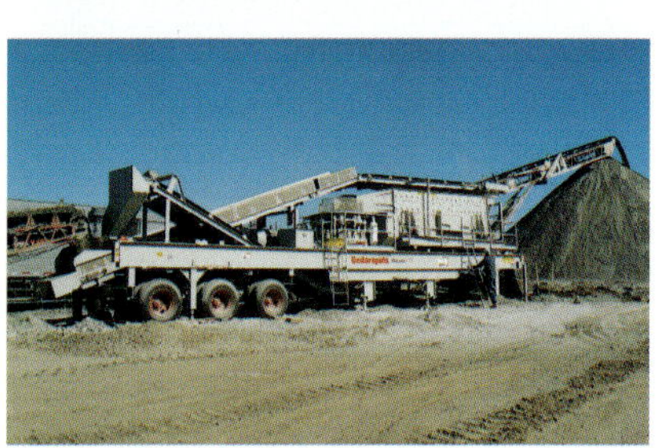

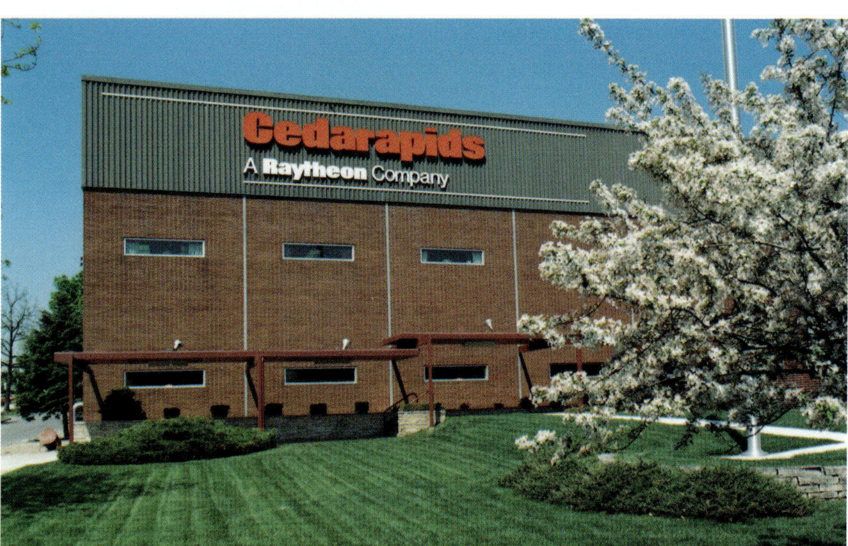

Muddy Roads

The automobile began its sensational climb as the preferred method of transportation over the horse and buggy in the early 1920s.

"Vote for good roads!" was a rallying cry across the nation. Getting the infrastructure "out of the mud" was a major objective of the government and the people.

Howard Hall, the Cedar Rapids industrialist, recognized the great business opportunities behind the good roads rhetoric. In 1923, he purchased the Bertschey Engineering Co. machine shop. He renamed it Iowa Manufacturing Co. of Cedar Rapids, Iowa, and opened its doors as manufacturers of crushing, screening and conveying machinery.

Crushers: Then and Now

Good roads could not be built without crushed stone (aggregate), and the demand for it was skyrocketing.

Aggregate production in the early 1920s was an inefficient process requiring many separate pieces of equipment. Moving the equipment to the raw material site was both costly and labor intensive.

This dilemma gave birth to an idea that was to revolutionize the road-building industry: build an easily transportable machine that receives unprocessed stone at one end, reduces it in size, and produces ready-to-use material at the other.

A team of engineers, led by company co-founder Guy Frazee, transformed this concept into the first truly portable aggregate plant, the "One Piece Outfit." It was easily moved between job sites and it shaved production costs to mere pennies per ton.

During World War II, the company

had the distinction of providing 80 percent of the U.S. military's crushing equipment needs. The 1700 plants built were used in every theater of the war, spreading the name Cedarapids throughout the world.

After the war, the company expanded its product offering to capitalize on increased demand and emerging markets. New Holland Equipment, purchased in 1950, added impact-type crushers. Twenty-six years later, ElJay Inc. was acquired for its world-renowned Rollercone cone crushers and associated equipment. Cedarapids' crushing and screening equipment line thus became the broadest offered in the industry.

Hot Mix Asphalt Plants

As the definition of better roads evolved from simple crushed stone surfaces to all-weather hard surfaces, Cedarapids kept pace. In 1929, the company introduced one of the very first hot mix asphalt plants.

Sixty years later, Standard Havens, a Missouri-based manufacturer of high-tech, counterflow, hot mix asphalt plants, was acquired to expand the product line.

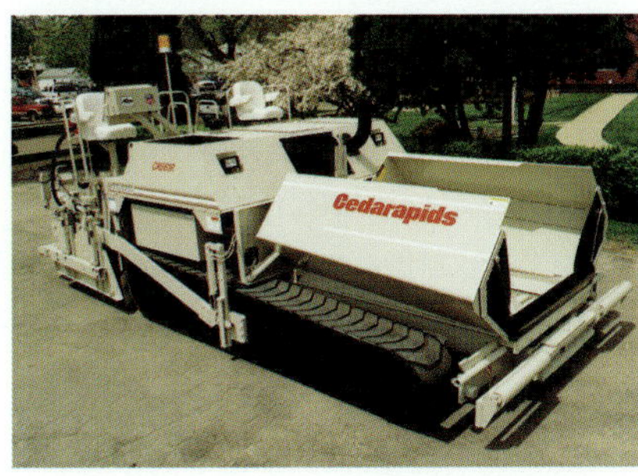

Remix and rubber track pavers were added in the 1990s to the existing line of rubber tire and steel track models.

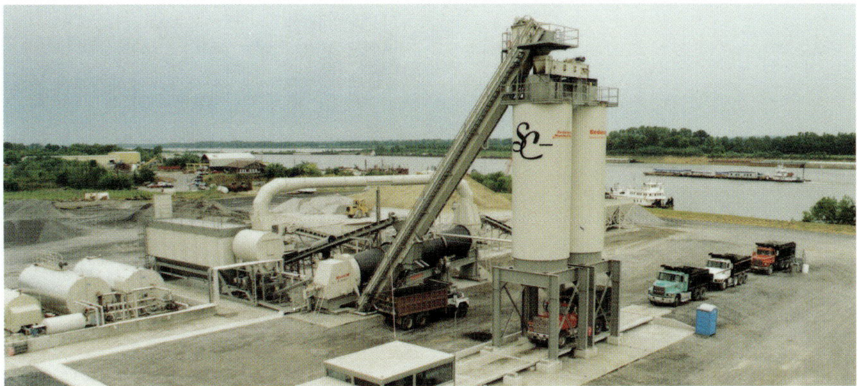

Environmentally sensitive counterflow plants meet today's emission control standards. They are part of a complete line of portable and stationary plants that give Cedarapids customers the most advanced asphalt mixing equipment available.

Hot Mix Asphalt Pavers

After World War II, the nation's attention returned to infrastructure expansion. Post-war prosperity brought a demand for more and better roads.

Cedarapids embraced the challenge. In 1956, it unveiled its first asphalt paver line, equipped with another first: the vibrating screed. The device substantially boosted both paving speed and volume over competitive models.

Less than 30 years later, the line was redesigned and renamed. The Grayhound paver ushered in a new era of innovative engineering and sleek appearance.

New Opportunities

Following the death of Howard Hall in 1971, Cedarapids became a subsidiary of Raytheon Company, a diversified, international, technology-based company.

Raytheon's vast resources and commitment to excellence have played a major role in Cedarapids' continued achievements in the construction equipment industry.

As the century draws to a close, Cedarapids crushing, screening, asphalt mixing and asphalt paving equipment is hard at work in almost every country in the world. Contractors can obtain equipment, parts and service through a worldwide network of distributors.

Road to Success

Each year the United States alone produces two billion tons of aggregate. Over 90 percent of the nation's highways are paved with asphalt.

Cedarapids' growth from a 12,000 square foot building in 1923 to over a million square feet under roof today, is a reflection of the world's ever-increasing demand for these materials.

Cedarapids, Inc. is proud of its pioneering role in the industry. From the One Piece Outfit that pulled our nation "out of the mud," to the revolutionary technology just over the horizon, Cedarapids is helping to build a better world.

Rockwell Collins

The list of Collins achievements reads like a history of electronics: radio telephony in the Antarctic with Byrd, automatic radio tuners for war pilots, and Armstrong's message from the moon.

Today, virtually all commercial air carriers worldwide fly with Collins avionics. And, Rockwell Collins is the leading producer of military communications systems for both airborne and ground-based communications.

The assembly area as it appeared in 1934 (below). The Collins hangar with a Twin Beech 18 in 1946 (far below).

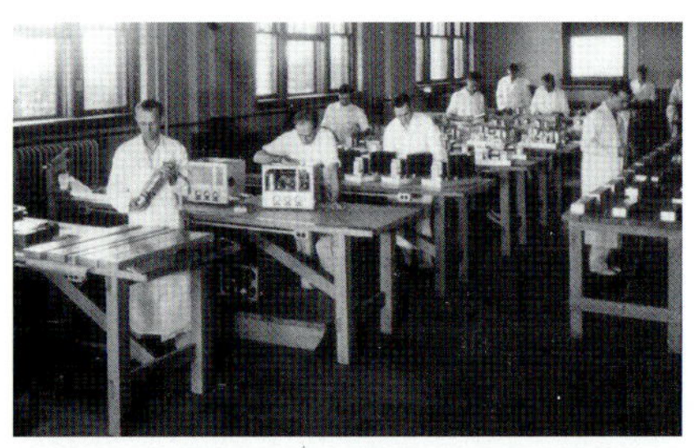

136

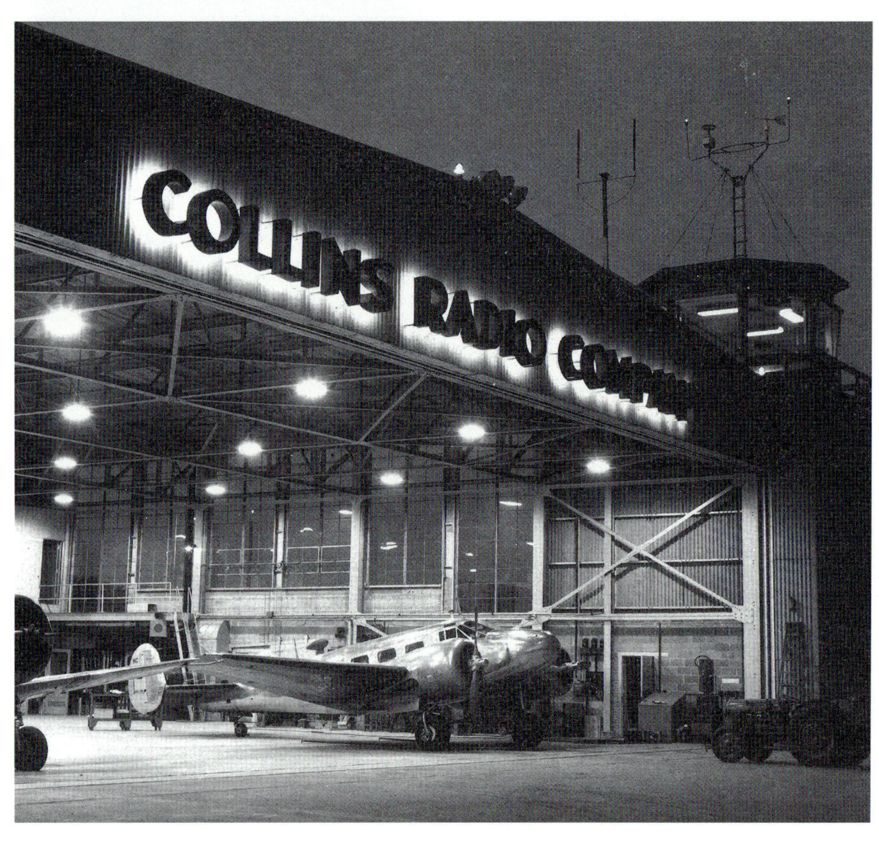

Home Office

In the basement of his Cedar Rapids home, 21-year-old Arthur Collins set up shop. Three years later, in 1933, Collins Radio Company became a corporation with eight employees and $29,000 in capital.

The company steadily grew, and captured the world's attention when Collins supplied the equipment to establish a communications link with the South Pole expedition of Rear Admiral Richard Byrd.

"It was a costly gamble for everyone if it failed," Byrd later wrote, "for involved was a 10,000-mile radio telephony circuit. The performance of the transmitter left little to be desired."

War Years

After the attack on Pearl Harbor, the main plant between 32nd and 35th streets in Cedar Rapids began to burst at the seams. With 3,332 workers, Collins Radio played an important role in World War II by supplying air-to-ground communication units credited with literally saving the lives of American pilots during the war.

Fabulous Fifties

The 1950s marked spectacular growth for Collins Radio. Avionics, a combination of "aviation" and "electronics," became the largest business segment, responding to demand for lightweight communication/navigation packages for use in aircraft.

Space Age

From the X-15 experimental rocket plane to the Apollo 11's landing on the moon, the company played a major role in the communications systems

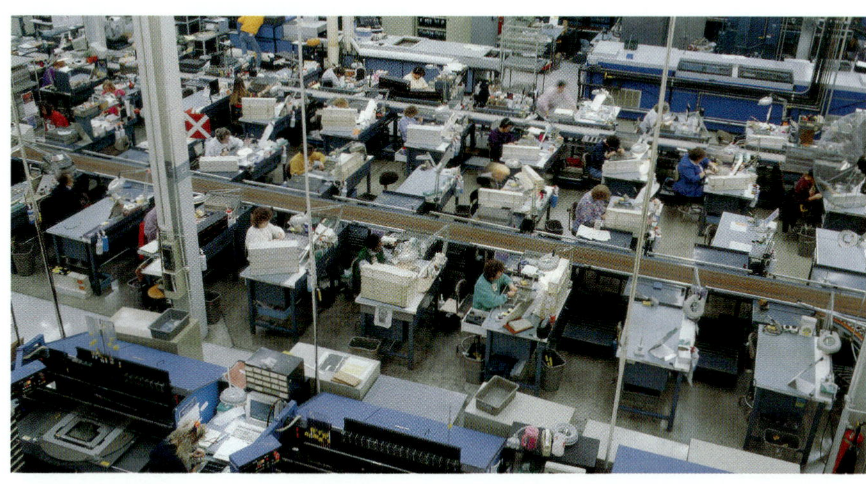

The modern manufacturing area at the "C" Avenue facility where employees do final assembly on Rockwell Collins products.

of Gemini, Mercury and Apollo.

Collins employees designed, developed and manufactured the communications equipment for the famous "giant leap for mankind" lunar landing. In fact, the voice of every American astronaut traveling through space at that time had been transmitted via Collins equipment.

Collins Rocks On

The latter half of the 1960s proved to be rough for defense contractors, with Collins being no exception. In 1969, the company repelled a hostile takeover by Texas businessman H. Ross Perot.

A later offer by North American Rockwell was accepted in 1971. The agreement of Willard Rockwell, Jr. and Arthur Collins resulted in a dramatic turnaround for the company, which was later merged into Rockwell and renamed Rockwell Collins in 1973.

More than 25 years later, Rockwell Collins has about 13,000 employees worldwide and 9,000 of them are in Iowa. With nearly 2,500 scientists and engineers, it is easily the largest technical work force in the state.

Flying Right

Rockwell Collins has now evolved from providing avionics components to offering total avionics systems. Completely integrated capabilities give both civil and military customers total solutions.

Data-intensive operations no longer begin and end in the cockpit. The company is now integrating the cockpit with the passenger cabin through in-flight entertainment and information systems for both commercial and business aircraft.

The Rockwell Collins Passenger Systems include newly emerging video-on-demand systems such as digital video/audio, direct broadcast satellite television and fax/phone connections.

Rockwell Collins is also exploring the potential of "synthetic vision" technologies. They show promise of allowing pilots to visualize not only their current situation relative to other aircraft, terrain and weather, but also their eventual situation based on the flight plan and aircraft performance.

The next century of flight presents significant opportunities and challenges for improving flight operations, efficiency and safety through developments in aviation electronics.

Rockwell Collins is addressing those challenges by creating the most trusted source of communication and aviation electronic solutions.

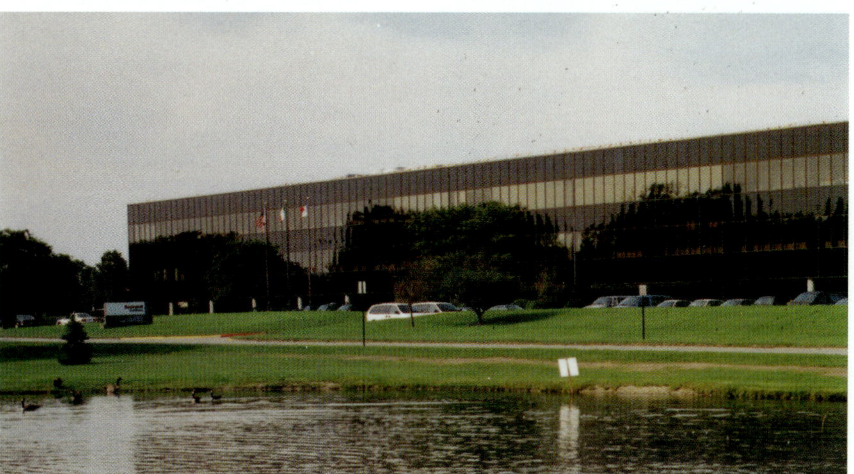

Rockwell Collins world headquarters building located in Northeast Cedar Rapids.

Farmers State Bank

LINN COUNTY'S LARGEST LOCALLY OWNED, INDEPENDENT BANK IS FARMERS STATE BANK. WITH OVER $275 MILLION IN ASSETS, IT IS TRULY A COMMUNITY BANK AS EVIDENCED BY ITS ONGOING COMMITMENT TO THE AREA IT SERVES.

Originally touted as "the bank built by its friends," FSB's mission has not changed much in the past 70 years. Today, the bank's slogan perfectly fits a community bank ... "You've got a good bank here at home."

Bank Beginnings

In 1927, a group of six prominent farmers and a local businessman rescued the failed Alburnett Savings Bank. With a mere $25,000 in capital, the bank was reorganized as the Alburnett State Bank after a charter was applied for and received from the Iowa Banking Department.

In 1945, the bank moved its charter to Marion and was renamed Farmers State Bank. With the relocation, the Alburnett office became FSB's first branch facility.

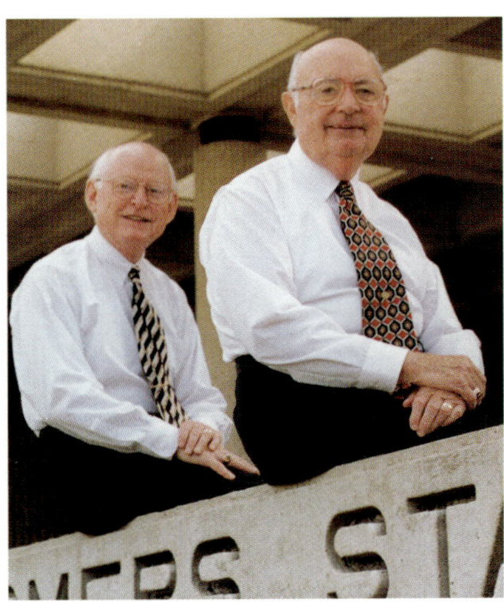

Clair Lensing, bank president, and Morris Neighbor, chairman of the board, in 1997.

Business, industry and employment in the Cedar Rapids area expanded during the postwar years. The local economy enjoyed extraordinary growth.

Farmers State Bank shared in that growth by expanding its products and services to meet the demands of new business endeavors, residential development and home buying needs.

During the past seven decades, FSB's assets have grown from essentially zero to more than a quarter-billion dollars.

"I attribute this significant growth to our loyal customers and our personalized service," said Clair Lensing, president and CEO of FSB. "We focus on change—particularly in technology. But, we have never lost sight of personal service. That's key in our industry."

Committed to the Future

FSB's success can be attributed to its strategic mission of providing what it refers to as the "best of both worlds."

By combining leading edge technology and good, old-fashioned service, FSB offers a variety of innovative banking options to meet the needs of today's consumers including computer banking, telephone banking, corporate cash management and investment services.

In addition to its six conveniently located offices at Collins Road Square, Lindale Mall, Edgewood Plaza Mall, Marion, Hiawatha and Alburnett, FSB owns or operates over 50 ATMs in Linn County.

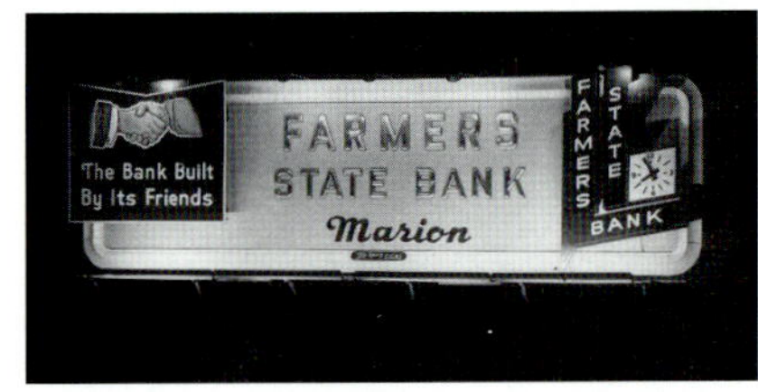

The Farmers State Bank billboard of the late 1940s still rings true today.

Technology helps the bank to operate faster, smarter and better. In fact, FSB was the first bank in Iowa to offer PC-based home banking, which allows customers to access their accounts via a modem.

Yet, it is the friendly, efficient, face-to-face interaction that helps create loyal customers who truly appreciate the old-fashioned, individualized service.

FSB and the Community

In the midst of all the advances of modern banking, Farmers State Bank continues its unequaled commitment to its customers and the community, thanks to the dedication of bank employees whose average length of employment exceeds eight years.

After more than 50 years in the banking business, chairman Morris Neighbor sums it up like this: "Our employees are our greatest asset. In fact, we think of ourselves as the FSB family. So many of our employees have contributed so much. They truly are the cornerstone of our success."

Nesper Sign Advertising, Inc.

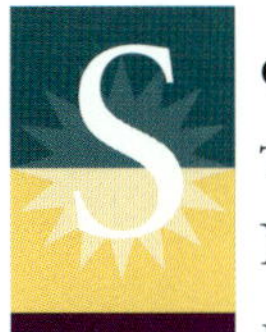

Scanning the Cedar Rapids skyline is like breezing through Nesper Sign Advertising, Inc.'s portfolio. Nearly every landmark sign is a Nesper product—proving that Nesper signs are the most direct and cost-effective method to reach consumers. Creating a niche in corporate signage, recent developments include the opening of two branches in Iowa and record financial growth.

Signing In

Established in 1925, Nesper Sign Advertising, Inc. has been a premier full service company. Over the years, integrity, craftsmanship and imagination have made its professional staff well-known.

Because its reputation is unsurpassed, many of Nesper's customers have been clients for over 50 years. Nesper signs are unlike other forms of advertising. Standing the test of time, their signs promote goods, services or images continually for years and years.

Beyond Brushes

Many employees at Nesper have been working there for more than 30 years. They bring a lifetime of experience and technical knowledge to each project. The combination of quality workmanship and innovative equipment positions Nesper as the dominant manufacturer of on-site signage.

The production facilities have evolved from a person with a paintbrush, hammer and welder to the most sophisticated CAD equipment available in the industry. All the fabrication equipment is electronically based. Today, the physical labor of a sign project requires much higher training.

In business to build business, Nesper's goal is to blend the newest technologies and most creative designs into the most effective image for their client.

Taking Care of Business

In 1990, two long-time Nesper employees, Phil Garland and Larry Sovern, purchased the company. Ever since, the growth of the business has been nothing less than phenomenal.

Nesper has grown from a local sign company to a national sign supplier. It now has a branch in Burlington and the future may see Nesper with other branches throughout Iowa as it becomes a regional company.

A recent study by the Institute of Signage Research in Palo Alto, California, listed Nesper as one of the top 100 sign companies in the nation. That rating is largely due to Nesper's focus on the future, as well as its dedication to providing full service to its clients.

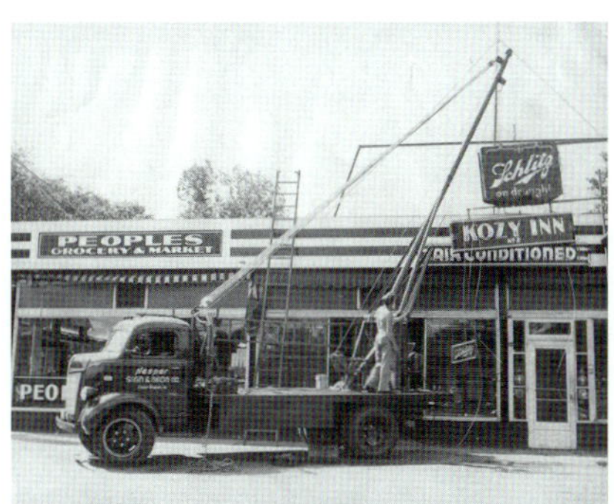

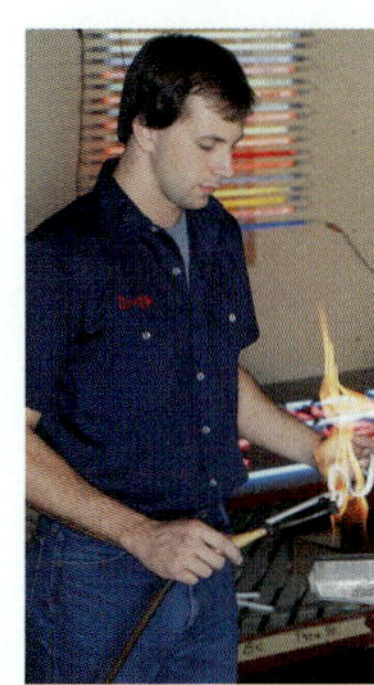

From yesterday (left) to today (right), neon-lighted signs have always been part of Nesper Sign Advertising, Inc.'s work. Nesper's famous electronic sign (below) welcomes travelers.

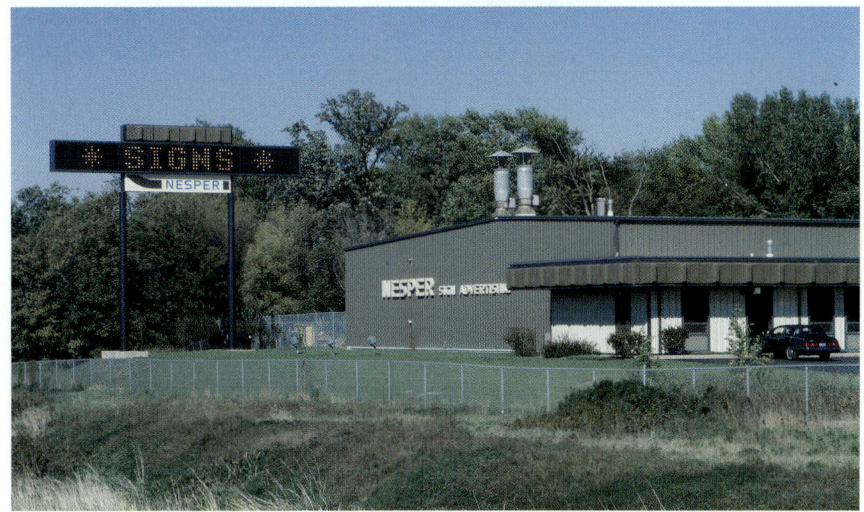

Guaranty Bank & Trust Co.

As "the local good bank," the Guaranty Bank & Trust Co. is a locally owned bank in Cedar Rapids, Marion and Hiawatha. The company provides quality financial services that contribute to the economic growth and vitality of the region.

Guaranty Bank & Trust employees are devoted to retaining the respect, confidence and loyalty of customers by maintaining the highest level of integrity, honesty and standards.

With personalized service, a handshake will always be the sign of good business at Guaranty Bank & Trust.

Financiers of the Round Table

The Guaranty Bank & Trust Co. was established in 1934 during a roundtable cafeteria luncheon of local businessmen.

Van Vechten Shaffer discussed his weariness of collecting bad loans for a Cedar Rapids bank. The 34-year-old Shaffer wished he had enough money to start his own bank.

The group of no more than ten gentlemen made his wish come true. One by one, they went around the table, each contributing thousands of dollars.

With the group's money and some additional shareholders, along with Shaffer's own cash, he had the nucleus for the necessary capital: $200,000.

Guaranty Bank & Trust was appointed agent for the deposits of the American Trust & Savings Bank and the Cedar Rapids Savings Bank, both of which had closed their doors in the early 1930s.

On May 5, 1934, the company opened its doors to the public in the former quarters of the Cedar Rapids Savings Bank at 3rd Ave. and 3rd St. SE, where its main bank resides today.

Architecturally Significant

Constructed in 1895, the building is the first all-steel and concrete structure built west of the Mississippi River.

The building was originally a rather slender structure measuring 30 feet by 140 feet, six stories high. It was expanded in 1909 and 1912.

The engineering and construction were novelties. Cedar Rapids citizens were amazed to see the courses of brick laid from top to bottom. This compelled each portion of the steel support to carry its full burden and

Constructed in 1895, the building was the first all-steel and concrete structure built west of the Mississippi River (below). Today, the main bank (far below) remains an architectural monument in downtown Cedar Rapids.

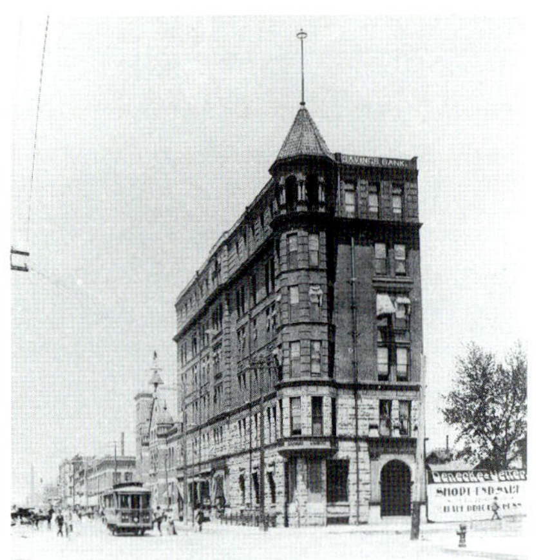

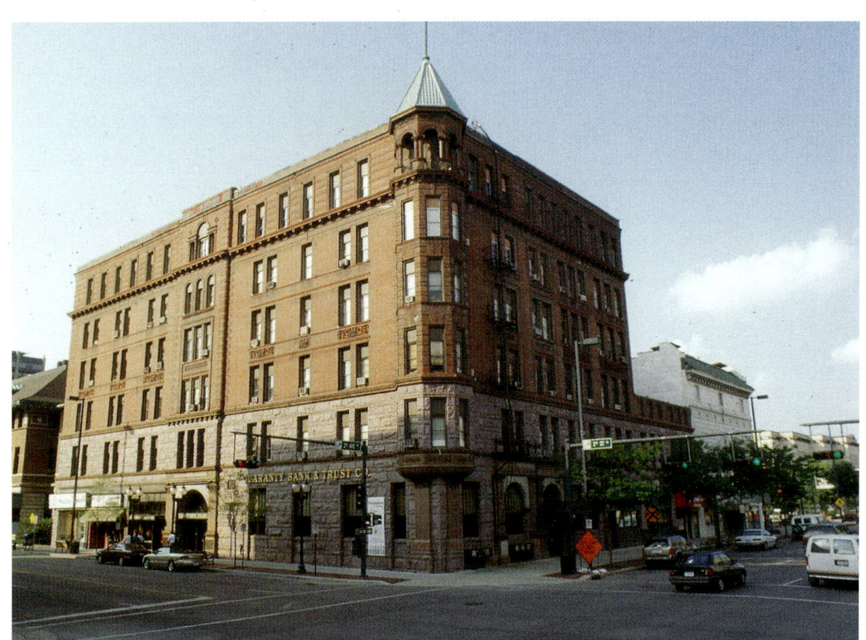

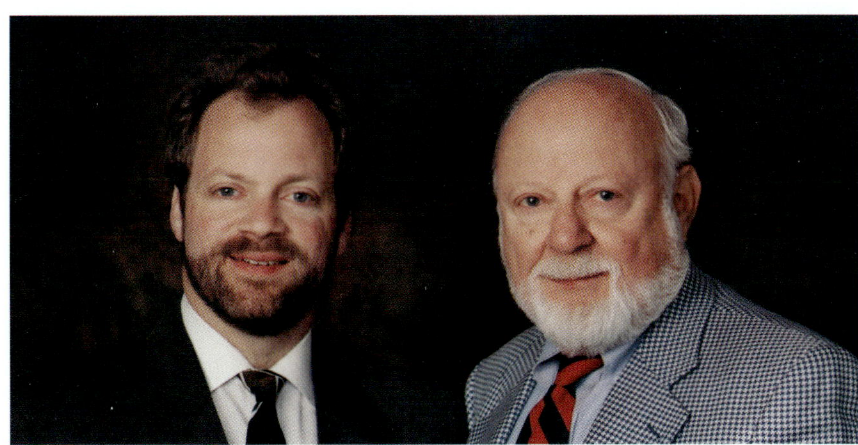

Robert D. Becker, Vice Chairman (left), and Harold M. Becker, Chairman of the Board (right), represent the local ownership and entrepreneurial spirit of the Guaranty Bank & Trust Co.

share in the load bearing equally.

Solid as a rock, it could be said the building is nearly as strong as Guaranty Bank & Trust's commitment to the community.

A New Era

In 1969, Van Vechten Shaffer planned to sell his shares of the company and eventually retire. He offered Harold Becker the opportunity to buy his interest.

Harold Becker had been a director of the bank. His father, Orrie, was one of the original "round-table" members of 1934.

With the buyout, Becker became Chairman of the Board and D. Bruce Gibson became President and CEO. Over the next three decades the bank's assets grew tenfold from $17 million to over $160 million.

Guaranty Bank has the distinction of having only three Presidents since its founding. Van Vechten Shaffer was the President from 1934 until 1969 at which time he was succeeded by D. Bruce Gibson. Gibson was succeeded by the current President, B. Larry Johnson, in 1994. Shaffer was Chairman of the Board until 1969 when was succeeded by Harold M. Becker. Robert D. Becker is the Vice Chairman assuring reliable succession and leadership. Such continuity in management is highly unusual in today's trend of revolving-door management due to mergers and acquisitions.

Trust Department

This aptly named department of Guaranty is second to none. With solid communication and strong client relationships, trust is a key factor in the department.

Guaranty Bank's trust professionals offer the kind of personal services rarely found in a *trust* department. They work with other financial planning professionals to formulate effective strategies that meet overall financial goals.

The trust professionals eliminate the difficulty of investing, transferring funds, and providing for a client's family members, as well as arranging meetings at a client's convenience on matters requiring personal attention.

Guaranty Bank & Trust offers services such as investment management, personal trusts, agencies, conservatorships, estate administration, custody and employee benefit plans. It also offers financial, tax and estate planning.

A Future to Bank On

Guaranty Bank & Trust has three locations in Cedar Rapids, one in Marion, and a new branch at 1195 Boyson Road in Hiawatha.

In addition to state-of-the-art offerings such as Guaranty Direct, a 24-hour bank-by-telephone service, the new Hiawatha bank is an exciting, totally innovative concept in banking.

"The current vogue is for banks to move to the supermarkets," said Harold Becker. "We're going to change that vogue and have markets come to the bank."

The plan is to have a diversity of high-demand businesses such as a service station, a convenience store, and smaller shops occupy space in the same structure as the bank.

The one-stop accessibility to the bank and its variety of stores will make arduous "errand running" a thing of the past.

The Guaranty Bank & Trust Co. is committed to the success of the people and businesses of the Cedar Rapids area. With a strong vision of how to make banking and living more productive, Guaranty Bank & Trust is truly "the local good bank—the bank that is good for you and our community."

SCI Financial Group, Inc.

SCI Financial Group, Inc. is home to the largest independently owned, full-service brokerage firm in the state. As the only independent firm in Cedar Rapids with an in-house research department, the company offers solid advice for a solid future.

Having always been located in the heart of downtown, the company will continue to provide comprehensive services to businesses, foundations and individuals for years to come.

Something Ventured

The company now known as SCI Financial Group was founded at a time when the country was beginning to climb out of a great depression. There was no guarantee of success. Nevertheless, Russell Knapp and Lowell Taylor organized Knapp & Company in 1938.

Eleven years later, the firm was incorporated and the name was changed to Securities Corporation of Iowa, with Knapp as the sole owner.

Growing Legacy

In 1965, Russell Knapp asked his son, John, to return from Africa.

John Knapp was in Kenya with Barbara, his wife, as a part of the Massachusetts Institute of Technology Fellows in Africa program. They agreed to return to Iowa.

Within four years, John Knapp was president of Securities Corporation of Iowa.

The company grew tremendously under his direction. He added investment advisor services and expanded brokerage services. He also added pension administration. By 1975, the company joined the Midwest Stock Exchange and moved from the Merchants National Bank building to the former Craemer Store building.

Moving into a building suitable to its legacy as a landmark business, Securities Corporation of Iowa would eventually occupy the entire downtown area historically known as the Mansfield Block.

Reorganizing

Due to extraordinary growth in the number of services, the company reorganized as SCI Financial Group, Inc. in 1978. With the new arrangement, SCI Financial Group, Inc. became a holding company for its three subsidiaries which now include: Securities Corporation of Iowa, SCI Capital Management and SCI Tower Pension Specialists Inc.

The two-story predecessor of the SCI Building (below) was built in 1872 by Dr. Eber Mansfield, believed to be the city's first physician. Over half a million dollars was invested in the renovation of the Craemer, SGA and Warriner buildings (built on the former Mansfield Block). SCI Financial Group, Inc. purchased the buildings.

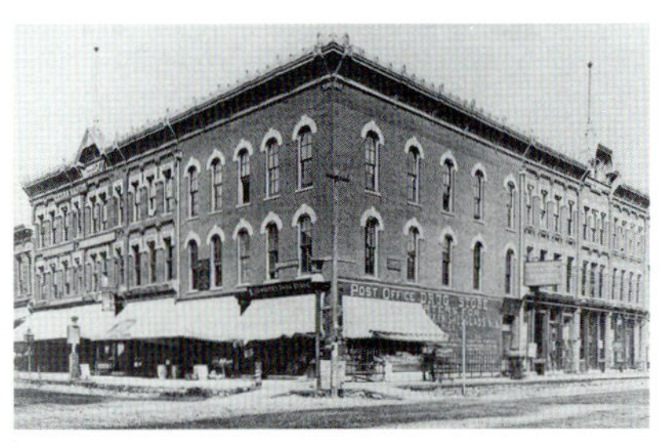

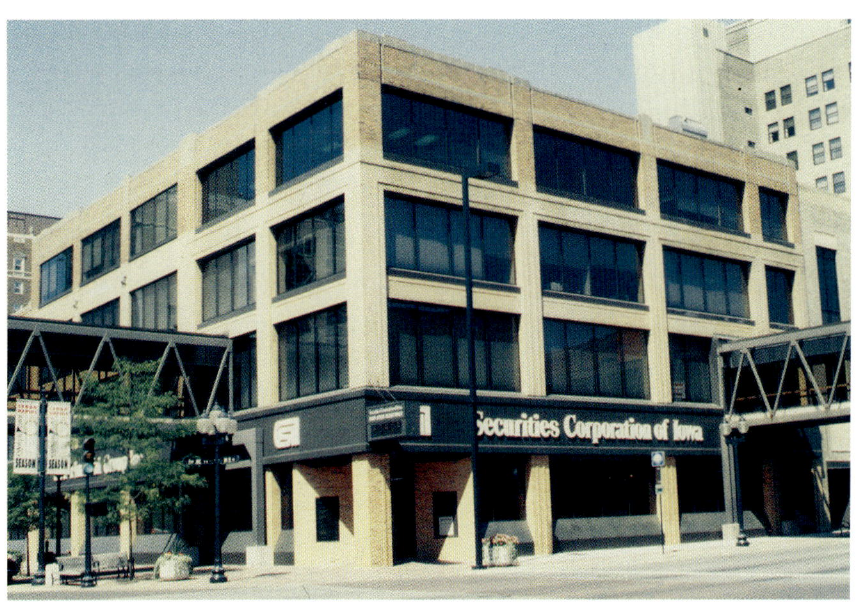

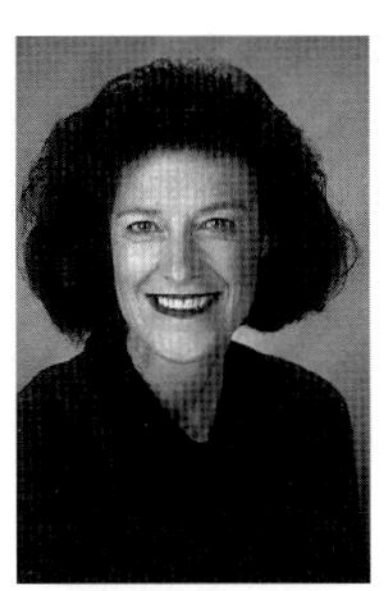

Barbara Knapp (left) runs SCI Financial Group. Chair Emeritus Russell Knapp (lower left). John Knapp (below).

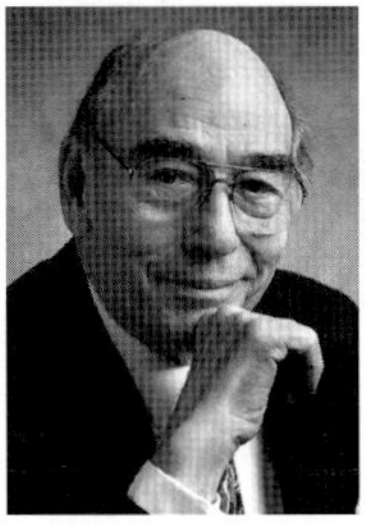

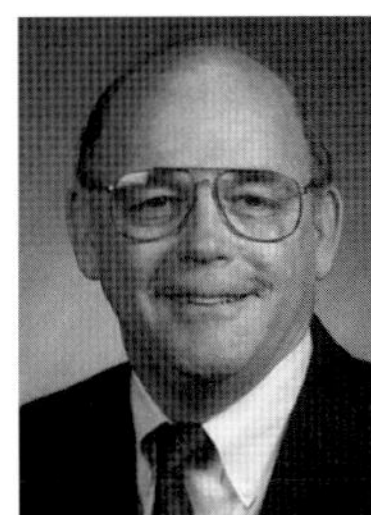

Following the death of John Knapp in 1994, Barbara Knapp was elected chairman of the board, CEO and president.

Today, Barbara Knapp and her father-in-law, Russell, perpetuate the vision of John Knapp.

Securities Corporation of Iowa

SCI Financial Group is a truly comprehensive company. Rarely will one find so many services under one roof.

One of the three subsidiaries is Securities Corporation of Iowa. It is the largest independent full-service brokerage firm headquartered in the state, and it has its own research department.

"We have four research analysts right on the premises," said Barbara Knapp. "They devote their full time to research."

The company's brokers seek to build diversified portfolios of stable, proven investments that provide the potential for long-term, dependable returns. Some investment options include not only exchange-listed and NASDAQ stocks but mutual and money market funds, and corporate and municipal bonds.

Securities Corporation of Iowa also specializes in investment banking and commodities trading.

The investment bankers offer a full range of financial and management services tailored to small and mid-sized midwestern companies. They offer valuation advice, merger partner identification and tactical advice. They also source capital for acquisitions, existing operations and growth companies.

The commodities department provides strategic market advice and trading services. Expert commodity brokers are heard daily on over 150 radio stations and are frequent guests on nationally broadcast television news programs.

Recognized nationwide for its solid analysis and independent thinking, the company has offices in Waterloo and Chicago.

SCI Capital Management

Another subsidiary of SCI Financial Group is SCI Capital Management. As a registered investment advisor, it specializes in the discretionary management of investment portfolios for individuals, profit sharing and pension plans, trusts, estates, foundations, endowments and corporations.

SCI Capital Management is founded on the principle that preservation and growth of capital is the highest priority. It follows a disciplined approach to investing, which provides the structure for the highest levels of professionalism.

Rather than adhere to a singular, restrictive investment style, the company's method allows it to capture the best attributes of the various market strategies that have provided consistent returns over time.

SCI Tower Pension Specialists Inc.

The third part of SCI Financial Group is SCI Tower Pension Specialists Inc., also known as Tower.

Tower provides complete plan design, consultation, installation, recordkeeping and investment services for all types of qualified retirement plans.

As Iowa's largest independent pension administration firm, Tower specializes in providing 401 (k) plan administration for all sizes of companies. Tower excels in clear, effective communication, which is key to strong employee participation. From effective plan kick-off meetings to easily understood quarterly individual account statements, the company guides clients every step of the way.

Investing in the Future

Proud of a rich tradition of providing the most comprehensive services available, SCI Financial Group, Inc. will continue to conduct business downtown far into the future.

"Downtown is a very gracious and lovely place," said Barbara Knapp. "We think it's a great environment to do business."

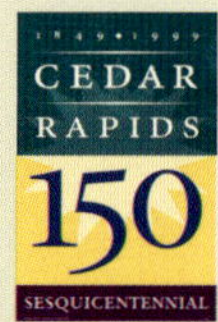

1940
1960

Diamond V Mills, Inc. - 1943

Climate Engineers, Inc. – 1947

In Tolerance – 1947

Acme Electric Co. – 1950

CRST International, Inc. – 1955

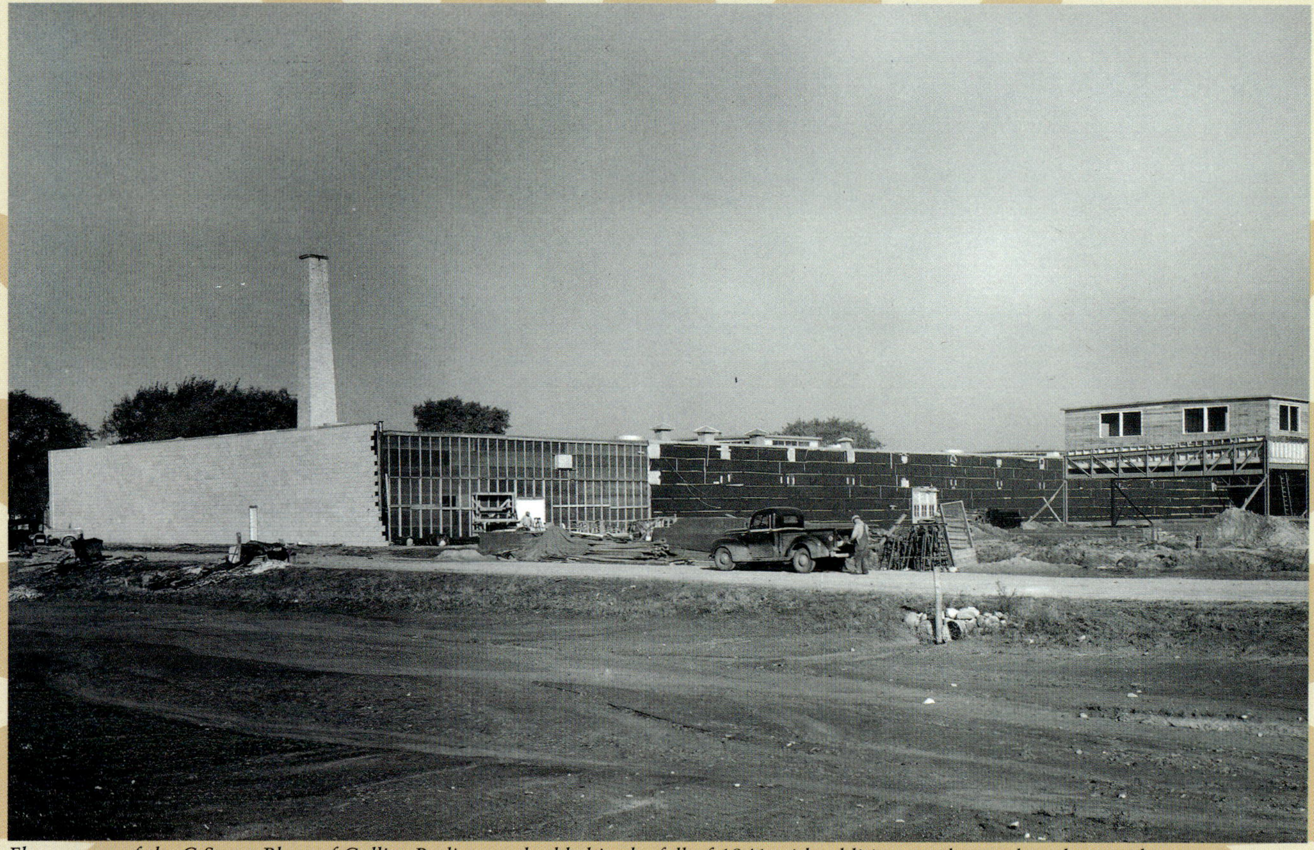

Floor space of the C Street Plant of Collins Radio was doubled in the fall of 1941 with additions to the south and east sides.

In Tolerance

One of the pioneers in its field, In Tolerance is Iowa's leading precision contract manufacturer. The company manufactures metal and plastic parts for industrial, medical and government applications.

Highly skilled employees with talents in programming, machining and tooling machine assemblies within exact specifications. Some dimensions are so tight that an error of 1/20 the width of a human hair will put the item out of tolerance. These employees and systems are responsible for In Tolerance becoming an officially certified manufacturer.

Basement Business

Norman Scott started his company in 1947, when Arthur Collins contracted him to make a special kind of screw for radios.

As the contracts grew, so did Scott's work area. Moving out of his basement workshop, he was soon operating from a series of buildings close to downtown Cedar Rapids that grew to 7,000 square feet.

Higher Standards

When Norman Scott died, his son John Scott took over the company and ran it until he retired in 1986.

He sold the business to Robert Becker, an entrepreneur from Cedar Rapids with education and experience in both finance and engineering.

As the new Owner/President, Becker aptly renamed the company In Tolerance and has quadrupled the revenue in just over 10 years.

The staff, led by Jack Hardin as General Manager and Russ Hess as Production Manager, has achieved certification by Rockwell and Boeing and most notably as an ISO-9002 manufacturer.

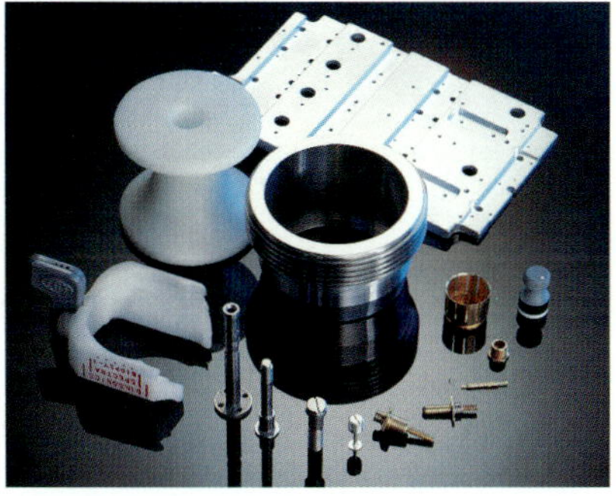

These parts were made for applications in medical, food distribution, avionics and military equipment.

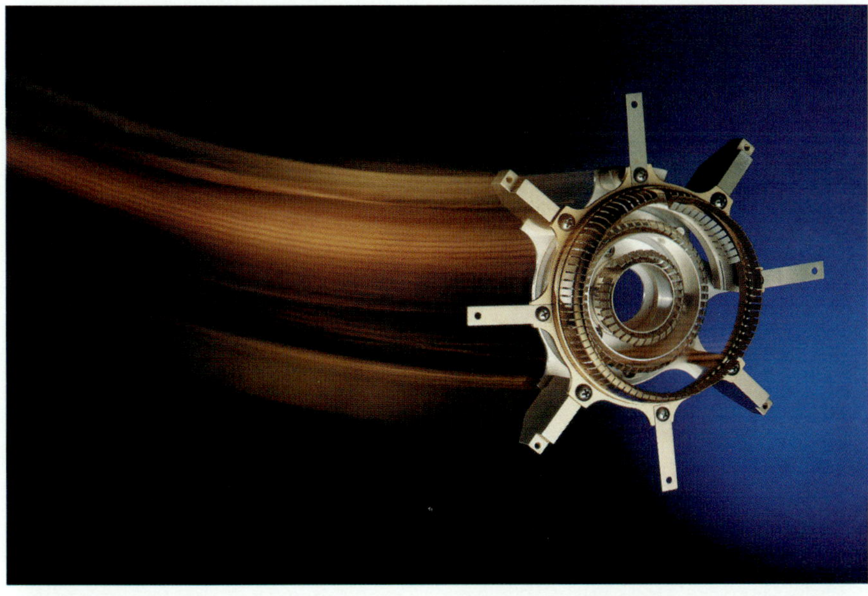

This "Electron Tube Socket" is an example of a reverse engineered assembly manufactured by In Tolerance. It appears on brochures and advertisements for the company due to its unique design and complexity.

The Future is Just in Time

In Tolerance is located in a 35,000 square-foot building that has ample space for manufacturing and future expansion.

Small and medium runs of machined parts and assemblies, and non-standard hardware with tight tolerances are produced. An increasing segment of the contracts is for rapid prototypes. Working with design engineers, the In Tolerance specialists create assemblies from non-production prints.

The company expects good growth, and credits trends in manufacturing to sub-contract out work and Just-In-Time inventory requirements. JIT helps customers control costs while providing purchase agreements for In Tolerance.

With plenty of business and a loyal work force, In Tolerance is the region's precision contract manufacturer for the new millennium.

Diamond V Mills, Inc.

GROWING ON A SINGLE PRODUCT LINE FOR MORE THAN HALF A CENTURY, DIAMOND V MILLS, INC. IS AN UNDISPUTED FEED INDUSTRY LEADER. DIAMOND V SERVES LIVESTOCK MARKETS AROUND THE GLOBE BY MAKING YEAST CULTURE PRODUCTS that improve feed palatability and digestibility. At Diamond V's recently constructed technical center, biotechnology scientists research, develop, test and improve products.

Before 1979, the Diamond V Mills production facilities (below) needed less than one-half of the 119,000 square feet of land in use today. Significant growth in domestic sales and a many-fold increase in export sales require the greatly expanded manufacturing facility (far below).

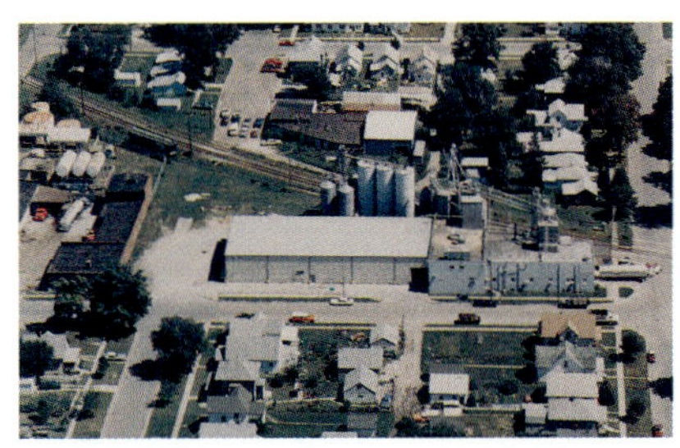

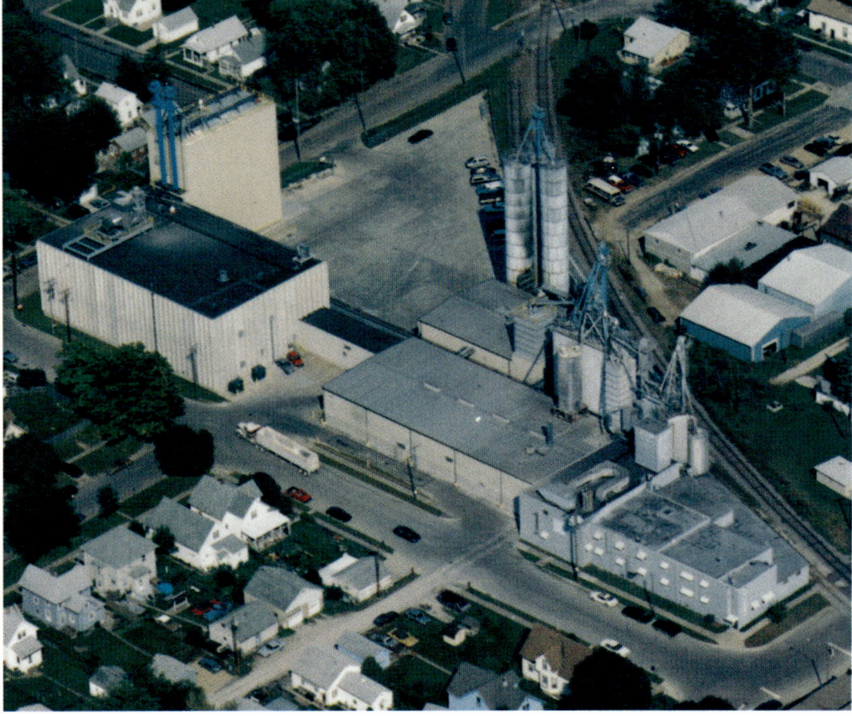

A Better Idea

C.W. Bloomhall worked in the milling industry for nearly 40 years. He believed that quality-controlled industrial fermentation could provide livestock producers with a consistent, affordable source of the nutritional metabolites found in fermented feeds.

When yeast ferments in a favorably controlled environment, the amount of nutrients produced can be maximized.

Knowing that properly fermented yeast culture would deliver greater productivity and better economic returns to livestock producers, Bloomhall started his own company in 1943.

"The origin of the 'Diamond V' name is a mystery to this day. We never got that out of him," said William A. Bloomhall II, Diamond V Mills, Inc. President and CEO. "He came from a ranching family in the Dakotas. It could have been a ranch brand that he had in mind."

Fully Fermented

There is no mystery to the origins of Diamond V's early success.

With an unwavering vision for his product and the subsequent development of a fully fermented yeast culture, C.W. Bloomhall set the standard for the livestock feed industry. In a few short years, Diamond V firmly established itself as the largest and most respected yeast culture manufacturer in North America. By 1961, the company began to trade internationally. Like the vigorous growth of yeast cells, Diamond V's business surged.

"Over twenty percent of our total business is international sales," said Bloomhall. "When I started in the business in 1972, we had one shift producing 30 tons a day. Today, in a highly automated facility, we run

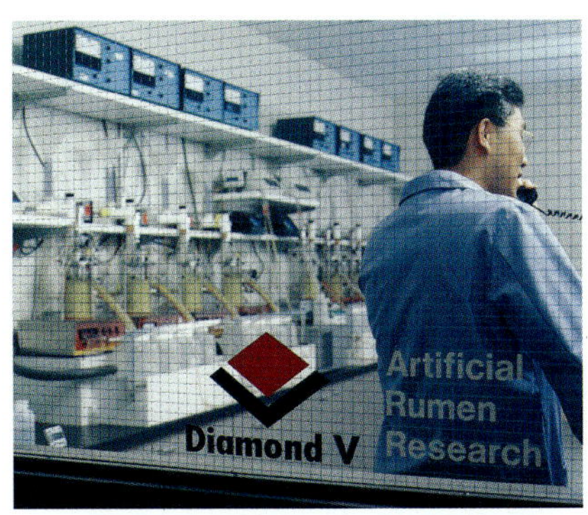

The Diamond V Technical Center is located on the Kirkwood Community College campus thanks to a unique partnership between the college and the agribusiness.

the plant around the clock and are capable of producing in excess of 400 tons daily."

In-house Improvements

The demand for increased production required major physical betterments and expansions to the plant in 1985, 1991 and 1994.

Expansion in 1994 included three developments: a new, highly automated bulk materials handling facility, a third fermenter/dryer unit, which skyrocketed finished product capacity by 50 percent, and a multimillion dollar, ultramodern yeast growth system.

The yeast growth system reduces dependence on outside suppliers and provides improved seed yeast quality. It also increases flexibility in producing varying strains of seed yeast.

Adding Value

The creation of yeast culture products requires several ingredients. Quality ground corn is one of those ingredients. By adding value to basic agricultural commodities, Diamond V Mills, Inc. brings dollars into the Iowa economy and higher profits for farmers.

Selling well in more than 30 countries, Diamond V has recently been honored with the Governor's Export Award as well as the "E" Award for Export Excellence from the President of the United States.

Leading the Way

Maintaining a lead position in the global marketplace takes dedication. Research of product potential is ongoing. Genetic engineering, one of the latest advancements of biotechnology, is helping scientists understand the mysteries of the nutritional metabolites found in Diamond V Yeast Culture products.

The Diamond V Technical Center, located on the Kirkwood Community College campus, was completed in 1997.

This corporate partnership is unique among community colleges. The college offers a location linked to its livestock and communication resources. Students provide a source for well-educated research assistants. Exposure to real-world corporate research helps the students and the college's ability to meet accreditation qualifications.

An especially remarkable feature of the center is the artificial rumen laboratory. One of only a few labs of its kind in the world, it provides a scientifically valid model of the extremely complex rumen ecologies found in live dairy cows, beef steers and other ruminant animals. A combination of flasks, tubes, electronic controls and monitors, the artificial rumen model plays an important role in new product development.

With innovative technology such as artificial rumens, Diamond V Mills, Inc. will continue investigating yeast fermentation and the quality of its fully fermented yeast culture products.

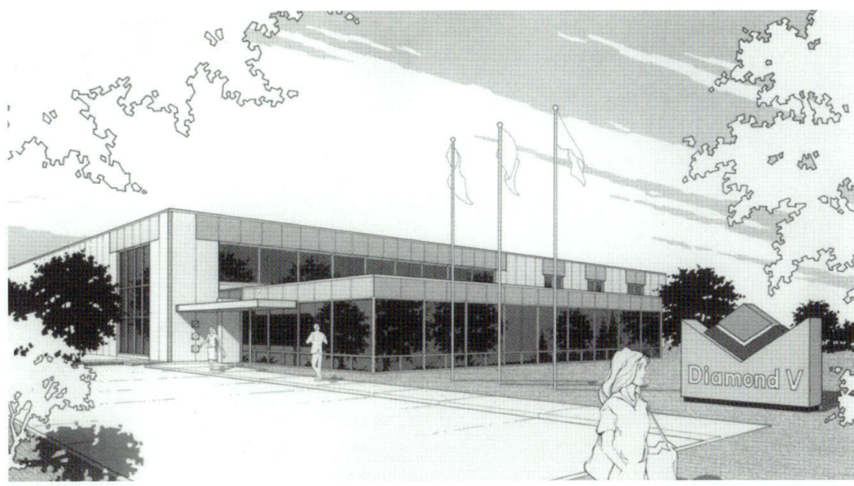

In 1998, to accommodate continued growth, Diamond V purchased the former Allied Glass office and warehouse building at 838 First St. NW. The planned renovation of the building is shown in this architect's drawing.

Climate Engineers, Inc.

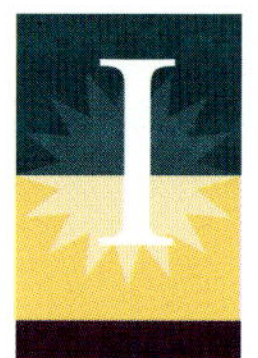

T TAKES MORE THAN A TRADITIONAL HEATING AND AIR CONDITIONING CONTRACTOR TO MEET THE CHALLENGES PRESENTED BY TODAY'S COMPLEX HEATING, VENTILATING AND AIR CONDITIONING (HVAC) SYSTEMS AND GOVERNMENT AIR-QUALITY STANDARDS.

Climate Engineers, Inc., which in 1997 celebrated the 50th anniversary of its founding, goes beyond the traditional by offering the commercial building market a team of experienced problem solvers along with its air-handling system design and manufacturing expertise.

Climate Engineers is one of the few companies capable not only of designing and installing HVAC systems, but also of manufacturing almost any type of sheet metal or plate structure. The company's work is a part of many Cedar Rapids and Eastern Iowa landmark buildings and manufacturing plants, including Quaker Oats, PMX Industries, General Mills, the Cedar Rapids Police Department's new facility, Mercy Medical Center and others.

The Climate Engineers Inc. main office in the early 1960s (below). The new look of the office today (bottom).

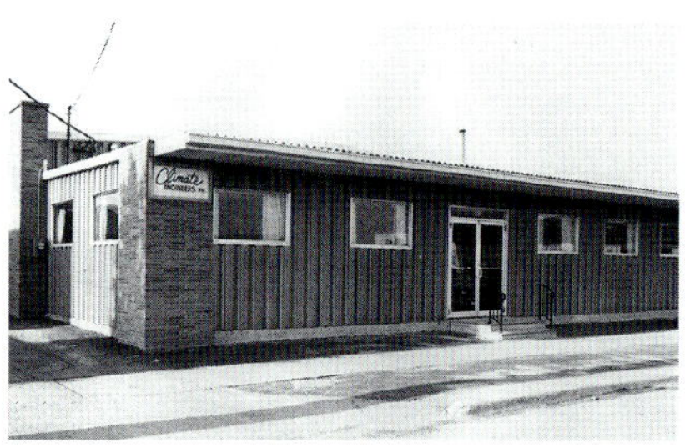

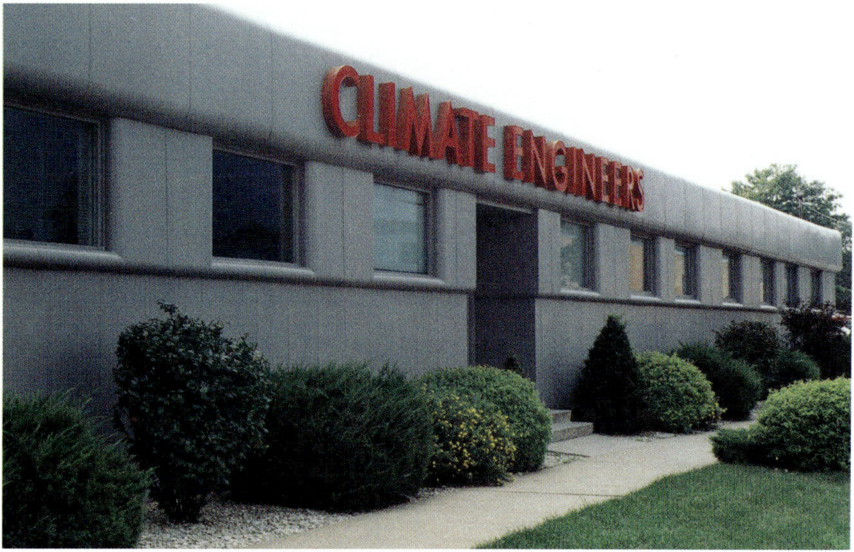

Big challenge in '70s

One of the company's first big challenges was installing the HVAC system for the Stouffer's Hotel (now the Crowne Plaza Five Seasons Hotel) and the Five Seasons Center in downtown Cedar Rapids, a two-year project that started in 1977. It required installation of 150 tons of sheet metal ductwork.

"The HVAC business has changed dramatically since the earliest days of the company," said Frank E. Kvach, who served as the company's president from 1976 to 1993 and who continues to be a consultant on special projects.

"Moving and handling air in these modern facilities is no easy task. You have more machinery and utilities to work around and there are more government regulations and employee concerns that have to be addressed. New manufacturing processes can also present some special demands."

Kvach said the company's computer-aided estimating and drafting capabilities give Climate Engineers an edge in meeting cost, performance and deadline requirements, and they let company engineers anticipate and avoid potential problems before fabrication.

"Our years of experience are also a great advantage," Kvach said. "We've been providing air-handling

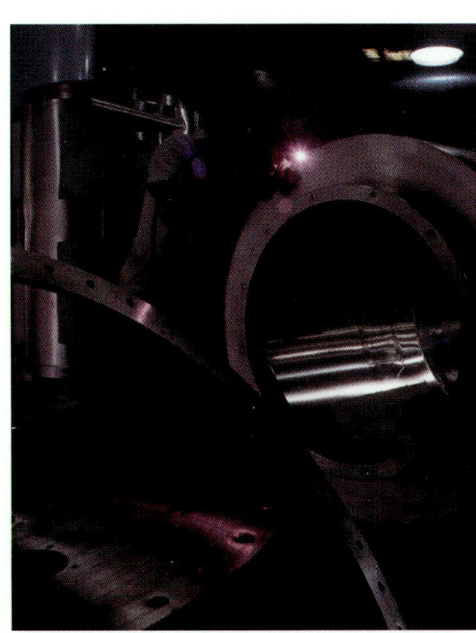

Custom fabrication and timely delivery of high-quality mechanical systems are important facets of the Climate Engineers mission.

solutions for businesses, factories and institutions since 1947."

Fabrication facilities expand

In addition to its HVAC capabilities, the company offers specialty manufacturing services. In its four fabrication facilities, Climate Engineers has manufactured everything from stainless steel surgical trays to six-foot-diameter welded pipe for a nuclear power plant. Any size component can be custom built using galvanized metal, aluminum, stainless steel, painted steel, PVS or copper.

Three of the facilities are recent additions. Berglund Sheet Metal in Des Moines was purchased in 1990. Climate River Valley was started in the Quad Cities in 1996, and Climate Engineers Seattle was started in 1997.

In Cedar Rapids, at 883 Shaver Road Northeast, Climate Engineers operates with 30,000 square feet of office and manufacturing space. A 5,000-square-foot building added in 1995 features a 40-foot ceiling and a 30-ton Canada Iron overhead crane running the length of the building to accommodate heavy manufacturing.

History of the company

Climate Engineers was founded in 1947 as a subsidiary of Continental Forest Products Co., which had spun off from Green Gable Builders Inc., an umbrella corporation formed by lumber broker James H. Maloney and headquartered in Onawa, Iowa. Climate Engineers originally was a metal-forming operation for Green Gable, which manufactured prefabricated metal buildings.

During its early years, Climate Engineers was engaged primarily in residential heating installation in rural areas. The company entered the commercial heating, cooling and ventilation market in 1955 with the growing popularity of air conditioning. By 1959, the company was working exclusively in the commercial building market.

In 1969, two years after Maloney's death, John C. Watson, who had run the company since 1953, purchased a controlling interest. During his tenure as president, major projects included installation of HVAC systems at Mercy Medical Center, St. Luke's Hospital, Kennedy High School, the University of Iowa Library and the Kitchens of Sara Lee in New Hampton.

The company was reorganized following John C. Watson's death in 1975, and longtime employee Frank Kvach became president. John C. Watson Jr. became president in 1993 when Kvach retired.

"We developed and continue to have a very good relationship with many local businesses, industrial plants and contractors because of performance and competitive pricing," Kvach said. "It's a feeling of great satisfaction to help the economy of Cedar Rapids."

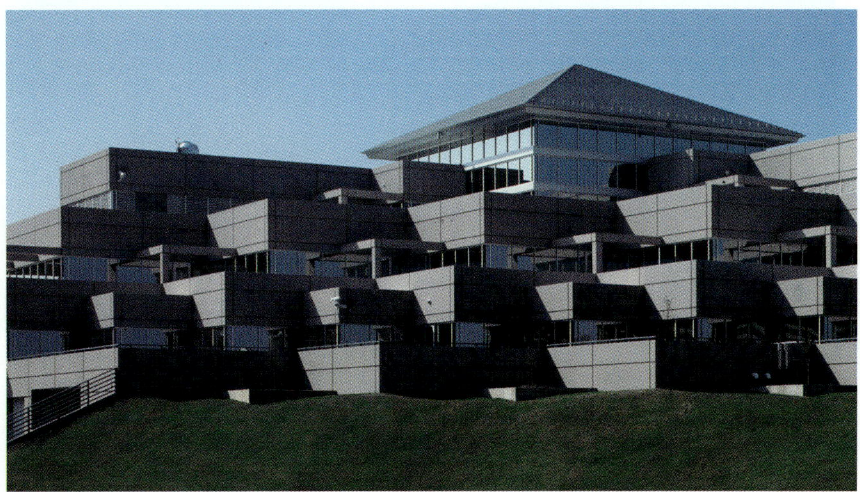

Climate Engineers installed the heating and air conditioning system in the Cedar Rapids Police Facility in 1997.

CRST International, Inc.

Following an aggressive program of expansion and growth, CRST International, Inc. is the largest family-owned trucking company in the United States. The spirit of resourcefulness that marked the company's foundation is still found today in its absolute dedication to customers. Having acquired smaller freight lines with unique capabilities over the years, CRST excels as a transportation company. Expertise in areas such as logistics, less-than-truckload expresses and dedicated services confirms that CRST International, Inc. is the "transportation solution."

The early years of CRST (below). John Smith (far below) continues the tradition of excellence started by his father, Herald "Smitty" Smith.

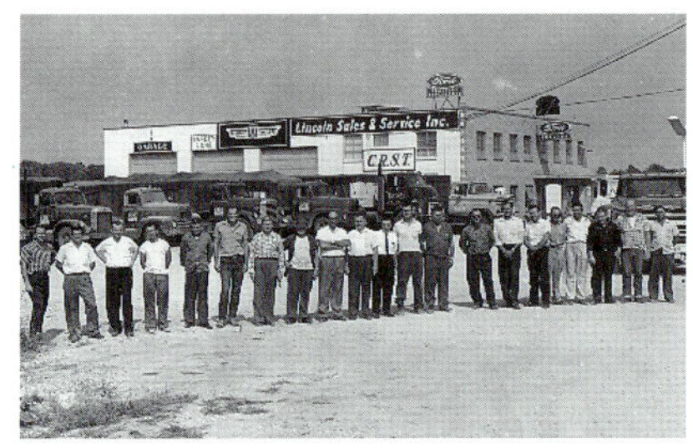

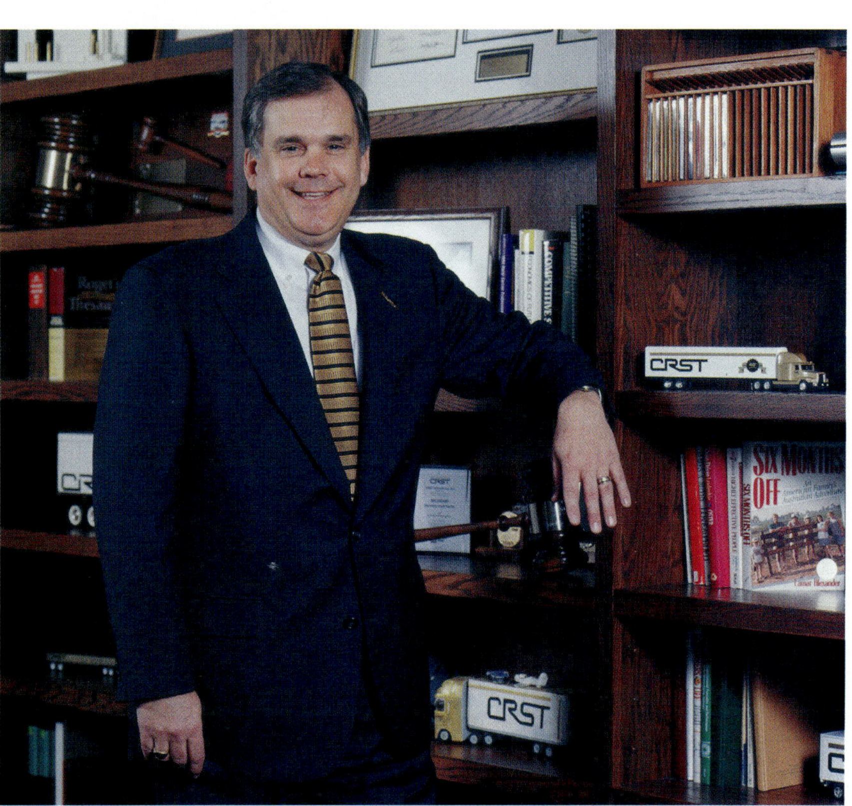

Long Shot

The year was 1955. Herald "Smitty" Smith found himself with a family to support, a mortgaged home and a standard of living to maintain. Yet, he and his wife, Miriam, had an ambitious scheme to pull themselves out of their financially leveraged situation.

With no customers, no trucks and virtually no working capital, they would start their own trucking business.

As a former district manager of a transportation company, he had experience in the trucking industry. He was an excellent salesman and relied on his ability to coax key persons. To begin, he needed a franchise.

It could have been impossible for Smith to find someone willing to sell a trucking franchise, the legal document that allows a company to operate. Luckily, he found an independent trucker who wanted to get out of the business. He purchased it for $10,000, payable within ten years with no interest.

Smith started his office in a refurbished chicken coop that he hauled into town. First, he used all of his finesse to convince five Cedar Rapids manufacturers that the new company would deliver steel from Chicago at competitive prices. Next, he contracted with owner/operators who hauled cattle to the Chicago stockyards and returned empty to Cedar Rapids.

With the "bullhaulers" hauling steel on their return trips, Cedar Rapids Steel Transportation, Inc.

made money. By the end of the first year, the company realized a total revenue of more than $100,000.

Merging

Hauling steel on the return trip decreased operating costs and eventually changed the way the entire trucking industry functioned.

Today's deregulated industry makes the advantages obvious.

Yet, strict regulations of the time did not create competition and the move was considered innovative.

Over the next two decades, the company increasingly entrenched itself in the industry. Smith attracted more business by passing savings on to the customers. He also invested capital back into the company for the purchase of additional franchises. The new authorities greatly expanded the parameters in which CRST Inc. could operate.

In the Family

Herald Smith's son, John, grew up with trucking and gained a thorough understanding of the CRST organization. After studying management methods at college, John Smith officially joined CRST in 1971. He administered every department within the company and by 1983 he was president.

A year later CRST Inc. bought Malone Freight Lines Inc., a national carrier that specialized in flatbed loads. Identifying regional flatbed hauls as another opportunity, Three I Truck Line Inc. was purchased.

In 1985 the new CRST International, Inc. integrated all four

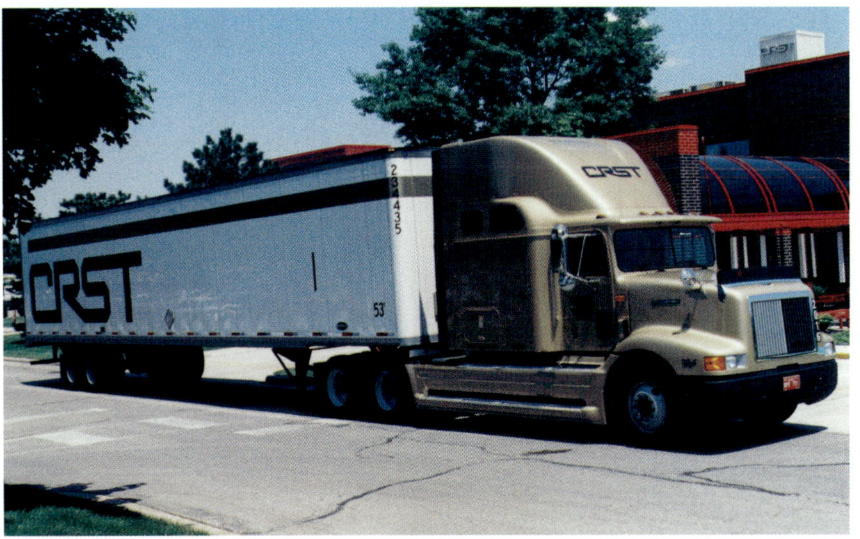

CRST's bold corporate colors of black and gold are easily recognizable on the road.

companies, including CRST Logistics, a ground-freight logistics advising service.

"Instead of every company trying to do everything for everybody, we decided each should become a specialist," said John Smith, president and CEO of CRST International.

Transportation Solutions

CRST International, Inc. is well situated to take on the future needs of the American economy.

Now, a single telephone call sets into motion the broadest scope of services in the industry. Customers can requisition any kind of van or flatbed service for either national or regional duty. Trucking, however, is just one of the services.

International air and ocean freight, truck, rail, intermodal, warehousing and distribution—Logistics Services can arrange it all. Featuring single-source accountability, one customer service person manages everything from booking loads to handling any special requests.

Express LTL (less than truckload) Services offers trucks equipped with a two-way satellite tracking system. It pinpoints their locations across the nation. Coordinated with EDI (Electronic Data Interchange) for fast booking, the transportation of goods has never been more efficient.

Dedicated Services can replace or supplement a customer's private trucking fleet. It administers all operational and regulatory issues, fees and paperwork. By outsourcing the headaches, Dedicated Services allows customers to return to their core business.

With a philosophy that has guided the business for nearly half a century, CRST International will continue to present transportation solutions.

"We never promise more than we can deliver," said Smith, "and we always strive to deliver more than we promise."

Acme Electric Co.

As the area's electrical contractor of choice, Acme Electric Co. provides expert service in commercial, industrial and residential projects. The company's electricians use the latest technology to plan and execute installations and maintenance.

As Acme Electric nears its 50th anniversary, the company is poised to take on the future needs of its customers in the next century.

Electrical History

Donald L. Barrigar and Howard Smith pooled their resources and founded Acme Electric in 1950. Three years later, they purchased assets of another electrical contractor business, Standard Electric.

Within 20 years, significant growth occurred as the company developed industrial and commercial niches beyond their residential work.

Today, Donald D. Barrigar, Donald L. Barrigar's son, is president of Acme Electric. The history of excellence continues in the 1990s with big projects at the Cedar River Paper Co., ADM Corn Sweetners and the Coral Ridge Mall.

Professional Employees

Acme Electric Co. employs approximately 100 field and 20 office people.

Through the International Brotherhood of Electrical Workers, all company electricians complete a 5-year apprenticeship program and are licensed by the city.

Their education continues with involvement in professional groups and supplier-sponsored programs.

Trio of Services

Acme Electric Co. has three divisions to serve the electrical needs of customers: construction, controls, and technical services.

Acme Electric Construction Division tackles new installations using computerized estimating and project scheduling software. The technology helps the company keep a project on track, on time, and within budget.

Design/Build, a construction and control capability, brings together Acme's electrical experts and a customer's process engineers to create a manufacturing system that achieves optimal electrical performance.

A part of Acme Electric since 1974, **Acme Controls Division** specializes in computerized process controls.

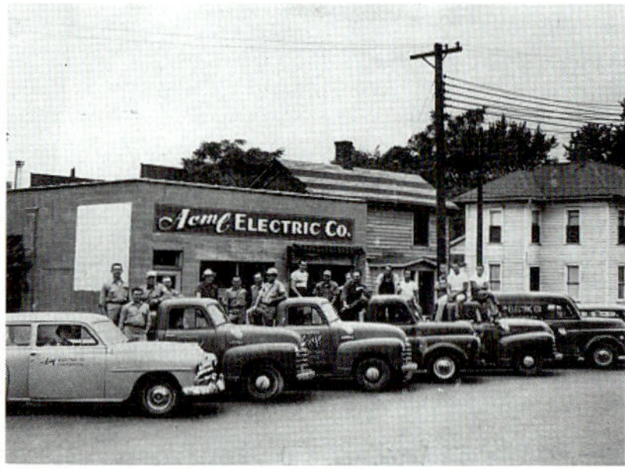

The controls are programmed by knowledgeable technicians.

The **Technical Services Division** is active in predictive and preventive maintenance of new and existing electrical systems. The experience of service technicians from all fields blend together in one organization to provide customers swift and accurate service.

Bright Future

The future is bright as the company approaches its half century mark.

Providing the latest in business systems, data cabling and computer aided design, Acme Electric Co. will continue as the electrical contractor of choice in the next century.

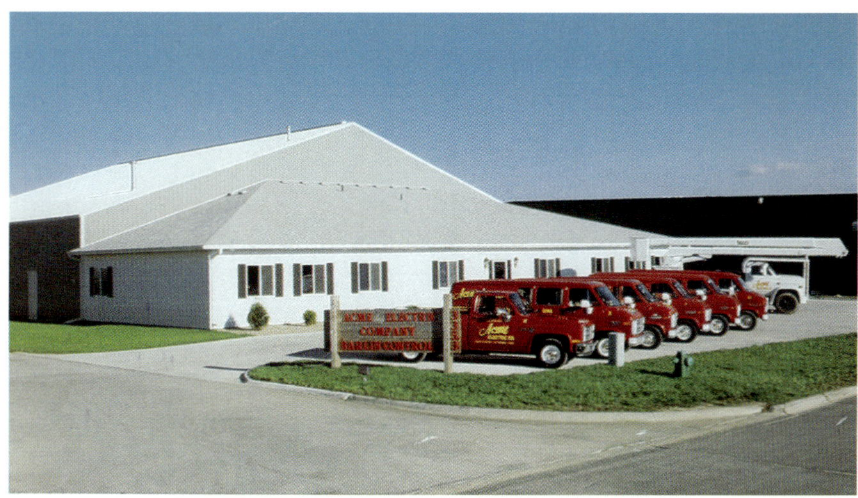

An early photograph (top) of the Acme Electric office and crew shows a young, but thriving company. The Acme Electric offices and fleet today at 3353 Southgate Court SW (above).

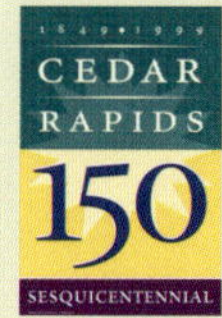

1960 1980

The Meth-Wick Community – 1961

Apache Hose & Belting, Inc. – 1963

Goss Graphic Systems, Inc. – 1965

Intermec/Norand Mobile Systems Division – 1968

Midamar Corporation – 1972

APAC Teleservices, Inc. – 1973

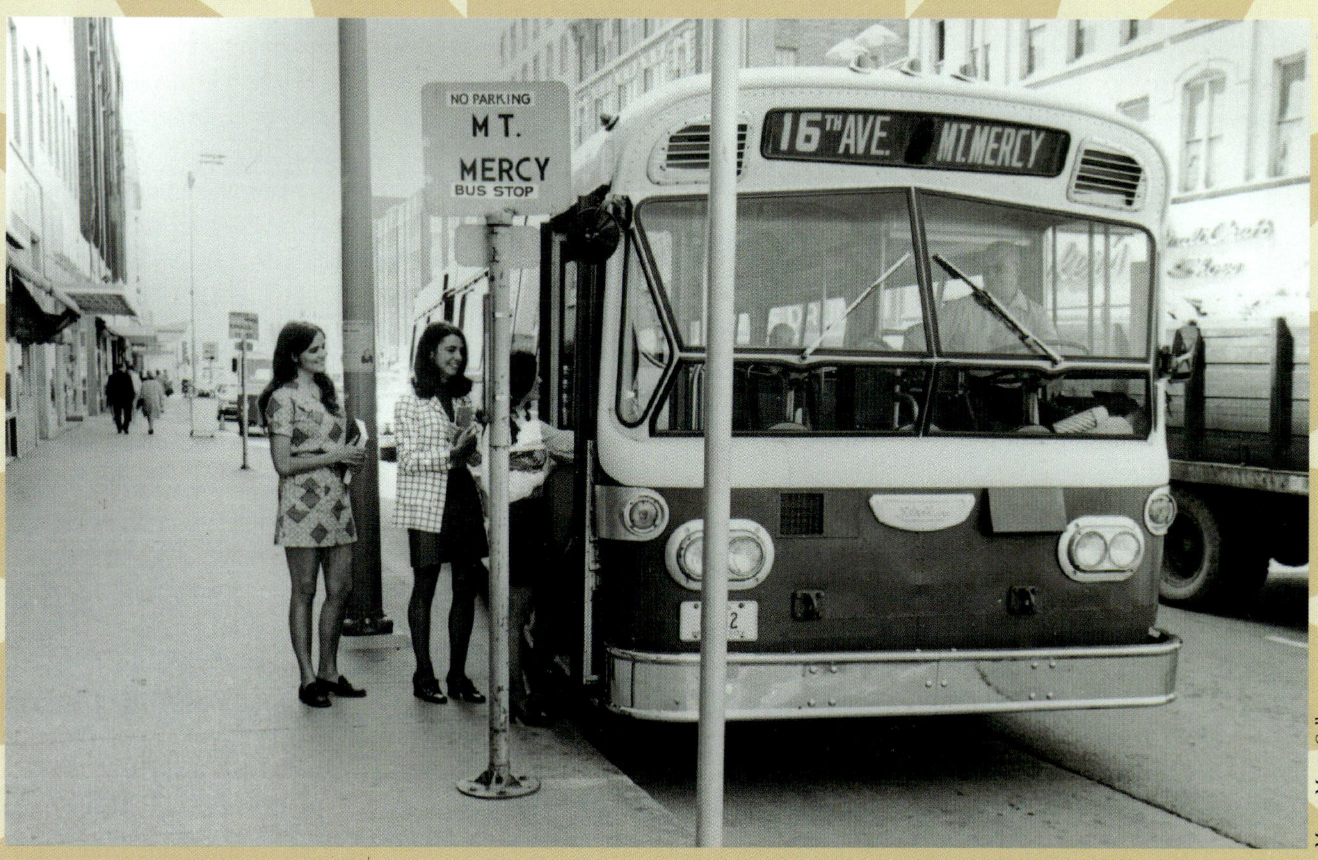

Mount Mercy College

The Meth-Wick Community

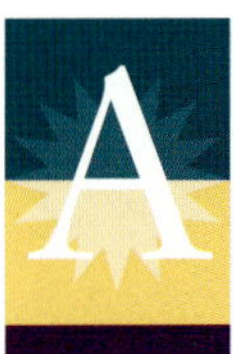

America's seniors have sought independent styles of living in recent years. Sensitive to this new desire, The Meth-Wick Community has living arrangements designed for the full continuum of lifestyles and care levels. Plans for the future include expansion of its 63 acre campus in northeast Cedar Rapids.

Where There's a Will...

Barthinius L. Wick, a Cedar Rapids attorney, was concerned with the welfare of the elderly and admired the efforts of the Cedar Rapids Home for Aged Women (known today as Kingston Hill). At the time, no similar home for men existed.

Dying a bachelor in 1947, he left behind a considerable estate for the foundation of a Cedar Rapids Home for Aged Men. However, the trustees of his estate struggled for several years to materialize his dream of a large-scaled facility. Progress was achieved only after they united their efforts with a former Iowa governor.

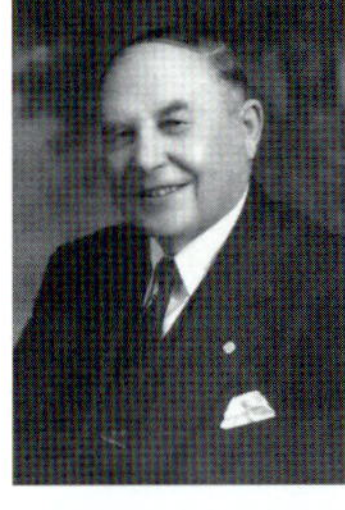

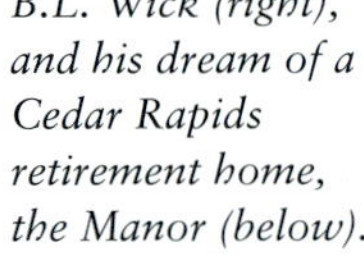

B.L. Wick (right), and his dream of a Cedar Rapids retirement home, the Manor (below).

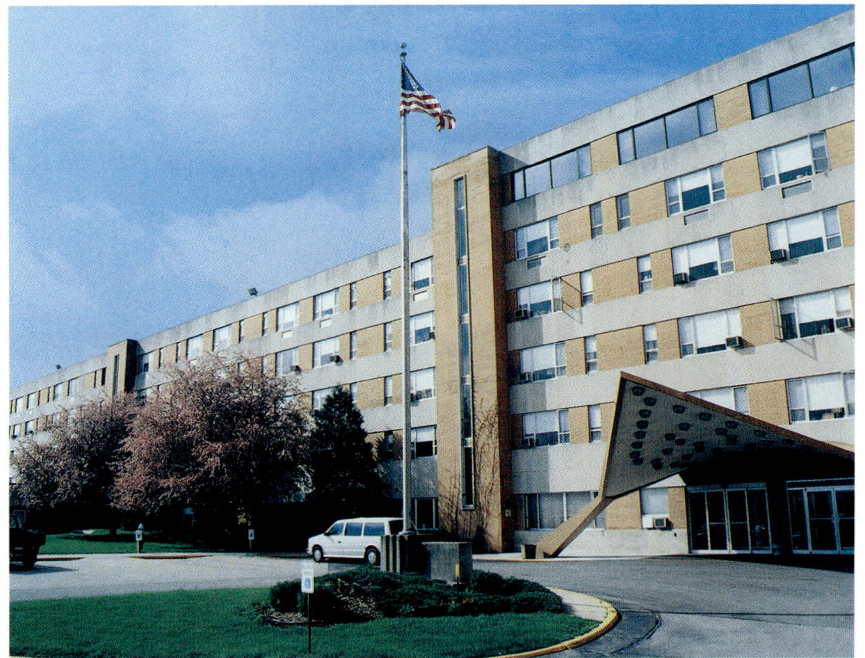

Former Governor Robert Blue was an instrumental member of the Methodist Retirement Homes of the North Iowa Conference. This group supervised the administration of several retirement communities in the state. When additional financial support from the organization was received, ground was broken for the Manor in the summer of 1960. Finally, a home for *all* the retired in Cedar Rapids was realized.

The Early Years

When the Manor opened in 1961, its system of bundled services were the latest in retirement care. The independent living quarters were studio apartments and everyone ate in the same dining room for all three meals. If residents were no longer self-reliant, they lived in the Health Center of the Manor.

This concept of bundled services met the needs of the residents for more than two decades. However, as the value systems of seniors started to change, so did the view of the total care package. Once regarded as a reassuring comfort, the bundled services started to be viewed as a style-cramping restriction.

"You must consider the changes in our society," said John Swanson, Meth-Wick director of foundations and marketing services. "People in

1961 were comfortable in studio apartments. That was your world and you thought that was great. Today's retired people are leading more active lives and they're finding that it's just not enough. They can afford more; they want more."

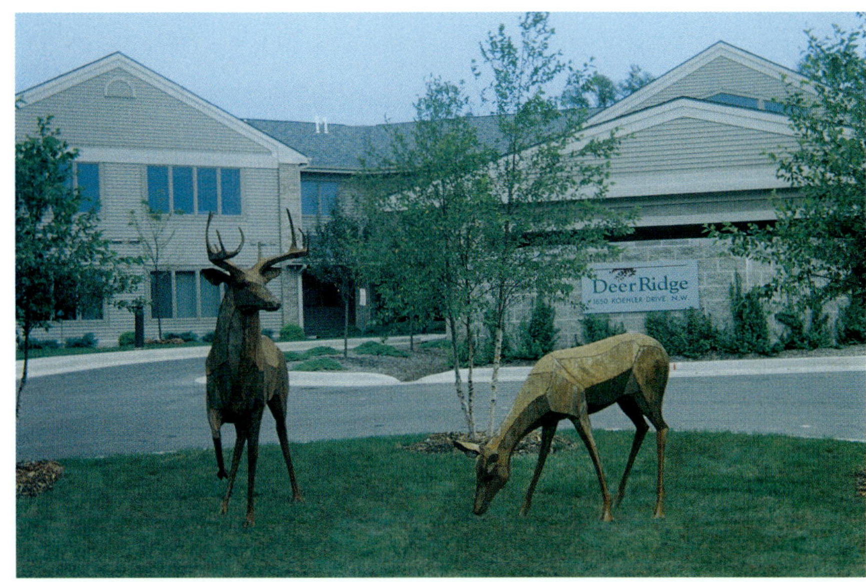

Deer Ridge is the latest condominium-style living unit to have been built on The Meth-Wick Community campus. All apartments feature a full kitchen, a large living and dining area, and an all-year sunroom.

The Spirit Continues

The foresight of two men marked a grand turning point for The Meth-Wick Community. Board president John Knapp and chief executive officer Bernie Bowman had a shared vision of betterment, which began with Greenwood Terrace in 1987.

The spacious condominium-style apartments in Greenwood Terrace were a remarkable innovation. They combined private residential living with Community Care, a house-call-by-request service. Each apartment included a complete kitchen and private sunporch. There were even exercise facilities and activity rooms in the lower level. The duality of carefree living with the a la carte Community Care made Meth-Wick a very attractive choice for seniors in the Cedar Rapids area.

However, with retirees more healthy than ever before, an even greater degree of trouble-free living was desired. Five years after the opening of Greenwood Terrace, Brendelwood Village was created to provide the ultimate in privacy and spaciousness.

Nestled in the rolling hills of the Meth-Wick campus, it gave seniors the independence for which they had yearned. Each townhome unit featured a private entrance, two bedrooms and an attached two-car garage.

A few years later, Deer Ridge was created to provide more living quarters. Even the original Manor was remodeled to create better accommodations.

The Meth-Wick Health Center was reorganized with an emphasis on the dignity of independent living. Previously, when residents asked for assistance, they received the full package of care, whether it was needed or even wanted. The Health Center established new, specialized levels of care more sensitive to individual needs.

Arbor Place, Meth-Wick's Alzheimer's and dementia unit, has the individual distinction of being the only facility of its kind in the state. Built in 1998, Arbor Place consists of four cottages that duplicate the surroundings of typical American homes.

Arbor Place's soothing, homey atmosphere calms much of the stress associated with Alzheimer's and dementia.

A Future of Dedication

Development will continue at The Meth-Wick Community. More living units are planned at Brendelwood Village. Meth-Wick's Board of Directors is now looking to new opportunities: Crosstown, a 12-acre site between Marion and southeast Cedar Rapids marks the first of these off-campus developments.

Keeping the convictions of its founders in mind, The Meth-Wick Community will continue to offer a full continuum of care and independent living styles that is unique in Cedar Rapids.

Apache Hose & Belting, Inc.

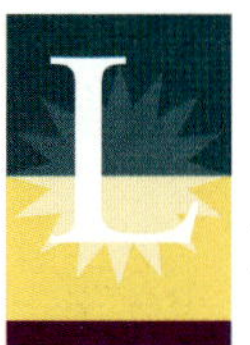

LIKE THE STEEP INCLINES THAT SOME OF THEIR CONVEYOR BELTS MUST CONQUER, THE ACCOMPLISHMENTS OF APACHE HOSE & BELTING, INC. KEEP GOING UP AND UP. WITH A PERSONAL STAKE IN THE SUCCESS OF THEIR COMPANY, employees have made it one of the best conveyor belting, industrial hose, hydraulic hose and die cut parts suppliers in the world. Aggressive plans include broadening its product line and acquiring other companies.

Belting It Out

The multi-million dollar company that is Apache Hose & Belting started in 1963, in an old garage at the rear of a former Cedar Rapids service station.

Robert South had an idea of starting his own belting company. He began selling a few products, but the real opportunity came when he experimented with rubber compounds and vulcanizing.

He believed a specialized rubber company could be successful. Less than twenty years later, Apache Hose & Belting was selling hundreds of products, including several that the company fabricated itself.

With branch offices in Chicago, Minneapolis, North Kansas City and St. Louis, Apache Hose & Belting is now one of the largest conveyor belt fabricators in the United States.

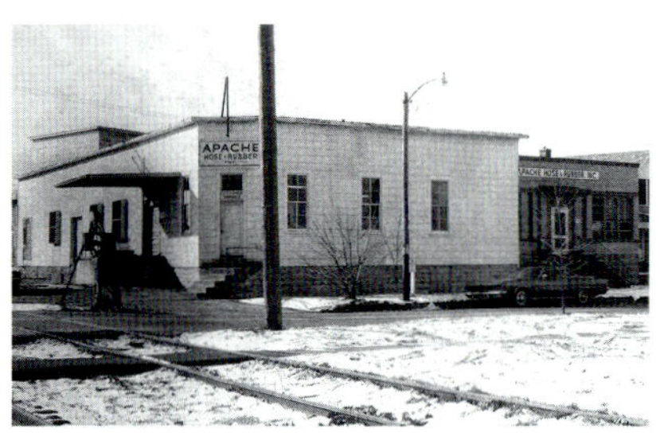

Truly a Fabrication

Over the past ten years, the company has invested over a million dollars in conveyor belt fabrication equipment.

Computerized machinery and a testing laboratory contribute to the quality of the fabricated products.

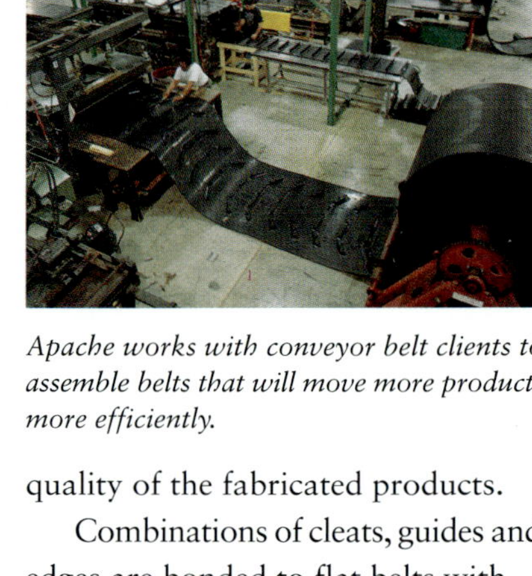

Apache works with conveyor belt clients to assemble belts that will move more product, more efficiently.

Combinations of cleats, guides and edges are bonded to flat belts with the company's own Hot Vulcanizing process to increase conveying capacity.

Apache's Durowall, for example, features flexible sidewalls that can continuously haul huge amounts of material in almost any conceivable configuration. Durowall fits into the most confined spaces, saving valuable conveyor belt space. It also eliminates product loss, which often occurs at transfer points.

An extensive value-added product line of fabricated conveyor belting and high volume hose assemblies makes the company the leader of its industry.

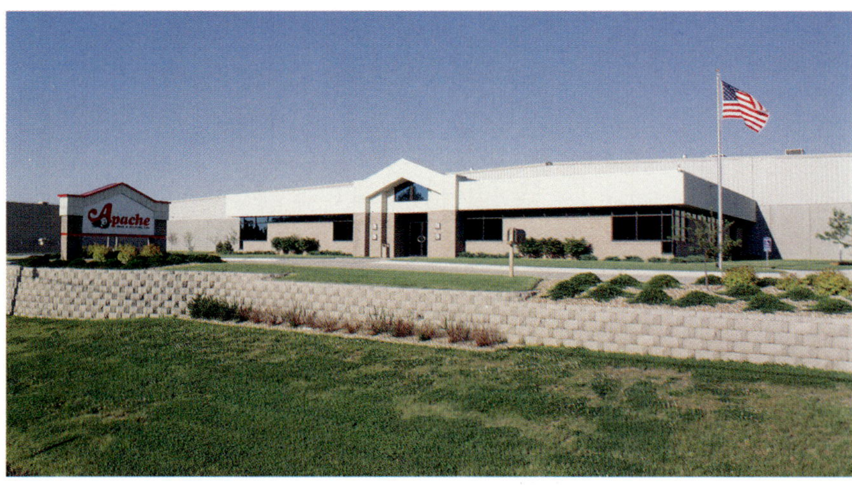

Apache moved from the back of an old gas station to an F Avenue NW location in 1970 (far above). Today's inviting corporate headquarters on Bowling Street SW (above).

Conveying the Future

In addition to expanding fabrication, the employee-owned company will expand its consultation service, increase its geographic coverage, and grow in the areas it already serves.

"We believe continued growth is essential," said Bill Nissen, Apache Hose & Belting, Inc.'s president. "Apache is committed to aggressively developing new opportunities."

Intermec/Norand Mobile Systems Division

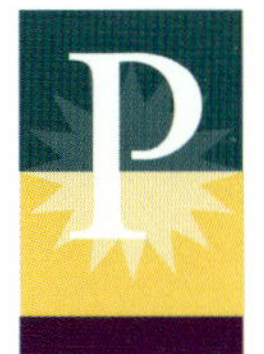

PROVIDING PRODUCTS AND TECHNOLOGIES THAT DEFINE AN INDUSTRY, THE NORAND MOBILE SYSTEMS DIVISION OF INTERMEC TECHNOLOGIES CORPORATION IS THE INTERNATIONAL LEADER IN MOBILE COMPUTING. WITH ANNUAL revenue over $180 million, the division offers mobile computing hardware, application software, network communications products, and integration and support services to businesses worldwide.

World's First

George Chadima founded Norand Corporation as a privately financed business in May 1968. The name Norand was derived from four computer terms: NOR, OR, AND, and NAND.

Because of the high cost to develop computerized devices, the company patented and sold humidifiers as an early source of revenue. With income established, work on the company's intended inventions could proceed.

A series of significant innovations followed. In 1969, Norand invented the world's first hand-held order-entry terminal. In 1971, the company invented the first portable bar code scanner. A year later, Norand created the world's first computerized cash register.

Pioneers of an Industry

Norand became a wholly owned subsidiary of Pioneer Hi-Bred International in 1976. The acquisition happened when the rapidly growing company was expanding into national and international sales.

By the early 1980s, three businesses began to emerge within Norand: route accounting for route-distribution salespersons, point of sales systems for restaurant or store management, and wireless communications for inventory control.

In 1988 the company sold its point-of-sale division to PAR Micronics to concentrate on handheld data and wireless data systems. In 1988 a leveraged buyout (LBO) led by Bob Hammer resulted in Pioneer divesting itself of the company.

Five years later, in 1993, Norand went public with a stock issue. Norand grew rapidly from a $70 million company in 1988 to over $200 million by 1997.

Partnership

In 1996, it became apparent that the portable data collection industry was due for significant consolidation. The company decided to maintain its high market position by partnering with another business.

Intermec was a leader in automatic identification equipment sales to the government and manufacturing systems. Norand was strong in developing and selling hand-held data systems into route sales and warehousing applications. In 1997, Norand was sold and merged with Intermec. At that time the warehousing data collection business was transferred to Intermec's Everett, WA location. Cedar Rapids became dedicated to mobile computing.

Innovation

Today, Intermec is a subsidiary of UNOVA, Inc., a spin-off from Western Atlas. As part of a new $2.2 billion industrial technologies company, Intermec's Norand Mobile Systems Division continues to provide innovative solutions such as pen-based, hand-held computers with desktop PC performance.

The markets served are direct store delivery, field service, pick-up and delivery, and sales automation. Norand continues to value innovative solutions that come from the creative Cedar Rapids workforce. These innovative ideas have been the root of Norand's success for over 30 years.

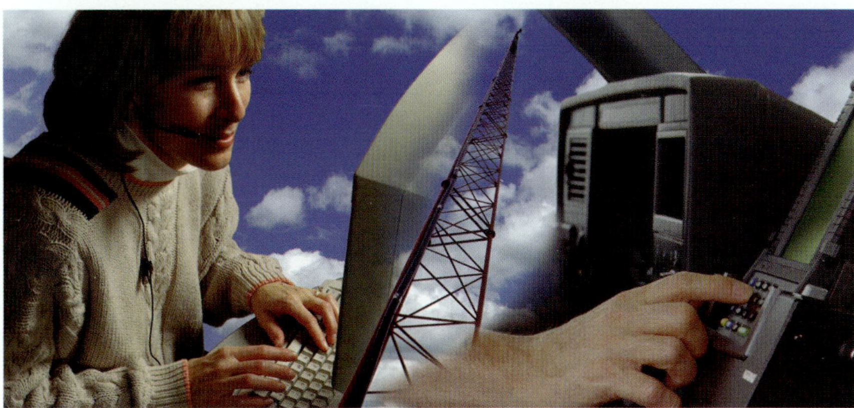

Intermec's Norand Mobile Systems Division provides mobile computing systems solutions to businesses worldwide.

Goss Graphic Systems

Newspaper publishers in more than 120 countries rely on Goss Graphic Systems for their printing equipment. Two out of three North American daily newspapers and more than half the dailies in the world are printed on Goss presses.

The Goss plant in Cedar Rapids is the company's largest production plant. Corporate Headquarters are in Westmont, Ill., with other plant locations in Reading, Pa.; Preston, England; Nantes, France; Sayama, Japan; and a joint business venture with a company in Shanghai, China.

The Cedar Rapids plant employs 650 and has a partnership with the International Association of Machinists and Aerospace Workers, AFL-CIO, Harmony Lodge No. 831.

From Chicago to Cedar Rapids

In 1885, the Goss brothers, Sam and Fred, of Chicago invented a faster version of the rotary printing press for use in producing the daily news. Since then, Goss Graphic Systems, an independent company, has been the printing industry leader in technological innovation.

Over the years, Goss has generated an impressive list of "firsts," from the first straight-line newspaper press in 1892 to the first newspaper web offset press in 1962 to digital press designs for the 21st Century.

Goss began operations in Cedar Rapids when a $7 million, 150,000-square-foot plant opened in March 1965.

The plant was originally built as a manufacturer of presses for magazines and small newspapers. In the late 1960s, the facility became a major manufacturer of large newspaper presses.

The Goss Metro-Offset press was the first double-width offset machine with a guaranteed speed of 50,000 papers an hour, larger capacity and facilities for spot and multicolor work.

Goss in the 1980s

As America's thirst for print increased in the 1980s, significant developments occurred at Goss in Cedar Rapids.

The beginning of the decade brought plant expansion to accommodate the growing production needs of the large newspaper presses. A year later, the largest newspaper press ever was shipped to the *Chicago Tribune*.

One of the early Goss presses (below). Newsliner press manufactured in Cedar Rapids (far below).

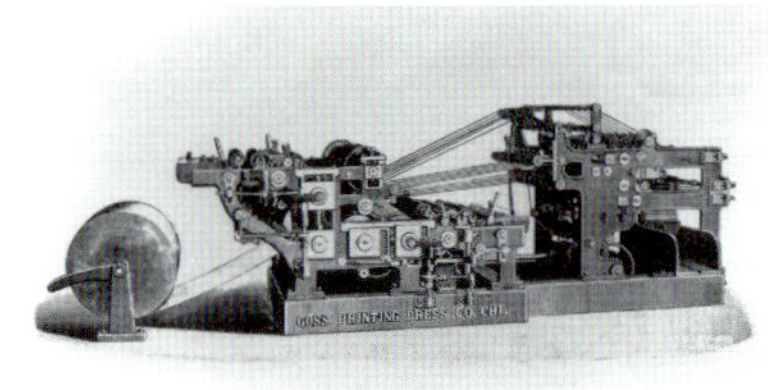

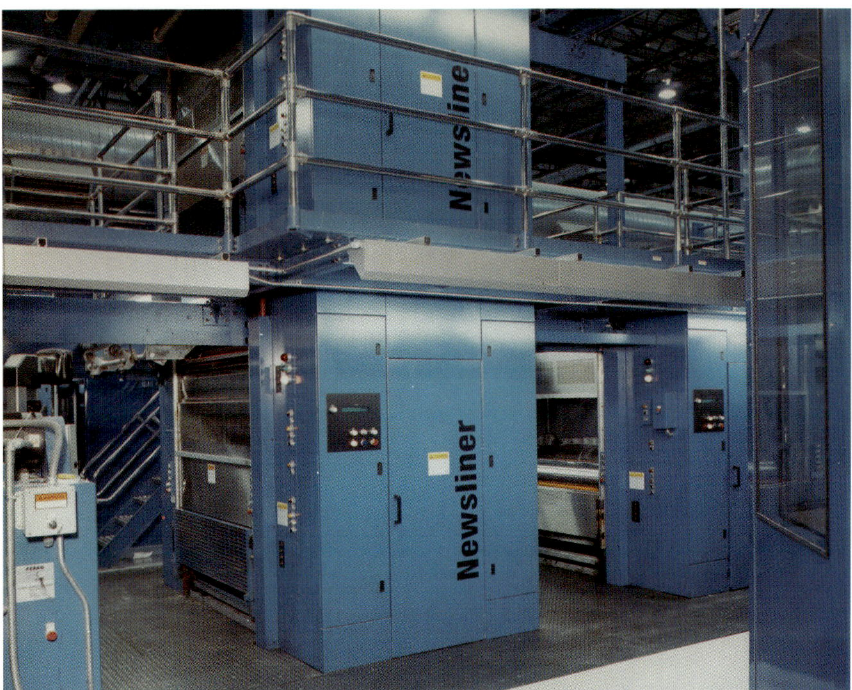

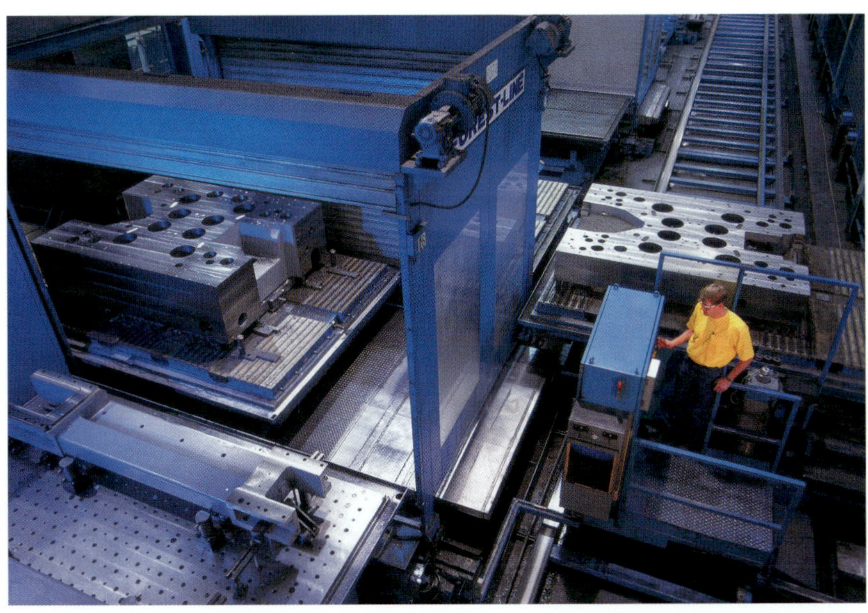

The Flexible Manufacturing System (FMS), which is the largest machining system in the world.

In 1984, the Headliner offset press was introduced. The product gave customers the ability to print 60,000 newspapers per hour and gave customers much more color capacity.

The ante was raised in 1987 with the Colorliner. With an 85,000 newspapers-papers-per-hour printing capability and an automated press control system, the Colorliner took Goss into a new leadership role in press operation.

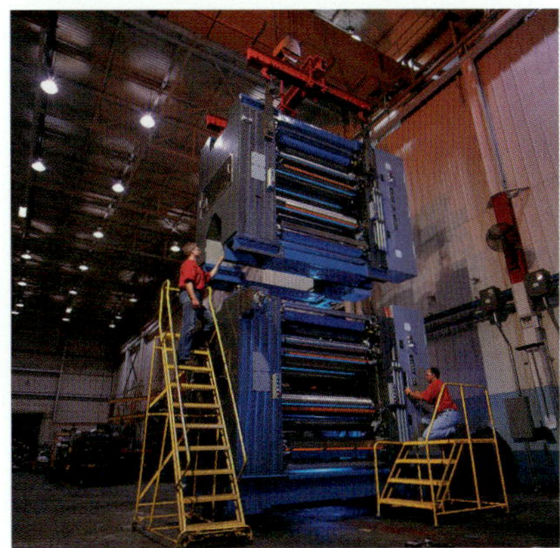

Assembly of the Newsliner press in the Cedar Rapids plant.

The next few years saw the expansion of the Cedar Rapids plant to two buildings for the increased sales of the Colorliner presses. The largest "flexible manufacturing system" in the world was installed to machine the largest castings required for the printing presses.

By the late 1980s, several of the largest newspaper press installations ever were created for the *Los Angeles Times*, the *Philadelphia Enquirer* and the *Cleveland Plain Dealer*.

Goss in the 1990s

Changes continued in 1991 with the introduction of the Metro Color offset press. The press was designed as an add-on to older newspaper presses for additional color capacity.

In 1992, the Goss facility in Cedar Rapids consolidated to one plant.

Within a year presses which printed magazines and catalogs (G14, G25, G25W), and advertising inserts (C700) were introduced to the Cedar Rapids plant.

1998 brought a new inking system (Color Flow) which would help customers reduce waste. Additionally, the Goss engineering groups from around the world came together to create a press which would give customers higher productivity and higher print quality and would be manufactured worldwide. This press was the Newsliner.

Printing in the Future

Goss Graphic Systems produces the highest quality printing equipment in the industry.

As its customers' businesses evolve with changing technologies, Goss Graphic Systems will work with them to develop new products. Goss is committed to helping its customers assure that print remains a cost-effective choice for the growing communications needs of the world's population.

The company is excited about the future of digital technology, which offers the prospect of directly sending and erasing an image on a press cylinder, without using printing plates. This promises simplified production flow and improved printing quality.

Goss Graphic Systems is prepared for business now and in the 21st Century.

MIDAMAR Corporation

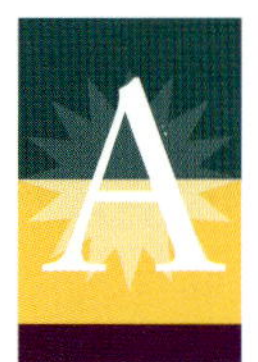

N EXPERIENCED EXPORTER AND INTERNATIONAL SALES AND DEVELOPMENT GROUP, MIDAMAR CORPORATION SUPPLIES QUALITY U.S.A. PRODUCTS TO MORE THAN 30 COUNTRIES. MIDAMAR IS IN ITS THIRD DECADE OF SERVICE TO ASIA, the Middle East, Africa, Europe, North and South America and Caribbean. MIDAMAR was developed and built on a commitment of service to international customers. In the dynamics of our changing world order, MIDAMAR strives to outperform the competition by continually setting higher standards and working diligently to develop new areas to further serve the international market.

World Observation

Bill Aossey, President of MIDAMAR, was born and raised in Cedar Rapids. His maternal grandparents emigrated from Lebanon to Iowa in 1888 and his father followed in 1907. They were a part of the original Iowa Islamic community that helped build the first Mosque in North America in Cedar Rapids, Iowa. Bill's father, Hadj Yayha William Aossey, in 1948, established the first Islamic cemetery in North America also located in Cedar Rapids.

Coming from an immigrant family and thinking of a larger world than Iowa, Bill Aossey joined the Peace Corps and served in Senegal, West Africa as the national Olympic wrestling coach. After completing two years in Senegal, Bill traveled and worked in more than 85 countries.

In 1966, Bill was awarded a scholarship from the Fulbright Foundation and the Institute of International Education to develop an agricultural research paper in Viet Nam. From 1967 to 1969 he worked in Saudi Arabia. These international experiences created an interest and desire to assist in projects for protein, food and agricultural development.

MIDAMAR was established in 1972 as an international development company. With the strong support of a very loyal, knowledgeable and committed team of staff and company officers, MIDAMAR has grown from an idea to a multi-million dollar company.

In 1993, MIDAMAR moved into its newly constructed facility at 1105-60th Avenue SW.

Recognition of Excellence

MIDAMAR has been a leader of international trade, development and consulting since its inception.

MIDAMAR was awarded the Iowa Governor's Award in 1983 and 1988. In 1990, MIDAMAR officers were invited by President Bush to the White House to accept the "President's E-Star Award for Export Expansion"—the U.S. Government's highest export award. Further, MIDAMAR has received: U.S. Department of Commerce "E" Award; S.B.A. Exporter of the Year - 1993; U.S. Department of Transportation and Merchant Marine Shipping Award; Cedar Rapids' 1st Annual International Trade Achievement Award for Export Excellence.

Building Excellence

MIDAMAR has maintained its primary center of international activities in Cedar Rapids, Iowa. Located in the very center of the nation, MIDAMAR provides access to most major U.S. manufacturers and suppliers. In 1993, the corporation moved into a newly constructed 55,000 square-foot building. This facility houses the company's offices, warehouse, shipping facilities and a USDA inspected cold storage.

This modern facility, combined with a dedicated and experienced staff of multi-lingual personnel, ensures MIDAMAR's continued leadership in the export industry.

MIDAMAR's motto is "Our most valuable Asset is our Customer. The Customer's success is MIDAMAR's success!

APAC Teleservices, Inc.

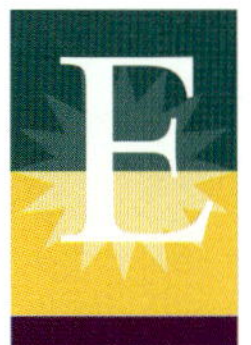

ENJOYING TREMENDOUS SUCCESS AS THE NATION'S BIGGEST TELESERVICES COMPANY, APAC TELESERVICES, INC. IS PREPARING FOR THE FUTURE. THE DEVELOPMENT OF MANAGERS AND THE EXPANSION OF CUSTOMER INTELLIGENCE ARE some of the ways APAC is setting the pace for an entire industry. With the current $97 billion market for teleservices, APAC intends to capitalize on its opportunity to gain more than a fair share of that market.

Telehistory

APAC Teleservices, Inc. was founded in 1973 by chairman and CEO Ted Schwartz. Before the word "teleservices" even existed, the company commenced selling radio and cable television advertising time over the telephone.

APAC anticipated the increased potential of the telephone as a channel for large-scale sales, marketing and customer service. In 1986 the decision was made to expand services into telesales. An investment was made and a modern teleservices facility was constructed next to the Chicago O'Hare International Airport.

In 1990 operations were initiated at Cedar Rapids with administrative offices and a customer contact center. Within a year, APAC optimized the value of their clients' customer relationships. It introduced the first fully dedicated, outsourced customer service group.

Calling Attention

Three acquisitions over the course of three years have established APAC as the premier teleservices provider.

APAC purchased the Shechtman Group in 1996 to become its People and Learning Division. From initial recruitment to ongoing education, this division helps employees grow themselves, meet challenges, accept responsibility and demand accountability.

The next purchase was Paragren Technologies in 1997. This innovative marketing leader helped APAC's clients know the value of each customer relationship. By integrating innovative software, services and market intelligence, it enabled business to expand profitable customer relationships.

The third purchase was ITI Marketing Services Inc. in 1998. This major acquisition catapulted APAC into the lead position as the largest teleservices company in the United States.

With over 14,000 workstations and 25,000 employees in 19 states, APAC is the best provider of customer optimization services. Expanded capabilities and resources enable even the largest companies to bolster their customer relationships through outsourcing APAC Teleservices.

By expanding, innovating, and seizing and extending competitive advantage, it has increased revenues from $5 million in 1990 to more than $356 million in 1997. As APAC grows, so does its tradition of continual prosperity.

APAC's letters proclaim "All People Are Customers" to downtown Cedar Rapids (below).

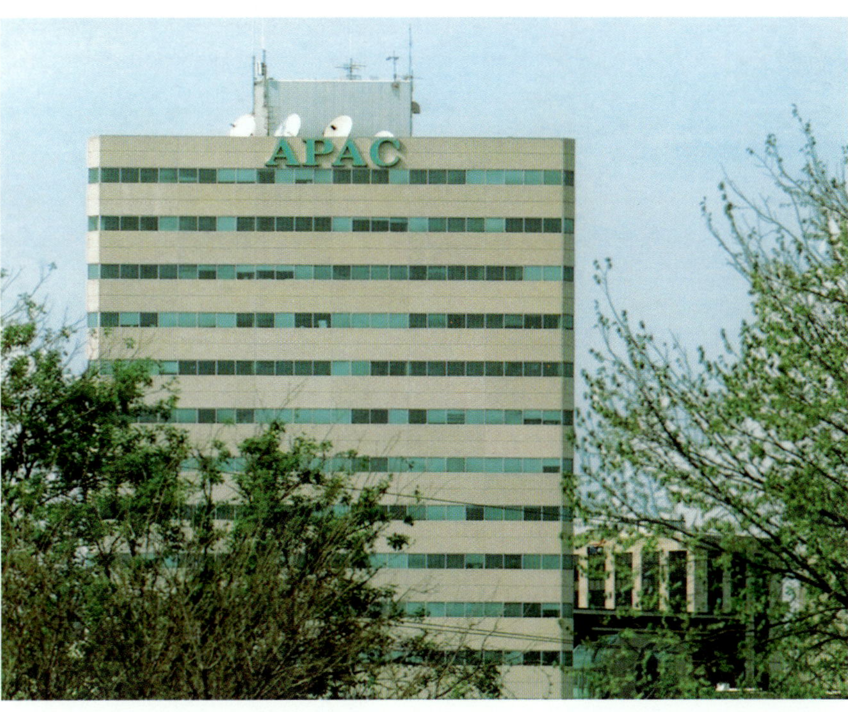

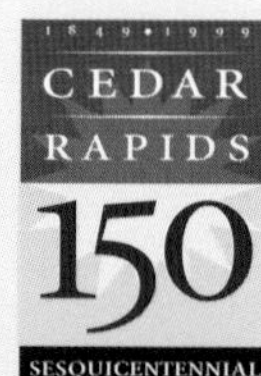

1980 2000

Point Builders, Inc. – 1988

McLeodUSA Incorporated – 1991

Cedar River Paper Co. – 1993

MCI WorldCom – 1990

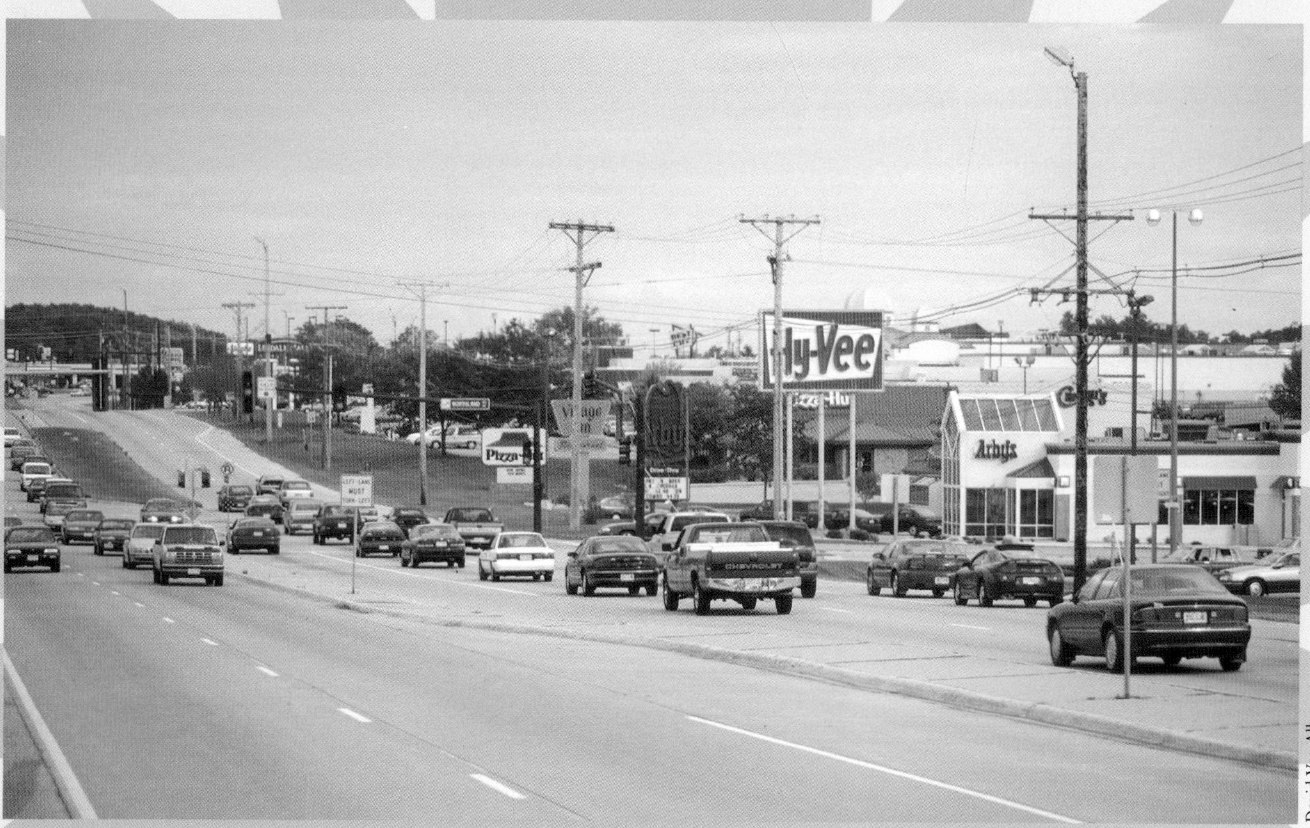

David Van Allen

Collins Road has been the scene of considerable retail expansion in the 1980s and '90s.

Point Builders, Inc.

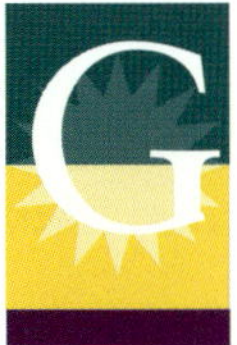

GROWING SINCE ITS FOUNDING 10 YEARS AGO, POINT BUILDERS, INC. IS A LEADING CONSTRUCTOR OF NON-RESIDENTIAL, LOW-RISE AND MID-RISE BUILDINGS IN EASTERN AND CENTRAL IOWA.

Building on Experience

With 25 years of experience in the real estate and construction industries, and the help of a financial backer, Fred Timko founded Point Builders in 1988.

It was a wise time to start the company. The Iowa economy was rebounding.

"Because of the economic condition, the business grew much faster than was anticipated," said Timko, president of Point Builders.

The company has expanded offices to Charles City, Cedar Falls and Des Moines.

Building Right

Business for Point Builders is taking off because the company matches the owner's needs with a solution, then provides the expertise to turn that solution into a quality building.

Point Builders offers complete design, construction and development services. The company can even assist in site selection.

Concentrating on projects that involve pre-engineered buildings, they design 90 percent of what they build. The company can offer the best in pre-engineered building systems products, custom concept design and superior construction service.

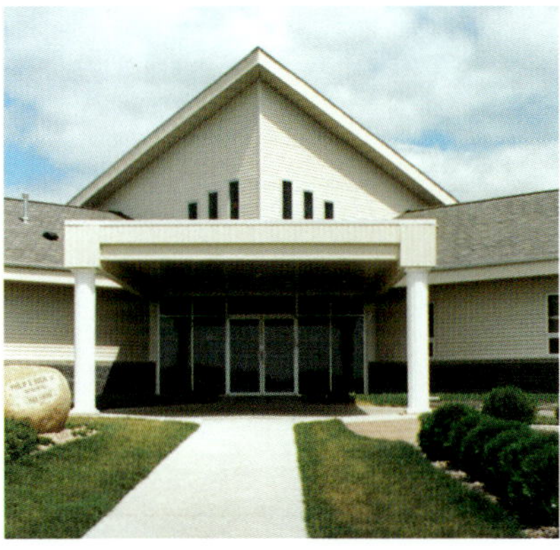

Christ Community Church in Marion.

Becoming deeply involved with an owner and his or her needs, Point Builders constantly suggests ideas and improvements which will enhance the completed project or save money.

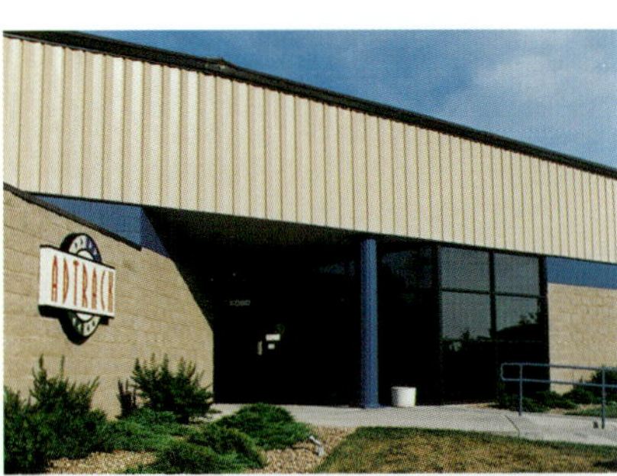

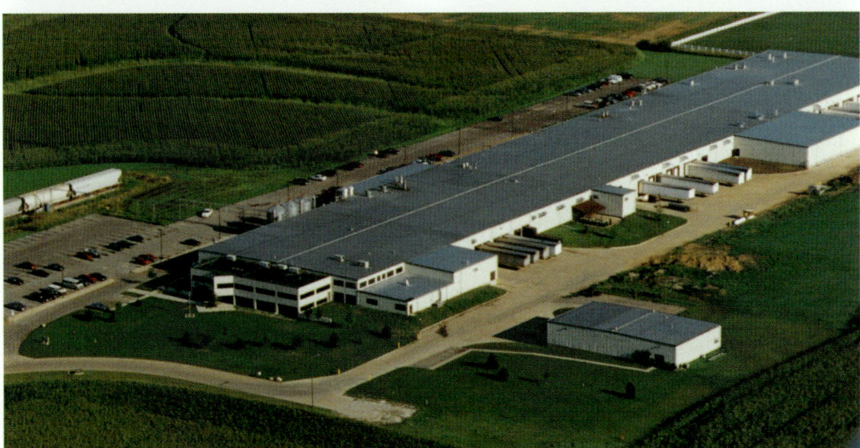

The corporate headquarters of Point Builders, Inc. (top, left). The Adtrack building (top, right). The Centro Inc. building of North Liberty, Iowa (above).

Building for the Future

Repeat business is an important part of the company's volume, so they invest heavily in customer satisfaction.

Point Builders' strong financial position and adequate bonding capacity, along with lease-back and building trade-in programs, allow the company to offer owners extraordinary support in developing the right financial package for a totally successful project.

Point Builders will be committed to its customers far into the future.

"We will remain an Iowa contractor," said Timko. "We want to serve our customers here."

McLeodUSA Incorporated

McLeodUSA is the first super-regional telecommunications company in the nation, offering integrated services to business and residential customers in ten Midwest and Rocky Mountain states. The company is achieving substantial growth. Revenues for 1997 totaled $267.8 million, up 229 percent from the prior year; total revenues for the first half of 1998 exceed $290 million.

Entrepreneur

Founded in Cedar Rapids in 1991 by local entrepreneur Clark McLeod, McLeodUSA has been building customer share since 1994 through excellent customer service.

The company has nearly 175,000 local telephone customers, 345,000 local lines in service, 5,600 route miles of fiber optic network, and 5,000 total employees in 60 locations.

The company's stock (symbol: MCLD) has been traded on NASDAQ since June 1996.

The Plan

The company's strategy is to build customer share; concurrently build network; and begin to migrate customers to that network resulting in enhanced services for customers and improved margins for McLeodUSA.

Capturing Customer Share

McLeodUSA focuses primarily on second and third-tier markets. The company now controls over 35 percent of the business lines in its Iowa markets and nearly 30 percent in its core Illinois markets.

In the first half of 1998, nearly 60 percent of new lines sold and installed were in expansion states.

Business and residential customers select McLeodUSA because they prefer the simplicity of "one company, one call, one bill" telecommunications for their local service, long distance, voice mail, Internet access and paging.

McLeodUSA Publishing Company is the company's phone directory publishing subsidiary and the foundation of the corporation's branding strategy.

By mid-year 1999, 16 million white and yellow page directories with a black cover and gold star will reach 27 million people in 20 states.

Other Cedar Rapids area business units include Ruffalo Cody & Associates non-profit fund raising, Digital Communications of Iowa telephone systems, and McLeodUSA ATS cable television services.

Building Network

Total network miles rose from 2,400 at the end of 1996 to nearly 5,600 at mid-year 1998.

The company is adding 2,000 miles per year. Approximately 60 percent of the company's network miles are operational, capable of transporting advanced voice, video and data services.

Migrating Customers

The important third step in the corporate strategy is the migration of customer calls to McLeodUSA network and switches. It brings financial benefits and greater control to the company. It also provides digital clarity, superior reliability, and advanced functionality for customers.

"The future holds the excitement of greater promise," said Clark McLeod, Chairman and CEO. "We are eager to achieve that promise."

The corporate headquarters of McLeodUSA are located at a new, 190-acre technology park in Cedar Rapids (below).

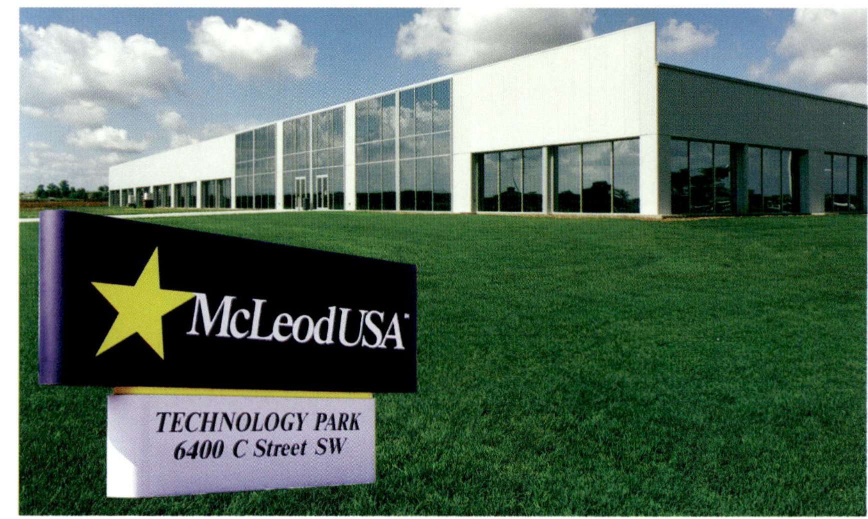

Cedar River Paper Co.

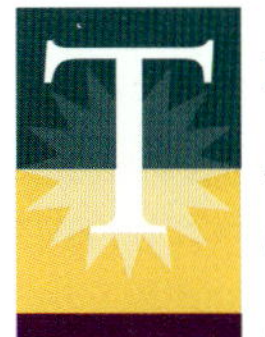

THE CEDAR RIVER PAPER CO. PRODUCES ENOUGH PAPER IN A SINGLE DAY TO CREATE AN INTERSTATE RUNNING FROM CEDAR RAPIDS TO DENVER AND BACK. EACH YEAR, THE COMPANY RECYCLES OVER 700,000 TONS OF WASTE THAT would otherwise end up in landfills.

As a joint venture between two corporations, the company is independently operated. The absence of a corporate hierarchy encourages teamwork, which pushes production levels beyond previous expectations.

A Unique Organization

Cedar River Paper was formed in 1993 as a general partnership joint venture between Weyerhaeuser Midwest Inc., a subsidiary of Weyerhaeuser Co., and Midwest Recycle Co., a subsidiary of BE&K.

The creators of the company wanted to build a unique organization that would be the most competitive in the world.

The teamwork concept, molded from strategies of some of the world's leading companies, recognizes employees as key team members. Empowered to make decisions on a daily basis, individuals operate the company at optimal performance.

How to Make Paper

Cedar River Paper uses superior technology to turn recyclable corrugated containerboard and mixed waste paper into high-quality corrugated medium and linerboard.

The first step in the process places 500 to 600 tons of paper waste every day into a large blender called a pulper. Next, the raw recyclables are mixed with a water solution that is blended into liquid form. From there, the mixture passes through three filtering systems to remove coarse and fine debris.

The liquefied substance is then spread onto a mesh screen conveyor and sent through a series of presses that remove excess water with vacuums and rollers. Heat and recirculated steam remove more moisture; the dried paper is then wound onto rollers. The paper is rolled onto giant reels weighing 45 tons each. The paper is then passed through a "winder" that slits it into "customer sized" rolls. The rolls are then labeled and banded for shipment.

The next step of the process involves taking samples from the rolls and testing them for strength and appearance. Finally, they are loaded into semi trailers and railroad cars, where they are shipped across the country to corrugated container plants.

Tearing Up the Competition

Most recycling plants are unable to use old corrugated containers and mixed waste paper. Cedar River Paper thrives on the waste—waste that would normally have ended up in landfills. By doing this, the company is changing the way others operate in the industry and the way they interact with nature.

The largest and most sophisticated 100 percent recycling paper mill in the United States, Cedar River Paper's process continues to complement a clean environment.

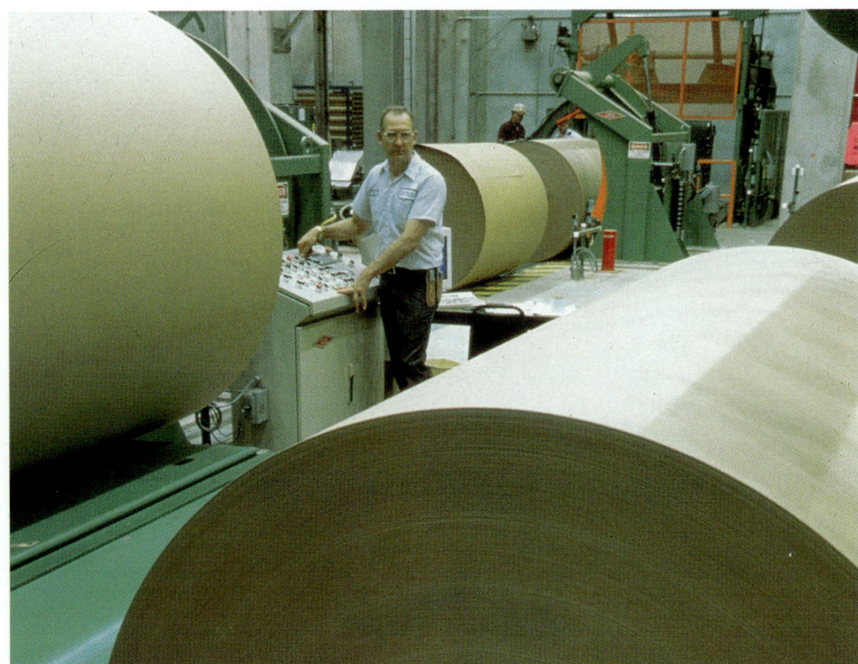

Cedar River Paper Co.'s equipment produces a product of superior quality (above).

MCI WorldCom

IOWA'S LARGEST TELECOMMUNICATIONS COMPANY IS LOCATED IN THE HEART OF DOWNTOWN CEDAR RAPIDS. MCI WORLDCOM IS A WORLD LEADER IN PROVIDING LOCAL-TO-GLOBAL COMMUNICATION SERVICES.

Its digital communication system spans the world, offering data, Internet, local and international communications services. MCI WorldCom in Cedar Rapids is an essential link in that global network.

MCI Comes to CR

In 1990, Telecom*USA merged with MCI. On September 14, 1998, MCI joined with WorldCom to form a communications company with revenue of more than $30 billion and established operations in over 65 countries.

Bert Roberts Jr., chairman of MCI WorldCom says, "MCI WorldCom is open for business. We have created a new kind of communications company with a unique set of assets, a top-flight group of employees, and a heritage for delivering the benefits of competition to our customers."

Heritage of Service

MCI WorldCom in Cedar Rapids is an important part of that heritage of excellent service. MCI WorldCom groups in Cedar Rapids support network services including commercial billing, ISTT (Internet Services Technical Training), along with engineering support for Internet services.

MCI WorldCom employees in Cedar Rapids develop and test new products, receive inbound customer calls, set up conference calling, offer operator services, and business-market sales and service. MCI WorldCom in Cedar Rapids is an essential link in the world's largest and most advanced digital network, connecting local markets in the United States to hundreds of locations worldwide.

Setting Competitive Standards

MCI WorldCom is setting competitive standards in the communications industry. Bernard J. Ebbers, president and chief executive officer of MCI WorldCom, says, "We have the right network—built for the explosive demand for high-speed data and Internet services—the right talent, and the right strategy at the right time. Simply put, MCI WorldCom is out in front and sets the standard by which all other communications companies will be measured."

The 2,000+ employees working at MCI WorldCom in Cedar Rapids, operate 24 hours a day to serve customers around the globe. They occupy 550,000 square feet of facility space in eight buildings, most of which are located in downtown Cedar Rapids. Several of these buildings have been restored inside and out. The facade of each building has been carefully restored—not to change the character of the original structure.

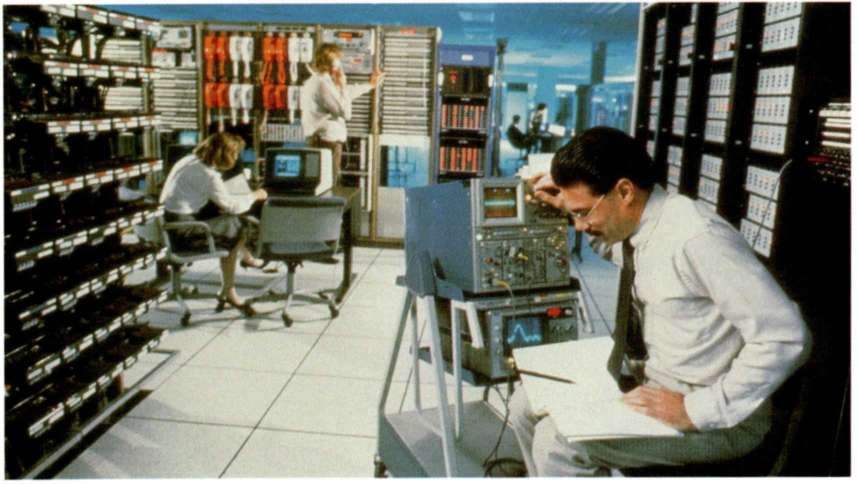

Software engineers design and improve products like MCI's 1-800-Collect in Cedar Rapids. The software is tested in labs like the one featured in this photograph. MCI WorldCom also employs customer service, billing, network conference calling and sales in Cedar Rapids.

Acting Locally

MCI WorldCom strongly believes in supporting the needs in the local community. Annually over $150,000 has been donated to local charities, educational institutions, and cultural organizations in the Cedar Rapids area. Employees are encouraged to give and are recognized for thousands of volunteer hours each year. Honoring their employees with this kind of respect has made MCI WorldCom one of the top ten private employers in Iowa.

By thinking globally and acting locally, MCI WorldCom in Cedar Rapids has created value for all stakeholders. The healthy relationship between MCI WorldCom and the Cedar Rapids community is evidence of that.

Photographers

Ron Dreasher

Ron Dreasher, through his company Dreasher Photography, has been providing award-winning professional photography services since 1992. Ron provides these services on location and at his 4400 square foot studio located in a converted movie theater in downtown Marion, Iowa. Dreasher Photography provides business-to-business, business-to-consumer, and editorial imaging services to advertising agencies and design firms, and directly to clients.

When away from the studio, Ron enjoys bicycling, cross-country skiing, and spending time with his wife and two small children.

French Studios, Inc.

In 1967 with 10 years of commercial photography experience, Robert French began his own photography company at his home in Marion, Iowa. By 1990, the move was made to a custom-designed, 16,500-square-foot building just off the Highway 100-Marion bypass. Under today's direction of Ronald French, president of technical and production operations, and Kathleen Bice, president of business/marketing operations, French Studios sustains its reputation as the area's largest, most comprehensive photographic facility of its kind.

Mark Tade

A native of Iowa City and a graduate of The University of Iowa School of Art, Mark Tade has been a commercial photographer for The Gazette Company since 1993. Originally specializing in the photography of fine art and ethnographic objects for museums, artists and collectors around the country, he has branched out since joining the Gazette's photo department to include editorial, aerial, illustration and portrait photography in his portfolio using both traditional film-based and state-of-the-art digital technologies. His panoramic photographs included in this book were created by combining several overlapping images using the computer program Adobe Photoshop™.

David Van Allen

With a B.A. in English from St. Olaf College and an M.F.A. in photography from the University of Iowa School of Art and Art History, David Van Allen is the photography instructor, college photographer and art gallery director at Mount Mercy College in Cedar Rapids. He does some free-lance photography when he has time, with a special affinity for service organizations, arts organizations and other non-profits. He moved from Iowa City to Cedar Rapids in 1987. David currently operates out of his studio-loft in the old Cherry building on 10th Avenue Southeast, where he does his personal photographic work, meets with students and makes portraits.

Index

ADM Corn Processing, 1
APAC Teleservices, 1, 103
Acme Electric Co., 152
Advance Program, 40
Ahn, Yang, Dr., 91
All Iowa Fair, 58, 59
Aller, Tom, 96, 97
Alliant Tower, 8
Alliant Utilities, 1, 97, 116-117
Amana Colonies, 61
Anaheim Angels, 48
Andringa, Mel, 70, 72, 74
Apache Hose & Belting Inc., 1, 156
Armitage, Tom, 36
Armstrong Family, 8
Armstrong-Race Realty, 9
Armstrong Department Store, 9

Baldwin, Dan, 14, 15
Barber, Martin L., Mayor, 80
Barker, Richard, 66, 69
Beck Motor Works, 125
Becker, Abraham, 6, 92
Becker, Harold, 92
Bender, Elizabeth, 36
Bender Pool, 14, 36
Bever, Sampson, 6
Blood, Sweat and Tears, 57
Blouin, Mike, 20
Bluesmore, 50
Boland, Jan, 67
Boyd, Lydia Jane, 28
Boyd, Jane, Community House, 14, 28, 36
Boyz II Men, 51
Brewer, Luther A., 4
Briggs, Ansel, Governor, 80
Broulik Painting, 129
Brown Healey Stone & Sauer, 128
Brucemore, 13, 50, 72, 73, 91, 97
Byrd, Richard E., 92

CRST International, 1, 5, 150-151
CSPS Hall, 8, 70, 72, 74
Camp Conservation, 28
Canney, Donald, Mayor, 86, 87, 88, 97
Cargill, 1
Carmody Foundry, 97
Carpenter, Frank, 6
Cedar Memorial, 99
Cedar Rapids Art Association, 64
Cedar Rapids City Hall, 78
Cedar Rapids Community School District, 39, 41, 69
Cedar Rapids Country Club, 54
Cedar Rapids Efficiency and Reform Commission, 79
Cedar Rapids Inter-Religious Council, 26, 28
Cedar Rapids Kernels, The, 48
Cedar Rapids Metropolitan Arts Council, 70
Cedar Rapids Municipal Band, 45
Cedar Rapids Museum of Art, 62, 63, 64, 70, 74
Cedar Rapids Police Department, 89
Cedar Rapids Public Library, 19, 36, 37, 38, 70
Cedar Rapids Symphony, 62, 65, 69, 70, 71, 72
Cedar Rapids' Five Seasons Center, 50, 51
Cedarapids Inc., 1, 134-135
Cedar River Houseboat Harbor, 52
Cedar River Paper Company, 1, 40
Cedar Valley Nature Trail, 46
Chamber of Commerce, 20, 97, 106, 110
Charter Commission, 79, 80
Cherry Sisters, 70
Christopher, William, 69
Clancey, Lee, Mayor, 80, 81, 84, 89
Classics at Brucemore, 72
Clifton Hotel, 22
Climate Engineers, Inc., 1, 148-149
Clinton, Bill, President, 15
Coe College, 36, 39, 40, 42, 103, 109
College Community School District, 41
Collins, Arthur, 8, 92, 93
Collins Radio Company, 92, 93
Committee of 100, 97
Community Character Initiative, 29
Cone, Marvin, 62, 64
Coralville Lake, 33, 52, 53
Cornell College, 43
Cosgrove, Jack, 93
Curran, Mary Russell, 38
Czech Heritage Foundation, 70
Czech National Cemetery, 14
Czech Cottage, 1
Czech Village, 8,12, 70

Diamond V Mills, Inc., 1, 40, 146-147
Doe, Donald, 62, 64, 65
Douglas Family, 6, 13, 97
Douglas Starch Works, 22, 23
Dowdall, John, 67
Downtown Cultural Alliance (Cedar Rapids Area Cultural Alliance), 70
Dows, Stephen L., Captain, 39
Dows Fine Arts Building, 39
Dows, Sutherland C. 6, 39
Dows, William G., 39
Dusek, Jon, 9

Eastern Iowa Airport, 75, 76, 77, 88, 106
Elmcrest Country Club, 55
Ely, Alexander, 6
Ely, John, 6
Evans, Jack, 91
Evans, Nancy, Public Safety Commissioner, 80, 81
Evergreen Packaging Equipment, 1, 115

Farm Crisis, 96
Farmers State Bank, 1, 138
Farmer's Market, 34, 35
Farmstead Foods, 99
Farr, Jamie, 69
Finch, Lew, 39
First Lutheran Church, 27
First National Bank, 1

Fifth Season Race, 46
Five Seasons Center, 105
Foresight 2020, 20, 104
Franklin Middle School, 30
Freedom Festival, 33, 56, 74

Gage, Harry Morehouse, Dr., 28
Gazette Company, The, 1, 120-121
Genencor, 91
General Mills, 32
Gibson, Viola, 14
Gibson Park, 14
Goss Graphic Systems Inc., 1
Granby Family, 8
Granger House, 60
Great Depression, 28, 92
Greater Cedar Rapids Foundation, The, 18
Greene, George, Judge, 6, 9, 18
Greene, Joseph, 80
Greene Square Park, 6, 9
Greene's Opera House, 66
Guaranty Bank, 1, 6, 92, 141-142

Hall Family, 6
Hall, Howard, 91, 97, 103
Hall, Kathy, 66, 69
Hall (Douglas), Margaret, 13, 97
Hall-Perrine Foundation, 18, 19, 20, 91, 97, 103
Hancher Auditorium, 44
Hanson, Lyle, 80
Haskell, Billy, Senator, 87
Havel, Vaclav, 15
Hawkeye Downs, 58, 59
Healthy Linn Care Network (Healthy Linn 2000), 30
Hennessy, Dr. David, 40
Herbert, F. John, 69, 70, 72
Herbert Hoover Presidential Museum and Library and National Historic Site, 60
Hickenlooper, Bourke B., 85
Higley Family, 8
History Center, 28
Hoffman, Jim, 86, 97, 99
Holy Redeemer Lutheran, 26
Home Rule Charter, 80
Hotel Frasier, 125
Hoover, Herbert, 60

IES Industries, 97
Indian Creek Nature Center, 33, 34
Intermec/Norand, 1
In Tolerance, 1, 145
Iowa Electric Light & Power Co., 39
Iowa Midland Supply , Inc., 1
Iowa Manufacturing Co., 97
Iowa Steel and Iron Works, 14, 97
Islamic Center of Cedar Rapids, 27
Jay, John, 97
Jazz in the Park, 51
Johnson Gas Appliance, 87
Junge, Steve, 105, 106
Junior League, 19

Kennedy, Homer, 80
Kenwood Neighborhood, 8
Killians Department Store, 9
King's Material, Inc., 1, 119
Kirkwood Community College, 40, 43
Kingston Neighborhood, 8
Kingston Stadium, 46
Kovac, Michal, 15
Kuba, Edward Rudolf, 12
Kubias Family, 8

Lake Macbride State Park, 52, 53
LaSalle High School, 41
Langston, Linda, 28
Larson, P.T., 79
Lattner, P.M., Manufacturing Company, 105
League of Women Voters, 79
Leverich, James, 80
Liu, Lee, 97
Lindale Mall, 9, 98
Linn County, 20, 30
Linn County Courthouse, 84
Linn County Historical Museum, 70
Linn County Day Care Center, 14
Lofdahl, Cedric, Rev., 26
MCI, 102, 103
MCI WorldCom, 1
Marion, Iowa, 1
Mayor's Committee for Oak Hill Citizens, 14
McGladrey & Pullen, 133
McHugh, Nancy, 36
McLeod, Clark, 99, 102, 103
McLeodUSA, 1, 40, 103
McLeodUSA Publishing, 103
Mercy Cancer Center, 103
Mercy Challenge Criterium, 47
Mercy Medical Center, 1, 30, 32, 126-127
Meth-Wick Community, The, 154-155
Metropolitan Arts Council, 70
Metropolitan Museum of Art, 62
Mother Mosque, 28
Mound View Neighborhood, 8
Mount Mercy College, 40, 42, 132

National Association for the Advancement of Colored People (NAACP), 14
National Czech and Slovak Museum and Library, 12, 14, 15, 70
National Oats, 92
Neighborhood Living Initiative, 89
Neilsen, Norm, 40
Nesper Sign Advertising Inc., 139
Networking Data Processing, 1
Nordstrom Fulfillment Center, 91

OB-GYN Associates, P.C., 1
Oak Hill Cemetery, 36
Oak Hill Neighborhood, 14, 36
O'Donnell, Jean, 34

PMX Industries, 91
Paramount Theater, 6, 66, 68, 69, 74
Patton, Dennis, 77
Patterson, Rich, 34
Penford Products (Penick & Ford), 12, 14, 92, 124
Pentacrest, The, 44

Perrine, Irene Hall, 103
Perrine, Beahl T., 103
Peoples Savings Bank, 8
People's Unitarian Church, 28
Phillips, Madge, Center, 19
Pinney, Richard, 37
Pineview Properties, 1
Pioneer Office Products, 1, 131
Point Builders, Inc., 1
Pollock, Stephen L., 80
Poongsan Corporation, 91
Prairie High School, 41
Priority One, 86, 97

Quaker Oats, 1, 12, 22, 92, 111, 112-113

Red Cedar Chamber Music, 67
Regis High School, 41
Riley, Nan, 62, 64
Riley, Tom, 62, 64
Rinderknecht Associates, Inc., 1, 118
Rockwell Collins, 1, 12, 92, 93, 105, 106, 136-137
Roosevelt, David, 18, 19
Rome on the Prairie, 62
Ruffalo Cody and Associates, 103
Ryu, Chung, 91

16th Avenue Bridge, 12
SCI Financial Group Inc., 1, 142-143
Sac and Fox Trail, 34
St. George's Greek Orthodox Church, 27
St. Jude's Sweet Corn Festival, 57
St. Ludmila Catholic Church, 14
St. Luke's Hospital, 1, 30, 31, 122-123
St. Patrick Catholic Church, 26, 27
St. Wenceslaus Catholic Church, 14
St. Wenceslaus Day Care Center, 14
Saturn, 103, 104
Science Station, 37, 70
Selk, Liz, 30
Senate Agriculture Committee, 85
Serbousek, Larry, Mayor, 80, 81
Shay, Dave, 80, 81, 84, 85
Shepherd, Osgood, 6
Shive Hattery, Inc., 1
Shuttleworth & Ingersoll, 104
Sinclair, Carolyn, 13
Sinclair Family, 6, 13
Sinclair, T.M., Meatpacking, 14, 92
Smith, Dave, 34
Smith, J.D., 80
Smulekoff, A.M., 6
Smulekoff Furniture Store, 9
Solomon, Oscar, 6
SouthernNet, Inc., 102
Souvenir Group, 1
Square D Company, 1
Stamats, B.B., 34
Streit, Gary, 104
Sullivan, Louis, 8
Sutherland C. Dows and Frances M. Dows Treatment Diagnostic and Trauma Center, 39
Sykora's Bakery, 19

3M, 62
2001 Development Corporation, 96
Taste of Iowa, 57
Teahen Funeral Home, Inc., 1
Telecom*USA, 102
Telecom*USA Publishing, 103
Teleconnect, 99, 102
Tiemeyer, Christian, 71
Theatre Cedar Rapids (TCR), 65, 66, 70, 72
Torchlight Theatre, 72
Toyota Motor Insurance Services, 91
Town Centre, 96
Tree of Five Seasons, 25
Turner Family, 8
Turner, John B., II, 64
Turner, Happy, 64
Tyler School, 28

United Way of East Central Iowa, 1, 19
University of Iowa, The, 44, 61, 87
University of Iowa School of Law, 85
Ushers Ferry Historic Village, 45

Van Vechten, Ada, 36
Van Vechten, Carl, 74
Vegetable Girls, 70
Vernon Heights Neighborhood, 8
Veterans Memorial Coliseum, 64
Veterans Stadium, 48

Walker Art Center, 62
Washington High School, 41
Wellington Heights Neighborhood, 8
Wells, Al, Homes, Inc., 1
Wendler, Nancy, 33
West Side Sewing, 1
Westdale Mall, 9, 98
Western Fraternal Life Insurance, 8
Whipple, William, 18, 40
Whittam, Isaac, 80
Wick, Barthinius L., 4
Wiederspan, Stan, 74, 75
Winterfest, 57
Wilson Foods, 14
Wood, Grant, 6, 7, 62. 64, 65, 74

Xavier High School, 41

YWCA Festival of Races, 47

Bibliography

Ken C. Braband, *The First 50 Years: A History of Collins Radio Company and the Collins Divisions of Rockwell International,* 1983.

Luther A. Brewer and Barthinius L. Wick, *History of Linn County, Iowa,* 1911.

Gary Cartwright, *Galveston: A History of the Island,* 1991.

Shirley M. Cutchlow, *The Biography of Mrs. Viola A. Gibson,* 1991.

Elinor Day, *Call Me Howard: The Story of the Hall-Perrine Foundation,* 1998.

Harold Ewoldt, *Jane Boyd and Her Times,* 1989.

Friends of Elizabeth Bender, *Remembering Elizabeth Bender,* 1991.

Bruce Kellner, *Carl Van Vechten and the Irreverent Decade,* 1968.

Edward Lueders, *Carl Van Vechten and the Twenties,* 1955.

John J. Murray, *It Took All of Us: 100 Years of Iowa Electric Light & Power Co.,* 1982.

Charles A. Laurance, *Pioneer Days in Cedar Rapids,* 1936.

Other Sources

African American Heritage Foundation

The Cedar Rapids Gazette

Cedar Rapids Public Library Information Center

History Center

State Historical Society of Iowa

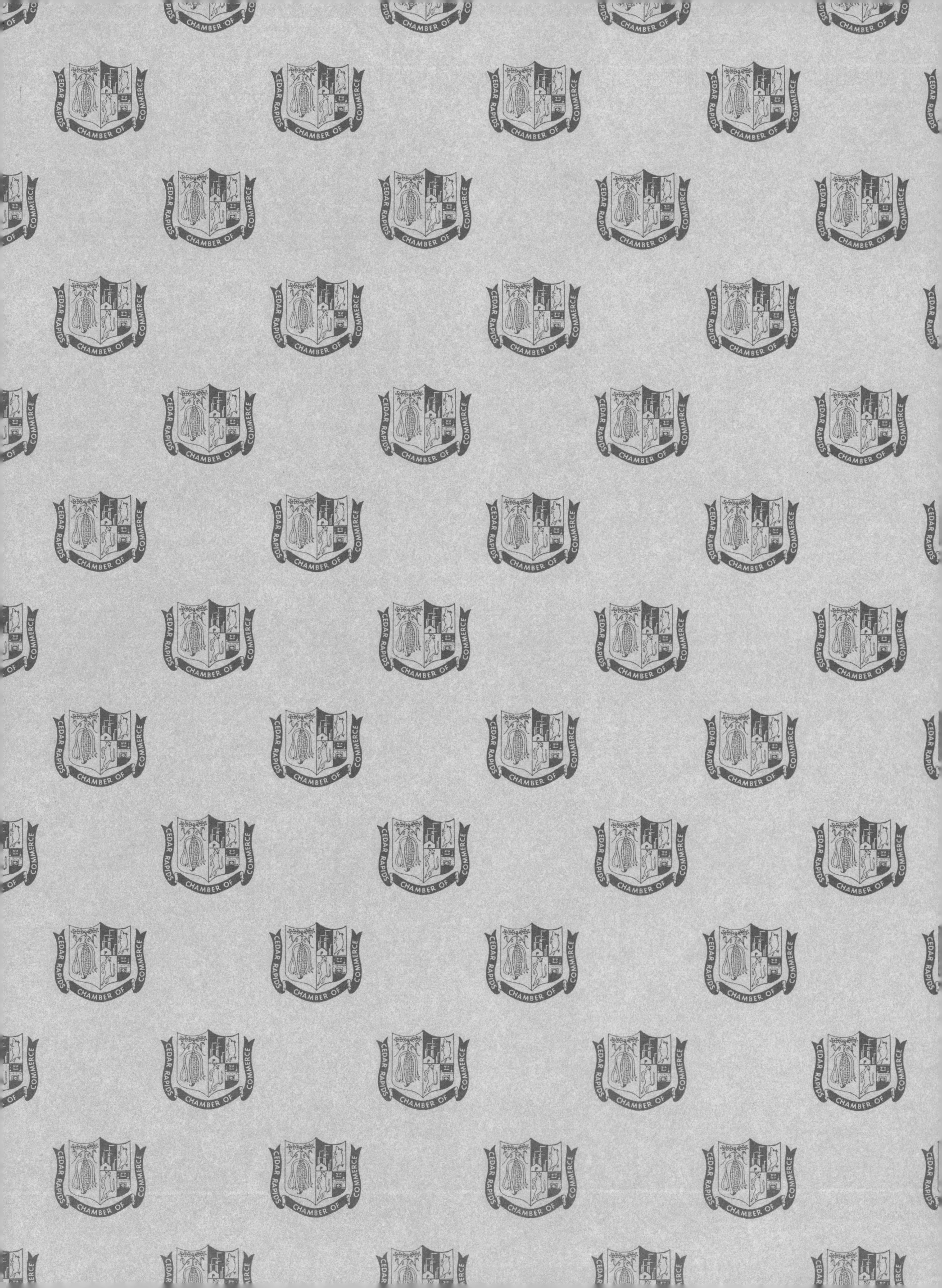